TEXAS AND TEXANS IN WORLD WAR II

Summerfield G. Roberts
Texas History Series

TEXAS AND TEXANS IN WORLD WAR II 1941–1945

EDITED BY
CHRISTOPHER B. BEAN
FOREWORD BY
RANDOLPH "MIKE" CAMPBELL

Texas A&M University Press College Station

First edition

This paper meets the requirements of ANSI/NISO Z39.48–1992 (Permanence of Paper).
Binding materials have been chosen for durability.
Manufactured in the United States of America

Library of Congress Control Number: 2021945249
ISBN (hardcover) 979-1-62349-969-3
ISBN (ebook) 979-1-62349-970-9

CONTENTS

Foreword, by Randolph "Mike" Campbell viii
Introduction 01

1
Before the Storm: Texas, 1939–41
Joseph G. Dawson III 17

2
The New Negro Moves Forward:
Black Texans Earn Their Citizenship in World War II
Christopher B. Bean, Bernadette Pruitt, and Michael Hurd 43

3
Volunteers All: Texas Women in the Military in World War II
Katherine Sharp Landdeck 100

4
Tejanos: On Two Battlegrounds
Arnoldo De León 128

5
Opportunity and Organized Labor in Wartime Texas, 1939–45
Zachary Montz 153

6
Victory Crude: Texas Oil in World War II
Houston Faust Mount II 184

7

The Better Half: Women, the Home Front, and World War II Texas
Christopher B. Bean 203

8

Oral History and World War II, 1941–45:
From the Front Line to the Lone Star State
Stephen M. Sloan 229

9

Texas Agriculture and World War II
Christopher B. Bean and Henry C. Dethloff 254

10

Serving the Nation in Time of War: Training Camps, Prison Camps, and Major Texas Units in the Second World War
Kelly E. Crager 284

11

A New Texas Emerges: The Long-Term Impact of World War II, 1945–60
Keith J. Volanto 317

Index 347

FOREWORD

World War II touched the lives of virtually all Texans and permanently transformed the Lone Star State. Approximately 750,000 Texans, including 12,000 women, served in the armed forces of the United States between 1941 and 1945, and 22,022 died in defeating the Axis powers. Texas entered the war as a largely impoverished, rural, agricultural state and emerged as a productive giant well on the road to urbanization and industrialization. Massive government spending on the war effort, building on the New Deal's expenditures on relief for individuals and economic recovery programs, ended the Great Depression. Texas recovered, and Texans have rarely, if at all, looked back to study and evaluate what the war meant to their state.

In *Texas and Texans in World War II: 1941–1945*, ten historians offer a much needed look back at the transformative effect on the Lone Star state brought by the greatest challenge to American arms and society in the twentieth century. An introduction by Joseph G. Dawson III, the "Dean" of Texas military historians, sets the stage with a description of the state on the eve of war in 1939. The following eight essays reveal the roles of Texas units in the war and the great diversity of the war's reach into Texas. Particularly notable is the emphasis in four essays on how different groups of the population—women, Tejanos, African Americans, and organized labor—responded to the war and sought to improve their circumstances as they supported the state during a time of great need. Key aspects of the Texas economy such as agriculture and oil receive due attention as well. Oral history, an approach that first proved itself as a way to develop sources on the military past, is explored. A concluding essay by Keith J.Volanto summarizes the long-term impact of the war in creating a "new Texas."

World War II ended less than seventy-five years ago, a very short time in the run of history, and yet its memory appears to be fading rapidly. These essays will remind Texans that four years of war with such momentous results for our state deserve to be remembered by anyone who wishes to understand where we are today.

—Randolph "Mike" Campbell

TEXAS AND TEXANS IN WORLD WAR II

INTRODUCTION

Christopher B. Bean[1]

The long and illustrious history of Texas has demarcations, events that mark the end of one era and the beginning of another. Spanish rule gave way to Mexican rule with the Mexican victory in the War of Independence in September 1821. Mexican rule lasted but a decade and a half, ending with the Texas Revolution in 1836. The Republic of Texas ceased being an independent country when it joined the United States in late 1845. Texas entered the Union as a slaveholding state, and when most of its fellow southern, slaveholding states seceded from the United States in late 1860 and early 1861, Texas followed. Now part of the Confederate States of America, Texas remained a vital source of men and resources for the Confederacy until its ultimate defeat in 1865.

Soon after its defeat in the US Civil War, Texas, which escaped the devastation experienced by other members of the Confederacy (e.g., Virginia, South Carolina, and Georgia), became a beacon of opportunity and renewal for hundreds of thousands in the late nineteenth and early twentieth centuries. Cattle, cotton, railroads, and oil transformed the Lone Star State into an emerging economic power by the twentieth century. Some of this transformation continued slowly with World War I and in the years that followed. But one event transformed the state like few occurrences have—World War II. This turned Texas from being primarily an agricultural and rural state to an urban one, moving beyond cotton and cattle and entering the burgeoning manufacturing, banking and finance, and oil and petrochemical industries. About the war's consequence to the state, "Old, Romantic Texas, with its ranches and cattle drives," concluded James Ward Lee, a leading student on Texas during the Second World War, "lived after the war only in the popular imagination." It further continued this economic modernization and diversification into the postwar years. A short three generations later, Texas had the second largest economy in the country, and if it had been a separate country (something many Texans still likely dream of), its economy would be the tenth largest in the world (below Italy's and above Canada's).[2]

The Texas that existed on December 6, 1941, would be much different from the one that experienced the internal and external forces unleashed and magnified by four years of war in 1945. With massive migration, the state's population witnessed a 50 percent increase from 1940 to 1960, something matched only by California. Provincialism, although not nearly as endemic as other states in the country since Texas shared a border with Mexico, continued to diminish. Mexican immigration, mainly due to the need for field labor, increased during the war and continued to do so in subsequent years. Many Americans, particularly from the South and Midwest, were attracted to Texas' industrial and manufacturing jobs during the war and remained afterward. Houston, Dallas, Fort Worth, and San Antonio drastically increased in population, marked by their national and international businesses. Modern culture accompanied this expansion. Educational institutions and cultural entertainment further developed, setting the state on a course of national prominence.[3]

Historian Studs Terkel, in his monumental work *The "Good War": An Oral History of World War II*, referred to the Second World War as "the Good War." If any war could be described such, it would be this one. Forces truly evil menaced the world, killing entire populations of people toward complete annihilation. In addition, it ultimately destroyed the colonial system that had bound the aspirations of hundreds of millions of people and an entire continent. A new world order, full of promise and hope, looked to have sprung from the ashes of the old. The war proved "good" for the United States as well. Relatively untouched by the war's more damaging aspects, at least compared to other major belligerents, the United States stood upon what was once the old world as its preeminent superpower. Diminished were Europe's and Asia's powers, such as those of Great Britain, France, Germany, Italy, and Japan, which had dominated their region of the globe. They now stood in the shadow of the United States, beholden to its money and technology, conforming to its principles and values, and respecting its military and influence. For fear of plagiarizing Tony Montana in *Scarface* (a cautionary tale not recommended quoting too often), for Uncle Sam the world was his.[4]

The war also proved "good" for Texas, which witnessed the war's elevating nature. On the eve of the war, Texas was a state, in certain aspects, that had changed little since the turn of the century. Agrarian-based, predominantly rural, with its citizens having a parochial outlook, still glorifying to the point of self-identification its nineteenth-century image of cattle drivers, gunslingers, and masculine, no-nonsense Texas Rangers, as well as its icons of individualism, fearlessness, and nobility who struggled against Mexico for independence. In fact, its governor at the time, W. Lee "Pappy" O'Daniel, highlighted his "hillbilly image." The state, to say the least, had more than one foot still in the past. Joseph G. "Chip" Dawson III, in a great narrative titled "Before the Storm," examines this provincialism in the years prior to the country's entry into the war. He suggests how Texas citizens, by being so affixed to the past, glacially moved into the future. Rural Texans still lacked many of the household amenities increasingly necessary in a country increasingly urbanized and industrialized. Few had telephones, relying instead on public phones, and still fewer had indoor plumbing, farms characterized by the ubiquitous outhouse and water drawn in a fashion that Sam Houston would have recognized.[5]

Despite the massive governmental effort of the New Deal to bring the amenities of urban society to rural America, many Texans still lacked electricity, pushing back the night as their forefathers would have, through candles or, in the manner of late-nineteenth-century America, by kerosene lamp. Many still preferred (perhaps due to economics, perhaps due to reliability) horse-drawn carriages as their primary mode of travel. There were forty-one colleges and universities in the state. Few Texans, however, went to school, and only one school ranked above national academic standards. As Dawson further points out, Texans in the urban centers of Houston, Dallas, and San Antonio were not much more advanced than their rural brethren. Few Texans earned a living in industry, although the oil industry and all its derivatives were on the precipice of dominance within the state and fewer industries called the state home. This began to change, as Dawson notes, as war neared. Although most Texans, similar to the country as a whole, did not want war with the Axis powers, they benefited from the production of war machines. Uncle Sam's need for the impending war soon made Fort Worth a major area for aircraft construction. The country's need for ships redounded, to the benefit of the coastal region. To fuel these craft, Houston's oil refineries greatly expanded. The state's vast expanses proved inviting for the construction of many military facilities to train the expanding armed forces. What began prior to the war was greatly magnified with entry into the war, and Texas began its transition to industrializing and urbanizing and becoming the economic superpower that would emerge from the Second World War.[6]

The state's military experience and role in the conflict is the focus of Kelly E. Crager's essay. Texas was appealing to the United States armed forces. Throughout the war, the federal government expanded or constructed 175 military facilities in the Lone Star State. One and a half million personnel passed through the state during the war, most either training for combat or in transit to overseas duty. An accessible coastline and nearby population centers appealed to the country's shipping industry and US Navy. For the army, along with housing Axis prisoners of war, the state's vastness, year-round-activity climate, and open skies were attractive. Tens of thousands of pilots, bombardiers, navigators, and aerial gunners trained in the Lone Star State. This included, most memorably, the famed Women Airforce Service Pilots, better known as WASP, who eventually made West Texas their home. On the coast, Corpus Christi became known as the "University of the Air." Amid the influx of military personnel, Texans also rallied to the country's defense. Three quarters of a million people entered the armed forces; some became famous, while many served in obscurity. By war's end, 23,000 paid the ultimate sacrifice. Crager argues that the state's military experience during the war was foundational. Construction of facilities and manufacturing of machines of war pumped billions into the state's economy. Thus, with the end of hostilities, it was poised to enter an era of profound growth.[7]

The military's "invasion" of Texas further affected the agricultural system. It greatly accelerated recent trends, irreparably relegating agriculture in Texas from a position of prominence to subordination, behind burgeoning industry and manufacturing. Cotton, in fact, lost its crown. Ironically, as Christopher B. Bean and Henry C. Dethloff argue in their essay, the demands placed on agriculture by the necessity of war resulted in the greater reliance on industrialization, technology, and specialization. Farmers did tap unused labor pools, such as women, Mexican immigrants, and prisoners of war. Mechanization proved more promising. During the war, to be sure, the number of farms and farmworkers noticeably decreased, yet the output per acre and total acreage in production increased. The same relationship also occurred in the livestock industry. As Bean and Dethloff note, resistance to mechanization, fertilizers, and, in a way, governmental cooperation abated, while cooperation between rival organizations in the industry occurred in the name of patriotism. Technological innovation, in large part through the efforts of Texas A&M University, became the norm. War's demand further resulted in the adoption of measures previously resisted. Farmers and ranchers embraced science. This allowed greater flexibility in the selection of crops and greater yields. The war's need further resulted in war production. Crops and livestock previously unheard of in Texas soon became leading exports for the state. In four short years, as these two authors show, Texas diversification resulted in the state becoming the leading producer of everything from cotton to sorghum, from pecans to tomatoes, from spinach to roses. Peanut production shifted from the Northeast to the South, with Texas becoming one of the leading producers of "the goober," behind only Georgia. In addition, Texas, the land of cattle and horses in popular image, now became the land of the chicken, sheep, goat, and turkey. The era of agribusiness was eclipsing the bucolic family farm.[8]

The Lone Star State would be vitally important to what fueled the tools of modern war. World War II was a mechanized war. It could only be won by ships, planes, tanks, and trucks, all fueled by oil and its derivatives. Texas was capital for oil in the country. In an illuminating essay, Houston Faust Mount II examines the essential role the war effort played in the state's oil industry. Petroleum was necessary in modern conflict and thus mandated that belligerents develop new tactics and strategies. It also, as Mount points out, presented strategic problems. Denied access to oil relegated the fighting force to a nineteenth-century capability, land-bound and reliant on the power and speed of horses. Prior to the war, the world's oil production registered 2.08 billion barrels—61 percent of which came from the United States. Nearly 40 percent of US production, and thus nearly one-quarter of the world's production, came from Texas. The maximization of this resource required cooperation between private enterprise and the state and between the state to the federal government. Mount chronicles the successes and failures of these relationships, as well as the conflicting bureaucracies and personalities. One such personality was Everette Lee DeGolyer. Mount details the industry during the war through DeGolyer's biography. Similar to Texas agriculture, oil producers and state officials recognized the necessity of federal involvement yet soon became frustrated by what they believed to be intrusiveness. The Texas oil industry proved vital to victory, and the expansion experienced by the industry due to the war helped lay the foundation for the massive industrialization of the state in the postwar years.[9]

Mobilization did not simply include resources. It also comprised workers. This was to be an industrial war. Ships needed to be built, aircraft constructed, and oil refined. The federal government pumped billions into urban centers to provide the necessities of war. Seven billion in defense contracts, in fact, came into Texas, first to construct or expand the necessary facilities, then the necessary products. Dallas and Fort Worth became centers of the aircraft industry, Beaumont and Galveston boomed with shipbuilding, and East Texas surged as a center of steel production. Houston, however, became an industrial center rivaled by few. In the "Bayou City," there were shipbuilding facilities, oil-refining facilities, tool-producing facilities, and even steel production. Paralleling this growth was the growth of industrial unions.

Zachary Montz examines the contribution made by these workers in Texas to the war effort. He details the efforts made by labor unions to use the war (and the subsequent growth in industrial workers) to increase their membership and leverage with industrialists. As Montz shows, many industrial workers in Texas, despite the state's hostile attitude toward unionization, saw labor unions as the personification of democracy. The war injected new life into a struggling union effort. Unions, however, did not see all workers the same. Some recruited all workers, regardless of race and sex, while others were more discriminatory, even to the point of colluding with industrialists and management against fellow industrial workers. Despite certain unions' hostility to them, African American workers and female workers were attracted to unions, not only for greater agency within the particular industry they labored, but also as a possible means to greater citizenship. The war spurred those marginalized to greater advocacy for rights denied and participation limited. These workers' struggle against economic discrimination and the growth of labor unions during the war, Montz argues, were related developments and commenced an era of labor unions in Texas previously unseen.[10]

Of all the resources mobilized for the war effort, none was more important than the citizenry. The monumental task necessitated the government to mobilize not just men—all able bodies were needed to acquit the effort. Women were needed for sowing and reaping the crops as well as performing livestock husbandry. They were instrumental in filling the administrative and clerical positions when the federal government swelled its ranks for the immense paperwork required during the war. The country still needed them to manage the home and, in a soldierly twist, defend against inflation, price gouging, and evasions of rationing. Combat notwithstanding, Texas women performed exactly the same tasks as their male counterparts. Texas had "Rosie the Riveters" as well as "Rosie the Shipbuilders," "Rosie the Oil Worker," and "Rosie the Farm Worker." In fact, 310,000 Texas women entered the workforce for the first time. He notes that without female participation, the country would have struggled to acquit a two-front strategy, perhaps having to focus on one enemy at the benefit of the other.[11]

As Christopher B. Bean shows, this effort had profound significance for postwar America. The female mobilization pebble tossed into the pool of American society, although making a little splash, produced monumental ripples well beyond the war. Although returned to the home immediately following the war, women during the war forced society in subsequent years to redefine female capability and offered a glimpse of a different future for Texas women. While female mobilization was considered necessary at the time, Bean demonstrates how it exposed societal concerns about the "proper role" for women. Many in society worried how this inclusion into men's spaces would affect the family and marriage, child care, and traditional male–female relations. Society, the author further notes, was even more uncomfortable with the specter of loosed moral norms. Female sexuality, free from the constraints during peacetime, was now uninhibited. Prostitution, infidelity, and illegitimate pregnancy, always concerns for society's vanguards, now imperiled not just gender roles but also the war effort. While applauding women's patriotism during the Second World War, society also expressed anxiety with women moving beyond generally accepted gender roles.[12]

Most memorable and high-profile than any other occupation they endeavored during the war, women were even admitted into the armed forces, primarily under the campaign "free a man to fight." As the need for manpower increased with the war's progression, government officials looked to women to replace men in noncombat positions. Women entered the services to perform clerical and administrative duties. They also acquitted themselves in positions not necessarily considered "women's work," such as mechanics, technicians, instructors (generally teaching males how to use a particular piece of military equipment), radio operators, and parachute technicians, to name a few. This most glamorous aspect of the women's contribution during the war, perhaps, was the all-female Women Airforce Service Pilots. These women, in order to free a man for combat, ferried planes to specified destinations, test-piloted new and repaired aircraft, and assisted ground troops in antiaircraft practice. They also assisted male cadet pilots in learning the ins and outs of new aircraft and helped assuage their concerns about the "flyability" of certain aircraft. If a woman can fly it, so the argument went, so can they.

Detailing this vital role of Texas women during World War II is Katherine Sharp Landdeck. Landdeck details the struggles that WASP's champion, Jacqueline Cochran, experienced in getting the organization accepted by policy and military officials. Once it was created, Cochran jealously protected WASP independence and operations, realizing the uncertainty that each day brought. Landdeck further chronicles the varied ways the WASP women served the war effort. Texas also had the unique honor as being the "hive" of WASP. More than a thousand WASP members comprised a fraction of the 12,000 Texas women who served in the nation's armed forces in units such as WAVES (Women Accepted for Volunteer Emergency Service) and WAC (Women's Army Corps). The stories of Texas women in both these units, WAVES and WAC, are also stressed. Landdeck details the indispensable ways Texas women contributed to the military's mission to defeat the Axis powers—a contribution that otherwise would have inhibited the execution of a two-front war, where in one theater the United States essentially carried the entire load.[13]

No part of the population remained untouched by forces unleashed by the Second World War. This included the state's largest minority group. Tejanos, although legally classified as white, faced uncertainties and discrimination few Anglos experienced. Despite being treated as a marginalized group, Tejanos were present at the beginning of what would ultimately become Texas, from its earliest days as a Spanish province to contemporary times as a prominent state in the United States. In the state's most trying times, Tejanos were present. They contributed to its independence from Mexico. Acquitted themselves in France "over there." And they mobilized to defend it against fascism. Tejanos are enmeshed in Texas culture and history to a point of indistinguishability. One chapter in their story is the focus of Arnoldo De León's essay. Tejano mobilization mirrored that of Anglo Texans. They labored in war mobilization work and served in the armed forces. It is generally estimated that between 500,000 and one million served, with a quarter of a million from Texas. Tejanos, unlike many African Americans placed in service units, were not generally excluded from combat roles. In fact, Texas produced 57 percent of the Spanish-speaking armed forces personnel. Tejanos in Texas, as De León details, combated fascism abroad and struggled against discrimination at home. A spirit of activism prompted that community to demand "Caucasian rights." Those fighting for others' equality returned to Texas to demand it for themselves. This egalitarianism, however, was not just pillared by racial equality, as will be seen with the struggle for black Texans. De León shows how intertwined labor rights were in the Tejano struggle. They demanded equality in society as well as in the fields. Hispanic labor was critical to the Texas agricultural economy and thus to the war effort. Fair treatment of field-workers meant fair treatment for the greater Tejano community and vice versa. The two were synonymous. Although predating the war, as De León shows, the struggle for equality and respect intensified during the conflict. The momentum carried the community into greater activism in the postwar years.[14]

Ideological forces, highlighting both the best of man and, at times, the worst, were unleashed by the profound measure necessary to acquit the Second World War. Black Texans also responded to the country's needs, the same country that assigned them second-class citizenship, maligned them as inferior, and relegated them to the extreme margins of society. This attitude was embodied in the dominant racial system known as Jim Crow. Texas society and politics was bifurcated, with one for African Americans and the another for whites. Black Texans, shown no dignity at home, were expected to defend others' dignity abroad. Little could anyone know that the war would unleash dynamic forces that would ultimately end the legal bifurcated system and transform society in the process. The attitude of African Americans in Texas during World War II and their expectations that involvement in the conflict is the focus of the essay by Christopher B. Bean, Bernadette Pruitt and Michael Hurd. Despite their treatment at home, approximately 84,000 African American Texans entered military service. These men and women entered a segregated service. Black men rarely saw combat, often relegated to labor or mess units. Black women, also experiencing racial exclusivity in the armed forces, rarely were sent overseas. Compared to their numbers, few reached officer ranks. Furthermore, African Americans assisting the country at its time of need had their patriotism questioned and involvement diminished. The civil rights movement of the 1950s and 1960s had its roots in the war. Wartime civil rights leaders initiated the Double V campaign ("Victory against fascism abroad and victory against racism at home") to defeat fascism abroad and racism at home. Black Texans faced the same limitations in the state's war industries, often at the hands of unions, despite these organizations proclaiming to be defenders of workers and agricultural sectors. As shows, this encouraged black citizens to take action to do their part for greater dignity and citizenship. With a newfound sense of empowerment, African Americans' challenges to racial exclusion initiated cracks in Jim Crow that would eventually result in its complete shattering. Lulu B. White was a truly monumental force in the Texas civil rights struggle. Passivity within the black community was a casualty of the war. Vitally important to molding the National Association for the Advancement of Colored People (NAACP) into an organization for effective change in Texas, White further focused the struggle on what she believed were the two pillars of equality for black Texans—economic and voter equality. This struggle, greatly intensified by the war's glaring hypocrisy of fighting for democracy abroad and denying it at home, magnified the struggle for black Texans, lending to civil rights advocates an undeniable moral gift to spotlight the inequities for an American populace sensitive to fulfilling the country's founding principles and ideals.[15]

World War II in popular culture is thought of as the "good war."

Americans—including Texans who contributed more than their fair share to victory—pride themselves on being on the side of the angels as they fought the forces of true evil. How Texans contributed to the defeat of fascism was a story that they not only wanted to tell, but also one that had to be told. Stephen M. Sloan focuses on these World War II oral histories by Texans. Oral histories allow for the complete presentation of those involved. Sloan shows how this approach proves invaluable in two ways. First, it expands understanding of the war, and, second, it proves invaluable to how Texans remember the war experience. Furthermore, as he highlights, oral history, with its long form, deep listening, and co-creation, is extremely valuable in recording the human experience of the war. In the United States, according to Sloan, no subject has received more attention from oral historians than the Second World War. He notes that almost immediately following the war, oral historians collected participants' experiences.

The initial focus by oral historians was on personnel serving overseas. However, in recent decades, they have shifted their attention to the conflict's long reach. Stories have been collected from the home front, including those mobilized to manufacture the tools of war, those mobilized to work the fields, and those mobilized in any other conceivable manner. Focus has also shifted to those who, for the most part, passively experienced the effects of the conflict. This includes children, the elderly, and housewives. As Sloan shows, oral history adds voices that enrich the refrain, voices that bring texture, color, and depth to the piece. It humanizes events that otherwise seem beyond those not in the positions of power and influence, and constantly reminds contemporaries that there was no one World War II experience, but millions.[16]

Change was occurring in Texas prior to the outbreak of the Second World War. Social, political, and economic forces were afoot. The war, however, accelerated much of that change and initiated still more into the decades immediately following. War compresses time and space. Change that otherwise would have occurred years later happens earlier. Change that perhaps may never have occurred happens due to energies unleashed only by war's disruptive and liberating nature. Texas in the decades immediately following World War II is examined by Keith J. Volanto. As Volanto describes, the average Texan in the early 1960s lived in a state that was transforming beyond anything previous generations could have imagined. Texans, already leaving the farm in the immediate prewar years, increased that exodus during the war and afterward. By 1950, more Texans lived in cities than in rural communities. The state's demography benefited its industrialization as well as internationalization. Volanto further chronicles the importance of Texas Instruments, which contributed to the rise of computers in the second half of the twentieth century. Furthering industrialization and computerization of Texas as well as the United States was the onset of the Cold War. Texas had a hand in this struggle against communism and its goal of global dominance.

Beyond its strategic resources, such as oil, and its technological industries, Texas was home to a burgeoning defense industry. Aircraft continued to be built in the Metroplex (Dallas-Fort Worth), and the state continued to be a central hub for the military. Its coastline was inviting to the navy, its open skies continued to appeal to the air force (officially created as a separate branch in 1947), and its spacious lands still attracted the army for bases. In addition, according to Volanto, West Texas became home to nuclear missiles aimed at the Soviet Union and its communist satellites. No sooner had Texans rallied to defend the country in one war than they found themselves once again called upon to defend the country against a force considered even more dangerous and threatening to the United States than fascism.[17]

Notes

1. Christopher B. Bean is Professor and Chair of the Department of History and Native American Studies at East Central University.

2. James Ward Lee, Carolyn N. Barnes, Kent Adam Bowman, and Laura Crow, eds., *1941: Texas Goes to War* (Denton: University of North Texas Press, 1991), vii; Mark J. Perry, "Economic Output: If States Were Countries, California Would Be France," *Newsweek* June 11, 2016, accessed June 11, 2021, https://www.newsweek.com/economic-output-if-states-were-countries-california-would-be-france-467614.

3. For the migration into the state, see Randolph B. Campbell, *Gone to Texas: A History of the Lone Star State*, 3rd ed. (New York: Oxford University, 2017). For education in the state during the Second World War, see Thomas D. Snyder, ed., *120 Years of American Education: A Statistical Portrait* (Washington, DC: US Department of Education, 1993); Henry C. Dethloff, *Centennial History of Texas A&M University*, 2 vols. (College Station: Texas A&M University Press, 1976), particularly volume 2; George R. Woolfolk, *Prairie View: A Study in Public Conscience, 1878–1946* (New York: Pageant Press, 1962); Michael R. Heintze, *Private*

Black Colleges in Texas, 1865–1954 (College Station: Texas A&M University Press, 1985); and Charles W. Funkhouser, ed., *Education in Texas: Policies, Practices, and Principles*, 9th ed. (New York: Prentice Hall, 2000).

4. Studs Terkel, *The "Good War": An Oral History of World War II* (New York: The New Press, 1984); Universal Pictures' *Scarface* stars Al Pacino as Tony Montana. The 1983 movie is directed by Brian De Palma and the screenplay was written by Oliver Stone.

5. For Texan's self-identification at the time, see Kenneth B. Ragsdale, *The Year America Discovered Texas: 1936* (College Station: Texas A&M University Press, 1987), and Mark E. Nackman, *Nation within a Nation: Rise of Texas Nationalism* (Port Washington, NY: Kennikat Press, 1975).

6. For works detailing the New Deal and Texas, see Walter L. Buenger, "Between Community and Corporation: The Southern Roots of Jesse H. Jones and the Reconstruction Finance Corporation," *Journal of Southern History* 56 (August 1990); Keith J. Volanto, *Texas Cotton and the New Deal* (College Station: Texas A&M University Press, 2005); and Michael Barr, "A Comparative Examination of Federal Work Relief in Fredericksburg and Gillespie County," *Southwestern Historical Quarterly* 96 (January 1993). For electricity in Texas, see *Historical Statistics of the United States, Colonial Times to 1957* (Washington, DC: US Department of Commerce, 1960), *County Data Book*; and Henry Robert Hodges, "Rural Electrification Co-ops in Texas" (master's thesis, University of Texas, 1962).

7. For a snippet of the works detailing "when the military comes to town," see Priscilla Myers-Benham, "Texas City: Port of Industrial Opportunity" (PhD diss., University of Houston, 1987); Irene Paulette, "Odessa during the War Years, 1941–1945: A Microcosm of the Nation," *Permian Historical Annual* 22 (December 1982); Tracy M. Shilcutt, "'Soldiers Were Everywhere': Camp Barkeley and Abilene, Texas 1940–1945," *Sound Historian: Journal of the Texas Oral History Association* 12 (2009); and Priscilla Myers-Benham, "Texas City Port of Opportunity," *Houston Review* 10 (1988). For surveys of Texans serving during the war, see Stephen M. Sloan, Lois E. Myers, and Michelle Holland, eds., *Tattooed On My Soul: Texas Veterans Remember World War II* (College Station: Texas A&M University Press, 2015); Ronald E. Marcello, "Lone Star POWs: Texas National Guardsmen and the Building of the Burma-Thailand Railroad, 1942–1944," *Southwestern Historical Quarterly* 95 (January 1992); Alexander Mendoza and Charles David Grear, *Texans and War: New Interpretations of the State's Military History* (College Station: Texas A&M University Press, 2012); Kelly E. Crager, *Hell under the Rising Sun: Texan POWs and the Building of the Burma-Thailand Death Railway* (College Station: Texas A&M University Press, 2008); and Kelly E. Crager, "'God Knows What's Going to Happen to Us': The Lost Battery of Texas's 'Lost Battalion' during World War II," *Southwestern Historical Quarterly* 112 (July 2008).

8. The numbers came from *Historical Statistics of the United States: Colonial Times to 1970* (Washington, DC: US Department of Commerce: Bureau of the Census, Part 1, Series K 1–81, 1975). For brief introductions to the material here,

see Seth S. McKay and Odie B. Faulk, *Texas After Spindletop: The Saga of Texas, 1901–1965* (Austin, TX: Steck-Vaughn Company, 1965); Henry C. Dethloff, *From Field to Fork: A History of Texas Grain and Feed Association, 1898–1998* (Fort Worth: Texas Grain and Feed Association, 1998); and Garry L. Nall, "The Cattle-Feeding Industry on the Texas High Plains," in *Southwestern Agriculture: Pre-Colombian to Modern*, ed. Henry C. Dethloff and Irvin May Jr. (College Station: Texas A&M University Press, 1982).

9. For this, see American Petroleum Institute, *Petroleum Facts and Figures*, 7th ed. (New York: American Petroleum Institute, 1941); Diana Davids Olien and Roger M. Olien, *Oil in Texas: The Gusher Age, 1895–1945* (Austin: University of Texas Press, 2002); C. A. Warner, "Texas and the Oil Industry," *Southwestern Historical Quarterly* 50 (July 1946); Paul Alejandro Levengood, "For the Duration and Beyond: World War II and the Creation of Modern Houston, Texas" (PhD diss., Rice University, 1999); Murray Polakoff, "The Development of the Texas State CIO Council" (PhD diss., Columbia University, 1955); Irene Paulette, "Odessa during the War Years, 1941–1945: A Microcosm of the Nation," *Permian Historical Annual* 22 (1992); Houston Faust Mount, II, *Oilfield Revolutionary: The Career of Everette Lee DeGolyer* (College Station: Texas A&M University Press, 2014); and James R. Pfluger, "Fuel for Victory: Texas Panhandle Petroleum, 1941–1945," *Panhandle-Plains Historical Review* 62 (1989).

10. For a more detailed examination, see Ernest Obadele-Starks, *Black Unionism in the Industrial South* (College Station: Texas A&M University Press, 2000); Gary J. Rabalais, "Humble Women at War: The Case of Humble's Baytown Refinery, 1942–1945," *Houston Review of History and Culture* 2 (Spring 2005); Joseph Abel, "African Americans, Labor Unions, and the Struggle for Fair Employment in the Aircraft Manufacturing Industry of Texas, 1941–1945," *Journal of Southern History* 77 (August 2011); and Zachary Montz, "'Negro Laborers to the Crossroads': Organized Labor and the Traditions of Black Unionism in Houston, Texas, 1935–1964" (PhD diss., University of Texas, 2013).

11. See Judy Barrett Litoff and David C. Smith, *We're in This War, Too: World War II Letters from American Women in Uniform* (New York: Oxford University Press, 1994); Cindy Weigand, *Texas Women in World War II* (Lanham, MD: Republic of Texas Press, 2003); and Mattie E. Treadwell, *The Women's Army Corps*, in *United States Army in World War II, Special Studies*, rev. ed. (1991; Washington, DC: Office of the Chief of Military History, Department of the Army, CMH Pub. 11–8, 1954).

12. See Leisa D. Meyer, *Creating GI Jane: Sexuality and Power in the Women's Army Corps during World War II* (New York: Columbia University Press, 1998); D'Ann Campbell, *Women at War with America: Private Lives in a Patriotic Era* (Cambridge, MA: Harvard University Press, 1984); and Maureen Honey, *Creating Rosie the Riveter: Class, Gender, and Propaganda during World War II* (Amherst: University of Massachusetts Press, 1984).

13. See footnote 10 of this essay.

14. For more on the Tejano story during the war, see Maggie Rivas-Rodriguez, Juliana Torres, Melissa Dipiero-D'Sa, and Lindsay Fitzpatrick, *A Legacy Greater Than Words: Stories of US Latinos & Latinas of the WWII Generation* (Austin, TX: US Latino & Latina WWII Oral History Project, 2006); Emilio Zamora, *Claiming Rights and Righting Wrongs in Texas: Mexican Workers and Job Politics during World War II* (College Station: Texas A&M University Press, 2009); and Raúl Morín, *Among the Valiant: Mexican-Americans in WW II and Korea* (Alhambra, CA: Borden Publishing Company, 1966).

15. Robert F. Jefferson, *Fighting for Hope: African American Troops of the 93rd Infantry Division in World War II and Postwar America* (Baltimore, MD: Johns Hopkins University Press, 2008); Bernard C. Nalty, *Strength for the Fight: A History of Black Americans in the Military* (New York: Free Press, 1986); Bruce A. Glasrud and Merline Pitre, eds., *Black Women in Texas History* (College Station: Texas A&M University Press, 2008); Ruthe Winegarten, ed., *Black Texas Women: 150 Years of Trial and Triumph* (Austin: University of Texas Press, 1995); Michael R. Botson Jr., *Labor, Civil Rights, and the Hughes Tool Company* (College Station: Texas A&M University Press, 2005); and Obadele-Starks, *Black Unionism in the Industrial South.*

16. A brief survey of oral history works concerning Texas, see Christopher N. Koontz, Ronald E. Marcello, and Kelly E. Crager, *Heroes: Oral History Interviews with World War II Veterans* (Denton: Oral History Program, University of North Texas Press, 2002); Rivas-Rodriguez et al., *A Legacy More than Words*; Louis Fairchild, *They Called It the War Effort: Oral Histories from WWII Orange, TX*, 2nd ed. (Denton: Texas State Historical Association, 2012); Rebecca Craver, "Homefront with a Border Twist: El Paso During World War II," *Sound Historian: Journal of the Texas Oral History Association* 5 (1999); Fred H. Allison, "Patriotic Prosperity and Social Change in World War II: The Impact of Majors Field on Greenville, Texas," *Sound Historian: Journal of the Texas Oral History Association* 5 (1999); J'Neil L. Pate, *Arsenal of Defense: Fort Worth's Military Legacy* (Denton: Texas State Historical Association, 2011); and Dawn Letson, "Girl Pilots of Avenger Field: Sweetwater's Romance with the WASP of World War II," *Sound Historian: Journal of the Texas Oral History Association* 13 (2011).

17. A few works examining some of the changes in postwar Texas are Randolph B. Campbell, *Gone to Texas: A History of the Lone Star State* (New York: Oxford University Press, 2003); Pete Daniel, *Breaking the Land: The Transformation of Cotton, Tobacco, and Rice Cultures since 1880* (Urbana: University of Illinois Press, 1985); Karen Gerhardt Britton, *Bale o' Cotton: The Mechanical Art of Cotton Ginning* (College Station: Texas A&M University Press, 1992); Charles A. Warner, "The Oil Industry in Texas since Pearl Harbor," *Southwestern Historical Quarterly* LXI (January 1958); Merline Pitre, *In Struggle Against Jim Crow: Lulu B. White and the NAACP, 1900–1957* (College Station: Texas A&M University Press, 1999); and Barbara Ganson, *Texas Takes Wing: A Century of Flight in the Lone Star State* (Austin: University of Texas Press, 2014).

1

Before the Storm

Texas, 1939–1941

Joseph G. Dawson III[1]

In the summer of 1939, Texans, regardless of social status or ethnicity, looked to the future with mixed emotions. Throughout the 1930s, the Great Depression devastated the American economy. In response, President Franklin D. Roosevelt, known to Americans as "FDR," initiated his "New Deal," which consisted of federal interventionist programs, but elements of the Depression still gripped America. At its height in 1933, unemployment of adult men had approached 25 percent nationally. By 1939, however, it had declined to 14 percent. The unemployment rate in Texas by war's eve hovered around 10 percent. War in Europe suddenly changed the outlook of Texans. War loomed for some time before Germany invaded Poland on September 1, 1939, thus prompting Britain and France to declare war on the invader. By New Year's Day 1940, war news from Asia as well as Europe dominated the front pages of newspapers. Analysts had marked the start of international conflicts in Asia with Japan's attack on China in 1937. They quickly moved southward into the Asian mainland with plans to seize most of the islands in the Pacific Ocean. This objective pitted Japan against the empires of Britain, France, the Netherlands, and the United States, with their colonial holdings in Asia and the Pacific.[2]

Under the pressures of a world war, the Texas economy expanded. The Lone Star State's industries grew, adding thousands of workers. The US government established new military bases in the state and supplemented existing ones. The war changed Texas even before the United States was officially involved. Notable Texans could influence national decisions for the coming war. President Roosevelt had appointed prominent Houston banker and businessman Jesse H. Jones to be director of the federal Reconstruction Finance Corporation (RFC) and then moved him into the cabinet to be secretary of commerce in 1940. Managing both the RFC and the Federal Loan Agency, Jones channeled huge federal loans to states and businesses. In the US House of Representatives, Congressman Martin Dies held the chair of the controversial House Committee on Un-American Activities. Dies investigated individuals suspected of communism and Nazism or others with subversive sympathies. Another energetic member of the House, Congressman Lyndon B. Johnson was former director of the National Youth Administration's Texas branch from 1935 to 1937. Remarkably ambitious, Johnson had already set his sights on election to the US Senate. John Nance "Cactus Jack" Garner attracted national attention as Speaker of the House of Representatives, and many delegates supported his presidential ambitions at the Democratic National Convention in 1932. FDR wisely chose Garner as his vice president.[3]

Texas was located a great distance from the cultural and political centers of New York City and Washington, DC, in the East and Los Angeles and San Francisco in the West. Pleased to draw distinctions about themselves, Texans, especially Anglos, boasted about their state with what seemed to outsiders as inordinate pride. They touted their hats, boots, manner of speaking, and military heritage. They praised the Texas Rangers, the Alamo, and the former Republic of Texas, which was independent from 1836 to 1845. And Texans enjoyed proclaiming that their state was the country's biggest (and remained so until Alaska's admittance in 1959). Indeed, to anyone traveling during the 1940s, Texas was truly gigantic, totaling 268,597 square miles. Crossing the state from the town of Orange in the east to El Paso in the west, people traveled more than 875 miles. The distance from north of Dalhart in the northern Panhandle, south to Brownsville on the Rio Grande border was a separate trip of 900 miles. Publicizing their state's centennial, Texans had celebrated in 1936 by staging an extravagant fair in Dallas, drawing millions of visitors, including President Roosevelt.[4]

Texas appeared economically more connected to the nineteenth century than to the mid-twentieth century. Grown in 223 of the state's 254 counties, cotton still dominated the lives of many Texans. Second to cotton was raising cattle, sugar cane, rice, and pecans—traditional crops and pursuits important for decades. Approximately 35 percent of farms and ranches were modest, producing an income of $400 per year (around $7,187 in 2021 dollars). Oil, by contrast, represented the future. Since its commercial production began in 1901, oil greatly supplemented and diversified the state's economy. In December 1941, the Dallas Chamber of Commerce released a report decorated by artwork on its cover perpetuating an iconic image of a cowboy herding cattle—though airplanes were depicted flying overhead.[5]

Politically, the governor of Texas from 1939 to 1941 (and later US senator), W. Lee "Pappy" O'Daniel, gloried in his hillbilly image, similar to the era's other Southern provisional politicians like Theodore Bilbo from Mississippi and Huey P. Long from Louisiana. Prior to running for governor, Pappy O'Daniel attracted a popular following hosting a weekday radio program sponsored by the Burrus Mills Company makers of Light Crust Flour. The program featured singer Bob Wills and a hillbilly vocal troupe, the "Light Crust Doughboys." O'Daniel advertised Light Crust Flour, introduced songs, and spun stories. The show's theme song resounded with the phrase "Pass the biscuits, Pappy!" Announcing his run for governor in 1938, he charmed surprisingly large crowds and ran on a platform that vaguely promised more jobs but was otherwise nearly empty of substance. As the hillbilly candidate, O'Daniel swept into office. In 1940, opponents failed to unseat him. His rivals included Miriam "Ma" Ferguson, herself a controversial former Texas two-term governor (1925–27 and 1932–35). US senator from Texas Morris Sheppard died in 1941, and O'Daniel seized the moment, appointing a short-term replacement and arranging a special election. Dozens challenged him. Congressman Lyndon B. Johnson campaigned energetically and took an early lead. In the end, however, O'Daniel narrowly won. Lieutenant Governor Coke Stevenson assumed the governorship and immediately elevated the office. O'Daniel's undistinguished years in the Senate did nothing to alter the impression of Texas provincialism.[6]

In education, Texas demonstrated notable deficiencies, partly due to the state legislature's low funding and partly to costly duplications created by segregating whites and blacks. Of the state's 6,414,824 residents, Anglos comprised 5,487,545—about 85 percent. The Texas population divided approximately 2,911,000 urban and 3,500,000 rural—with the rural majority adding to the air of provincialism. Among Texans aged fourteen and older, 2.9 percent were illiterate in any language, including 2 percent of Anglos. More than 11 percent of African Americans were illiterate. Only 24.5 percent of the state's population had graduated from high school, though Texas did not begin requiring twelve years of basic education until 1942. Texas counted several urban metropolitan areas of more than 100,000 people. These areas included:

Houston: 528,900 people, 32.9 percent of whom were high school graduates in the city;

Dallas: 398,500 people, 39.2 percent;

San Antonio: 338,100 people, 28.1 percent;

Fort Worth: 226,500 people, 32.8 percent;

Beaumont: 178,000 people, 26.6 percent;

El Paso: 131,000 people, 26.8 percent;

Austin, the capital: 111,000 people, 35 percent; and

Waco: 101,900 people, 25.2 percent.[7]

Texans could pick from forty-one public and private colleges in 1940. Only one state university ranked above average academically—the University of Texas at Austin, with a student enrollment of 11,600. Located in College Station, the Agricultural and Mechanical College of Texas, known as the A&M College, was an all-male military college mustering 6,500 cadets. More than 4,000 enrolled at Texas Technological College in Lubbock, but only 2,700 registered at the University of Houston, recently elevated to full university status. Texas also funded several teachers' colleges in each region of the state. Among a number of private colleges, Baylor University and Rice University enrolled 2,550 and 1,450 students, respectively. A segregated society, Texas woefully underserved its black citizens. More than 1,300 black youths matriculated at a state college, Prairie View A&M, most majoring in agriculture. The city of Houston had established the Houston College for Negroes (today Texas Southern University). In 1940 it registered only 400 pupils. Small private black institutions struggled to remain open. For example, Wiley College and Bishop College, both in Marshall, enrolled 420 students and 450 students, respectively.[8]

In some ways America itself seemed provincial. Nationally and in Texas some elements of modern technology were still too expensive for many who resided in America's rural expanses. For instance, electricity in private homes had significantly increased due to New Deal electrification programs in the 1930s, but in 1940 only one-third of *rural* American residences and farms had electric power. In Texas, only 18.4 percent of rural homes had electricity. Pertaining to other basic services, one-third of rural American homes did not have an indoor toilet. Less than 20 percent of rural Texas homes had running water. Widely available, a new car in 1940 cost around $800 (approximately $15,493 in 2021 dollars) but the economic hard times of the Depression meant that not everyone owned a car. Numbers of rural Americans still relied on animal power. For example, a 1939 photograph taken at the Harrison County courthouse parking lot in Marshall, Texas (population 20,000), showed more than twenty motor vehicles and fourteen wagons pulled by horses and mules. Without cars, people relied heavily on streetcars and buses, as trains, though reliable, were more expensive. The telephone was common in cities but unavailable in many rural areas. Urban residents could place calls on ubiquitous public pay telephones, but at the price of a loaf of bread (5 cents). Radios transmitted music, programs, and news, but many Americans did not own one. In rural Texas, only about one in five homes had a radio.[9]

Prewar social attitudes of many Anglos in Texas maintained the "Jim Crow" system of segregation. Discrimination against African Americans created a bifurcated society regarding service to blacks in many businesses and daily life. Jim Crow also pertained to America's military forces. Black men were allowed to enlist in the US Army, but segregated in only four regiments, routinely led by white officers. Black men rarely obtained a commission to become an army officer, and the navy and the Marine Corps did not permit them as officers. When the US Congress convened in 1940, only one African American had been elected by voters to the House of Representatives. In fact, it had been forty-three years since an African American man had represented any Texan, either in the state legislature or Congress. Contributing to this was the individual state poll tax. Costing between $1 and $2, it required all adult citizens to pay it prior to voting. This extra expense fell heaviest on society's poorest and minority. Northern and Southern states had a poll tax. Like most Southern states, Texas mandated it. However, a few former Confederate states—North Carolina, Florida, and Louisiana—had repealed theirs. Southern states also used the restrictive "white primary," designed by Anglos to discourage minorities from voting in primary elections scheduled before a state's general election. The violent and intimidating scourge of lynching (hanging and torturing African Americans) remained present in the South, though its occurrence declined in the 1930s in Texas. Since the early twentieth century, the National Association for the Advancement of Colored People (NAACP) actively challenged all forms of discrimination. The NAACP operated chapters in Dallas and Houston, initiating court cases against poll taxes, white primaries, and segregation in Texas. Discrimination was not limited to blacks; it also inhibited the lives of Tejanos, although it was not as intense nor pervasive as against African Americans.[10]

America's educational levels had improved but still remained low in the views of some educators. Based on a summary of one federal study, states had made notable improvements since the Great War. As of 1916, nationwide, approximately 1,700,000 American students attended high schools and 400,000 enrolled in colleges and universities. Thirty-four years later, the numbers had risen dramatically to 7,100,000 and 1,400,000, respectively. While only about one-fourth of Texas students finished high school, according to a federal report, about 30 percent of US high school students were graduating. About 6 percent of American men and 4 percent of women had earned bachelor's degrees.[11]

On the other hand, one of President Roosevelt's most successful programs, the Civilian Conservation Corps (CCC), improved the circumstances and broadened the horizons of young men in Texas and America. The CCC brought about "a more national outlook" and accomplished multiple goals during its existence from 1933 to 1942. Recruiting thousands of unemployed men aged 18 to 25, many from cities, the CCC placed them in work camps, often in rural areas outside of their home states. Operating under the leadership of US Army soldiers, the CCC set up camps in every state. Government-issued uniforms identified its workers. A few of the camps in the North were racially integrated, but in the South the CCC segregated blacks and whites. However, Latinos worked alongside Anglos in many of the more than ninety camps active in Texas. The CCC built or improved roads, campgrounds, and parks; cut firebreaks; and planted millions of trees, usually in federal lands, parks, and forests, but also in state parks and recreation areas. CCC workers handled various tools, drove and repaired motor vehicles, and learned alongside skilled craftsmen, all the while meeting men from other states. Furthermore, CCC members took the opportunity to improve their literacy and education, attending class levels ranging from grammar school through high school with some college courses. Bettering the capabilities and qualifications of Texas workers meant the state might attract new business and industry.[12]

In 1940, the war in Europe took an abrupt turn. Germany defeated and occupied several European nations, including Norway, Denmark, the Netherlands, Luxemburg, and Belgium. This string of German success culminated with its defeat of France in June. Germany posed an immediate threat to Great Britain. These military campaigns stunned America's leaders, and in September 1940, Germany, Japan, and Italy agreed to the Tripartite Pact—the Axis alliance. President Roosevelt and Congress responded by expanding the US armed forces and allocating funds to purchase all sorts of military supplies, equipment, ships, vehicles, and aircraft. Thousands of civilian jobs, many in Texas, directly followed as a result of these steps. In an inspiring radio address to the nation, the president asserted that America "must be the great arsenal of democracy."[13]

Throughout 1940 and 1941, after a decade of decline in the state's manufacturing base during the Depression, Texas' industrial activities, many connected to military matters, experienced a significant upswing. Sparking the state's economy during this time, the War Department authorized contracts for construction at both established and new military installations. To produce the needed building materials for such projects, Texans expanded existing industries. Businessmen also erected new plants, especially for aircraft and ships. The oil industry, to be sure, boomed. All of these activities sent economic ripples through the state's growing population. Accommodating the influx of new residents, Texans greatly expanded existing infrastructure and built much-needed housing for both military personnel and civilians.[14]

Texans welcomed the stepped-up business activities without necessarily linking them to military preparation. Leaders and workers recognized their state's dependence on agriculture, including cattle raising, and most encouraged economic diversification. Americans responded to George Gallup's national polling company with clear opinions opposed to entering the wars in either Europe or Asia, without wanting to acknowledge that as those wars intensified, so, too, did the state's economic growth. But as the wars intensified, the probability for America to become embroiled in both conflicts also increased. A Gallup poll taken in May 1941 showed that 29 percent of Texans favored the United States going to war with Germany. Thus, a vast majority did not want war even if they were benefiting from economic growth propelled by military activities.[15]

Manufacturing motor vehicles and airplanes rapidly bolstered the economies of the Dallas and Fort Worth metropolitan areas during 1940–41. Workers flocked to those cities as businessmen built new factories, such as the North American Aviation plant, to turn out single-engine fighter aircraft. Ford Motor Company's Dallas plant added lines producing tank motors. A major takeoff occurred when Consolidated Aircraft Corporation constructed a giant complex in Fort Worth to manufacture four-engine bombers and cargo planes. When completed, Consolidated's facility rivaled Ford Motor Company's bomber factory at Willow Run, near Detroit, Michigan. As a writer proclaimed in March 1941, "Dallas is Defense-Minded." Regarding North American Aviation's contract to manufacture 1,000 warplanes for Britain, another writer reinforced the same by stating, "Our job is Making Planes." In contrast to September 1939, by December 1941, observant Texans understood that many military products rolled out of factories flourishing in the Dallas–Fort Worth vicinity.[16]

To the south, several Houston companies also benefited from the military's business. One firm made tents for the army. Others became subcontractors, with one producing machine-gun parts and a second fabricating landing gear for bombers. These components went to plants in Texas and other states for further assembly. Public high schools prepared students as auto mechanics, radio operators, cooks, and typists—skills that businesses and the military needed. Businessmen encouraged workers' efficiency by installing air-conditioning in more than 160 of Houston's buildings in 1940—the leading edge of a technology in the coming years that transformed life for people in Texas and the rest of the "sunbelt." If some businessmen had yet to notice the military-related activities of the previous twenty-two months, the artwork on the cover of Houston's Chamber of Commerce magazine for November 1941 pictured an army convoy snaking out of the city. Guarded by eight four-engine bombers flying overhead, a twelve-ton M-3 "Stuart" tank led a column of trucks pulling artillery. Perhaps the convoy rolled toward one of the army posts near Houston, such as Camp Wallace in Hitchcock (near Galveston), Fort Crockett in Galveston, or Camp Hulen at Palacios, Matagorda County, a coastal county approximately halfway between Galveston and Corpus Christi.[17]

Though Houston lagged behind Dallas and Fort Worth in heavy industry, the Bayou City surpassed its rivals in the ever-important shipbuilding industry. President Roosevelt and Congress agreed to greatly strengthen and expand the US Navy. Around Houston from 1940 through 1941, new port facilities popped up like mushrooms. Existing shipyards added more berths and docks. Hiring doubled at Todd Shipbuilding Corporation and other businesses along the Houston Ship Channel. By December 1941, the Chamber of Commerce trumpeted that Houston and its Ship Channel amounted to the "First Port of the South" and ranked only behind the ports of New York City and Philadelphia in volume of cargo. With increased traffic, Houston's port required more longshoremen to load and unload the vessels. Although Anglos landed most of these good jobs, African Americans and Latinos also benefited from the better job situation.[18]

Elsewhere on the upper Texas coast, shipbuilding and associated industries prospered. Workers in Beaumont fabricated oceangoing cargo vessels, while in nearby Orange, Consolidated Steel Corporation received the contract to build twelve destroyers for the US Navy. Just when it seemed that available housing and other businesses had reached their capacity to meet the increased needs during 1940–41, a second wave of shipbuilding contracts swamped the Gulf Coast the following year. The director of the Federal Bureau of Investigation (FBI), J. Edgar Hoover, recognizing the state's importance to national security, urged Texans to be vigilant, especially for German spies who might try to obtain industrial or military information.[19]

Throughout 1940 and 1941, both the US Army and US Navy expanded existing bases and opened new ones in Texas as thousands of military personnel arrived for training in the state. The very characteristics that previously made Texas seem "provincial" now became attributes. Abundant and inexpensive land for the federal government to buy or lease made Texas an attractive state for military installations, especially for army maneuvers. In 1939, the *Texas Almanac* listed fifteen army installations, some with airfields. The next edition listed twenty-three army posts. Some of the largest had been active for many years, such as Fort Bliss, established in 1849 near El Paso, and Fort Crockett, established in 1897 on Galveston Island. The heart of a complex of military facilities and airfields in San Antonio, Fort Sam Houston, established in 1876, spread across 3,000 acres. The fort contained 1,000 buildings, including Brooke General Hospital, one of the army's largest health care centers.[20]

Other army facilities, termed "camps," typically ranked below forts in size and permanency. Both camps and forts began to fill with troops during 1940 and 1941. FDR issued an executive order on August 31, 1940, calling the entire US National Guard into federal service for one year. The War Department put the plan in motion in September, and in the coming months, Guard units moved to training camps. Several tripled in acreage as Texas units and outfits from other states relocated to the Lone Star State. Camp Hulen, near Palacios, had opened in 1926 as a modest National Guard training site. Beginning in January 1941, civilians employed at Hulen by the federal Works Progress Administration (WPA) built a variety of new structures on more than a thousand acres. Near the town of Brownwood in Brown County, in Central Texas, Camp Bowie expanded from about 2,000 to more than 20,000 acres. The primary outfit at Bowie was the National Guard's

36th Infantry Division, nicknamed the "Texas Division." Soon, artillery, armor, signal, and engineer units also trained at Bowie. Camp Barkeley, near Abilene, in West Texas, opened in December 1940 with the arrival of the 45th Infantry Division, an Oklahoma National Guard unit manned from men from Arizona, New Mexico, Colorado, and Oklahoma. Accompanying that division was a young Guardsman named Bill Mauldin, who got his start as a cartoonist drawing for the camp newspaper before becoming America's most notable illustrator of soldier life during World War II. The next year, other major units began arriving at Barkeley, including tank brigades, containing 5,000 men each. Adding a touch of nostalgia, a Texas National Guard horse cavalry unit, the 112th Cavalry Regiment, reported to Fort Bliss. After a few weeks, its commanding officer observed that his troopers understood that they may be headed to war—even if FDR had stated that American "boys are not going to be sent into any foreign wars."[21]

In addition to ground combat units, the army also opened or expanded Army Air Corps airfields during 1940 and 1941. The clear and open skies appealed to the army for pilot and aircrew training. One of the most important facilities was Randolph Field in San Antonio. Praised as the "West Point of the Air," Randolph Field added classrooms, built new barracks, and poured more runways for training thousands of pilots. Kelly Field, Lackland Field, and Brooks Field supplemented Randolph. Together they comprised "one of the largest military airdromes in the world." The War Department also reactivated Ellington Army Airfield in Houston and opened Sheppard Army Airfield in Wichita Falls in June 1941, the same month that Congress renamed the Air Corps the Army Air Forces. Officials also scouted possible airfield sites throughout the state at Amarillo, Austin, Bryan, Dalhart, Laredo, Lubbock, San Angelo, San Marcos, and Waco.[22]

Though not as active as the army, the US Navy also increased its presence in Texas in the early forties. A fairly prosperous town of 92,600, Corpus Christi was the perfect location for a naval air station to train pilots. In June 1940, FDR signed a military budget that tripled funds for naval aviation. The Department of the Navy allocated some of that money for new buildings, support facilities, and airfields at Corpus Christi. Attending a ceremony in the city in March 1941, Congressman Lyndon B. Johnson accompanied the secretary of the navy, highlighting the base's expansion. A class of fifty naval aviators started training in April. One month later, 200 cadet pilots trained at Corpus Christi. Near Dallas, the Naval Reserve had operated a small base at Grand Prairie, with a hangar, a repair building, and a fuel depot. The Department of the Navy expanded all of these facilities and included a barracks in 1941. Thirty-five student fliers arrived, and plans estimated 600 total training there. Texans residing near these cities noticed the army and navy's surging pace of activities.[23]

In addition to these developments, President Roosevelt further prepared America for the prospect of war. He appointed two respected Republicans to his cabinet. Chicago newspaper publisher Frank Knox became secretary of the navy, while former secretary of state Henry L. Stimson became secretary of war. To assist Great Britain, the president exchanged fifty aging US Navy destroyers for leasing rights for naval bases on English territory in the Western Hemisphere. The Royal Navy needed the warships to guard the Atlantic convoys against German U-boats, while the Americans needed the bases to extend its defensive perimeter into the Atlantic. Conscription was another major consequence of the pressures of the war on America. After calling the National Guard to federal service for one year, President Roosevelt asked Congress to approve a draft law. Always a controversial policy, conscription, the president argued, was necessary to strengthen America's defenses. Congress passed and President Roosevelt signed the Selective Service Act into law in September 1940. Under its terms, men could be drafted for one year. The *Dallas Morning News* front page headline read "1,573 Texans Ordered for First Draft," part of 30,000 Americans conscripted by the end of November. This law changed the tone of life in the country. Within months, many knew someone who had received a draft notice.[24]

On May 11, 1941, a college student issued his own warning to Texans about the possibility of being drawn into the Second World War. Texas A&M's Corps of Cadets marched in a campus parade for its annual "Mother's Day Program." Cadet Colonel Mayo J. Thompson delivered a sobering speech to the Corps. A senior student, Thompson was only a few days away from being commissioned as a lieutenant in the US Army. He reminded attendees that "all the world is struggling in the midst of chaos and destruction," sliding into "a world in flames." Thompson emphasized Texas mothers, like British mothers, must be vigilant, since "we are confronted with the problem of preserving the

Democratic [*sic*] way of life that the founders of this nation established." He advised all present to look to their mothers for "keeping up public morale, the foundation of which is laid in the home." Thompson's speech prepared his listeners and other Texans for US entry into the war. When the country finally entered the conflict approximately six months after his speech, Thompson would be among the 20,000 Aggies who served in it.[25]

Mayo "Joe" Thompson was born on May 12, 1919, and received a diploma from Paschal High School in Fort Worth. In 1937, he enrolled in the Agricultural and Mechanical College of Texas (later Texas A&M University). Cadet Thompson excelled at several activities, most notably as an accomplished public speaker and debater. His skills won him awards for four consecutive years with the student debate club. As a cadet in his senior year, he was the personnel officer on the staff of the cadet Artillery Regiment with the rank of cadet captain. He graduated with a bachelor's degree in economics in May 1941. Having established himself as one of the most notable student speakers, Thompson was selected in May 1941 to give the public address to the entire cadet corps and campus visitors during the annual Mother's Day Program. He addressed a crowd estimated at nearly 5,000 people, one of the largest crowds on campus for a nonsporting event. Commissioned as a second lieutenant in the US Army's Artillery Branch in June 1941, Thompson served in the Pacific Theater during World War II. He commanded an artillery unit in the army's 7th Infantry Division against Japanese forces. In the last year of the war, Captain Thompson successfully completed the program of study in the Ground Forces Course from early January to mid-March 1945 at the US Army Command and General Staff College, Fort Leavenworth, Kansas. After the war, he remained in the US Army National Guard, eventually rising to the rank of colonel before retiring from the National Guard in 1958. Leaving active military duty in the postwar years, Thompson graduated from the South Texas College of Law in 1949 and entered into the practice of admiralty law. In addition to a successful law practice, he also devoted himself to Texas A&M by endowing student scholarships at the university and becoming president of the Alumni Association, among other activities. He was made a Distinguished Alumnus of the university in 1980. Thompson died in Houston on July 15, 2007.[26]

Texans, meanwhile, still sought entertainment by playing and watching sports. Although Texas was not represented in the big leagues, the state gave its name to baseball's Class A "Texas League." The Texas League had teams in Houston, Dallas, Fort Worth, San Antonio, and Beaumont, as well as in cities in Oklahoma and Louisiana. Texans played baseball in neighborhood sandlots and on club teams representing churches, towns, and counties. High schools and colleges also fielded many teams. Baseball justly deserved the appellation of "America's game." At the same time Americans faced threats of war, the "Friday Night Lights" began to blare as high school and college football gained in popularity in Texas. Among the rabid rivalries, the Texas A&M Aggies challenged the University of Texas' Texas Longhorns, both members of the Southwest Conference, which comprised six Texas teams and one from Arkansas. The Aggies throttled the Longhorns 20–0 to secure the conference championship and secured the national championship in 1939 with a win over Tulane in the Sugar Bowl on January 1, 1940. The next season, though Texas upset A&M 7–0 in their annual Thanksgiving Day contest, A&M won the Southwest Conference and went to Dallas to play in the Cotton Bowl. With 40,000 people in attendance, the Aggies defeated Fordham University on January 1, 1941. During the fall of 1941, A&M again won the conference title despite losing to the Longhorns 23–0. Two weeks later, on December 7, Japan attacked Pearl Harbor in Hawaii. Four days later, Germany declared war on America. Infuriated by such treachery, Americans and Texans were in the war. As planned, the Aggies made it to the Cotton Bowl on January 1, 1942, and 38,000 watched the visiting team, Alabama, defeat A&M 29–21. By then, the nation had turned its attention to the Second World War.[27]

For most Texans born between 1900 and 1925, two developments dominated their lives: the Great Depression and World War II. Prior to the United States entering the war, the intensifying conflict produced consequences for Texas. During 1940 and 1941, Houston, Dallas, Fort Worth, Beaumont, and San Antonio experienced significant population increases. As happened nationally, more Texas women willingly entered the workforce, answering the nation's call. Setting an exceptional example, Oveta Culp Hobby of Houston, a college graduate and wife of former Texas governor William P. Hobby, operated a radio station and published the *Houston Post*, one of the state's major newspapers. Having worked in the public relations office of the War Department, she came to the attention of the army chief of staff, General George C. Marshall. The general was considering a plan for women to serve in a new Women's Army Auxiliary Corps (WAAC), and Marshall appointed Mrs. Hobby to direct the WAAC.[28]

During 1940 and 1941, thousands of soldiers and sailors were sent to Texas. Jobs in the state's burgeoning economy attracted many people from around the country. By December 1941, Texans of all ages were highly patriotic and nationalistic. Each school day, students pledged, in unison, allegiance to the US flag. At sporting events, their parents stood for the National Anthem. The song "God Bless America," written by Irving Berlin, was phenomenally popular. Singer Kate Smith's recording of "God Bless America" became a smash hit on jukeboxes, radio shows, and sheet music. Men sang the song in public at club meetings such as Kiwanis, Rotary, Elks, Lions, Masons, Knights of Columbus, and the American Legion. Women joined in singing "God Bless America" at Junior League meetings and garden clubs. Delegates sang "God Bless America" at the Republican and Democratic Party nominating conventions. Patriotism even permeated into children's comics. The most popular hero was Superman. In the early days of the war, "the Man of Steel's" main adversaries were foreign agents, saboteurs, and their traitorous henchmen threatening America.[29]

Federal art programs contributed to patriotism and national pride. Prominent were the New Deal's Federal Art Project of the Public Works Administration and the Section of Fine Arts in the Treasury Department. From 1934 to 1943, the US government commissioned hundreds of pieces of art throughout Texas. Many were influenced by the state's history or culture. These programs placed paintings, murals, and posters in every US Post Office, federal building, and courthouse in Texas, as well as throughout train stations and airports.[30]

After December 7, 1941, Texans were confident that, somehow, America would defeat the Axis powers. Given the contingencies of war, no one knew how long it would take to achieve victory. Texans could expect to be directly involved in multiple ways.

Chapter 1, Appendix A: Southern States, Percentage of Students Completing High School*

Southern States
Percent Completing High School
[National Average approx. 30%]

Florida	26.2
Texas	*24.5*
North Carolina	18.2
South Carolina	18.2
Tennessee	17.9
Louisiana	7.5
Mississippi	15.9
Alabama	15.7
Arkansas	14.9

*Reference: *County Data Book, A Supplement to the Statistical Abstract of the United States* (Washington, DC: Government Printing Office, 1947), 2

Chapter 1, Appendix B: Selected US States, Percentage of Students Completing High School*

Selected States
Percent Completing High School
[National Average approx. 30%]

Texas	*24.5*
California	36.9
Colorado	31.7
Massachusetts	30.4
Nebraska	28.7
Michigan	24.5
New York	22.9
Wisconsin	22.1
Pennsylvania	20.9

*Reference: *County Data Book, A Supplement to the Statistical Abstract of the United States* (Washington, DC: Government Printing Office, 1947), 2.

Notes

1. Joseph G. "Chip" Dawson III is Professor of History at Texas A&M University at College Station. Former Director of A&M's Military Studies Institute, Dawson has authored and edited many works on military history.

2. William E. Leuchtenburg, *Franklin D. Roosevelt and the New Deal, 1932–1940* (New York: Harper, 1963), 263, 346; Roger Biles, *The South and the New Deal* (Lexington: University of Kentucky Press, 1994), 20–21; Roger Biles, "The New Deal in Dallas," *Southwestern Historical Quarterly* 95 (July 1991): 1–19; *Houston Post* and *Dallas Morning News*, January 1, 1940. The *Morning News* ran a frequent article on its front page of section one, "The War Today," reporting the war's notable events and giving the number of days the war had lasted. The survey covering Texas, 1941–1945, is from Ralph A. Wooster's, *Texas and Texans in World War II* (Austin, TX: Eakin Press, 2005). For more on the New Deal and the Depression in the late 1930s and early 1940s in Texas, see Lionel V. Palenaude, *Texas, Politics and the New Deal* (New York: Garland, 1983); Jesse Jones and Edward Angly, *Fifty Billion Dollars: My Thirteen Years with the Reconstruction Finance Corporation, 1933–1945* (New York: Macmillan Company, 1951); and Seth Shepherd McKay, *W. Lee O'Daniel and Texas Politics, 1938–1942* (Lubbock: Texas Tech University Press, 1944).

3. Walter L. Buenger, "Between Community and Corporation: The Southern Roots of Jesse H. Jones and the Reconstruction Finance Corporation," *Journal of Southern History* 56 (August 1990), 481–510; Carol Weisenberger, *The National Youth Administration in Texas* (New York: Peter Lang, 1994); August R. Ogden, *The Dies Committee*, rev. ed. (Westport, CT: Greenwood Press, 1984); Patrick Cox, "John Nance Garner," in *Profiles in Power: Twentieth Century Texans in Washington*, eds. Kenneth E. Hendrickson Jr., et al. (New Edition; Austin: University of Texas Press, 1993), 42–63. The literature on the Great Depression defies the limited space here. For an introduction to this time period on the New Deal and New Deal agencies like the National Youth Administration, Works Progress Administration, and the Reconstruction Finance Administration, see Christie Lynne Bourgeois, "Lyndon Johnson's Years with the National Youth Administration" (master's thesis, University of Texas, 1986); Bascom N. Timmons, *Garner of Texas: A Personal History* (New York: Harper & Brothers Publishers, 1948); Michael Barr, "A Comparative Examination of Federal Work Relief in Fredericksburg and Gillespie County," *Southwestern Historical Quarterly* 96 (January 1993); Sheila D. Collins and Gertrude Schaffner Goldberg, eds., *When Government Helped: Learning from the Successes and Failures of the New Deal* (New York: Oxford University Press, 2014); William H. Chafe, ed., *American Liberalism: The New Deal and Its Legacies* (New York: Columbia University Press, 2003); Erich Rauchway, *The Great Depression & and the New Deal: A Very Short Introduction* (New York: Oxford University Press, 2008); Christie Lynne Bourgeois, "Stepping over the Lines: Lyndon Johnson, Black Texans, and the National Youth Administration," *Southwestern Historical Quarterly* 91 (October 1987); Jason Scott Smith, *A Concise History of the New Deal*

(New York: Cambridge University Press, 2014); Alan Brinkley, *The End of Reform: New Deal Liberalism in Recession and War* (New York: Vintage Books, 1996); Searle F. Charles, *Minister of Relief: Harry Hopkins and the Depression* (Syracuse, NY: Syracuse University Press, 1963); and Arthur M. Schlesinger's three volumes titled *The Age of Roosevelt*. Less favorable views of FDR and governmental action to combat the Depression are Gary Dean Best, *Pride, Prejudice, and Politics: Roosevelt Versus Recovery, 1933–1938* (New York: Praeger, 1990); Amity Schlaes, *The Forgotten Man: A New History of the Great Depression* (New York: Harper Perennial, 2007); and Burton W. Folsom Jr., *New Deal or Raw Deal?: How FDR's Economic Legacy Has Damaged America* (New York: Threshold Editions, 2008).

4. Kenneth B. Ragsdale, *The Year America Discovered Texas: 1936* (College Station: Texas A&M University Press, 1987), 225, 295, 305; Mark E. Nackman, *Nation within a Nation: Rise of Texas Nationalism* (Port Washington, NY: Kennikat Press, 1975); Walter L. Buenger and Robert W. Calvert, "Introduction," in *Texas through Time: Evolving Interpretations*, eds. Buenger and Calvert (College Station: Texas A&M University Press, 1991), ix–xxxv; Walter L. Buenger, "Three Truths in Texas," in *Beyond Texas through Time: Breaking Away from Past Interpretations*, eds. Walter L. Buenger and Arnoldo DeLeon (College Station: Texas A&M University Press, 2011), 1–49. Another point of debate is whether Texas is more a "Western" state or a "Southern" state—or some hybrid combination of South and West. For this argument, see Sue B. Beckham, *Depression Post Office Murals and Southern Culture* (Baton Rouge: Louisiana State University Press, 1989); and Randolph B. Campbell, *Gone to Texas: A History of the Lone Star State* (New York: Oxford University Press, 2003). Two works chronicling the Texas Centennial in 1936 are Kenneth B. Ragsdale, *The Year America Discovered Texas-Centennial '36* (College Station: Texas A&M University Press, 1987); and Jesse O. Thomas, *Negro Participation in the Texas Centennial Exposition* (Boston: Christopher Publishing House, 1938).

5. Keith J. Volanto, *Texas Cotton and the New Deal* (College Station: Texas A&M University Press, 2005), 5–6. On agriculture, see *County Data Book: A Supplement to the Statistical Abstract of the United States* (Washington, DC: US Government Printing Office, 1947); and *Annual Report of the Dallas Chamber of Commerce*, special supplement to the Chamber's monthly magazine, *Dallas* 20 (December 1941). For Texas in the initial years of the Great Depression, see Donald W. Whisenhunt, *The Depression in Texas: The Hoover Years* (New York: Garland Publishing, 1983).

6. Kenneth E. Hendrickson Jr., *Chief Executives of Texas: From Stephen F. Austin to John B. Connally* (College Station: Texas A&M University Press, 1995), 195–202; Seth S. McKay, *Texas after Spindletop*, vol. 6, *Saga of Texas, 1901–1965* (Austin, TX: Steck-Vaughn Company, 1965), 152–58, 161–64, 168–75. A more detailed account of O'Daniel and the Light Crust Doughboys is John Mark Dempsey's, *The Light Crust Doughboys Are on the Air: Celebrating Seventy Years of Texas Music* (Denton: University of North Texas Press, 2002). See also T. Harry Williams, *Huey Long: A Biography* (New York: Knopf, 1969); William Ivy Hair, *The Kingfish and His Realm:*

The Life and Times of Huey P. Long (Baton Rouge: Louisiana State University Press, 1997); Richard D. White, *Kingfish: The Reign of Huey P. Long* (New York: Random House, 2006); and Chester M. Morgan, *Redneck Liberal: Theodore Bilbo and the New Deal* (Baton Rouge: Louisiana State University Press, 1985).

7. Thomas D. Snyder, ed., *120 Years of American Education: A Statistical Portrait* (Washington, DC: US Department of Education, 1993), 21; *Texas Almanac and State Industrial Guide 1939–40* (Dallas: A. H. Belo Corporation, 1939), 486; *Texas Almanac and State Industrial Guide, 1941–42* (Dallas: A. H. Belo Corporation, 1941), 326–28; *County Data Book*, 2, 356. See this chapter's Appendix A and Appendix B comparing and contrasting Texas to other former Confederate states and selected Northern and Western states in percent of population that completed high school in 1940.

8. *Texas Almanac 1939–40*, 486; *Texas Almanac 1941–42*, 326–28; Henry C. Dethloff, *Centennial History of Texas A&M University*, 2 vols. (College Station: Texas A&M University Press, 1976), 2:442; George R. Woolfolk, *Prairie View: A Study in Public Conscience, 1878–1946* (New York: Pageant Press, 1962), 315, 321, 354; Michael R. Heintze, *Private Black Colleges in Texas, 1865–1954* (College Station: Texas A&M University Press, 1985), 129–39, 150–51. See also Anna Victoria Wilson, "Education for African Americans," *Handbook of Texas*, accessed August 3, 2016, https://tshaonline.org/handbook/online/articles/pkaan; Henry A. Bullock, *A History of Negro Education in the South from 1619 to the Present* (Cambridge, MA: Harvard University Press, 1970); Charles W. Funkhouser, ed., *Education in Texas: Policies, Practices, and Principles*, 9th ed. (New York: Prentice Hall, 2000); Alwyn Barr, *Black Texans: A History of Negroes in Texas, 1528–1971* (Norman: University of Oklahoma Press, 1996); Michael L. Gillette, "The NAACP in Texas, 1937–1957" (PhD diss., University of Texas, 1984); Chandler Davidson, *Race and Class in Texas Politics* (Princeton, NJ: Princeton University Press, 1990); Melvin J. Banks, "The Pursuit of Equality: The Movement for First Class Citizenship among Negro Schools, 1920–1950s" (PhD diss., Syracuse University, 1962); and William Joseph Brophy, "The Black Texan: A Quantitative History" (PhD diss., Vanderbilt University, 1974).

9. On electricity, toilets, and radios, see *Historical Statistics of the United States, Colonial Times to 1957* (Washington, DC: US Department of Commerce, 1960), *County Data Book*; Henry Robert Hodges, "Rural Electrification Co-ops in Texas" (master's thesis, University of Texas, 1962); James E. Banks and John E. Babcock, *Corralling the Colorado: The First Fifty Years of the Lower Colorado River Authority* (Austin, TX: Eakin Press, 1988); Comer Clay, "The Lower Colorado River Authority: A Study in Politics and Public Administration" (PhD diss., University of Texas, 1948); John A. Adams Jr., *Damning the Colorado: The Rise of the Lower Colorado River Authority, 1933–1939* (College Station: Texas A&M University Press, 1940); Carroll Pursell, *A History of Technology in Postwar America* (New York: Columbia University Press, 2007); David E. Kyvig, *Daily Life in the United States, 1920–1939* (Westport, CT: Greenwood Press, 2002), 27–90; Eugenia Kaledin, *Daily Life in the*

United States, 1940–1959: Shifting Worlds (Westport, CT: Greenwood Press, 2000); and Richard Schroeder, *Texas Signs On: The Early Days of Radio and Television* (College Station: Texas A&M University Press, 1998). For radios and telephones, see *Texas Almanac 1939–40*. The 1939 photo is in Robert L. Reid, *Picturing Texas: The FSA-OWI Photographers* (Austin: Texas State Historical Association, 1994). A wide-ranging discussion is in David E. Nye, *Electrifying America: Social Meanings of New Technology, 1880–1940* (Cambridge, MA: Massachusetts Institute of Technology Press, 1990). Examples of advertisements for train travel are in *Texas Almanac 1941–42*.

10. Bernard C. Nalty, *Strength for the Fight: A History of Black Americans in the Military* (New York: Free Press, 1986), 128–33 and passim; Donald Strong, "The Poll Tax: The Case of Texas," *American Political Science Review* 38 (August 1944), 693–709; Darlene Clark Hine, "Elusive Ballot: The Black Struggle Against the Texas Democratic White Primary, 1932–1945," *Southwestern Historical Quarterly* 81 (April 1978), 373–92; David L. Chapman, "Lynching in Texas" (master's thesis, Texas A&M University, 1973), 96; Merline Pitre, *In the Struggle against Jim Crow: Lulu B. White, 1900–1957* (College Station: Texas A&M University Press, 1999); Michael L. Gillette, "The Rise of the NAACP in Texas," *Southwestern Historical Quarterly* 81 (April 1978), 393–416; Zaragosa Vargas, *Crucible of Struggle: A History of Mexican-Americans* (New York: Oxford University Press, 2011), 236–37, 243–48. For other works on race, segregation, and politics in pre-World War II Texas, see John Mason Brewer, *Negro Legislators of Texas and Their Descendants: A History of the Negro in Texas Politics from Reconstruction to Disfranchisement* (Dallas: Mathis, 1935); Darlene Clark Hine, *Black Victory: The Rise and Fall of the White Primary in Texas* (Millwood, NY: KTO Press, 1979); Robert L. Zangrando, *The NAACP Crusade Against Lynching, 1909–1950* (Philadelphia: Temple University Press, 1980); Tyina Steptoe, *Houston Bound: Culture and Color in a Jim Crow City* (Oakland: University of California Press, 2016); Dwight D. Watson, *Race and the Houston Police Department, 1930–1990: A Change Did Come* (College Station: Texas A&M University Press, 2005); and Richard M. Valelly, *The Two Reconstructions: The Struggle for Black Enfranchisement* (Chicago: University of Chicago Press, 2004). For additional works on Tejanos, in conjunction with Arnoldo De Leon's subsequent essay on Tejanos, see Arnoldo De Leon, *They Called Them Greasers: Anglo Attitudes toward Mexicans in Texas, 1824–1900* (Austin: University of Texas Press, 1983); Arnold De Leon, *The Tejano Community, 1836–1900* (Albuquerque: University of New Mexico Press, 1982); Arnoldo De Leon, *Ethnicity in the Sunbelt: A History of Mexican-Americans in Houston* (Houston: University of Houston Press, 1989); David Montejano, *Anglos and Mexicans in the Making of Texas, 1836–1986* (Austin: University of Texas Press, 1987); Guadalupe San Miguel Jr., *Brown, Not White: School Integration and the Chicano Movement in Houston* (College Station: Texas A&M University Press, 2005); and Guadalupe San Miguel Jr., *"Let Them All Take Heed": Mexican Americans and the Campaign for Educational Equality in Texas, 1910–1981* (College Station: Texas A&M University Press,

2000). The sole black man elected to the HOR was Arthur Mitchell from Illinois.

11. The federal study is summarized in Samuel A. Stouffer et al., eds., *The American Soldier: Adjustment during Army Life*, 2 vols. (Princeton, NJ: Princeton University Press, 1949), 1:57. See also Snyder, ed., *120 Years of American Education.*

12. John A. Salmond, *The Civilian Conservation Corps, 1933–1942: A New Deal Case Study* (Durham, NC: Duke University Press, 1967), 47–54, 75–79, 85–88, quotation on 75. Covering the CCC in Texas is James W. Steely, *Parks for Texas: Enduring Landscapes of the New Deal* (Austin: University of Texas Press, 1999), esp. 20, 23, 25, 30–31, 33–35, 39, 59, 81, 94–95, 98, 156, 161, 168–71. Steely shows that the CCC was active in Texas through 1941.

13. Franklin D. Roosevelt, radio address to the nation ("Arsenal of Democracy"), December 29, 1940, reported in *Dallas Morning News*, December 30, 1940.

14. Edwin L. Caldwell, "Highlights of the Development of Manufacturing in Texas, 1900–1960," *Southwestern Historical Quarterly* 68 (April 1965), 405–31; Frederic C. Lane, *Ships for Victory: A History of Shipbuilding under the US Maritime Commission in World War II* (Baltimore, MD: Johns Hopkins University Press, 1951), 51, 55; George W. H. Reid, "30 Refineries on Texas Gulf Coast Manufacture 25 Percent of Nation's Gasoline," *Houston* magazine (April 1940), 111; Anonymous, "The Oil Industry Is Ready," *Houston* magazine (December 1940), 44; Anonymous, "Defense—One Year: A World Picture of Our Progressive Rearming," *Dallas* magazine (July 1941), 36; Robert L. Bobbitt, "Texas and Military Highways," *Texas Parade* (May 1940), 4. *Houston* and *Dallas* were the magazines of each city's Chamber of Commerce. *Texas Parade* was the magazine of the Texas Good Roads Association.

15. George Horace Gallup, *The Gallup Poll: Public Opinion, 1935–1971,* 3 vols. (New York: Random House, 1971), 1:279.

16. Francisco Millett, *Southwest Business* (January–December 1940), passim; Anonymous, "Dallas Wins Plane Factory," *Southwest Business* (September 1940), 5, 45; Anonymous, "North American Comes to Dallas," *Southwest Business* (October 1940), 9–17; Paul Carrington, "Dallas Is Defense Minded," *Dallas* magazine (March 1941), 9; Clyde Wallis, "Factories: Front Line of Defense," *Dallas* magazine (March 1941), 13; Jim Rivers, "Our Job Is Making Planes," *Dallas* magazine (April 1941), 22, 26, 41, 52, 64; Anonymous, "Giant Army Tank Engine Plant to Be Built Near Dallas," *Dallas* magazine ibid. (October 1941), 10–11. Other articles on military-related industries are in the December 1941 issue of *Dallas* magazine. Descriptions of the substantial investments by Consolidated Aircraft are analyzed in J'Nell L. Pate, *Arsenal of Defense: Fort Worth's Military Legacy* (Denton: Texas State Historical Association, 2011). Other works on economic statistics for Texas prior to the Second World War are Francis B. May, *Economic Statistics of Texas, 1900–1962* (Austin: University of Texas Press, 1964); Roger Bilstein and Jay Miller, *Aviation in Texas* (Austin: Texas Monthly Press, 1985); and E. C. Barksdale, *The Genesis of the Aviation Industry in North Texas* (Austin: University of Texas Press, 1958).

17. For the business activities, including tent production, see *Houston* magazine (February 1941), 5. Further information can be found in C. F. McElhinney, "The National Defense Training Program of the Houston Independent School District," *Houston* magazine (August 1941), 8–9; cover illustration of army convoy, *Houston* magazine (November 1941); R. L. Boyd, "Air Conditioning Does Pay," *Houston* magazine (May 1940), 8; and Anonymous, "Houston Leads in Air Conditioning," *Houston* magazine (May 1941), 26. See also Raymond Arsenault, "The End of the Long Hot Summer: The Air Conditioner and Southern Culture," *Journal of Southern History* 50 (November 1984).

18. Caldwell, "Manufacturing in Texas," 420; Anonymous, "First Port of the South," *Houston* magazine (April 1941), 60–61; Anonymous, "Houston, Still 3rd Port of the Nation," *Houston* magazine (November 1941), 2; Lane, *Ships for Victory*, 48, and photos of shipyards near Houston, opposite 75 and opposite 331; Marilyn M. Sibley, *Port of Houston* (Austin: University of Texas Press, 1968), 190; David G. McComb, *Houston: The Bayou City* (Austin: University of Texas Press, 1969), 178–80, 187; Ernest Obadele-Starks, *Black Unionism in the Industrial South* (College Station: Texas A&M University Press, 2000), 48. Additional works on the Port of Houston and the shipbuilding industry in Texas are Warren Rose, *Catalyst of an Economy: The Economic Impact of the Port of Houston* (Houston: University of Houston Press, 1965); A. L. Weinberger, "The Houston Ship Channel" (master's thesis, University of Texas, 1940); and Gerald J. Fischer, *A Statistical Survey of Shipbuilding Under the US Maritime Commission during World War II* (Washington, DC: US Maritime Commission, 1949).

19. Lane, *Ships for Victory*, 35, 55, 59; Louis Fairchild, *They Called It the War Effort: Oral Histories from WW II Orange, Texas* (Denton: Texas State Historical Association, 1993), xxix; J. Edgar Hoover, "Protect America!" *Houston* magazine (September 1940), 3. See also Works Projects Administration, *Beaumont: A Guide to the City* (Houston: Anson Jones Press, 1939). An evocative photo of Beaumont shipyard workers is found in Reid, *Picturing Texas: The FSA-OWI Photographers.*

20. *Annual Report of the Secretary of War 1940* (Washington, DC: Government Printing Office, 1940); *Annual Report of the Secretary of War 1941* (Washington, DC: Government Printing Office, 1941). Anyone interested could buy these reports from the GPO for fifty cents each. *Texas Almanac 1939–40*, 289–90; *Texas Almanac 1941–42*, 267, 316–18; and Mary Olivia Handy, *History of Fort Sam Houston* (San Antonio: Naylor Company, 1951). Under construction during 1941, Camp Hood, near Killeen, grew in importance during World War II and later became Fort Hood, the US Army's largest installation. A good photographic study is David Ford, *Fort Hood in World War II* (Charleston, SC: Arcadia, 2015).

21. Franklin D. Roosevelt, "Campaign Address at Boston, Massachusetts," October 30, 1940, the American Presidency Project, accessed August 5, 2016, http://www.presidency.ucsb.edu/; James M. Myers, "Camp Barkeley," "Camp Bowie"; Rachel Jenkins, "Camp Hulen"; Leon C. Metz, "Fort Bliss"; Maury Darst, "Fort Crockett"; John Manguso, "Fort Sam Houston"; Joseph G. Dawson III, "36th

Infantry Division," all in *Handbook of Texas*, accessed August 1, 2016, https://tshaonline.org/handbook/online/articles/qbc02. Richard A. Huff, ed., *A Pictorial History of the 36th Division* (Baton Rouge, LA: Army & Navy Publishing Company, 1940), 1–2; John Hatcher, "Camp Barkeley," *Texas Military History* 3 (Winter 1963), 219–27; Todd De Pastino, *Bill Mauldin: A Life Up Front* (New York: Norton, 2008), 62–63; Bill Mauldin, *Up Front* (New York: Henry Holt, 1945); Works Progress Administration, *Houston: A History and Guide* (Houston: Anson Jones Press, 1942), 123, on Camp Wallace; James S. Powell, *Learning Under Fire: The 112th Cavalry Regiment in World War II* (College Station: Texas A&M University Press, 2010), 1–7. See also *Houston* magazine (January 1941), 22, for a full page of "Army and Navy Assignments" for Houstonians, followed by *Houston*'s February 1941 issue with a cover photo of three military officers and a nurse. A more detailed account on Camp Hulen can be found in the Matagorda County Historical Commission's, *Historic Matagorda County* 3 vols. (Houston: Armstrong, 1986); and Ruby Penland, *Camp Hulen, Texas* (Palacios, TX: Palacios Area Historical Association, 1987).

22. Robert E. Hays Jr., "[Army] Air Force Training Expansion in Texas, 1940–1942," *Texas Military History* 4 (Spring 1964), 7–22; Roger D. Launius, "A New Way of War: The Development of Military Aviation in the American West, 1908–1945," *Military History of the West* 25 (Fall 1995), 167–90, esp. 177. For additional information on San Antonio and its military bases that effectively describes the expansion of flight officer training and is well illustrated, see Works Projects Administration, *Randolph Field* (New York: Devin-Adair Company, 1942); Works Projects Administration, *San Antonio: A History and Guide* (San Antonio, TX: Clegg Company, 1941), 100; and Thomas E. Alexander, *The Wings of Change: The Army Air Force Experience in Texas during World War II* (Abilene, TX: McWhiney Foundation Press, 2003), 225–26. Basic references are Robert Mueller, *Air Force Bases* (Washington, DC: Office of Air Force History, 1989), and Mary Moore Allen, *Origin of Names of Army and Air Corps Posts, Camps and Stations in World War II in Texas* (Goldsboro, NC: n/p, 1958). Evocative period photographs are found in Mel Brown, *Wings Over San Antonio* (Charleston, SC: Arcadia, 2001); Norman W. Brown, *Sheppard Air Force Base* (Charleston, SC: Arcadia, 2015); John M. Manguso, *Fort Sam Houston* (Charleston, SC: Arcadia, 2012); and Michael P. Hoffman, *Randolph Field* (Charleston, SC: Arcadia, 2014). All of the towns mentioned in the paragraph's last sentence, and others, became the sites of army airfields in Texas.

23. Paolo E. Coletta, ed., *United States Navy and Marine Corps Bases, Domestic* (Westport, CT: Greenwood Press, 1985), 152–54, 165; US Navy Department, *Building the Navy's Bases in World War II* (Washington, DC: Government Printing Office, 1947), 231, 246, 355, 357; Anonymous, "New Naval Base," *Southwest Business* (September 1940), 5, 45; Lt. W. W. Premo Jr. and Lt. H. Sartoris, "Dallas, New Nest for Navy Eaglets," *Dallas* magazine (May 1941), 7, 15; unnumbered pages of photos of the new Naval Air Training Base, *Dallas* magazine (July 1941), following

p. 37. For other works on Corpus Christi, see Bill Walraven, *Corpus Christi: The History of a Texas Seaport* (Woodland Hills, CA: Windsor Publications, 1982); *Yearbook, US Naval Air Station, Corpus Christi* (Corpus Christi: Texas Auxiliary of the Naval Relief Society, 1941); and Joseph A. Pratt and Christopher J. Castaneda, *Builders: Herman and George R. Brown* (College Station: Texas A&M University Press, 1999).

24. New cabinet members: *Houston Post*, June 21, 1940; destroyers for bases, *New York Times*, September 2, 1940; drawing draft numbers, *Dallas Morning News*, October 31, 1940; Flynn, *The Draft*, 10–12, 16–22. A work on Frank Knox is William Gardner Bell, *Secretaries of War and Secretaries of the Army: Portrait & Biographical Sketches* (Washington, DC: Center for Military History, 2010). For Henry L. Stimson, see Godfrey Hodgson, *The Colonel: The Life and Wars of Henry L. Stimson, 1867–1950* (New York: Knopf, 1990); Elting Elmore Morison, *Turmoil and Tradition: A Study of the Life and Times of Henry L. Stimson* (Boston, MA: Houghton Mifflin, 1960); and David F. Schmitz, *Henry L. Stimson: The First Wise Man* (Wilmington, DE: SR Books, 2001). The draft law called for men to meet minimum requirements, such as not being under five feet, five inches tall; passing a vision test with or without eyeglasses; possessing half of their own teeth; and not having a criminal record. Remarkably, nearly half of the men drafted in 1940–41 were not inducted due to not meeting one or more of these requirements. See Flynn, *The Draft*, 31–33, ibid., 31–33, and the report in the *Dallas Morning News*, May 12, 1941, explaining, "More Draftees Rejected than in World War [I]." See also J. Garry Clifford and Samuel R. Spencer Jr., *The First Peacetime Draft* (Lawrence: University Press of Kansas, 1986); and James Ward Lee et al., eds., *1941: Texas Goes to War* (Denton: University of North Texas Press, 1991). Some good works on the destroyers for bases deal are James R. Leutze, *Bargaining for Supremacy: Anglo-American Naval Collaboration, 1937–1941* (Chapel Hill: University of North Carolina Press 1977); F. F. Neary, "Newfoundland and the Anglo American Leased Bases Agreement of 27 March 1941," *Canadian Historical Review* 67 (December 1986); Richard M. Pious, "The Historical Presidency: Franklin D. Roosevelt and the Destroyer Deal: Normalizing Prerogative Power," *Presidential Studies Quarterly* 42 (March 2012); and Charlie Whitham, "The Thin End of the Wedge: The British Foreign Office, the West Indies and Avoiding the Destroyers-Bases Deal, 1938–1940," *Journal of Transatlantic Studies* 11 (September 2013).

25. Text of Mayo J. Thompson's speech, "A&M Cadets on Review," *Houston* magazine (June 1941), 12–13; *Bryan Daily Eagle*, May 12, 1941; Texas A&M *Battalion*, May 14, 1941; Association of Former Students, Texas A&M University, Silver Taps Notification, July 17, 2007, accessed online August 3, 2016, https://www.aggienetwork.com/news/148627/silver-taps-notification/. To find Texas A&M's contribution to the Second World War, see John A. Adams Jr., *We Are the Aggies: The Texas A&M University Association of Former Students* (College Station: Texas A&M University Press, 1979); and Henry C. Dethloff with John A. Adams Jr., *Texas Aggies Go to War* (College Station: Texas A&M University Press, 2006).

26. For the sketch of Mayo J. Thompson's biography, the information came from the Texas A&M Former Students Association (Alumni Association); the curator of the Texas A&M Corps of Cadets Center; and the file on Thompson at A&M's Cushing Memorial Library. A brief biography was published to accompany his speech in the collected work of Muster speeches edited by Jerry Cooper and published by Texas A&M University Press in 2015. A more detailed bio appeared in the lengthy obituary in the Houston *Chronicle* July 17, 2007. However, it stressed his postwar activities, including his law practice and the several ways he supported Texas A&M University. The reference librarian at the Combined Arms Library at the US Army Command and General Staff College provided the dates Thompson was enrolled there and his rank as of March 1945.

27. Marshall D. Wright, *The Texas League in Baseball, 1888–1958* (Jefferson, NC: McFarland & Company, 2004), 359–85; Kern Tips, *Football—Texas Style* (New York: Doubleday, 1964), 87–101; Dethloff, *Centennial History of Texas A&M*, 2:518–19. An entire history of the Cotton Bowl Classic is in Carlton Stowers, *Cotton Bowl Classic: The First Fifty Years* (Dallas: Host Communications, 1986). For an additional work on baseball in Texas, see Bill O'Neal, *The Texas League, 1888–1987: A Century of Baseball* (Austin: Eakin Press, 1987). The teams in the Southwest Conference in 1939, 1940, and 1941 were Texas A&M University, University of Texas, Texas Christian University, Baylor University, Rice University, Southern Methodist University, and the University of Arkansas.

28. Congress later simplified the name to the Women's Army Corps (WAC). Congress did not pass legislation for the WAAC until 1942, but proposals to create the new organization had been discussed for more than a year. For this information, see Mattie E. Treadwell, "The Women's Army Corps," in *United States Army in World War II, Special Studies* (Reprint Edition 1991; Washington, DC: Office of the Chief of Military History, Department of the Army, CMH Pub. 11–8, 1954). For works on George C. Marshall, see Ed Cray, *General of the Army: George C. Marshall, Soldier and Statesman* (New York: Cooper Square Press, 1990); and the four-volume work by Forrest C. Pogue. Fine secondary treatments of Texas women and the military are Ann Fears Crawford and Crystal Sasse Ragsdale, *Women in Texas* (Austin: State House Press, 1992); and Leisa D. Meyer, *Creating GI Jane: Sexuality and Power in the Women's Army Corps during World War II* (New York: Columbia University Press, 1996).

29. Sherl Kashowitz, *God Bless America: The Surprising History of an Iconic Song* (New York: Oxford University Press, 2013), 16–17, 51, 53; Ian Gordon, *Comic Strips and Consumer Culture, 1890–1945* (Washington, DC: Smithsonian Institution Press, 1998), 137. To compare Texas with nearby states, see Jerry Purvis Sanson, *Louisiana during World War II* (Baton Rouge: Louisiana State University Press, 1999); and C. Calvin Smith, *War and Wartime Changes: The Transformation of Arkansas, 1940–1945* (Fayetteville: University of Arkansas Press, 1986). For the tone of patriotism and nationalism, see Tom Brokaw, *The Greatest Generation* (New York: Random House, 1998); and selected accounts in Studs Terkel, *The*

the Baker boys with continued opportunities to thrive, notwithstanding the enduring elasticity of racism. As the sons of Jesse Baker, they found opportunities, even in the era of Jim Crow. They purchased or built homes, married, raised families, and, in the case of Wendell H. Baker, earned a chemistry degree and later desegregated the Golden Triangle petroleum industry. War service, to be sure, gave them confidence to challenge White supremacy and promoted the idea of civil rights and social justice among the brothers, as their experiences in the war advanced the idea of racial equality.[6]

Dogged by depression and oppression, Black Texans in the early 1940s crafted old and new strategies for survival and success during the Second World War. Building on the social-justice work of Reconstruction-era politicians and teachers, antisegregation and antilynching lobbyists of the late nineteenth and early twentieth centuries, and New Negro civil-rights advocates, Black Texans during the Second World War sought attainable solutions to reoccurring dilemmas. First, nearly 85,000 women and men challenged racial norms by enlisting, serving in all capacities, including stevedores, cooks, postal workers, ground troops, paratroopers, police officers, physicians, pilots, and commissioned and noncommissioned officers. Second, many knew that economic opportunities would help bring socioeconomic stability. These Black Texans thus stressed jobs ahead of social-justice initiatives, at least initially, as the former provided skill sets their White peers learned through technical training in New Deal programs and defense manufacturing plants. Third, with greater awareness for civil rights, Black Texans eventually made human rights, both worldwide and in the United States, a priority and thus forced the South to contemplate change. Particularly for those in the middle class, legal challenges to segregation would prove most effective in dismantling the institution. African Americans especially saw their struggle intertwined with that of other people of African descent, thereby embracing an African diasporic concept of intra-racial unity and hope.[7]

Despite a newfound awareness, reaction against African American agency prevailed, a fact that surprised probably no one, particularly African American Texans. Blacks still supported the war effort, investing in war bonds, rationing goods, enlisting and fighting as soldiers, and participating in the *Pittsburgh Courier*'s "Double V" crusade that demanded triumph against racism at home and fascism abroad. Their loyalty never wavering, Black Texans therefore remained determined to exercise their rights as citizens, never losing sight of the larger goal of achieving social acceptance, sociopolitical justice, and economic parity with their White peers, along with having greater embrace of transnational justice with Black people worldwide and an awareness of those suffering under European imperialism. Finally, Afro-Texans had the means to lead such an effort. Generally wealthier than other African American Southerners due primarily to the state's diversified economy that increasingly depended on oil refining and petrochemicals, as well as lumbering, transportation firms, and the manufacturing of steel and oil-production equipment, Black Texans and their growing middle class in several examples played a commanding lead in the twentieth-century fight for racial justice.[8]

This chapter builds upon a multilayered literature that in many ways remains scattered as it pertains to the history of African American Texans and World War II. The many works on Texas and World War II do mention African Americans but primarily concentrate on White Texans, often neglecting the contribution of marginalized groups. By examining the African American assault on poverty and structural racism in Texas and on the warfront during World War II, a fuller picture develops of their multifaceted contributions to victory. Blacks mostly sought better-paying jobs, especially stable work in the defense industry. Nevertheless, even those who searched for decent pay challenged the mainstream status quo, as they relied on labor unions and federal activism, all the while occasionally experiencing violence against them and their families. In addition, internal migration as an act of protest often motivated Black Texans to permanently abandon the state, particularly for California. Cultural awareness, too, proved transformative and expressly moved this community to action.[9]

These Texans' resilience in the wake of disappointment and commitment to a state and nation that denied them full citizenship remains the essence of Blackness in the United States. The New Negro Movement helped trigger the "Double V" construct of activism among Black Texans. This essay therefore begins in 1937—four years before the country declared war on Japan—when Texas celebrated its centennial and Blacks used the event to bolster African American credibility in the eyes of the world. It ends in 1947, when Black Texans used the war effort as a launchpad for racial equality and lasting change at home and abroad.[10]

The Fabulous Baker Boys: James (Jimmy) Otis "Pap" Baker

The middle brother to serve in World War II, James Otis "Pap" Baker, was born the seventh child of Fannie and Jesse Baker on January 24, 1919, in Walker County. A superb student, principally in mathematics, the nineteen-year-old was valedictorian at Sam Houston High School in 1938. He turned down Fisk University and Tuskegee University to attend Prairie View Normal and Industrial College (Prairie View). "Prairie View was close to home," he explained. "At that time," James Otis Baker remembered in 2004, "if you graduated from Prairie View, you were guaranteed a job in Texas." He took classes in math, mechanical arts, woodworking, and interior decorating. Although a superb student, Baker left school before his junior year. The National Youth Administration (NYA) offered him a position as a Negro division project supervisor, a job that paid $85 a month. He later noted his justification:

> They started the . . . National Youth Administration. . . . They [NYA] had to have Blacks . . . [T]hey couldn't just have Whites, with it being federal . . . so all they could think about in Huntsville—the Whites—was me. . . . They knew I was pretty smart . . . [be]cause they asked why I could write so good when I signed the bills for Sam Houston. . . . They called and asked if I would come to Huntsville to Supervise the NYA. I took the job because the teachers at Prairie View were only making $50 a month, the teachers in Huntsville were making $45–$50 a month, and I was going to be making $85 a month and had a car to drive and I was twenty-years-old![11]

He remained with the federal government until the summer of 1940. When the NYA consolidated its offices in Texas, Baker was asked to supervise all the East Texas programs for African Americans. Even though the job would allow him to remain in Huntsville, he declined the offer, instead desiring defense contract work in the big city.[12]

Defense manufacturing jobs opened throughout the state, although the majority could be found in cities. The owner of a local business in Huntsville, who also did business with his father, recommended young Jimmy "Pap" Baker for a job at his Houston firm. Pap saw Stanley in Huntsville one Sunday and coyly said to him, "Mr. Stanley, I've been supervising . . . [and] I would like to come to Houston and work for you. . . ." Stanley operated the materials warehouse for Houston Shipbuilding (currently Todd Shipyards Corporation)—one of the state's leading employers during the war that employed 20,000 and hired mostly African Americans as unskilled workers. Stanley responded enthusiastically to Baker's inquiry, "Okay, Pap. When your job closes, you come on to Houston; I'm going to give you my number at my house and you can call me, and I will tell you where to go from there." Pap called him at home on a Sunday once his job ended. Stanley told him to "be at the shipyard that Monday morning." Arriving at the shipyard, someone over the loudspeaker asked, "Is Jimmy Baker in the car? Come on in to Mr. Stanley's office." Perhaps seeing this as an important opportunity to integrate the firm, because he knew of Baker's reputation as an excellent skilled worker and preferred Blacks who could pass for White, Stanley gave him a job filing requisition orders at the warehouse, a position that normally went to "white boys." Stanley gave the following instructions to the warehouse supervisors: "Baker's well qualified and I want him to do what these white boys are doing. . . ." The highly intelligent, fair-complexioned Jimmy Baker would have a different experience from most African Americans, even those with similar qualifications.[13]

Baker did not have too many problems from Whites, although they certainly did not accept him as an equal coworker. Ironically, he had more difficulties with Blacks. They accepted orders only from Whites. "If you want them [requisition orders]," his Black coworkers would declare, "you bring them out yourself." He found himself in a perplexing situation. Although tall, handsome, fair-skinned, and highly intelligent, desired attributes within in the Black community, he did not make friends easily at his new job. Blacks resented him for gaming the system. In Jim Crow America, African Americans resigned themselves to being second-class citizens. They, however, would not tolerate special treatment for Black individuals other than celebrities. They, at least, bolstered the community's credibility while the unknown Baker unfairly attracted favorable attention from Whites. The Black community would not countenance a third-class ranking.[14]

Such hostility aside, he understood their point of view. Only twenty-one years old at the time, Baker was supervising men twice his age. Their pride would not allow them to get to know the young man because they resented his dad's connections, his "passable" characteristics, and his perceived "uppityness." Whites, on the other hand, also resented his relationship with the boss. Sensing the dilemma for young James Baker, Stanley built a smaller, adjacent warehouse for Baker to work. "I did that until the war broke out and I had to go to the Navy," Baker, who benefited from the isolation and higher pay, remembered. "And [Stanley] wrote the Navy the nicest letter saying I was qualified to do whatever." The army drafted Baker in early 1942 and assigned him to basic training in Louisiana. But after consultation with his older brother Herbert, who had been stationed in Louisiana before assignment overseas, he complained to his younger brother that the Gulf Coast environment made him sick. James, fearful of disease, immediately requested a transfer to the navy. Upon induction in the navy, he left for naval basic training, first for the Naval Air Station Grosse Ile in Michigan right along the Detroit River in late 1942 and subsequently in Southern California near Los Angeles.[15]

James "Pap" Baker served with the brand-new 34th Naval Construction Battalion (NCB), the first predominantly Black construction unit in the navy. The 1940 Selective Training and Service Act of 1940, which reinstituted the draft, prohibited racial segregation. The navy, nevertheless, continued segregation, with the vast majority of the 12,000 African American "Seabees" being segregated. The 34th NCB, however, proved the exception. Formed October 23, 1942, in Norfolk, Virginia, this integrated battalion became the first to be composed of Blacks with previous experience in trades, including steelworkers, electricians, and carpenters. The unit comprised 880 African Americans and 280 Whites. All the unit's officers, however, were Whites. Companies of the 34th trained across the country before being deployed in Southern California.[16]

A perfect fit for the former engineering major, the battalion comprised individuals like Baker, current college undergraduates and administrators and professionals. The individual experiences of those serving in the 34th differed considerably from other men of color in the navy during World War II, who, with few exceptions, served as stewards and messmen. Baker hoped this unit's success would open doors of inclusion to other outfits. They constructed warehouses, hospitals, roads, and airstrips along with other military facilities. Baker served as the only African American blacksmith on the ship (Shipfitter 2nd class with an F2 rating). Raised on a farm, he loved the work. Ultimately his charisma and talent landed him the job:

> They gave me a bunch of shovels to go out and dig, but I just kept getting behind the big tree and put my shovel down and went back to the shop where the blacksmith . . . was working, and I just volunteered and went to working with them just as if I had been sent there to work, and I was doing so good till by evening they asked the commander if I could work there for them. Then they let me go to school for it. So, when they got ready [to] give the examinations for pay raise and connect rate. They . . . had [it] for everything else but didn't have nothing [sic] on the ship for the blacksmith. So, he said, "Baker, you're the only one that knows anything about . . . blacksmith[ing]. So, I am going to take this paper and you write out your own questions and we'll type them up." And I took the examination that I had wrote out myself . . . so on Okinawa I ran the shop and on Guadalcanal I ran the shop.[17]

Departing Hueneme Naval Base in Oxnard, California, on January 7, 1943, the 34th arrived in the Solomon Islands, Southwest Pacific, after a forty-three-day voyage. Aware of his importance and optimistic about being in an integrated unit, Pap Baker was quickly disabused of any thoughts about racial equality. Where Americans go, so go their institutions and attitudes. According to Baker, "our commander was from Mississippi—an ole White guy," who accepted only White officers from the South, believing them the only ones capable of "handling" African American men. One of those officers, a native Texan, Baker remembered, "knew how" to deal with Blacks with prejudice and condescension. African American "Seabees" faced entrenched racism on the ship, often being addressed by superiors as "Nigger." Other indignities included White seamen cutting in front of Blacks when in line waiting for meals; qualified African Americans not being promoted to petty officer by the ship's commander; and, while in port in Australia and due to fear of sexual race-mixing, the lack of shore leave for Blacks but not their White counterparts. Baker recalled an incident when an older Black "Seabee" received a pass in Australia. The Whites, angry this "old man" might have had a sexual encounter, mutilated him "to keep him from going around messing with them White women. . . ."[18]

Such treatment shocked Baker. Shielded from such racism in his daily life, Baker admitted his experience during the war "was different from Huntsville." For those African Americans from the North, the degradation also came as a shock. "We got sick of that stuff," he declared. A generation removed from the earlier generation of New Negroes of World War I who approached racism with moderation, these servicemen, in the midst of fighting the country's enemies, attacked the problem with a two-pronged frontal assault of civil disobedience. The first prong occurred in late 1944. They knew that putting soap on their tongues would raise their temperatures, thus placing them in sick bay. The Seabees in essence "stopped working."

Upon returning to the United States, the 34th NCB initiated their second prong. With support from the National Association for the Advancement of Colored People (NAACP), the servicemen of color initiated a two-day hunger strike in March 1945. This newfound activism generated international attention, something that displeased the US government. The men this time continued to work even though they stopped eating. An investigation by the chief of the Bureau of Naval Personnel found widespread racism, concluding that the lack of promotion for qualified African Americans to petty officers adversely affected their morale and performance. The White officers were discharged and replaced by a new group commanded by Lester M. Marx, a Jewish American officer from Rochester, New York. Marx immediately instituted measures to boost morale, including equitable pay rates. Baker returned home a year later in 1946 and eventually settled in Los Angeles permanently. His experiences speak to an emerging activism, one in which younger African Americans would demand more of their nation following the war.[19]

The "Double V" War Front for Black Texans

Entering World War II, the biggest challenge facing Pap Baker and his fellow African American brethren was not the peril of combat but overcoming the US military's racism. With the benefit of hindsight, the economic possibilities for Black Texans, even more so for Black women, although better than prewar years, did not permeate the economy as a whole. Many employers hired African Americans only as a last resort, while others simply refused to hire them at all; in fact, such an approach resulted in Black women comprising just 4 percent of the approximately seven million African Americans in war production work. When hired, their employment, despite the pressing needs of the war effort, came with certain expectations: last hired, first fired; exhausting menial or unskilled, manual labor; and, most likely, lower wages than White counterparts. Furthermore, in addition to racial animus and stereotypes, Black women faced chauvinism. Despite this, they rallied to the nation's defense by boosting morale through volunteering and entertaining. They also worked in defense plants building the weapons of war and labored in the fields procuring vitally important foods and fibers. Black adolescent Texans also contributed in many ways. They joined 4-H clubs and grew victory gardens and canned food. The Washington County (northwest of Houston) 4-H club in East Texas raised chickens for the war effort. Girls knitted clothing for soldiers or the Red Cross, while the boys participated in scrap metal drives and efforts at conserving and preserving food. Maud A. B. Fuller in Austin was "constantly on the go." Selling war bonds, she noted how "[e]very fraternity meeting is greeted with her presence, and she does not run away empty handed." Black sorority girls volunteered in the United Service Organization (USO) by sending much desired luxuries from home like candy or writing letters to servicemen abroad. Those who could joined dance troupes. At Prairie View, female students learned radio communication, engineering, and the mechanics of the internal combustion engine. These workers, however, often did not find employment in Texas due to the racial climate. They instead went to Pennsylvania or California for work. Black women in Texas, regardless of the pressing need for labor, were relegated to essentially four occupations: meat packing, garment factories, railroads, and shipyards. The epicenter of most of these industries was Dallas, Fort Worth, and Houston.[20]

Those beyond adolescence worked. Some found employment with the government. The war effort required coordination. Each of the sixteen million in uniform and the billions of dollars in wartime contracts generated immense paperwork. To manage this information, the federal government quadrupled in size, from one million civilians in 1940 to four million by war's end. A growing constituency of this workforce were Black Americans. In 1938, African Americans accounted for 10 percent of the governmental workforce; six years later, 12 percent. Ruby Wyatt Mitchell from Houston and Ella Ruth White from Dallas worked for the War Department, relocating to Washington, DC. Congressman Lyndon B. Johnson appointed Annie Rucker Baker postmistress of a little town east of Austin. Many others benefited from mobilization. Approximately 60 percent of the one million African Americans who were in the wartime labor force worked in war-related industries (in total, 2.1 million women of color worked in the economy during the war).

In Fort Worth, Gladys Humphery found work in a meat processing plant. Among canning chili and Vienna sausage, she also sliced bacon. Although not as glamorous as assembling a B-17 or even entertaining troops, this work was not only vital to the armed forces, but also this simple act was profound. Prior to the war, such work was primarily a man's job. Not that many women were desiring this exhausting and messy job, for it required processing cuts of meat from hogs and cattle and stretching and drying the hides. But in the name of the war effort, Black women set aside reservations to do their part. Humphery eventually made inspector. Other African American women also did "man's work." The struggle against fascism was going to be a "metal-turning, engine-building, multiyear conflict." In Kingsville, South Texas, for instance, women of color washed locomotives. Others cleaned and steamed the engines. African American women worked all sectors of the war economy, including in shipyards, aircraft assembly, electrical equipment, and ordnance assembly. Workers in the garment industry, especially in the Metroplex (Dallas–Fort Worth area), sewed military uniforms. One such worker was Olivia Rawlston, who was president of the segregated union, International Ladies Garment Workers Union.[21]

In spite of the newfound employment opportunities the war demand created, it did not necessarily redound to Black women in loosening their traditional role as homemaker. Most still remained in the private household, either as dutiful wives and mothers (not employed outside the house) or as domestic help. Far more than being in the various acronymic military organizations for women like the WAC (Women's Army Corps) and WAVES (Women Accepted for Volunteer Emergency Service), Black women were more likely to be WIVES. The number of households without a male head in the war years nearly quadrupled. Not an insignificant number were headed by an African American woman who contributed by remaining the center of private life. War or not, homes still needed tending. These women remained primarily by choice. But, at times, the racial attitudes necessitated their return to housework. Keith Walton, born into one of the increasing middle-class households in 1966, remembers the situation his paternal and maternal grandmothers faced when they left Texas for the promise of California during the war. Both had been elementary school teachers in Texas and hoped to find such work in California. The Golden State's racial climate, however, not only precluded their hiring as teachers, but also wartime employers resisted employing too many workers of color. The women remained in the home throughout the war.[22]

When the war began, Whites held a "deeply ingrained image of a bandanna-crowned female domestic whose maternal nature derives more satisfaction from caring for her owners' or employers' children than her own." The war presented the opportunity to redress this demeaning stereotype by recasting—not without a tinge of class-consciousness and nonthreatening to the gendered-division of labor still prevalent in both the African American and labor communities—the Black homemaker as a respectable mother, devoted to her family and not simply for the satisfaction of White families. Furthering this makeover was new agency on the part of women of color. The allure and possibility of war work caused many White households to lose their domestic help. Still many others faced a more empowered and assertive domestic, or as their White female employer would assert, "spoiled," who now understood her increased worth. Until 1950, domestic work was the leading occupation for both Black and White women. The percentage of African American women working as domestics dropped from 60 percent at the beginning of the war to 44 percent by war's end (the percentage of the entire Black working population also dropped from 29 to 21 percent). These women were twice as likely as White women to be domestics: 29 percent compared to 15 percent. Racial barriers, among other interdictions, of course, limited the opportunities for African Americans, especially women, to follow their White counterparts into the war industries in comparable numbers. That said, the opportunities developed redounded to the benefit of domestics as better wages and better treatment became more prevalent. "Negro" or "Colored" replaced the more derogatory racial slurs by Whites in the presence of their help. In Dallas, Annie Mae Hunt remembered the changed situation for "kitchen mechanics" once the United States entered the war. "That's when housework begin [sic] to go up," she noticed. Hunt noticed her pay increase from around a dollar and a half a day to ultimately seven a day. Such reversals of fortune for African American female domestics caused resentment with White women, challenging their dominant status and the very hierarchy of American society and consequently proved to be a barrier "to interracial tolerance and good will."[23]

Not all contributions came from sweat and muscle. The US government, with millions of service personnel scattered throughout the world, wanted to provide a "little taste of home." Numerous actors, singers, and comedians crisscrossed the globe to entertain the boys overseas. Roberta Dodd Crawford was one of them. A native of Bonham, East Texas, Dodd was a young African American girl with "a voice that made the citizens of her hometown sit up and take notice." After graduating from Fisk University, a historically Black college in Tennessee, she moved to Chicago to improve her voice and French language skills. She made her singing debut at Kimball Hall in Chicago, before embarking on a national tour. Her proficiency in French proved beneficial when she relocated to France to continue her voice studies. She married an African activist with alleged royal ties and settled down in West Africa, until her husband's untimely death when she went back to France. Unfortunately, she could not have chosen a worse time to relocate to France, for shortly thereafter the Germans invaded and occupied the country until 1944. Dodd remained under Nazi occupation until France's liberation by the Allies. She then put her singing talents to use entertaining American forces, even going to hospitals to entertain the wounded. She also volunteered her time at the information desk of the Left Bank Red Cross club, which was for servicemen of color.[24]

The War Department initially resisted placing Black men in combat duty. Although they had served with distinction in combat roles in all the nation's wars, most recently in the Great War, a "collective amnesia" set in after each conflict to ignore their contributions. "We return from fighting," W. E. B. Du Bois declared in 1919. "We return fighting." In fact, the military did not care about the New Negro any more than it did about the old. Despite evidence to the contrary, the attitude of most military brass regarding the martial abilities of African American men was best personified by Lieutenant General Robert Lee Bullard, a Southerner and commander of the U.S Second Army during the First World War, who wrote in his 1925 memoirs: "Poor Negroes! They are hopelessly inferior. As fighting troops, Negroes were simply failures." His sentiments were still the norm on the eve of the Second World War. A 1937 study by the Army War College, dripping with the racial assumptions of the day, addressed the issue of Black soldiers and their "deficiencies":

> As an individual, the Negro is docile, tractable, lighthearted, care free and good natured. If unjustly treated he is likely to become surly and stubborn, though this is usually a temporary phase. He is careless, shiftless, irresponsible, and secretive. He resents censure and is best handled with praise and by ridicule. He is unmoral, untruthful and his sense of right doing is relatively inferior. Crimes and convictions involving moral turpitude are nearly five to one as compared to convictions of whites on similar charges. On the other hand, the Negro is cheerful, loyal, and usually uncomplaining if reasonably well fed. He has a musical nature and a marked sense of rhythm. His art is primitive. He is religious. With proper direction in mass, Negroes are industrious. They are emotional and can be stirred to a high state of enthusiasm. Their emotions are unstable and their reactions uncertain. Bad leadership in particular is easily communicated to them.[25]

The military, thus wanting to discourage African Americans from enlisting, created inane and shamelessly overt racist hurdles to excuse discrimination. Black officials, such as future judge William Hastie, and certain White advocates in the War Department, began to push harder for greater opportunities in the armed forces. Political expediency came into play when Franklin D. Roosevelt courted the Black vote during his presidential campaign in 1932 by promising concessions toward integration in the military and defense industries. The First Lady, Eleanor Roosevelt, joined with civil rights leaders for the push as a strong advocate for racial equality. Her advocacy for Black servicemen's advancement prompted White servicemen to coin the nickname "Eleanor's Niggers" for their Black peers.[26]

Such attitudes, however, did not dampen the New Negro's patriotism. As a result, there existed reservations about defending a country in war that did not respect them in peace. The majority of African Americans in Texas, however, saw mobilization not just as a way to contribute to the country's defense, but also as an opportunity for social mobility and racial equality. They would fight not necessarily for what some deemed, with slight exaggeration, "domestic Nazis," but "for personal survival" and expectations afterward. This struggle for Blacks should be one for "Victory Abroad & Victory at Home." Their demand was for the "elimination of the ban which prevents loyal and patriotic Negro Americans from full participation in the defense industries of the country." The African American community thus sought an end to the bifurcation of the military and American society. The "time was ripe for a new emancipation." This duality of conflict against fascism abroad and racism at home would further set in motion a renewed sense of pride and purpose in postwar Texas and the country at large. The war's sense of urgency opened new possibilities for the New Negro, including an "entrée into industry." Wartime employment might be a way to economic equality, wartime patriotism might bring about social equality, and wartime service and sacrifice might guarantee civic equality. The future was pregnant with uncertainty and possibility. Whether Black Texas would benefit from the war remained unclear. Less uncertain was how profoundly changed the 900,000 African American Texans (14 percent of the state's population) would come through the experience.[27]

Similar to when previous opportunities were presented, Black men boldly stepped forward, ready to raise their hands and swear allegiance to their country. They served for patriotism and for familial and social expectations. They joined for the chance to fight "for the opportunity to create a democracy—not to save a democratic society." Others joined simply to escape the boredom of home and earn a steady paycheck of $50 a month. Still others saw service as a positive upon their lives, whether instilling discipline or maturity or achieving social status. Whatever their reason, approximately 1.2 million African Americans would serve in the US armed forces, with an estimated 909,000 Black men and women serving in the army alone. The peak of Black service was in 1944, with 700,000—or 8.7 percent of the army's total strength. By war's end, 750,000 (this includes 12,000 women) Texans entered the armed services. Of those, 84,000 were African Americans, with most entering the army. They served in a generally segregated military (excluding the training of officers, the WAVES, and in most army hospitals), and facilities on all the installations had "little Harlems." The government wanted them mainly for their labor rather than their intellect, skills, and willingness to sacrifice their lives for their country. Their service and sacrifice (many the ultimate) mattered little, trumped by their skin color. The army agreed to the creation of a few all-Black combat units. This small victory, however, did not change the entrenched opinion about them. It is estimated that 78 percent of the Black men in the army served as cooks, drivers, and janitors. To determine place, the army used its Army General Classification Test and the Mechanical Aptitude Test. This determined a new recruit's ability and placement in "grade" levels. It also assisted in preserving a Jim Crow army, since nearly half the Black recruits, according to test results, were placed in the lowest grade (grade V). Slightly more than 8 percent of Whites scored in that grade. Even accounting for the poor education and access to educational materials for African American men, especially from the South, the armed forces, moved by racial stereotypes, simply put, believed them inferior. This mattered the most considering that since the Revolutionary Era, "bearing arms had been associated with the right to claim full citizenship privileges." Preclusion provided a convenient excuse for exclusion.[28]

Perhaps most galling, even more than fellow countrymen who at the same time championed freedom and liberty abroad while hardly practicing it at home, was the treatment of prisoners of war (POWs).

As Black Texans served their country, sweating in the fields to produce the necessary food, laboring in war industries to manufacture the necessary weapons, and risking their lives in the necessary battles, these same men and women were treated not much better and, at times, worse than the POWs from the very enemy countries the US military currently battled. As the war progressed, the number of enemy captured increased. Ultimately, 435,788 Axis POWs were held by the United States: 378,898 Germans, 51,455 Italians, and 5,435 Japanese. Of those, Texas held 78,982 prisoners in fourteen military installations and seven smaller installations constructed specifically for housing captives. The number of prisoner camps in the Lone Star State, in fact, was twice that of any other state in the Union. In order to earn a little more money at the commissary and perhaps to escape the boredom and passivity of confinement, POWs often worked for locals, especially for farmers who felt the brunt of the labor shortage. While outside camp, these men, so far from home and often housed in camps far beyond urban areas, experienced a modicum of freedom and the luxuries of American society. Although enemies, Italian and German prisoners were still White, and thus soon the White locals acclimated to their presence to the point of no longer being a novelty. Others formed bonds. These prisoners were often welcomed into the establishments of daily life. In one of the great ironies (or perhaps embarrassments) of the war in Texas, these POWs, actually could sit at the lunch counter at cafés or most other Whites-only facilities, while an African American Texan serving in uniform in defense of the country could not.[29]

Consider one such example. A troop train was passing through Texas. When time came to serve a meal, the Black troops had to eat behind a curtain. This convenient barrier, at least, created a separate portion within the rail car and secluded the White soldiers from the "indignity" of interracial eating. The point of racial superiority was the solution to where the German POWs, who were also on the train, would eat. Instead of a separate facility for them, authorities simply allowed them to eat with the White soldiers and guards. Harold Witter Bynner (his pen name was Emanuel Morgan, and he rarely went by Harold), an openly gay, White poet, highlighted this wound to both the African American community at large and the country as a whole in his poem "Defeat":

On a train in Texas German prisoners eat
With white American soldiers, seat by seat,
While black American soldiers sit apart
The white men eating meat, the black men heart.
Now, with that other war a century done,
Not the live North, but the dead South has won,
Nor yet a riven nation comes awake.
Whom are we fighting this time, for God's sake?
Mark well the token of the separate seat.
It is again ourselves whom we defeat.[30]

One German POW held at Camp Huntsville admitted after the war, "You have to see how they [Black Texans] lived. These people were so exploited." Most certainly, no wound of the flesh by the enemy could hurt more than this wound to the soul by one's countrymen.[31]

Although open to men of color, the navy initially segregated them in specified occupations such as cooks and labor; as the war progressed, the navy loosened that policy and slowly integrated previously prohibited occupations and allowed for promotion to previously prohibited ranks. Approximately 167,000 African Americans served in the navy during the war. An additional 17,000 served in the Marine Corps, with the majority as support or ammunition troops. African American women, on the other hand, were initially barred from naval service. In fact, not until late 1944 did the navy officially admit African American women (the Marine Corps refused these women from its ranks until 1949). WAVES, similar to the WAC in a sense, enabled women to perform necessary tasks for the navy, thus freeing a man for reassignment. It was not until early 1945 that WAVES could serve outside the continental United States. Unlike the nurses and WAC, WAVES, by law, were restricted to stateside service. In all, the navy trained only seventy-two African American women by war's end.[32]

Although relegated to one of the few positions historically open to African American men, messman Doris "Dorie" Miller engaged in one of the most memorable acts of heroism of the war. A burly nineteen-year-old former Waco Moore High School bruising fullback known as "The Bull," Miller, needing money for his sharecropping family, enlisted in the navy as a mess attendant in 1939. Assigned to the battleship USS *West Virginia*, he soon became the ship's heavyweight boxing champion. His real claim to fame, however, came on the "day of infamy," December 7. Miller was collecting laundry when the first Japanese wave of planes attacked. Ordered to his battle station, Miller dodged flames to rescue the ship's commander, Captain Mervyn Bennion, carrying him below deck to safety. Ordered to carry ammunition to an unmanned machine-gun station, Miller instinctively took control of the weapon and began firing. News stories credited him with as many as five confirmed "downings" of Japanese planes. These accounts have never been confirmed, and Miller thought he may have hit only one plane. Nonetheless, he was awarded the Navy Cross, the second highest military decoration awarded for combat, with many arguing he should have been awarded the Congressional Medal of Honor (CMOH). Ironically, the man pinning the medal on Miller's uniform was fellow Texan, Admiral Chester Nimitz, who stated, "This marks the first time in this conflict that such high tribute has been made in the Pacific Fleet to a member of his race, and I'm sure that the future will see others similarly honored for brave acts." Miller was eventually transferred to the aircraft carrier *Liscome Bay* (sometimes *Liscomb Bay*). He was lost at sea when it was sunk during the Gilbert Islands Campaign in late 1943.

Mess attendant Leonard Roy Harmon, a native of Cuero, Texas, southeast of San Antonio, served aboard the cruiser USS *San Francisco*. During the Battle of Guadalcanal in November 1942, Harmon, while evacuating wounded men to safety, shielded a shipmate with his own body during a Japanese strafing attack. This act of heroism cost Harmon his life. He was posthumously awarded the Navy Cross. The Navy further bestowed additional honors on these two fallen heroes by naming ships after them.[33]

In 1944, General George S. Patton's Third Army, in need of more tanks as he fought his way toward Germany, requested the best tankers available. Superiors notified him that the only available tank unit was Black. The general replied, "Who the ^%$& asked for color? I asked for tankers." The War Department sent "Old Blood and Guts," who had once doubted the ability of such soldiers, the 761st Tank Battalion, the first all-Black tank unit from Fort Hood in Killeen, Texas. The hard-nosed general was the first to greet the unit as only he could:

> Men, you're the first Negro tankers to ever fight in the American Army. I would never have asked for you if you weren't good. I have nothing but the best in my Army. I don't care what color you are as long as you go up there and kill those Kraut sonsofbitches. . . . Most of all your race is looking forward to your success. Don't let them down and damn you, don't let me down! They say it is patriotic to die for your country. Well, let's see how many patriots we can make out of those German sonsofbitches.[34]

The 761st engaged the enemy for 183 straight days. Few in the unit fought with as much ferocity as Sergeant Warren Crecy, the "baddest man" in the 761st. A football star from Corpus Christi, Texas, Crecy was known as a polite, mild-mannered, and driven individual. His fellow tankers, however, recalled how Crecy's demeanor changed after the death of one of his friends. He determined to exact revenge. Although he would be reprimanded for wild, irresponsible conduct, Crecy would display unbelievable heroism in late 1944. In a two-day action, on November 10 he fought through enemy positions to aid his men until his tank was destroyed. Commandeering another tank, he destroyed the enemy position that had destroyed his tank. Still under heavy fire, Crecy helped eliminate the enemy forward observers who were directing the artillery fire that had staunched the American advance. The next day, when his tank became bogged down in the mud, Crecy dismounted and, while facing heavy enemy fire, tried to extricate his tank. While doing so, he noticed the enemy was counterattacking. Climbing to the rear of his immobilized tank, he held the Germans at bay with his .50-caliber machine gun while the foot soldiers withdrew. Later that day, he again exposed himself to enemy fire as he wiped out several machine-gun nests and an anti-tank position with only his machine gun. Trezzvant Anderson, a Black journalist embedded with the 761st, testified to what he witnessed:

> To look at Warren G.H. Crecy (the G.H. stands for Gamaliel Harding) you'd never think that here was a "killer," who had slain

> more of the enemy than any man in the 761st. He extracted a toll of lives from the enemy that would have formed the composition of 3 or 4 companies, with his machine guns alone. And yet, he is such a quiet, easy-going, meek-looking fellow . . . But here was a youth who went so primitively savage on the battle field that his only thought was to "kill, kill, kill," and he poured his rain of death pellets into German bodies with so much reckless abandon and joy that he was the nemesis of all the foes of the 761st. By all human equations Warren G.H. Crecy should have been dead long ago, and should have had the Congressional Medal of Honor, at least![35]

Crecy was nominated for the CMOH but only received a battlefield commission to lieutenant.[36]

Texas was highly desirable for the placement of military facilities and bases. Thousands from Texas served in the armed forces, yet many more came through the Lone Star State for training or prior to departure overseas. With 175 military installations in the state during the war, many of the 80 percent of all Black soldiers who received training in the South passed through Texas. Many of those African Americans were from outside the Jim Crow South. Although familiar with racism, the experiences in the segregated South came as a shock. They learned that with "separate but equal," the emphasis was on *separate* . . . not equal. At Camp Wolters, near Mineral Wells, there existed only a White servicemen's club. Black personnel had to open their own. A similar situation existed at Camp Wallace near Galveston. At times, the White community actually rallied to the assistance of those men of color serving in their name. For instance, the approximately 200 soldiers stationed at the San Marcos Army Air Field lacked a separate recreational facility. Community leaders (in possibly one of the first examples of unconscious bias) converted several cells in the local jail into a makeshift USO club for the Black men. Other than it being in the municipal jail, all other reminders of its previous function were removed. The African American airmen at Hondo Army Air Field in late 1943 had it even better. The first Black pilot cadets to train outside of Tuskegee (famed Tuskegee Airmen in Alabama) trained at Hondo. Unlike similar situations throughout the South, Black cadets had comparable (although separate) barracks, as well as their own classroom. Moreover, despite grumblings, they dined in the desegregated mess hall and "had equal privileges and enjoyed equal access to the same recreational facilities." Black personnel described the situation at Hondo as "correct."[37]

This small, yet significant, victory did not represent the norm. Texas could be a hostile environment for African American soldiers. An environment that had roots in the First World War, yet continued into the Second. Consider what occurred in Houston in 1917. Government officials in the South lobbied for military installations in their districts for the economic benefits. But then, if the army posted Black units in those installations or even planned to, the lobbying took on a more vile, belligerent tone with myriad reasons why such a move would not be prudent. At the heart of White concerns was "race mixing" and the effect that Black men in uniform would have on the local African American community. This was an invitation to incite local Black citizens to demand equality. Those were among the prime factors that led to Houston's Camp Logan riots in 1917, an incident noted as the only race riot in US history where more Whites (sixteen) than Blacks (four) were killed. Sixty-three men of the 24th Infantry Regiment were tried in the largest court-martial in military history at Fort Sam Houston in San Antonio. Their legal representative was not adequate, and none of the defendants were positively identified as participants in the incident. Yet thirteen of the men were summarily hanged; forty-one others were sentenced to life; sixteen others were sentenced to hang in subsequent trials; and twelve more were also sentenced to life imprisonment. The incident and court-martial did force the army to institute a soldier's right to appeal, an option previously unavailable, and the staying of a death sentence until a review and determination of legality could examine the sentence. This, in fact, ultimately led to the current structure of the army's Court of Criminal Appeals. The Camp Logan Mutiny, as the event is also called, set a precedent for military justice but was also a huge setback for military race relations and precluded any movement toward desegregating the army for a generation.[38]

To ensure "tranquility" between the races, African Americans in the

South had to show deference to Whites, and by doing so, acknowledge their subservient and nonthreatening status. Blacks often referred to Whites as "Mr.," "Mrs.," or "Miss." "Sir" also qualified many a question or request toward Whites. White Texans routinely referred to African American men as "boy" or "uncle," rarely conveying respect or equality. Signs in public places informed outsiders of local racial attitudes and reminded Black Texans their business was not wanted. Those establishments that did generally serve African Americans only did after all Whites had been tended to, or they had to enter a "special section" out of sight of the general public. Clothing stores refused to allow them to try on clothes unless guaranteed a purchase. Houston, for example, was not as "Negro hating" as other Southern cities, in part because Whites completely controlled the city and Blacks accepted that "with little outward evidence or resentment." On the other hand, the city's culture was immersed in the biracial attitude of East Texas, thus hostile to anything that smacked of integration. In the "Bayou City," in fact, racial mingling in "eating establishments [was] 'a very sore spot in this town.'"[39]

Numerous soldiers and their wives commented about the conditions in Texas. One "Soldier's Wife," for instance, was offended, if not hurt, by the treatment she and her husband, as well as others in the African American community, received. Arriving in Temple, Texas (just northeast of Austin), she noticed the offensive caricatures and the White community's indifference to them. Shopping for groceries at Safeway, a national grocery chain, she was shocked to see offensive labels and caricatures on items on the shelves, such as "Nigger Head Brand Shrimp." Such products were quite pervasive throughout the South. By the tone of her letter to the *Crisis*, the official publication of the NAACP, she was not from the South, for she was shocked at the sight of the numerous signs of segregation that littered the area: "For Colored" and "For White." The writer further informed how people of color not only had to give their seats to White patrons, but also had to wait hours on end while "dozens of drivers refused to stop in colored areas until the whites had been accommodated. . . ." Such practices, "too numerous to go into detail," she noted, "are forcing the morale of our colored soldiers to a new low." She saves her most damning remarks for the country as a whole, focusing her ire on the complicit North, complicit War Department, and complicit President Roosevelt.

> "Why must our second lieutenants remain second lieutenants indefinitely, regardless of efficiency or capabilities?" she questions. "Why must our husbands and brothers go abroad to fight for principles they only 'hear' about at home? Does our War Department believe in the Constitution of our country? Are the 'Four Freedoms' excluding our Southern States? Does the 'Commander in Chief' realize what's going on in the hearts and minds of his colored soldiers? How long does he expect them to tolerate these deplorable conditions? Is he training them to be brave, courageous soldiers on foreign soil and mere mice here at home? Does it matter to him whether or not these men leave the shores of their homeland with the deep feeling of peace in knowing they must go to protect, and insure, Liberty and Justice to ALL here at home?
>
> Is the appeasement of the South worth the sacrifice of America's most loyal citizens? How long will this farce of Democracy continue before our President and War Department begin practicing what they preach? I wonder."[40]

White Southerners, although accustomed to African Americans, rarely welcomed those from outside the South. Their very presence, especially Black officers, posed a threat to the segregated society that necessitated a subservient and pliant population. Hostility, therefore, welcomed non-White units. "Texas," noticed secretary of war Henry L. Stimson, "particularly has protested against the stationing of colored troops in that State . . . We are suffering from the persistent legacy of the original crimes of slavery." The civilian police in Houston had an attitude (often referring to them as "you nigger soldier") toward Black troops that worried one observer for "contributing to a potential outbreak of violence which would rival the Houston race riot of 1917." Black troops stationed at Majors Field in Greenville noticed the White community's hostility toward them when they left the base and ventured into town. African American soldiers at Fort Bliss, near El Paso, celebrating Juneteenth were pelted with rocks and beaten and chased by White troops. The mayor of Bastrop contacted his congressman to inform the president that if any of the Black soldiers from nearby

Camp Swift come to town, he would personally shoot them. When a Black soldier sat in the White section on a Beaumont city bus, the incident escalated, ending with the soldier shot and killed. One African American soldier commented on his treatment in Bracketville, Texas (west of San Antonio near the border): "Few civilians never have the idea of what we boys are really going through down here in Texas, one of the worst states in this country," he remarked. "And now, way down in Texas, where we're not even good as dogs, much less soldiers, even our General on the post hates the sight of a colored soldier . . . [L]et me tell you it couldn't be any worse than hell itself." Another lamented the treatment he and his fellow soldiers received while at Camp Bowie in Brownwood, Texas:

> "[F]rom these 'white' soldiers we're jeered by them both day and night," he recounted, "calling us various unpleasing names as Niggers, Snow ball, and their Black Affrican [sic] Army . . . Also they don't allow us to ride the post busses . . . If we ride the busses we're talked about like dogs and pushed and shoved around in the same manner . . . This is our problem, I wish that you could help us in some respect, and if possible please publish this letter so that the rest of the country would know how they're treating colored soldiers in the US Army."[41]

In an interview in late 1945, the father of Doris Miller, Conery Miller, remarked, "I can't see where we've progressed . . . I am honestly sincere when I say many white people seemingly hate us more since the war. . . ."[42]

Most assuredly, Miller's comments notwithstanding, the war forced subtle beneficial changes. What segregation in Texas (and the South as well) required was not necessarily the violent racists such as the Ku Klux Klan, but the quiet support or indifference from the majority of Whites. Either from fear of social stigma or violence, they went about their daily routine ignoring (and perhaps participating in) the degradation of the Jim Crow system. Whether due to the patriotic spirit sweeping the country, or "wartime emergency," or concession to a gnawing conscience of the hypocrisy of Black men dying overseas yet denied dignity at home, some White establishments, in a small way, moved Texas toward an integrated society. In 1942, for instance, White army officers approached the manager of Kelly's Café in Houston. They inquired about serving their men. The manager agreed, assuming the men White. Naturally he was a bit surprised when he saw an all-Black unit. Nonetheless, he served the men. The local Black paper recounted the incident with a bit of sarcasm. "The soldiers ate," the editor noted. "They used knives and forks and spoons and deported themselves as any other gentlemen. Not even one poured his coffee into his saucer to sip it up. . . . There were no casualties . . . and the café is still open."[43] It would ultimately be the activism of the New Negro appeal to conscience that signaled the promise of ultimate defeat of segregation.

African American Women's Perseverance and Service

Black Texas women also served their country in uniform, in part to show "their worthiness for citizenship." The historical role, and the one generally accepted by the public since it was seen as a natural occupation for women, was the Nurse Corps. The first American women in theater (North Africa), in fact, were nurses, who arrived with the invasion forces. Wherever US forces advanced, nurses followed. In total, 76,000 women served throughout the world in this capacity. Of these, only 343 African American women served in the Army Nurse Corps (in 1941, only 2 percent of the registered nurses in the country were Black). This exclusion was mostly due to racism but also influenced by the armed forces' reluctance to accept married women. Houstonian Leola Grenn, a second lieutenant in the Army Nurse Corps, served about a year in North Africa. Upon returning home in 1943, she was interviewed by the Houston *Informer*, the city's most prominent African American newspaper. "An injured soldier ceases to be black and white in the fighting force," she confessed. Estelle Massey Lidele Osborne, born in Palestine, Texas, served on the staff of the National Nursing Council for War Service. Those who joined the various branches open to women of color wanted to contribute to the war effort, but also desired adventure. Others balked at spending another year as a domestic for White families or working in the fields (from 1940 to 1944, the percentage of Black men and women working in agriculture dropped from 43.3 percent in 1940, to 21 percent in 1941, to 31.3 percent in 1943, and to 10.9 percent in 1944), under White landowners' or prying parents' supervision. Eva Boggess, a native of Waco, served in Liberia in western Africa. An avid bug collector, she split her time tending the wounded and searching for exotic specimens for her personal collection.[44]

Needing manpower, the army, of course, turned to womanpower. Although needed, women never amounted to more than 2 percent of the armed forces. Created in early 1942 as an auxiliary to the army, the Women's Army Auxiliary Corps (WAAC) was to assist the army by allowing women, other than nurses, to perform numerous vital tasks short of combat (the organization was initially criticized by the NAACP, which hoped to use the unit as a wedge to force integration, but the army held fast). More than 150,000 women served in this unit during the war. Officially designated a supplement, these women did not initially receive the same benefits as the men nor, if captured by the enemy, the protection under international law regarding prisoner of war status. The unit's auxiliary status was officially dropped by late 1943, upon which the women received the same benefits as males and official status as a soldier. The unit also was now rechristened Women's Army Corps (WAC). Prominent Texan socialite and wife of former Texas governor William Hobby, Oveta Culp Hobby, headed the organization. Hobby toed the War Department attitude that marginalized Black women in WAC, and she worked to curtail their recruitment numbers. An attitude that believed these women were "fit only to do the dirtiest type of work" because "that's what Negro women are used to doing." Perhaps as a result, only 4,000 Black women served in WAC.

Culp's position raised some concerns that her Southern roots and perhaps her racial prejudices contributed to the low number. The appointment of her assistant, Mary McLeod Bethune, assuaged some concerns. Bethune, a Black woman and icon in the struggle for equality, worked diligently to enlist African American female officers. Open to both races, although segregated, and, in theory, possibly officered by Black women, the WAC performed everything from clerical and lab work to vehicle repair to telephone operations to financial services. Four women of color, all Houstonians and graduates from Prairie View, trained as officers. The "Woman's [sic] Army Auxiliary Corps," admitted Jones, "offers a splendid opportunity for colored women to help achieve success in the war effort." Black female WAC stationed in Texas generally served at Fort Sam Houston in San Antonio.[45]

Black women, indeed, did their part in World War II. Most served within the United States, never leaving its borders. Others served overseas assignments. Some White military commanders requested these female units simply for the "morale" of the Black troops in the area. Elizabeth "Tex" Williams of Houston served as a WAC photographer. She would serve as an army photographer until 1970. She often flew on maneuvers, filming combat techniques. Mary Bingham August Anderson answered the nation's call at the age of forty-one. When she arrived at Houston's city hall, she was dismissed as "Pee Wee." The four-foot, eleven-inch Anderson refused to give up, stating, "You asked for cooks, and I am an experienced cook." Her persistence prevailed, and during the war she passed on to cooks of both races her culinary knowledge. She later admitted that many of those she was training "didn't know you had to let the water boil for three minutes [to make coffee]."[46]

Mary Newson, a Black Texan, left her family's farm for California. Following a unfulfilling position cleaning train cars, she became a riveter in the booming naval industry. Her supervisor wanted to move her to the night shift. Needing to remain in the daytime due to her child, Newson found work at another plant but was soon assigned, although skilled, to janitorial work. Such positions were often reserved for Black employees. She luckily did not remain long in this menial position before reassignment to the assembly line. Aller Hunter also migrated to the Golden State. Working as a domestic for a White family in Texas, she moved for the better pay and greater dignity of war work in 1943. She soon found work as a welder in the naval industry in Richmond, California. Despite this lucrative occupation, Aller was not comfortable as a welder and eventually moved to the cleanup crew. She disposed of the metal shavings that littered the floor following the welding of the seams of the ships. Fanny Christina Hill, a native of Texas, migrated to Los Angeles, California, seeking work in the aircraft production industry. She found it at North American Aviation. Although her wages were high and she appreciated her employer's willingness to hire African Americans, she soon noticed how the workforce was segregated. "I could see where they made a different [approach] in placing you in certain jobs," she remembered. "They had fifteen or twenty departments, but all the Negroes went to Department 17 because there was nothing but shooting and bucking rivets . . . I just didn't like it."[47]

Community Agency and the Fight for "Double V" on the Home Front

During World War II, African American Texans adopted the "Double V" campaign, the two-pronged strategy against fascism abroad and racism at home. African Americans fought in the trenches, battling racism throughout their everyday lives. The year prior to Pearl Harbor, Andrew Webster Jackson, a principal in Fort Bend County, traveled the state documenting African American agency. His findings speak to a diverse community of givers, not takers, and hopeful activists, not passive victims, having the fortitude and courage to withstand the challenges of the day. "[A]ll we ask," declared Jackson, "is an equal chance in the field or endeavor and we will build a monument of honor and love in the hearts of all mankind that will stand as a sure foundation for us and even unborn generations who will have need to call us blessed." African Americans, with the opportunity presented by the war, resolved themselves to fulfill this "equal chance." New Negro artists found solace and agency through their crafts.

As they came of age in Texas, they found themselves drawn toward activism. Houston saxophonist Illinois Jacquet, for instance, left school and in 1939 eventually toured with the Lionel Hampton Orchestra. Still considered a jazz classic, Jacquet's recording of "Flying Home" perhaps ushered in the standard R&B sound. Jacquet, in his six-decade career, worked with Nat King Cole, Duke Ellington, Count Basie, Dizzy Gillespie, Lena Horne, and Ella Fitzgerald. Shortly after the war, he found the strength to use his influence to demand desegregation of Houston's Music Hall.

Most African Americans actually were employed in work that was necessary whether a war was on or not. For example, Black teachers in Houston wanted pay equalization. To offset costs, school boards generally cut wages by percentages according to the teacher's yearly salary. The application was not race neutral, with minority teachers disproportionately affected. Not until the war were these women willing to move against the school board's lack of pay equalization. A similar successful campaign in Dallas finally moved African American teachers in Houston to action, although more than a few senior teachers opposed the campaign. Fearing a legal battle that might turn against the board (recent opinions favored equalization), the Houston school board proposed a plan of incremental pay hikes until 1945. The concession was "the most inspiring example of racial cooperation and democracy at work," and one small, yet very profound, victory against racism.[48]

Civil rights activism in this era usually manifested itself most noticeably with the NAACP. Compared to the more activist postwar years, the war years are generally "the 'forgotten years' of the Negro revolution." The organization saw the war as an opportunity to achieve racial equality. It had chapters throughout the country, with each provincially working toward a national goal. Few chapters had the success let alone the acclaim than the chapter in Houston, mostly because of a force of nature known as Lulu B. White. Born in Elmo, Texas (east of Dallas), White was raised on a farm. She attended Butler College for a year before transferring to Prairie View. She was graduated in 1928 with a degree in English. She married and began teaching. Within a decade, a higher cause called, and she resigned to devote all her time to working for civil rights in the NAACP. White quickly moved up the ranks, along the way breaking glass ceilings: In 1943, she became the first female full-time executive secretary of the Houston branch and the first woman to hold such a position in any branch in the NAACP. The Houston branch, in fact, would more than double its membership during the war years, going from approximately 5,600 members in 1943 to 12,700 in 1945. In 1946, she assumed the head of the organization in Texas. Throughout the war years, under White's leadership, the NAACP would mobilize the African American community to vote (something White believed the most important act Black people could do); would press for a permanent Fair Employment Practice Committee; would work for greater cooperation between the civil rights community and labor unions; would organize boycotts, demonstrations, and letter-writing campaigns; and, in the postwar years, would spearhead the movement to integrate the University of Texas at Austin. "We cannot sit idly by and expect things to come to us," she firmly believed. "We must go out and get them."[49]

And that is exactly what White and her fellow activists did. Activists, in the initial years of the 1940s, began organizing efforts to challenge the White primary in Texas. In early 1941, to formalize the cooperative efforts of the movement in Texas, civil rights supporters created the Texas Council of Negro Organization and appointed as its chairman a masterful organizing and leading civil rights figure in Dallas, A. Maceo

Smith. In 1942, a Black dentist named Lonnie Smith filed suit against the Democratic Party's White primary rule. This rule effectively eliminated Black Texans from participating in party decisions. The state and national officials from the NAACP provided legal assistance that included a relatively unknown counsel named Thurgood Marshall. In 1944, with the war in full bloom, the Supreme Court ruled the White primary unconstitutional, a ruling that went relatively unnoticed at the time but would have astronomically significant repercussions in the coming decade. This significance, however, would not come before reactionary resistance tried to staunch and reverse the momentum toward African American voting equality.[50]

The Second Great Migration and the Expanding World War II Workforce

World War II especially raised the hopes of African Americans. Concentrating their efforts on securing defense-contract jobs, they initially restrained themselves politically, focusing instead on labor rights. War mobilization prompted a migration in what became known as the Second Great Migration. From 1940 to 1970, an estimated five to eight million African Americans abandoned rural communities across the South for better opportunities in cities throughout the nation, including Southern cities. This depletion adversely affected the Texas farm population: It declined from 2,149,187 in 1940 to 1,740,000 in June 1944. The number of Black tenants in Texas also declined from 50,941 in 1935 to 23,878 in 1945, while their number of sharecroppers decreased from 25,675 in 1935 to 9,847 in 1945. War mobilization transformed Texas into an urban, industrial center, prompting approximately 500,000 to migrate from rural to urban communities. By 1950, urban residents comprised 62 percent of the state's population. A total of 608,655 Blacks lived in urban centers, while 369,875 resided in rural areas by 1950. For example, Houston's African American workforce grew dramatically during the war decade, with their numbers nearly doubling from 23,394 to 40,487 between 1940 and 1950. Prior to 1940, industrial workers constituted approximately 40 percent of Houston's Black male labor force; after the war, they comprised a majority. Black male industrial workers increased from 14,345 in 1940 to 27,244 in 1950, comprising 61 percent of the state's overall African American male workforce for 1950.[51]

This shift in the Texas population brought about an occupational change among African American workers. Prairie View professor of sociology Henry A. Bullock conducted a survey on the war's impact. Surveying 1,000 Black families, he concluded that the war altered the occupational makeup of the African American family. Farming and domestic service comprised 68 percent of the occupational divisions prior to 1941; afterward, it represented only 17 percent. Farmers who abandoned the fields moved into the manufacturing and transportation employment sectors. Before the war, these two industries constituted only 14 percent of the work done by family workers; after 1941, it was 77 percent. Houston employed more African American industrial workers than Memphis, Atlanta, and New Orleans by the start of World War II. As the war effort demanded more workers, according to Bullock, some traditional barriers to African American employment diminished. Tolerance, however, only went so far.[52]

Further exacerbating racial tensions for Whites was the increased number of African Americans within their communities. Consider the example of Beaumont, Texas. Lying just east of Houston, Beaumont increased by 21,000 residents in a matter of three years. By 1943, in fact, nearly one-third of the city's 80,000 residents were Black. Housing and labor shortages forced limited integration. This racial component further added volatility. The situation reached a boiling point in Beaumont in the early summer of 1943. The wife of a Pennsylvania Shipyard worker accused an African American man of rape. Such a charge in the South by a White woman against a Black man set the White community off, akin to waving a red handkerchief in front of a bull. On the night of June 15, approximately 2,000 Whites marched on city hall (some accounts have the mob reaching as many as 4,000). The accused could not positively identify her rapist. But this mattered little to a mob wanting "justice" and many townsfolk needing catharsis for their frustrations and anxieties about the great disruptions the war brought to Beaumont. The Black community felt the brunt of this violent release. Moreover, for weeks the racial situation in Beaumont had been rising as the expected date of a scheduled Ku Klux Klan rally neared. This Klan rally, in part, was expected to be a response to the annual celebration of Juneteenth held by the African American community, the celebration of Texas ending slavery following the Civil War. The White vigilantes, armed with guns, axes, and hammers, descended on surrounding Black neighborhoods, ransacking more than a hundred homes and assaulting hundreds of residents. The orgy of violence was only quelled by 2,000 state guardsmen, police, and Texas Rangers and the governor's declaration of martial law. In the end, fifty were injured, with three fatalities: two Black and one White. Authorities arrested more than 206 people. After a review, 29 of the 206 were turned over to local authorities for prosecution. This incident was one of more than 200 racial incidents in 1943, a racially troubled year.[53]

A recent creation promised assistance. Created by Executive Order 8802 (in part from pressure by the A. Philip Randolph's planned "March on Washington") and charged with enforcing equal opportunity in war production as well as government employment by President Roosevelt, the Fair Employment Practices Committee (FEPC) held the aspirations for equality. Although strengthened in 1943, the Committee still lacked the power necessary to effect meaningful change. Even with the cooperation from the Dallas Negro Chamber of Congress under the direction of A. Maceo Smith; the NAACP in Texas under the leadership of Lulu White; Robert Weaver, the director of the War Manpower Commission's Minority Group Services; and Don Ellinger, the chief investigator with the FEPC Region X office, tirelessly working with FEPC officials to eliminate discrimination in the defense industry, progress remained slow. The FEPC lacked the ability to force change and instead looked to find common ground and compromise in the name of war mobilization. This allowed employers and unions alike to easily hinder any FEPC efforts considered unsavory or racially offensive. In one of those strange twists in life, racism could actually bridge the divide that naturally exists between management and unions. This occurred in the rail industry in Texas when executives and the all-White unions, in consensus, simply denied racial discrimination existed. This front left no fissure for the FEPC to maneuver. Such allegiance highlights the limitations experienced by the FEPC. In the early summer of 1943, as mentioned earlier, a race riot erupted in Beaumont. The FEPC investigated but was hindered by the shipyard unions. Union representatives simply refused to appear at any hearing when summoned by the FEPC. Employers acknowledged discrimination yet indicted union hostility and the racial riot for not hiring more Black workers beyond unskilled and menial positions. According to one student of the FEPC:

> The FEPC was created not out of a keen desire to insure the full participation of Negroes in the war employment, but rather out of the political necessity . . . to placate the growing insistence of the Negro communities for greater opportunities in the field of war employment.[54]

Industrial centers in Texas were rarely inviting to Black workers. Industrialists and unions often colluded to undermine efforts at racial progress. In 1940 there were 5.3 million African Americans (3.5 million males) employed in the US economy. Although a lack of education and means to relocate contributed to their exclusion from war mobilization defense jobs, the biggest hurdle was the racial sentiments of employers. According to a government survey, more than half of those who responded stated prejudice. Labor unions also contributed to this prohibition. To be sure, those industries that were barred to Black workers or only hired them for menial labor generally had dominant racist unions. Unions representing aircraft machinists, shipbuilding, boilermakers, or oil workers, to name a few, were often the most hostile to hiring African Americans (although there were exceptions). For instance, the International Brotherhood of Boilermakers with Todd Shipbuilding in Houston refused full membership to Black shipbuilding coworkers but demanded that they still pay the same dues as Whites and only report grievances to a White local. When railroads desperately needed workers, they seemed more compelled to operate below capacity rather than employ qualified African Americans. Such unions represented large percentages of these industries; as a result, their consent in personnel matters actually mattered and exclusion of Black workers was countenanced. This, along with the still strong free-market impulse and the weak federal willingness (and ability) to intervene, meant discrimination went unchallenged. Employers and federal officials further understood that forcing the matter (not that there were many in either camp that preferred to do that) would definitely impede war production.[55]

African Americans were not passive. When Todd Shipbuilding in Houston denied qualified Black welders' entry in the company's training school, Solomon Garrett filed a complaint with the FEPC. Felix

Ward, a fellow Todd Shipbuilding worker and race liaison between segregated unions, lost his job after investigating allegations of racism. Black railroaders testified in Washington, DC, in 1944 about racism in their industry. Not all unions, however, were racist. In fact, one of the more progressive on race was the umbrella organization to unskilled unions, Congress of Industrial Organizations (CIO). The CIO "generally fostered equal treatment, upgrading and promotion for the Negro worker, and only a few of its Southern locals were de facto segregated." This was in contrast to the skilled unions under the American Federation of Labor (AFL). The CIO focused primarily on unskilled "industrial" workers, regardless of race or sex. The AFL represented many unions in the shipbuilding, aircraft, and oil industry. Having previously failed at unionizing efforts in Texas, such as the failed efforts of the "industrial" Oil Workers International Union (OWIU) and United Steelworkers of America (USWA), which evolved to embrace the CIO's commitment to racial inclusion, the CIO looked to capitalize on the new wartime opportunities for labor. Their efforts were easily undermined, however, by fears of communism and integration—things one and the same to many. "Let any wild-eyed labor agitators . . . come to Texas and attempt . . . to slow down or stop work, and they will have plenty of time to rue their folly while they pick cotton on our Texas prison farms," Governor W. Lee "Pappy" O'Daniel notified labor unionizers. Despite such hostility, labor unions promised African American workers empowerment. They offered a way for workers to counter the arbitrariness of management; they offered meaningful representation in grievance proceedings; they offered predictable and fair systems of promotion and layoffs through the seniority system; and they offered negotiating power.[56]

Conclusion

By war's end, amid ticker-tape parades and joyous reunions, the situation for Black Texans appeared relatively unchanged. Segregation appeared as strong as ever, if not validated by the efforts of the state's mobilization and contribution to the war effort. The wartime gains and contributions of Black Texans had to be staunched or dismissed; for Whites, the pressing emergency had passed and it was time to return to "normalcy." Black soldiers, more so than their White counterparts, were administratively discharged from service by receiving a "blue discharge."

This classified them as neither "honorable" nor "dishonorable," a distinction that created difficulties for postwar employment and receiving benefits from the Servicemen's Readjustment Act of 1944, popularly known as the GI Bill. Unemployment for African Americans was increased at a much higher rate than other groups. African Americans who sacrificed for victory and "lived through a major war" now wondered if they could "make it through a minor peace." The Axis powers were vanquished, a defeat seen primarily at the hands of the Americans. Many Whites, although acknowledging the contribution by New Negroes, did not consider them essential to victory. To many, this victory was an American—that is, White American—victory. The major contributions, sacrifices, and even images of the "Good War" are of White "Rosie the Riveters" or "GIs." On the big screen, the war was fought in black and white, with only the white mattering. Italians and Jews from New York, Irish from Boston, Scots Irish from the South, and even Hispanics from the Southwest all relished in their shared victory. These peoples, still sensitive to their ethnic distinctions, came together for a common goal. Their victory was America's victory, and America's victory was theirs.[57]

The war, however, initiated developments that would, in the end, lead to the inclusion of African Americans. The war marked a profound stage between Reconstruction following the Civil War and the modern civil rights movement. "If it hadn't been for the Second World War," one Black migrant to Orange, Texas, admitted, "I think it would a-still been right where it was." He continued:

> That was simply because people had never had a chance to be together, to know each other. And then when they finally went in the service and met each other it made a big change. You'll find black soldiers bringing white boys home with 'em on their leave. White boys bringing black. . . . This soldier wanted that boy with him. They had been through a lot together. So it made a change.[58]

Although not nearly the agent of transformative change that many activists in Texas had hoped for, the initial bold steps taken by the federal government, certainly constrained and hesitant, represented a major precedent for future action and a noticeable break with the past idea that racial issues remain a local matter. There was a newfound optimism and confidence that no longer waited for change but instead initiated it. Passivity, in many ways, was the most important casualty of the war. This newfound vigor was personified by the New Negro.[59]

These victories, however, would have to come in subsequent decades, for the Double V campaign, in the end, failed to eradicate racism. White Texans, with very few exceptions, refused to recognize the patriotism and sacrifice of Black Texans. Unlike his peers, Pap Baker had the ability bypass many of the humiliations of the less privileged. Nonetheless, he represented a new generation who was proud, determined, and committed to the idea of Black equality. World War II did in fact alter the lives of African Americans. Currents were set in motion by the war that would fundamentally transform the country in the coming decades. Business and governmental leaders alike were more sensitive to, if not convinced of, the situation faced by African Americans. Increasingly, Black activists and labor activists realized their differences were not as strong as their similarities. Political equality was gaining momentum. Public perceptions were changing and, shortly, public policy. There was a newfound optimism and confidence within the African American community in Texas not seen since Emancipation. The New Negro–Double V construct would transition into the postwar civil rights movement and would appeal to a burgeoning awakening of conscience in the White community that found it harder to reconcile what it believed the country stood for in theory yet failed to practice in reality. Pap Baker and his fellow activists, using the skills learned in preceding decades, would find the means to penetrate the federal government and the nation in their attempt to force the nation to fulfill its founding promise.[60]

Notes

1. Bernadette Pruitt is Associate Professor of History at Sam Houston State University. She specializes in African American history and has authored several works on the subject in Texas, including *The Other Great Migration: The Movement of Rural African Americans to Houston, 1900–1941* (College Station: Texas A&M University Press, 2013). Michael Hurd is Director of the Texas Institute for the Preservation of History and Culture at Prairie View A&M University and former sportswriter for the *Houston Post*, *USA Today*, *Austin American-Statesman*, and the *Washington Post*. A Vietnam veteran, he has authored several works on African American football, including *Thursday Night Lights: The Story of Black High School Football in Texas* (Austin: University of Texas Press, 2018).

2. Historian W. D. Wright makes a compelling case for the use of *Black*, instead of *black*. According to Wright, middle-class and professional African Americans themselves have in recent years urged society to capitalize the first letter in the word *black*. This designates ethnicity, while *Black* defines race and color. To avoid controversy, I have also decided to use *White* when defining people of European descent. (See W. D. Wright, *Black History and Black Identity: A Call for a New Historiography* [Westport, CT: Praeger, 2001], 1–21; and John McWhorter, "Why I'm Black, Not African American," *Detroit News*, September 30, 2004).

3. Wendell H. Baker interview by Bernadette Pruitt, Huntsville, Texas, February 1, 2003 (all such interviews are in possession of the author and subsequent references will be by name and date); James Otis Baker interview, November 20, 2004; and Wendell Baker, *"If Not Me, Who?": What One Man Accomplished in His Battle for Equality*, eds. Bruce A. Glasrud and Milton S. Jordan (Nacogdoches, TX: Stephen F. Austin State University Press, 2014), 24–27; J. H. Freeman, "James Addison Baker," in *The New Handbook of Texas*, ed. Ron Tyler (Austin: Texas State Historical Association, 1996), I: 346–347; Nelda Woodall, "James Baker Has an Interesting Story to Tell," *Huntsville Item*, December 31, 1989; Charles L. Dwyer and Gerald L. Holder, "Huntsville, Texas," in *The New Handbook of Texas*, ed. Ron Tyler (Austin: Texas State Historical Association, 1996), III: 793–95; J. H. Freeman, "Baker and Botts," in *The New Handbook of Texas*, ed. Ron Tyler (Austin: Texas State Historical Association, 1996), I: 352–53; Kenneth Lipartito and Joseph Pratt, *Baker& Botts in the Development of Modern Houston* (Austin: University of Texas Press, 1991), 2–63; "James Addison and Rowena had 9 children," Unidentified and undated note, Huntsville—Baker Family—Vertical Files, Thomason Room, Newton Gresham Library, Sam Houston State University, Huntsville, Texas (hereafter "Baker Family Vertical File").

4. Having recently suffered the loss of his first wife—Caroline Hightower Baker—widower James Addison Baker followed the advice of friends and family and moved to the sprawling yet thriving East Texas slaveholding community. Founded in 1835 or 1837 by Ephraim Gray as an American Indian trading post, Huntsville and Walker County attracted many from northern Alabama. James Addison Baker's in-laws, the Hightower family, had moved to Texas in 1841. James Addison Baker established a lucrative law practice specializing in business law. He teamed up with his father-in-law, attorney Lewis B. Hightower, before establishing a law practice with Andrew P. Wiley. As an influential member of the Austin College board of trustees, he helped create the state's first law school in 1855. His peers and constituents also elected him to the Ninth Texas Legislature during the Civil War and—while serving in the Confederate Army—the Eleventh District Court of Harris County. In 1872, Judge Baker joined the Houston-based law firm Gray & Botts (Peter Gray and Walter Browne Botts) and soon formed the law firm of Gray, Baker & Botts. Three years later in 1873, after Peter Gray's appointment to the Texas Supreme Court, the firm became Baker & Botts. Railroad lawyer James A. Baker remarried and raised a family in Huntsville as well. In 1853, Baker wedded Rowena Crawford, the principal of the Huntsville Female Brick Academy. The couple had a total of five children, including Captain James Addison Baker,

Sr., of Baker & Botts—grandfather of former secretary of state James A. Baker, III. (See Manuscript Census, Walker County, 1860, roll 1307, Bureau of Census, Series M653, Clayton Genealogy Library, Houston Public Library, Houston, Texas and footnote 2.)

5. Wendell Baker interview, February 1, 2003; Freeman, "James Addison Baker," 346–47; Nelda Woodall, "James Baker Has an Interesting Story to Tell," *Huntsville Item*, December 31, 1989; Dwyer and Holder, "Huntsville, Texas," III: 793–95; Freeman, "Baker and Botts," I: 352–53; Lipartito and Pratt, *Baker& Botts*, 2–63; "James Addison and Rowena had 9 children," Unidentified and undated note, Baker Family Vertical File. Most obituaries and biographies on Judge Baker and the Baker family fail to give the full names of the female children of James and Rowena. These women are generally listed as follows: Mrs. D. M. Parish, Mrs. George Thompson, and Mrs. Duncan. Judge James A. Baker is generally listed as James A. Baker, Senior. His son, Captain James A. Baker, was listed in the 1860 census as James A. Baker Jr.; in later years, however, after Captain Baker grew in stature and prominence, he was not listed as a junior. His son, James A. Baker, was listed as Jr., and his son's son—Secretary of State Baker—was given the name James A. Baker III. (See Wendell Baker interview, November 20, 2004; James O. Baker interview, November 20, 2004; Alain Locke, *The New Negro: An Interpretation* (New York: Simon & Schuster, 1992), 3–18; John Hope Franklin and Elizabeth Brooks Higginbotham, *From Slavery to Freedom: A History of the United States*, 9th ed. (New York: McGraw-Hill, 2011.) Most associate the term *New Negro* with the New Negro Movement, the period between World War I and World War II, when African Americans more confidently formulated new strategies of resistance to racism through political mobilization. Alain Locke, the first Black Rhodes Scholar at Oxford University and noted Howard University professor and scholar/artist of the Harlem Renaissance, borrowed the term *New Negro* in 1925. The "New Negro" combined Booker T. Washington's self-help and accommodation philosophy, Marcus Garvey's Pan-Africanism, and W. E. B. Du Bois's social and political integrationist creed with economic radicalism. In truth, the term, according to literature scholar Gabriel Briggs, derived from the Black community-building efforts of free Blacks during the Reconstruction era and years that followed. Blacks used politics, farming, business formation, education, and community agency to improve their material and social conditions in the United States. For Brigs, the term surprisingly began with the efforts of Southern Blacks, not northern African American communities. Scholars also associate the term with Booker T. Washington. In 1900 he published *A New Negro for a New Century* (1900; New York: Arno Press, 1965). St. Croix native and socialist activist Hubert Harrison also borrowed the term *New Negro*, ultimately expanding it to New Negro Movement by 1917. Locke's work came several years later. Locke popularizes the use of the term. For a criticism of Alain Locke and call for transition from his definition of the New Negro, see Gabriel A. Briggs, *The New Negro in the Old South* (New Brunswick, NJ: Rutgers University Press, 2015). For a comprehensive list of works about the New Negro Movement, see Jeffery B. Perry, *Hubert Harrison: The Voice of Harlem*

Radicalism, 1883–1927 (New York: Columbia University Press, 2010); Henry Lewis Gates and Gene Andrew Jarrett, eds., *The New Negro: Readings on Race, Representation, and African American Culture, 1892–1938* (Princeton: Princeton University Press, 2007); Cary D. Wintz and Paul Finkelman, eds., *Encyclopedia of the Harlem Renaissance*, 2 vols. (New York: Routledge, 2004); *Encyclopedia of the Great Black Migration*, vol. 2, s.v. "New Negro" (by Davarian L. Baldwin), ed. Steven A. Reich (Westport, CT: Greenwood Press, 2006); and William M. Tuttle, *Race Riot: Chicago in the Red Summer of 1919*, 1st THUS ed. (Urbana: University of Illinois Press, 1996).

6. Wendell Baker interview, 20, November 2004; Wendell Baker interview, February 1, 2003; James O. Baker interview, November 20, 2004; Bernadette Pruitt, "Wendall H. Baker," in *Pathfinders: A History of the Pioneering Efforts of African Americans, Huntsville, Walker County, Texas: A Publication of the African American Documentary Committee in Cooperation with the Walker County Historical Commission*, ed. Naomi Ledé (Virginia Beach, VA: Donning Company Publishers, 2004), I: 155–57; James Otis Baker, Draft Registration Cards for Texas from Ancestry.com, *US WWII Draft Cards Young Men, 1940–1947* (database online), Fold3.com, accessed March 13, 2019, https://www.fold3.com/image/625458242; James Otis Baker, United States, *Muster Rolls of US Navy Ships, Stations, and Other Naval Activities*, 8443926, F2, February 9, 1946, accessed June 12, 2021, https://www.ancestry.com/interactive/1143/32860_245214–00674?pid=34654886&backurl=https://search.ancestry.com/cgi-bin/sse.dll?dbid%3D1143%26h%3D34654886%26indiv%3Dtry%26°_vc%3DRecord:OtherRecord%26rhSource%3D2441&treeid=&personid=&hintid=&usePUB=true&usePUBJs=true&lang=en-US; James Otis Baker, Find a Grave, from Ancestry.com. US, Find a Grave Index, accessed March 13, 2019, https://www.findagrave.com/memorial/142455417; James Otis Baker, US Social Security Death Index, 1936–2014, from Ancestry.com, accessed June 12, 2021, https://search.ancestry.com/cgi-bin/sse.dll?dbid=3693&h=87749781&indiv=try&o_vc=Record:OtherRecord&rhSource=60525; Wendell Harold Baker, Find a Grave, from Ancestry.com, accessed March 13, 2019 https://www.findagrave.com/memorial/120461464; Wendell Harold Baker, US World War II Army Enlistment Records, 1938–1946, accessed June 12, 2021, https://search.ancestry.com/cgi-bin/sse.dll?indiv=1&dbid=8939&h=3035420&tid=&pid=&usePUB=true&_phsrc=UdQ28&_phstart=successSource; Herbert Baker, US World War II Draft Cards, Young Men, 1940–1947, from Ancestry.com, accessed March 13, 2019, https://www.fold3.com/image/625457580?xid=1022.

7. For such works, see Ramona Houston, "The NAACP State Conference in Texas: Intermediary and Catalyst for Change, 1937–1957," *Journal of African American History* 94 (Fall 2009); Merline Pitre, *In Struggle against Jim Crow: Lulu B. White and the NAACP, 1900–1957* (College Station: Texas A&M University Press, 1999); Jacqueline Ann Rouse, "Out of the Shadow of Tuskegee: Margaret Murray Washington, Social Activism, and Race Vindication," *Journal of Negro History* 81 (Winter-Fall 1996); Darlene Clark Hine, *Black Victory: The Rise and Fall of the White Primary in Texas*, New Edition (Columbia: University of Missouri Press,

2003); Michael R. Botson Jr., *Labor, Civil Rights, and the Hughes Tool Company* (College Station: Texas A&M University Press, 2005); Dwight Watson, *Race and the Houston Police Department, 1930–1990: A Change Did Come* (College Station: Texas A&M University Press, 2005); Bernadette Pruitt, *The Other Great Migration: The Movement of Rural African Americans to Houston, 1900–1941* (College Station: Texas A&M University Press, 2013); Amilcar Shabazz, *Advancing Democracy: African Americans and the Struggle for Access and Equity in Higher Education in Texas* (Chapel Hill: University of North Carolina Press, 2004); Amilcar Shabazz, "Carter Wesley and the Making of Houston's Civic Culture before the Second Reconstruction," *Houston Review of History and Culture* 1 (Summer 2004); Eric Arnesen, *Brotherhoods of Color: Black Railroad Workers and the Struggle for Equality* (Cambridge, MA: Harvard University Press, 2002); Randy J. Sparks, "'Heavenly Houston' or 'Hellish Houston'?" *Southern Studies* 25 (Winter 1986); Steven A. Reich, "Soldiers of Democracy: Black Texans and the Fight for Citizenship, 1917–1921," *Journal of American History* 82 (March 1996); and Robin D. G. Kelley, *Race Rebels: Politics, Culture and the Black Working Class* (New York: Free Press, 1996).

8. See Walter White, "What Caused the Detroit Riot of 1943?" in *Detroit*, ed. Melvin Hall (New York: New Viewpoints, 1976); Thomas J. Sugrue, *The Origins of the Urban Crisis: Race and Inequality in Postwar Detroit*, rev. ed. (Princeton, NJ: Princeton University Press, 2006); Dominic J. Capeci Jr., "Black-Jewish Relations in Wartime Detroit: The Marsh, Loving, Wolf Surveys: The Race Riot of 1943," *Jewish Social Studies* 47 (Summer–Autumn 1985); Harvard Sitkoff, "The Detroit Race Riot of 1943," *Michigan History* 53 (Fall 1969); Dominic J. Capeci Jr. and Martha Wilkerson, *Layered Violence: The Detroit Riot of 1943* (Jackson: University Press of Mississippi Press, 1991); "The 1943 Race Riot," *Detroit News*, January 21, 2013; Richard W. Thomas, *Life for Us Is What We Make It: Building Black Community in Detroit* (Bloomington: Indiana University Press, 1992); James G. Thompson, "Letter to the Editor," *Pittsburgh Courier*, January 31, 1942; Matthew Delmont, "Why African-American Soldiers Saw World War II as a Two-Front Battle," Smithsonian.com, https://www.smithsonianmag.com/history/why-african-american-soldiers-saw-world-war-ii-two-front-battle-180964616/#m3alSCb5YOLq1gRH.99; Pat Washburn, "The *Pittsburgh Courier's* Double V Campaign in 1942" (paper presented at the annual meeting of the Association for Education in Journalism, East Lansing, Michigan, August 8–11, 1981); Lee Finkle, "The Conservative Aims of Negro Rhetoric: Negro Protest during World War II," *Journal of American History* 60 (December 1973); Richard M. Dalfiume, "The Forgotten Years of the Negro Revolution," *Journal of American History* 55 (June 1968); and Lewis H. Fenderson, "The Negro Press as a Social Instrument," *Journal of Negro Education* 20 (Spring 1951).

9. Works not already mentioned that examine Black Texans' struggle for racial equality during the war years are Max Krochmal, *Blue Texas: The Making of a Multiracial Democratic Coalition* (Chapel Hill: University of North Carolina Press, 2017); Michael L. Gillette, "The NAACP in Texas, 1937–1957" (PhD diss., University of Texas, 1984); Brian Behnken, *Fighting Their Own Battles: Blacks, Mexican Americans, and the Struggle for Civil Rights in Texas* (Chapel Hill, NC: University

of North Carolina Press, 2013); Tyina L. Steptoe, *Houston Bound: Culture and Color in a Jim Crow City* (Oakland: University of California Press, 2015); "African Americans in World War II," National WWII Museum----New Orleans, accessed June 12, 2021, http://www.pacificwarmuseum.org/your-visit/african-americans-in-wwii; "The African American Experience in the US Navy," *Naval History and Heritage Command*, accessed March 14, 2019, https://www.history.navy.mil/browse-by-topic/diversity/african-americans.html; Dwonna Goldstone, *Integrating the 40 Acres: The Fifty Year Struggle for Racial Equality at the University of Texas* (Athens: University of Georgia Press, 2012); Yvonne Davis Frear, "Making the Invisible Visible: African American Women in the Texas Civil Rights Movement," in *Southern Black Women in the Modern Civil Rights Movement*, eds. Bruce Glasrud and Merline Pitre (College Station: Texas A&M University Press, 2013); Michael Philips, *White Metropolis: Race, Ethnicity, and Religion in Dallas, 1841–2001* (Austin: University of Texas Press, 2006); Karen Kossie-Chernyshev, ed., *Recovering Five Generations Hence: The Life and Writings of Lillian Jones Horace* (College Station: Texas A&M University Press, 2013); Karen Kossie-Chernyshev, "A 'Grand Old Church' Rose in the East: The Church of God in Christ (COGIC) in East Texas," *East Texas Historical Journal* 31 (Winter 2003); Howard O. Beeth and Cary D. Wintz, *Black Dixie: Afro-Texas History and Culture in the Bayou City* (College Station: Texas A&M University Press, 1992); Thomas R. Cole, *No Color Is My Kind: The Life of Eldrewey Strearrns and the Integration of Houston* (College Station: Texas A&M University Press, 1995); Neil Foley, *White Scourge: Mexicans, Blacks, and Poor Whites in Texas Cotton Culture* (Berkeley: University of California Press, 1999); Rob Fink, *Playing in Shadows: Texas and Negro League Baseball* (Lubbock: Texas Tech University Press, 2010); James M. SoRelle, "The Darker Side of 'Heaven': The Black Community in Houston, Texas, 1917–1945" (PhD diss., Kent State University, 1980); Bruce Glasrud and Deborah Liles, eds., *African Americans in Central Texas History* (College Station: Texas A&M University Press, 2019); Michael Hurd, *Thursday Night Lights: The Story of Black High School Football in Texas* (Austin: University of Texas Press, 2018); Carroll Parrot Blue, *The Dawn at My Back: Memoir of a Black Texas Upbringing* (Austin: University of Texas Press, 2003); Will Guzmán, *Civil Rights in the Texas Borderlands: Dr. Lawrence A. Nixon* (College Station: Texas A&M University Press, 2015); and William H. Kellar, *Make Haste Slowly: Moderates, Conservatives, and School Desegregation in Houston* (College Station: Texas A&M University Press, 1999).

10. See Blue, *The Dawn at My Back*; Hine, *Black Victory*; Pruitt, *The Other Great Migration*; Pitre, *In Struggle Against Jim Crow*; Jesse O. Thomas, *Negro Participation in the Texas Exposition* (Boston, MA: Christopher Publishing, 1938); John David Boswell, "Negro Participation in the 1936 Texas Centennial Exposition" (master's thesis, University of Texas, 1969); and Kevin Mooney, "Texas Centennial 1936: African-American Texans and the Third National Folk Festival," *Journal of Texas Music History* 1 (Spring 2001). The centennial museum further corroborates the argument that Blacks saw Blackness in a transnational context. This awareness further motivated African Americans in the US to not only attack racism at home,

but also to focus on the racism that formed the foundation of colonialism. For such global awareness, see James H. Meriwether, *So Proudly We Can Be Africans: Black Americans and Africa, 1935–1961* (Durham: University of North Carolina Press, 2002); Thomas Borstelmann, *The Cold War and the Color Line: American Race Relations in the Global Arena* (Cambridge, MA: Harvard University Press, 2001); and Mary L. Dudziak, *Cold War Civil Rights: Race and the Image of American Democracy* (Princeton, NJ: Princeton University Press, 200).

11. James Otis Baker interview, November 20, 2004. For more on the National Youth Administration in Texas, see Christie Lynne Bourgeois, "Stepping over the Lines: Lyndon Johnson, Black Texans, and the National Youth Administration," *Southwestern Historical Quarterly* 91 (October 1987); and *Handbook of Texas Online*, s.v. "National Youth Administration" by Kenneth E. Hendrickson Jr., accessed March 14, 2019, https://tshaonline.org/handbook/online/articles/ncn04.

12. James Otis Baker interview, November 20, 2004.

13. James Otis Baker interview, November 20, 2004.

14. James Otis Baker interview, November 20, 2004. For context, see Lawrence Otis Graham, *Our Kind of People: Inside America's Black Upper Class*, rev. ed. (New York: Harper-Perennial, 1993); and Kathy Russell, Midge Wilson, and Ronald Hall, *The Color Complex: The Politics of Skin Color in the New Millennium*, rev. ed. (New York: Anchor Books, 2013).

15. James Otis Baker interview, November 20, 2004; Wendell H. Baker, November 20, 2004; "Grosse Isle Naval Air Station," *Military History of the Upper Great Lakes*, accessed March 14, 2019, https://ss.sites.mtu.edu/mhugl/2017/11/17/grosse-ile-naval-air-station/; Warren A. Beck and Ynez D. Hasse, "Major Navy and Marine Corp Installations during World War II," *Historic California Posts, Camps, Stations and Airfields*, accessed March 14, 2019, http://militarymuseum.org/NvPosts.html. Baker's pay even exceeded some White workers' at the company while working at this adjacent warehouse.

16. James Otis Baker interview, November 20, 2004; "Breaking Down Barriers: The 34th Naval Construction Battalion Construction," US Navy Seabee Museum, accessed March 14, 2019, https://seabeemuseum.wordpress.com/2018/02/07/breaking-down-barriers-the-34th-naval-construction-battalion/; Dr. Frank A. Blazich Jr., "Building for a Nation and Equality: African American Seabees in World War II," US History Blog, US Naval Institute, accessed March 14, 2019, https://www.navalhistory.org/2014/03/04/building-for-a-nation-and-for-equality-african-american-seabees-in-world-war-ii; and *Thirty-Fourth Navy Construction Battalion*, published by Lester M. Marx, Commander, accessed June 12, 2021, https://www.history.navy.mil/content/dam/museums/Seabee/Cruisebooks/wwii-cruisebooks/ncb-cruisebooks/34%20%20NCB%20%201942–45.pdf, 58.

17. James Otis Baker interview, November 20, 2004; "Breaking Down Barriers"; Blazich Jr., "Building for a Nation and Equality"; *Muster Rolls of US Navy Ships, Stations, and Other Naval Activities*; and *Thirty-Fourth Navy Construction Battalion.*

18. James O. Baker interview, November 20, 2004; and *Thirty-Fourth Navy Construction Battalion.*

19. James Otis Baker interview, November 20, 2004; "NAACP Makes Seabee Investigation: Asks Immediate Probe of Findings," *Negro Star*, March 23, 1945; David Middlecamp, "When Pismo Beach Lots Cost $100: World War II Week by Week," *Tribune*, March 11, 2015, https://www.sanluisobispo.com/news/local/news-columns-blogs/photos-from-the-vault/article39515748.html; "Ends Hunger Strike: Work Battalion of 1000 Negroes Eats First Meal in Two Days," *New York Times*, March 5, 1945; and *Thirty-Fourth Navy Construction Battalion*.

20. Ruthe Winegarten, ed., *Black Texas Women: 150 Years of Trial and Triumph* (Austin: University of Texas Press, 1995), 231–32; Glasrud and Pitre, eds., *Black Women in Texas History*, 137; Neil A. Wynn, *The Afro-American and the Second World War* (New York: Holmes & Meier Publishers, 1976), 56; Ruthe Winegarten and Sharon Kahn, *Brave Black Women: From Slavery to the Space Shuttle* (Austin: University of Texas Press, 1997), 77–78. For more on the industries Black women worked and hurdles they experienced during the war, see Carolyn Cott Webber, "Negro in Texas Industrial Market, 1940–1947" (master's thesis, University of Texas, 1948); Susan M. Hartmann, *The Home Front and Beyond: American Women in the 1940s* (Boston: Twayne Publishers, 1982); Neil Gary Sapper, "Survey of the History of Black People in Texas, 1930–1954" (PhD diss., Texas Tech University, 1972); William Brophy, "The Black Texan, 1900–1950: A Quantitative History" (PhD diss., Vanderbilt University, 1974); and Philip S. Foner and Ronald L. Lewis, eds., *Black Workers: A Documentary History from Colonial Times to the Present* (Philadelphia: Temple University Press, 1989), especially section 122. A fantastic snapshot of one month on the home front at the height of the war is the National Urban League's *Opportunity: Journal of Negro Life*, January 1943. The story of the USO can be found in Julia M. H. Carson, *Home Away from Home: The Story of the USO* (New York: Harper and Brothers, 1946).

21. Joshua Freeman et al., *Who Built America? Working People and the Nation's Economy, Politics, Culture, and Society*, 2 vols. (New York: Pantheon Books, 1992), II: 445; Maureen Honey, ed., *Bitter Fruit: African American Women in World War II* (Columbia: University of Missouri Press, 1999), 2; D'Ann Campbell, *Women at War with America: Private Lives in a Patriotic Era* (Cambridge, MA: Harvard University Press, 1984), 19; Harold G. Vatter, *The US Economy in World War II* (New York: Columbia University Press, 1985), 130; Winegarten, *Black Texas Women*, 234; Winegarten and Kahn, *Brave Black Women*, 79.

22. Campbell, *Women at War with America*, 81; Honey, ed., *Bitter Fruit*, 8. 186; Lois Benjamin, *Three Black Generations at the Crossroads: Community, Culture, and Consciousness*, 2nd ed. (New York: Rowman & Littlefield Publishers, 2007), 69–70.

23. Melinda Chateauvert, *Marching Together: Women of the Brotherhood of Sleeping Car Porters* (Urbana: University of Illinois Press, 1998), 96–97, 107; Winegarten, *Black Texas Women*, 234; Wynn, *Afro-American and the Second World War*, 16; Phyllis Palmer, "Black Domestics during the Depression: Workers, Organizers, Social Commentators," *Prologue: The Journal of the National Archives* 29 (Summer 1997), 127; Jacqueline Jones, *Labor of Love, Labor of Sorrow: Black Women, Work, and the Family, from Slavery to the Present* (New York: Basic Books,

2011), 235, 237; Phyllis Palmer, *Domesticity and Dirt: Housewives and Domestic Servants in the United States, 1920–1945* (Philadelphia: Temple University Press, 1989), 12; Alwyn Barr, *Black Texans: A History of Negroes in Texas 1528–1971* (Austin, TX: Jenkins Publishing Company, 1971), 198; Vatter, *The US Economy in World War II*, 130; Judith Rollins, *Between Women: Domestics and Their Employers* (Philadelphia: Temple University Press, 1985), 56; Amy Bentley, *Eating for Victory: Food Rationing and the Politics of Domesticity* (Urbana: University of Illinois Press, 1998), 77–78. The experience of Annie Mae Hunt during the war is in Ruthe Winegarten and Annie Mae Hunt, *I Am Annie Mae: An Extraordinary Woman in Her Own Words: The Personal Story of a Black Texas Woman* (Austin: University of Texas Press, 1983). For more on domestic servants during the war and their changing image, see David M. Katzman, *Seven Days a Week: Women and Domestic Service in Industrializing America* (New York: Oxford University Press, 1981); Bonnie Thornton Dill, "Across the Barriers of Race and Class: An Exploration of the Relationship between Work and Family among Black Female Domestic Servants" (PhD diss., New York University, 1979); K. Sue Jewell, *From Mammy to Miss America and Beyond: Cultural Images and the Shaping of US Social Policy* (London, UK: Routledge, 1993); Patricia Morton, *Disfigured Images: The Historical Assault on Afro-American Women* (Westport, CT: Greenwood Press, 1991); John Langston Gwaltney, *Drylongso: A Self-Portrait of Black America* (New York: Random House, 1980); Margaret Allen, "The Domestic Ideal and the Mobilization of Womanpower in World War II," *Women's Studies International Forum* 6 (1983); and Daniel E. Sutherland, *Americans and Their Servants: Domestic Service in the United States from 1880–1920* (Baton Rouge: Louisiana State University Press, 1981).

24. Cheryl Mullenbach, *Double Victory: How African American Women Broke Race and Gender Barriers to Help Win World War II* (Chicago: Chicago Review Press, 2013), 225–26.

25. John Virtue, *The Black Soldiers Who Built the Alaskan Highway: A History of Four US Army Regiments in the North, 1942–1943* (Jefferson, NC: McFarland & Company, 2013), 21; Robert Lee Bullard, *Personalities and Reminiscences of the War* (Garden City, NY: Doubleday, 1925), quoted from Ulysses Lee, *The United States Army in World War II: Employment of Negro Troops* (Washington, DC: US Government Printing Office, 1966), 15; W. E. B. Du Bois, "We Return from Fighting, We Return Fighting," *The Crisis: A Record of the Darker Races*, May 1919, accessed March 24, 2019, https://www.marxists.org/history/usa/workers/civil-rights/crisis/0500-crisis-v18n01-w103.pdf; and "W. E. B. Du Bois," World War I and America, http://wwiamerica.org/web-dubois2.php.

26. Blanche Wiesen Cook, *Eleanor Roosevelt, V. 3: The War Years and After, 1939–1962,* rev. ed. (New York: Penguin, 2017); and Ilene Cooper, *Eleanor Roosevelt, Fighter for Justice: Her Impact on Civil Rights, the White House, and World* (New York: Abrams, 2018).

27. *Handbook of Texas Online*, s.v. "Texans in World War II" (by Ralph A. Wooster), Texas State Historical Association, accessed March 24, 2019, https://tshaonline.org/handbook/online/articles/qdw02. For works on the history of

African Americans in combat in the United States, see Gail Lumet Buckley, *American Patriots: The Story of Blacks in the Military from the Revolution to Desert Storm* (New York: Random House, 2002); Mary P. Motley, *Invisible Soldier: The Experience of the Black Soldier, World War II* (Detroit, MI: Wayne State University Press, 1975); Franklin and Higginbotham, *From Slavery to Freedom*; Ivan J. Houston, *Black Warriors: The Buffalo Soldiers of World War II: Memories of the Only Negro Infantry Division to Fight in Europe during World War II* (Bloomington, IN: iUniverse, 2011); Hondon B. Hargrove, *Buffalo Soldiers in Italy: Americans in World War II* (Jefferson, NC: McFarland & Company, 2003); Debra J. Sheffer, *The Buffalo Soldiers, Their Epic Story and Major Campaigns* (Santa Barbara, CA: Praeger, 2015); Bernard C. Nalty, *The Right to Fight: African-American Marines in World War II* (Ann Arbor: University of Michigan Library, 1995); Melton E. McLaurin, *The Marines of Monford Point: America's First Black Marines* (Chapel Hill: University of North Carolina Press, 2007); Carolyn Ross Johnston, *Finding My Father's War: Fighting with the Buffalo Soldiers in World War II* (Tuscaloosa: University of Alabama Press, 2012); Gina M. DiNicolo, *The Black Panthers: A Story of Race, War, and Courage—the 761st Tank Battalion in World War II* (Yardley, PA: Westholme Publishing, 2014); Stephen L. Harris, *Harlem's Hell Fighters: The African-American 369th Infantry in World War I* (Washington, DC: Brassey's, 2003); Chad L. Williams, *Torchbearers: African American Soldiers in the World War I Era* (Chapel Hill: University of North Carolina Press, 2010); Arthur E. Barbeau and Florette Henri, *The Unknown Soldier: Black American Troops in World War I* (Philadelphia: Temple University Press, 1974); and Emmett J. Scott, *The True Story of the Harlem Hellfighters in World War I* (Brighton, MI: Cornell Publications, 1919). Surprisingly, Black women have fought in combat units. For one fascinating example, see Philip Thomas Tucker, *Cathy Williams: From Slave to Buffalo Soldier*, 2nd ed. (Mechanicsburg, PA; Stackpole Books, 2009). For hesitancy and reservations in Black America about fighting for an oppressive society, see Christin Knauer, *Let Us Fight as Free Men: Black Soldiers and Civil Rights* (Philadelphia: University of Pennsylvania Press, 2014); and Jerrold M. Packard, *American Nightmare: The History of Jim Crow* (New York: St. Martins Griffin, 2002). The quotations are on page 2. The quotation regarding the Double V Campaign can be found at NewseumED, "Unsung Heroes: Double V Campaign," accessed June 12, 2021, http://www.newseum.org/2015/02/19/unsung-heroes-double-v-campaign/. The quotation about a new emancipation came from *The Crisis*, November 1943, 328–329. Those reservations and White concerns about Black America and subsequent governmental censorship can be found in Patrick Washburn, *A Question of Sedition: The Federal Government's Investigation of the Black Press during World War II* (New York: Oxford University Press, 1986); Clayton Koppes and Gregory Black, "Blacks, Loyalty, and Motion-Picture Propaganda in World War II," *Journal of American History* 73 (September 1986); and Thomas Cripps, *Making Movies Black: The Hollywood Message Movie from World War II to the Civil Rights Era* (New York: Oxford University Press, 1993). For more on the Double V Campaign, both in Texas and at the national level, see Jerry Gershenhorn, "Double V in North Carolina:

The Carolina Times and the Struggle for Racial Equality During World War II," *Journalism History* 32 (Fall 2006); Byron R. Skinner, "The Double V: The Impact of World War II on Black America" (PhD diss., University of California, Berkeley, 1978); Beth Bailey and David Farber, "The 'Double V Campaign' in World War II Hawaii: African Americans, Racial Ideology, and Federal Power," *Journal of Social History* 26 (July 1993); and Bruce Tyler, "The Black Double V Campaign for Racial Democracy during World War II," *Journal of Kentucky Studies* 8 (September 1991).

28. Sapper, "A Survey of the History of the Black People of Texas," 368, 378; Wynn, *Afro-American and the Second World War*, 27; Michael C. C. Adams, *The Best War Ever: America and World War II* (Baltimore, MD: Johns Hopkins University Press, 1994), 83; Malvern Hall Tillitt, "Army-Navy Pay Tops Most Civilians," American Merchant Marine at War, accessed June 12, 2021, http://www.usmm.org/barrons.html; John Modell, Marc Goulden, and Sigurdur Magnusson, "World War II in the Lives of Black Americans: Some Findings and an Interpretation," *Journal of American History* 76 (December 1989), 841–42; Ron Tyler et al., *The New Handbook of Texas* 6 vols. (Austin: Texas State Historical Association, 1996), VI: 1081. For numbers of Texans who entered armed service, see Robert L. Wagner, *The Texas Army: A History of the 36th Division in the Italian Campaign* (Austin: State House Press, 1972); and James Lee Ward et al., eds., *1941: Texas Goes to War* (Denton: University of North Texas Press, 1991). To see why the army agreed to all-Black units, see John Morton Blum, *V Was for Victory: Politics and American Culture during World War II* (New York: Harcourt Brace Jovanovich, 1976); and Lee, *United States Army in World War II: Employment of Negro Troops*. For the information regarding the army's General Classification Test and Mechanical Aptitude Test, see *Atlanta Black Star*, June 16, 2015, http://atlantablackstar.com/2015/06/16/10-things-mistreatment-black-soldiers-world-war-ii-may-not-know/5/. A telling statistic about the government's role for Black men is that as late as 1943, when theaters throughout the Allied war effort experienced shortages in manpower, the US Army stationed 425,000 of the 504,000 Black servicemen in the United States.

29. *Washington Post*, September 10, 1997. For the numbers of prisoners of war in the United States and those in Texas, see the essay by Kelly Crager, specifically footnote 9. For a few works that examine the internment of Axis POWs in Texas and other states, and their treatment compared to the local community and Black populace and, at times, assimilation, are Danny Steelman, "German Prisoners of War in America: Oklahoma's Prisoner of War Operations during World War II," *Oklahoma State Historical Review* 4 (Spring 1983); George T. Mazuzan and Nancy Walker, "Restricted Areas: German Prisoner of War Camps in Western New York, 1944–1946," *New York History* 59 (January 1978); Anita Buck, *Behind Barbed Wire: German Prisoner of War Camps in Minnesota* (St. Cloud, MN: North Star Press, 1998); Hazel Wages, "Memphis Armed Service Forces Depot Prisoner of War Camp: 1944–1946," *Tennessee Historical Quarterly* 52 (Spring 1993); John J. Culley, "World War II and a Western Town: The Internment of the Japanese Railroad Workers of Clovis, New Mexico," *Western Historical Quarterly* 13 (January 1982);

Robert C. Doyle, *The Enemy in Our Hands: America's Treatment of Prisoners of War from the Revolution to the War on Terror* (Lexington: The University of Kentucky Press, 2010); James Richard Keen, "The Captive Enemy?: Italian Prisoners of War in Texas during World War II" (master's thesis, University of Texas at the Permian Basin, 1998); Arnold P. Krammer, "Japanese Prisoners of War in America," *Pacific Historical Review* 52 (February 1983); and Richard Paul Walker, "Prisoners of War in Texas during World War II" (PhD diss., University of North Texas, 1980). Memoirs and oral histories by German POWs in Texas and America are Lewis H. Carlson, *We Were Each Other's Prisoners: An Oral History of World War II American and German Prisoners of War* (New York: Basic Books, 1997); Heino R. Erichsen, *The Reluctant Warrior: Former German POW Finds Peace in Texas* (Austin: Eakin Press, 2001); Helmut Hörner, *A German Odyssey: The Journal of a German Prisoner of War*, trans. and ed. Allan Kent Powell (Golden CO: Fulcrum, 1991); Berneda Koller, *An Ironic Point of Light: A Story of a German from Russia Who Survived an American World War II Prisoner of War Camp* (Freeman, SD: Pine Hill Press, 1994); Kathy Roe Coker, "World War II Prisoners of War in Georgia: German Memories of Camp Gordon, 1943–1945," *Georgia Historical Quarterly* 76 (Winter 1992). Walter Schmid, *A German POW in New Mexico*, ed. Wolfgang T. Schlauch, trans. Richard Rundell (Albuquerque: University of New Mexico Press, 2005); Fritz Ensslin, "A German Soldier Tells What It Is Like to Visit Ft. Leonard Wood in 1943 as a POW," *Essayons* (June 1991); and Jeffrey E. Geiger, *German Prisoners of War at Camp Cooke, California: Personal Accounts of 14 Soldiers, 1944–1946* (Jefferson, NC: McFarland & Company, 1996).

30. Kenneth D. Rose, *Myth and the Greatest Generation: A Social History of Americans in World War II* (New York: Routledge, 2008), 136. This work has other examples of such indignities experienced by Black Americans in the presence of enemy White prisoners. For a brief biography of Witter Bynner, see James Craft, *Who Is Witter Bynner? A Biography*; and "Harvard Square Library: A Digital Library of Unitarian Universalist Biographies, History, Books, and Media," http://www.harvardsquarelibrary.org/cambridge-harvard/witter-bynner/. For more on the indignities experienced by Black soldiers regarding White enemy POWs, see Andrew Carroll, ed., *War Letters: Extraordinary Correspondence from American Wars* (New York: Washington Square Press, 2001); Honey, ed., *Bitter Fruit*, particularly chapter 2; and Matthias Reiss, "Icons of Insult: German and Italian Prisoners of War in African American Letters during World War II," *Amerikastudian/American Studies* 49 (2004). For a work on contemporary Black literature chronicling their experiences both on the war front and home front during the Second World War, see Jennifer C. James, *A Freedom Bought with Blood: African American War Literature from the Civil War to World War II* (Durham: University of North Carolina Press, 2007).

31. Heather Gilligan, "Even Nazi Prisoners of War in Texas Were Shocked at How Black People Were Treated in the South," *Timeline*, accessed June 12, 2021, https://timeline.com/nazi-prisoners-war-texas-f4a0794458ea.

32. The numbers for the US Navy and Marine Corps came from "African

Americans in WWII" National WWII Museum----New Orleans, accessed June 12, 2021, http://www.pacificwarmuseum.org/your-visit/african-americans-in-wwii/.

33. Mullenbach, *Double Victory*, 117; Jeanne Holm, *Women in the Military: An Unfinished Revolution* (Novato, CA: Presidio Press, 1992), 81; Judy Barrett Litoff and David C. Smith, eds., *American Women in a World at War: Contemporary Accounts during World War II* (Plymouth, UK: SR Books, 1997), 74. Those interested in Doris Miller can read Thomas W. Cutrer and T. Michael Parrish, *Doris Miller, Pearl Harbor, and the Birth of the Civil Rights Movement* (College Station: Texas A&M University Press, 2017); Bill O'Neal, *Doris Miller: Hero of Pearl Harbor* (Austin: Eakin Press, 2007); Richard E. Miller, *The Messman Chronicles: African Americans in the US Navy, 1932–1943* (Annapolis, MD: Naval Institute Press, 2004); and Neil Gary Sapper, "Aboard the Wrong Ship in the Right Books: Doris Miller and Historical Accuracy," *East Texas Historical Journal* 18 (January 1980). The information for Harmon came from Cuero *Record*, December 3, 1943; Ibid., February 13 and April 30, 1976; Houston *Informer*, May 29, 1943; *New York Times*, May 22, 1943; and Robert Ewell Greene, *Black Defenders of America, 1775–1973* (Chicago: Johnson Publishing Company, 1974). Although Black men did not have the opportunities for combat and thus limited in "acts of heroism," those few who were on the front lines unfortunately had their service judged by their skin color and not gallantry or bravery. Like so much of their contribution, Black servicemen's actions were rarely acknowledged or appreciated. After a review of the war years to determine whether race determined acknowledgment of heroism, the federal government took a profound step of rectifying past wrongs and acknowledging the heroism and sacrifice of seven African American men. President Bill Clinton, in a publicized ceremony in 1997, presented the families of six of the men the Congressional Medal of Honor for actions during World War II: Staff Sgt. Edward A. Carter Jr.; 1st Lt. John R. Fox; Pfc. Willy F. James Jr.; Staff Sgt. Ruben Rivers; 1st Lt. Charles L. Thomas; and Pvt. George Watson. The seventh and only living recipient from the war, 1st Lt. Vernon Baker, had the president personally drape it across his neck. See Vernon J. Baker and Ken Olsen, *Lasting Valor: The Story of the Only Living Black World War II Veteran to Earn American's Highest Distinction for Valor, the Medal of Honor* (New York: Bantam Books, 1999); Tiara Dunlap, "Families of African-American WWII Soldiers Awarded Medals of Honor 50 Years Later: These Men Were National Heroes and Almost All of Them Died without Recognition," *People*, October 14, 2015; *DoDNews*, January 16, 1997; and *New York Times*, January 14, 1997. Works that look to correct the neglect of Black servicemen are Linda Hervieux, *Forgotten: The Untold Story of D-Day's Black Heroes at Home and at War* (New York: HarperCollins, 2015); and Denise George and Robert Child, *The Eleven: The Forgotten Story of Black American Soldiers Brutally Massacred in World War II* (New York: Caliber, 2017). The USS *Harmon* (DE-678) was a destroyer-escort commissioned in 1943, and the USS *Dorie Miller* (DE-1091) was also a destroyer-escort commissioned in 1973.

34. Charles W. Sasser, "761st Tank Battalion: Patton's Panthers Would Not Quit," *The History Reader*, July 12, 2011, http://www.thehistoryreader.com/modern-history/761st-tank-battalion-pattons-panthers-quit/. For more on the

761st, see Charles W. Sasser, *Patton's Panthers: The African-American 761st Tank Battalion in World War II* (New York: Pocket Books, 2004); Kareem Abdul-Jabbar and Anthony Walton, *Brothers in Arms: The Epic Story of the 761st Tank Battalion, WWII Forgotten Heroes* (New York: Broadway Books, 2004); and Joe Wilson Jr., *The 761st "Black Panther" Tank Battalion in World War II: An Illustrated History of the First African American Armored Unit to See Combat* (Jefferson, NC: McFarland & Company, 1999).

35. "Lt. Warren Crecy," 761st Tank Battalion, accessed June 12, 2021, http://www.761st.com/18update/2018a/index.php/history/lt-warren-crecy.

36. Michael Lee Lanning, *The African American Soldier, from Crispus Attucks to Colin Powell* (Secaucus, NJ: Birch Lane Press, 1997), 182.

37. Sapper, "A Survey of the History of the Black People of Texas," 381, 378; *Texas in World War II* (Austin: Texas Historical Commission, 2005), 5. The number of Texans who trained in Texas military facilities can be found at Texas Historical Commission's online site, which proves to be one of the better and more reliable educational sites, accessed June 12, 2021, www.thc.texas.gov/preserve/projects-and-programs/military-sites/texas-world-war-ii. By war's end, 1.5 million servicemen passed through the state.

38. For works on the Camp Logan Incident, see Robert V. Haynes, *A Night of Violence: The Houston Riot of 1917* (Baton Rouge: Louisiana State University Press, 1976); Robert V. Haynes, "The Houston Mutiny and Riot of 1917," *Southwestern Historical Quarterly* 76 (April 1973); C. Calvin Smith, "The Houston Riot of 1917, Revisited," *Houston Review* 13 (1991); Thomas Richards Adams, "The Houston Riot of 1917" (master's thesis, Texas A&M University, 1972); Edgar A. Schuler, "The Houston Race Riot, 1917," *Journal of Negro History* 29 (July 1944); Phocion Samuel Parker Jr., "The Twenty-Fourth Infantry Regiment and the Houston Riot of 1917" (master's thesis, University of Houston, 1971); Rawn James Jr., *The Double V: How Wars, Protest, and Harry Truman Desegregated America's Military* (New York: Bloomsbury Press, 2013); and Sig Christenson, "A Century Ago, Executions at Fort Sam Sparked Change in Military Law," *San Antonio Express-News*, December 10, 2017, https://www.expressnews.com/sa300/article/A-century-ago-executions-at-Fort-Sam-sparked-12420513.php.

39. James M. SoRelle, "Race Relations in 'Heavenly Houston,' 1919–1945," in *Black Dixie: Afro-Texan History and Culture in Houston*, eds., Howard Beeth and Cary D. Wintz (College Station: Texas A&M University Press, 1992), 186, 175–76.

40. *The Crisis*, January 26, 1944. The "Four Freedoms" were freedom of speech, freedom of worship, freedom from want, and freedom from fear. President Roosevelt delivered these freedoms in his annual "State of the Union Address" in early 1941 and proposed them as the benchmark for all humanity around the world. The entire text of the speech can be found in Franklin D. Roosevelt, *The Public Papers and Addresses of Franklin D. Roosevelt 1940 Volume*, War and aid to democracies: with a special introduction and explanatory notes by President Roosevelt, [Book 1], compiled by Samuel Irving Rosenman (New York: Harper & Brothers Publishers 1950), 663–78. For more on the speech, see Elizabeth Borgwardt, *A New Deal for the World: America's Vision for Human Rights* (Cambridge, MA: Harvard

University Press, 2007); Laura Crowell, "The Building of the 'Four Freedoms' Speech," *Speech Monographs* 22 (November 1955); Samuel I. Rosenman, *Working with Roosevelt* (New York: Harper & Brothers, 1952); and Halford R. Ryan, *Franklin D. Roosevelt's Rhetorical Presidency* (Westport, CT: Greenwood Press, 1988). The letter by a Black WAC detailing the treatment of African Americans in uniform by Whites at Camp Forrest, Tennessee, is in Judy Barrett Litoff and David C. Smith, eds., *We're in This War, Too: World War II Letters from American Women in Uniform* (New York: Oxford University Press, 1994). A firsthand account of the ordeal experienced by wives following their husbands around the country, although from a White woman's point of view, is Barbara Klaw, *Camp Followers: The Story of a Soldier's Wife* (New York: Random House, 1944). There were self-help books for those women waiting at home for the return of a husband in the service. For this, see Ethel Gorham, *So Your Husband's Gone to War!* (Garden City, NY: Doubleday, Doran and Company, 1942).

41. Phillip McGuire, ed., *Taps for a Jim Crow Army: Letters from Black Soldiers in World War II* (Lexington: University of Kentucky Press, 2015), 184, 192, 104–5; Maria Höhn and Martin Klimke, *A Breath of Freedom: The Civil Rights Struggle, African American GIs, and Germany* (New York: Palgrave Macmillan, 2010), 23–25; Fred H. Allison, "Patriotic Prosperity and Social Change in World War II: The Impact of Majors Field on Greenville, Texas," *Sound Historian: Journal of the Texas Oral History* 5 (1999), 47–48; Sapper, "A Survey of the History of the Black People of Texas," 378, 382–83; Honey, ed., *Bitter Fruit*, 127.

42. *Houston Informer*, December 22, 1945.

43. SoRell, "Race Relations in 'Heavenly Houston,' 1919–1945," 186; John Egerton, *Speak Now Against the Day: The Generation before the Civil Rights Movement in the South* (New York: Alfred A. Knopf, 1994), 327; *Houston Informer*, October 17, 1942.

44. Winegarten and Kahn, *Brave Black Women*, 74–76; Doris Weatherford, *American Women and World War II* (Edison, NJ: Castle Books, 2008), 21; Campbell, *Women at War with America*, 53; Litoff and Smith, eds., *American Women in a World War at War*, 35; Honey, ed., *Bitter Fruit*, 2; Wynn, *Afro-American and the Second World War*, 57; Winegarten, ed., *Black Texas Women*, 228. The details of Osborne can be found in *Brenham Banner Press*, December 30, 1981. A firsthand account of a nurse during the war is Theresa Archard, *G.I. Nightingale: The Story of an American Army Nurse* (New York: W.W. Norton and Company, 1945).

45. Rita Victoria Gomez, "Black WACs and Bad Times in the Good War," *Washington Post*, November 10, 1991, accessed June 12, 2021, https://www.washingtonpost.com/archive/opinions/1991/11/10/black-wacs-and-bad-times-in-the-good-war/f8e770db-2a12–48b8-ac3f-5c81bf677f6f/?utm_term=.683a19fbba00; John W. Jeffries, *Wartime America: The World War II Home Front*, 2nd ed. (New York: Rowman & Littlefield, 2018), 76; Mullenbach, *Double Victory*, 90–111, 123; Glasrud and Pitre, eds., *Black Women in Texas History*, 140; Merline Pitre, "At the Crossroads: Black Texas Women, 1930–1954," in *Black Women in Texas History*, eds. Bruce A. Glasrud and Merline Pitre (College Station: Texas A&M University

Press, 2008), 140; Holm, *Women in the Military*, 77–78, 80, 91. The four female Houstonians were Annie Lois Brown-Wright, Ruth L. Freeman, Geraldine Bright, and Alice Marie Jones. For Hobby's prejudices, see Sandra M. Bolzenius, "The Black Women Soldiers Who Demanded Opportunities," *What It Means to Be American*, November 15, 2018, https://www.whatitmeanstobeamerican.org/engagements/the-black-women-soldiers-who-demanded-opportunities/; and Debra L. Winegarten, *Oveta Culp Hobby: Colonel, Cabinet Member, Philanthropist* (Austin: University of Texas Press, 2014). For the experiences of an all-Black WAC unit, see Brenda L. Moore, *To Serve My Country, to Serve My Race: The Story of the Only African-American WACs Stationed Overseas during World War II* (New York: New York University Press, 1996). For more on the WACs in World War II, see Mattie E. Treadwell "The Women's Army Corps," in *United States Army in World War II, Special Studies* (Washington, DC: US Government Printing Office, 1954); Bettie J. Morden *The Women's Army Corps, 1945–1978* (1954; repr., Washington, DC: Office of the Chief of Military History, Department of the Army, CMH Pub. 11–8, 1991); The Women's Army Corps Veterans Association, *Daughters of Pallas Athene: Cameo Recollections of Women's Army Corps Veterans* (Independence, MO: Print America, 1983); Jesse J. Johnson, *Black Women in the Armed Forces, 1941–1974* (Hampton, VA: Hampton Institute, 1974); Margaret Flint, *Dress Right, Dress: The Autobiography of a WAC* (New York: Dodd, Mead & Company, 1943); Karen Anderson, *Wartime Women: Sex Roles, Family Relations and the Status of Women during World War II* (Westport, CT: Greenwood Press, 1981); Leisa D. Meyer, *Creating GI Jane: Sexuality and Power in the Women's Army Corps during World War II* (New York: Columbia University Press, 1998); Martha S. Putney, *When the Nation Was in Need: Blacks in the Women's Army Corps during World War II* (Matuchen, NJ: Scarecrow Press, 1992); Ethel A. Starbird, *When Women First Wore Army Shoes: A First-Person Account of Service as a Member of the Women's Army Corps during WWII* (Bloomington, IN: iUniverse, 2010); and Anne Bosanko Green, *One Woman's War: Letters Home from the Women's Army Corps, 1944–1946* (St. Paul: Minnesota Historical Society Press, 1989). For the experiences of a female Black officer in the WACs, see Charity Adams Earley, *One Woman's Army: A Black Officer Remembers the WAC* (College Station: Texas A&M University Press, 1989).

46. Lynsey Weatherspoon, "Black Women in Photography // Elizabeth "Tex" Williams," *Medium*, February 2, 2017, https://medium.com/@lnweatherspoon/black-women-in-photography-elizabeth-tex-williams-a3edebfa60e2; Winegarten and Kahn, *Brave Black Women*, 75; Holm, *Women in the Military*, 78. For the experience of an all-Black female unit that sorted mail overseas, see Don Vaughan, "All-Black Female Battalion Made History," *Voices for America's Troops*, accessed June 12, 2021, http://www.voicesfortroops.org/Learn_More/From_the_Newsletter/All-Black_Female_Battalion_Made_History.html; and Alexis Clark, "These Black Female Heroes Made Sure US WWII Forces Got Their Mail," *History*, https://www.history.com/news/black-woman-army-unit-mail-world-war-ii.

47. Honey, ed., *Bitter Fruit*, 9; Mullenbach, *Double Victory*, 20–21. A detailed examination of the issues faced by women in the aircraft industry during World

War II is Sherna B. Gluck, *Rosie the Riveter Revisited: Women, the War, and Social Change* (Boston: Twayne Publishers, 1987). For more on African American women and their aspirations and disappointments in the California shipyards, see Amy Kesselman, *Fleeting Opportunities: Women Shipyard Workers in Portland and Vancouver during World War II and Reconversion* (Albany: State University of New York Press, 1990); Marilynn S. Johnson, *The Second Gold Rush: Oakland and the East Bay in World War II* (Berkeley: University of California Press, 1993); and Kevin Starr, *Embattled Dreams: California in War and Peace, 1940–1950* (New York: Oxford University Press, 2002).

48. *Houston Informer*, March 1941, September 1942, and April 1943; SoRelle, "The Darker Side of 'Heaven,'" 89–92; Kellar, *Make Haste Slowly*, 35–46; Shabazz, *Advancing Democracy*, 9–33; Houston, "The NAACP State Conference in Texas," 509–28; Pitre, *In Struggle against Jim Crow*, 56–80; Andrew Webster Jackson, *A Sure Foundation: A Sketch of Negro Life in Texas* (Houston: Wester-Richardson Publishing Co., 1940), 1–5; Pruitt, *The Other Great Migration*, 194–206, 277–83; Steptoe, *Houston Bound*, 157–71; *Handbook of Texas* Online, s.v. "McDavid, Percy"; *Handbook of Texas*, s.v. "Larkin, Milton Sr," accessed June 12, 2021, https://tshaonline.org/handbook/online/articles/flajb; Reginald Buckner, "A History of Music Education in the Black Community Kansas City, Kansas, 1905–1954," *Journal of Research in Music Education* 30 (1982): 94–100; Horace Tapscott, *Songs of the Unsung: The Musical and Social Journey of Horace Tapscott*, ed. Steven L. Isoardi (Durham, NC: Duke University Press, 2001), 25–29, 90–95; "Illinois Jacquet: Jazz at the Philharmonic Crowd Favorite in the 1940s and 1950s," *Legends of Jazz History. Swingmusic.net,* http://www.swingmusic.net/Illinois_Jacquet_Big_Band_And_Jazz_Legend_Biography.html; Aimee L'Heureux, "Illinois Jacquet: Integrating Houston Jazz Audiences . . . Lands Ella Fitzgerald and Ella Fitzgerald in Jail," *Houston History* 8 (2010): 6–8, 49; *Handbook of Texas Online*, s.v. "Jacquet, Jean Baptist [Illinois]" (by Grant Mazak), accessed March 14, 2019, https://tshaonline.org/handbook/online/articles/fja39; and *Handbook of Texas Online*, s.v. "Cobb, Arnette Cleophus" (by Stephen Williams and Kharen Monsho), accessed March 14, 2019, https://tshaonline.org/handbook/online/articles/fcobs. A noted painter was Staff Sgt. Samuel Albert Countee, who was commissioned in 1942 to produce a painting for the Black Officer's Club Negro Officers Club at Fort Leonard Wood in Missouri. Today, his murals are considered great works of art. (See Steven Smith, *US Army Corps of Engineers Construction Engineering Research Laboratories and US Department of Defense Legacy Resource Management Program: A Historic Context Statement for a World War II Era Black Officers' Club at Fort Leonard Wood, Missouri, November 1998*, http://www.cas.sc.edu/sciaa/PDFdocs/military-research/FLWBlackOfficersClub.pdf, 87–99).

49. The first quote comes from Wynn, *Afro-American and the Second World War*, 1. The second quote comes from Glasrud and Pitre, eds., *Black Women in Texas History*, 150. The biography of White can be found in Pitre, *In Struggle against Jim Crow*; Michael L. Gillette, "The Rise of the NAACP in Texas," *Southwestern Historical Quarterly* 81 (April 1978); *Houston Informer*, July 13, 1957; and

Merline Pitre, "Building and Selling the NAACP: Lulu B. White as an Organizer and Mobilizer," *East Texas Historical Journal* 39 (Fall 2001). For the integration of the University of Texas, see Goldstone, *Integrating the 40 Acres*. Works that examine the burgeoning midcentury movement for racial equality at the national level are Glenda Gilmore, *Defying Dixie: The Radical Roots of Civil Rights, 1919–1950* (New York: W. W. Norton, 2009); Patricia Sullivan, "Movement Building during the World War II Era: The NAACP's Legal Insurgency in the South," in *Fog of War: The Second World War and the Civil Rights Movement*, eds. Kevin M. Kruse and Stephen Tuck (New York: Oxford University Press, 2012); Thomas J. Sugrue, *Sweet Land of Liberty: The Forgotten Struggle for Civil Rights in the North* (New York: Random House, 2008); Shana Bernstein, "Building Bridges at Home in a Time of Global Conflict: Interracial Cooperation and the Fight for Civil Rights in Los Angeles, 1933–1954" (PhD diss., Stanford University, 2004); Cornelius L. Bynum, *A. Philip Randolph and the Struggle of Civil Rights* (Urbana: University of Illinois Press, 2010); John Hope Franklin, *From Slavery to Freedom: A History of African Americans*, 7th ed. (New York: Knopf, 1994); Manning Marable, *Race, Reform, and Rebellion: The Second Reconstruction in Black America, 1945–1968* (Jackson: University Press of Mississippi, 2007); August Meier and Elliott Rudwick, *CORE: A Study in the Civil Rights Movement, 1942–1968* (New York: Oxford University Press, 1973); Dorothy K. Newman et al., *Protest, Politics, and Prosperity: Black Americans and White Institutions, 1940–1975* (New York: Pantheon Books, 1978); Brenda Gayle Plummer, *Rising Wind: Black Americans and US Foreign Affairs, 1935–1960* (Chapel Hill: University of North Carolina Press, 1996); Jennifer E. Brooks, *Defining the Peace: World War Veterans, Race, and the Remaking of Southern Political Tradition* (Chapel Hill: University of North Carolina Press, 2004); Christopher Parker, *Fighting for Democracy: Black Veterans and the Struggle Against White Supremacy in the Postwar South* (Princeton, NJ: Princeton University Press, 2009); Ronald R. Krebs, *Fighting for Rights: Military Service and the Politics of Citizenship* (Ithaca, NY: Cornell University Press, 2006); and Martha Biondi, *To Stand and Fight: The Struggle for Civil Rights in Postwar New York City* (Cambridge, MA: Harvard University Press, 2003).

50. Barr, *Black Texans*, 173–175. For the Court's ruling on the White primary in Texas, see Hine, *Black Victory*; and Darlene Clark Hine, "The Illusive Ballot: The Black Struggle against the Texas Democratic White Primary, 1932–1945," *Southwestern Historical Quarterly* 81 (April 1978). The resistance to gains in the civil rights movement in the midcentury can be found in Jason Morgan Ward, *Defending White Democracy: The Making of a Segregationist Movement and the Remaking of Racial Politics, 1936–1965* (Chapel Hill: University of North Carolina Press, 2011); George Lewis, *Massive Resistance: The White Response to the Civil Rights Movement* (London: Hodder Arnold, 2006); Kari Frederickson, *The Dixiecrat Revolt and End of the Solid South* (Chapel Hill: University of North Carolina Press, 2001); Keith M. Finley, *Delaying the Dream: Southern Senators and the Fight Against Civil Rights, 1938–1965* (Baton Rouge: Louisiana State University Press, 2008); Herbert Shapiro, *White Violence and Black Response: From Reconstruction to*

Montgomery (Amherst: University of Massachusetts Press, 1988); and Jason Sokol, *There Goes My Everything: White Southerners in the Age of Civil Rights, 1945–1975* (New York: Vintage, 2006).

51. Pruitt, *The Other Great Migration*, 1–14, 277–90; Bureau of Census, *Sixteenth Census of the United States, 1940: Population: Characteristics of the Population*, V. 2, Part 6: Pennsylvania-Wyoming (Washington, DC: US Government Printing Office, 1943), 763; Bureau of Census, *A Report on the Seventeenth Census of the United States: Census of Population: 1950*: V. II: Characteristics of the Population: Part 43: Texas (Washington, DC: US Government Printing Office, 1953), 43–63; Bureau of Census, *Sixteenth Census of the United States: 1940*: Population, V. 3: The Labor Force, Part 5: Pennsylvania-Wyoming, 506–7; Bureau of Census, *A Report of the Seventeenth Decennial Census of the United States: Census of Population: 1950*: V. II: Characteristics of the Population: Part 43: Texas, 509–10.

52. "Negro Workers and the National Defense," 2–3, Records of the Bureau of Training Industry Service, General Records, 1940–45, Records of the War Manpower Commission, Record Group 211, National Archives at College Park, College Park, Maryland (hereafter cited as War Manpower Commission, "Negro Workers," RG 211); Housing and Urban Development, War Housing Program, WHP No. 5-Q3-C4, RG 207; Henry Allen Bullock, "Some Readjustments of the Texas Negro Family to the Emergency of War," *Southwestern Social Science Quarterly* 25 (June 1944–March 1945): 102–3; Pratt, *Growth of a Refining Region*, 94; Housing and Urban Development, War Housing Program, No., 6-Q4, RG 207; Bureau of Census, *Sixteenth Census of the United States, 1940: Population: Characteristics of the Population*, V. 2, 763; Bureau of Census, *A Report on the Seventeenth Census of the United States: Census of Population: 1950*: V. II: *Characteristics of the Population: Part 43: Texas*, 43–63.

53. The best works on the Beaumont Race Riot are James A. Burran, "Violence in an 'Arsenal of Democracy,'" *East Texas Historical Journal* 14 (Spring 1976); James A. Burran, "The Beaumont Race Riot, 1943" (master's thesis, Texas Tech University, 1973); Maury Klein, *A Call to Arms: Mobilizing America for World War II* (New York: Bloomsbury Press, 2013); and James S. Olson and Sharon Phair, "Anatomy of a Race Riot: Beaumont, Texas, 1943," *Texana* 11 (1973). The number of racial incidents during 1943 is in Eugenia Kaledin, *Daily Life in the United States, 1940–1959* (Westport, CT: Greenwood Press, 2000). For the history of lynching in the Lone Star State, see David L. Chapman, "Lynching in Texas" (master's thesis, Texas Tech University, 1973). Prior to the war, yet during mobilization, Dallas experienced similar racial strife in 1940 and 1941. For this, see Sapper, "A Survey of the History of the Black People of Texas," 388–91. The works on the racial incidents throughout the war and during the summer of 1943 are Jack Hamann, *On American Soil: How Justice Became a Casualty of World War II* (Chapel Hill, NC: Algonquin Books of Chapel Hill, 2005); Quintard Taylor, *The Forging of a Black Community: Seattle's Central District from 1870 through the Civil Rights Era* (Seattle: University of Washington Press, 1994); *Seattle Times*, August 18 and November 16, 1944; *Seattle*

Times, October 17, 2007; Dominic J. Capeci Jr., *Race Relations in Wartime Detroit: The Sojourner Truth Housing Controversy of 1942* (Philadelphia: Temple University Press, 1984); *New York Times*, October 27, 2007; Dominic W. Moreo, *Riot at Fort Lawton, 1944* (New York: iUniverse, Inc., 2004); Capeci Jr. and Wilkerson, *Layered Violence*; Cheryl Greenberg, "The Politics of Disorder: Reexamining Harlem's Riots of 1935–1943," *Journal of Urban History* 18 (August 1992); Charles A. Gallagher and Cameron D. Lippard, eds., *Race and Racism in the United States: An Encyclopedia of the American Mosaic*, 4 vols. (Santa Barbara, CA: Greenwood 2014); Marc Favreau, ed., *A People's History of World War II: The World's Most Destructive Conflict, As Told by the People Who Lived Through It* (New York: Free Press, 2011); James Wolfinger, *Philadelphia Divided: Race and Politics in the City of Brotherly Love* (Chapel Hill: University of North Carolina Press, 2007); Bob Korstad, "Those Who Were Not Afraid: Winston-Salem, 1943," in *Working Lives: The Southern Exposure History of Labor in the South*, ed. Marc S. Miller (New York: Pantheon Books, 1980); Allan M. Winkler, "The Philadelphia Transit Strike of 1944," *Journal of American History* 59 (June 1972); and Janet L. Langlois, "The Belle Isle Bridge Incident: Legend Dialectic and Semiotic System in the 1943 Detroit Race Riots," *Journal of American Folklore* 96 (April–June 1983).

54. Arnesen, *Brotherhoods of Color*, 181–202. For the details on the struggles of the FEPC in Texas, see Obadele-Starks, *Black Unionism in the Industrial South*; Botson Jr., *Labor, Civil Rights, and the Hughes Tool Company*; Emilio Zamora, "The Failed Promise of Wartime Opportunity for Mexicans in the Texas Oil Industry," *Southwestern Historical Quarterly* 95 (January 1992); and Joseph Abel, "African Americans, Labor Unions, and the Struggle for Fair Employment in the Aircraft Manufacturing Industry of Texas, 1941–1945," *Journal of Southern History* 77 (August 2011). For the Committee's limitations, see Richard M. Dalfiume, "The Forgotten Years of the Negro Revolution," *Journal of American History* 35 (June 1968); William J. Collins, "Race, Roosevelt, and Wartime Production: Fair Employment in World War II Labor Markets," *American Economic Review* 91 (March 2001); and James A Burran, "Violence in an 'Arsenal of Democracy,'" *East Texas Historical Journal* 14 (Spring 1976). On Black pressure and the origins of the FEPC, see Paula F. Pfeffer, *A. Philip Randolph, Pioneer of the Civil Rights Movement* (Baton Rouge: Louisiana State University Press, 1996); Jervis Anderson, *A. Philip Randolph: A Biographical Portrait* (Berkeley: University of California Press, 1986); Daniel S. Davis, *Mr. Black Labor: The Story of A. Phillip Randolph, Father of the Civil Rights Movement* (New York: E. P. Dutton, 1972); Andrew E. Kersten, *A. Philip Randolph: A Life in the Vanguard* (New York: Rowman and Littlefield Publishers, 2006); and Andrew E. Kersten and Clarence Lang, eds., *Reframing Randolph: Labor, Black Freedom, and the Legacies of A. Philip Randolph* (New York: New York University Press, 2015). A generally favorable assessment is Merl Elwyn Reed, *Seedtime for the Modern Civil Rights Movement: The President's Committee on Fair Employment Practice, 1941–1946* (Baton Rouge: Louisiana State University Press, 1991). Other works include Herbert Garfinkel, *When Negroes March: The March*

on Washington Movement in the Organizational Policies for FEPC (Glencoe, IL: Free Press, 1959); Andrew E. Kersten, *Race, Jobs, and the War: The FEPC in the Midwest, 1941–1946* (Urbana: University of Illinois Press, 2007); Clete Daniel, *Chicano Workers and the Politics of Fairness: The FEPC in the Southwest, 1941–1945* (Austin: University of Texas Press, 1991); Louis C. Kesselman, *The Social Politics of FEPC: A Study in Reform Pressure Movements* (Chapel Hill: University of North Carolina Press, 1948); and Louis Ruchames, *Race, Jobs, and Politics: The Story of FEPC* (Westport, CT: Negro Universities Press, 1953). Local studies of the FEPC include Alex Lichtenstein, "Exclusion, Fair Employment, or Interracial Unionism: Race Relations in Florida's Shipyards during World War II," in *Labor in the Modern South*, ed. Glen T. Eskew (Athens: University of Georgia Press, 2011); and Bruce Nelson, "Organized Labor and the Struggle for Black Equality in Mobile during World War II," *Journal of American History* 80 (December 1993). Those interested in examining the limits of reform during the war can see Alan Brinkley, *The End of Reform: New Deal Liberalism in Recession and War* (New York: Vintage Books, 1995); and Wendy L. Wall, *Inventing the "American Way": The Politics of Consensus from the New Deal to the Civil Rights Movement* (New York: Oxford University Press, 2008).

55. William L. O'Neill, *A Democracy at War: America's Fight at Home and Abroad in World War II* (Cambridge, MA: Harvard University Press, 1993), 238–39; Arnesen, *Brotherhoods of Color*, 181–202; Franklin and Higginbotham, *From Slavery to Freedom*, 449–509; Obadele-Starks, *Black Unionism in the Industrial South*, 101–27; and Charles D. Chamberlain, *Victory at Home: Manpower and Race in the American South during World War II* (Athens: University of Georgia Press, 2003), 150–80; and Botson Jr., *Labor, Civil Rights, and the Hughes Tool Company*, 74–120. For more on the attitudes of the Congress of Industrial Organizations (CIO) and American Federation of Labor (AFL) affiliates toward African Americans, see Philip S. Foner, *Women and the American Labor Movement* (New York: Free Press, 1979); Quintard Taylor, "Swing the Door Wide Open: World War II Wrought a Profound Transformation in Seattle's Black Community," *Columbia Magazine* 9 (Summer 1995); Emily Yellin, *Our Mothers' War: American Women at Home and at the Front during World War II* (New York: Free Press, 2004); Katherine Turk, "'A Fair Chance to Do My Part of Work': Black Women, War Work, and Rights Claims at the Kingsbury Ordnance Plant," *Indiana Magazine of History* 108 (September 2012); Judith N. McArthur and Harold L. Smith, *Texas through Women's Eyes: The Twentieth-Century Experience* (Austin: University of Texas Press, 2010); Jacqueline Jones, *American Work: Four Centuries of Black and White Labor* (New York: W. W. Norton and Company, 1998).

56. Richard Lingeman, *Don't You Know There's a War On? The American Home Front 1941–1945* (New York: Nation Books, 1970), 170. For more on Black unionism and civil rights as well as hostility toward Blacks, see Arnesen, *Brotherhoods of Color*; Botson Jr., *Labor, Civil Rights, and the Hughes Tool Company*; and Obadele-Starks, *Black Unionism in the Industrial South*. An elaboration of the AFL's actions during the war is Andrew E. Kersten, *Labor's Home Front: The*

American Federation of Labor during World War II (New York: New York University Press, 2006). The CIO during the war can be found in Rebecca Anne Montes, "Working for American Rights: Black, White and Mexican American Dockworkers in Texas during the Great Depression" (PhD diss., University of Texas, 2005); Ray Davidson, *Challenging the Giants: A History of the Oil, Chemical and Atomic Workers International Union* (Denver, CO: Oil, Chemical and Atomic Workers International Union, 1988); Nelson Lichtenstein, *Labor's War at Home: The CIO in World War II* (New York: Cambridge University Press, 1982); Murray Polakoff, "The Development of the Texas State CIO Council" (PhD diss., Columbia University, 1955); Martin Glaberman, *Wartime Strikes: The Struggle Against the No-Strike Pledge in the UAW during World War II* (Detroit, MI: Bewick Press, 1980); James Green, *The World of the Worker: Labor in Twentieth-Century America* (New York: Hill and Wang, 1980); Rick Halpern, "Interracial Unionism in the Southwest Fort Worth's Packinghouse Workers, 1937–1954," in *Organized Labor in the Twentieth-Century South*, ed. Robert H. Zeiger (Knoxville: University of Tennessee Press, 1991); Zachary A. Montz, "Negro Laborers to the Crossroads: Organized Labor and the Traditions of Black Unionism in Houston, Texas, 1935–1964," (PhD diss., Texas A&M University Press, 2013); and Herbert Northrup, *Organized Labor and the Negro* (New York: Harper & Brothers, 1944). A more elaborate exploration of unions and race, including the CIO, during the war is in Zachary Montz's essay.

57. For a snapshot of the despair, anxiety, and frustration within a portion of Black America about the unfilled promises regarding equality, see Maya Angelou, *Gather Together in My Name* (New York: Random House, 1974), 5. For the classification of "blue discharge," see J. Michael Martinez, *A Long Dark Night: Race in America from Jim Crow to World War II* (Lanham, MD: Rowman & Littlefield, 2016).

58. Louis Fairchild, *They Called It the War Effort: Oral Histories from WWII Orange, Texas*, 2nd ed. (Denton: Texas State Historical Association, 2012), 220.

59. Hadley Cantril, *Public Opinion, 1935–1946* (Princeton, NJ: Princeton University Press, 1951), 141.

60. Hadley Cantril, *Public Opinion, 1935–1946* (Princeton, NJ: Princeton University Press, 1951), 141; James Otis Baker, November 20, 2004. Pap Baker would retire as a postal inspector in Los Angeles. Wendell Harold Baker, a surgical technician in the Army Medical Corp in the Pacific Theater during World War II, returned home to Huntsville after earning his bachelor of science in chemistry in 1949 from TSUN (today Texas Southern University). He taught biology, chemistry, and physics at Sam Houston High School for twelve years, before being fired because he decided to build a ranch-style brick home near a new White subdivision in Huntsville. In 1961, the year of his termination, he landed a job as a chemical engineer with the Goodyear Tire Company in Beaumont. Wendell Baker became the first African American professional with the Golden Triangle petroleum sector. His experience would lead him toward political agitation in Huntsville.

3

Volunteers All

Texas Women in the Military in World War II

Katherine Sharp Landdeck[1]

When it comes to Texas and women in World War II, there are many important groups and individuals worthy of discussion. Women throughout the state volunteered for the Red Cross, sang with the United Service Organizations (USO), and donated their time wherever it was needed. Some 310,000 Texas women entered the workforce for the first time, while other women, including women of color across the state, left low-paying jobs to take on the better-paying defense positions. They worked making tools and ships in Houston, making guns and transmissions in Angelina (East Texas), and making planes for Consolidated Aircraft in Fort Worth. Texas women joined the military, too, with over 12,000 Texans serving in the army (WAC), Navy (WAVES), Coast Guard (SPARS, which is an acronym from the US Coast Guards motto, *Semper Paratus* and its English translation, "Always Ready"), and Marines (US Marine Corps Women's Reserve, simply known as the Reserve). Oveta Culp Hobby, wife of former Texas governor William P. Hobby and vice president of the *Houston Post*, became Colonel Hobby when she spent World War II serving as head of WAC. Most states across the nation can claim a similar story for their women during the war. But only Texas was home to the first all-women's pilot training base in the country—indeed, in the world. The Women Airforce Service Pilots (WASP) were pilots for the US Army Air Forces (USAAF) from September 1942 to December 1944 and trained for a short time in Houston before finding their final home at Avenger Field in Sweetwater, Texas (West Texas). They completed the same flight training as male cadets and proved to the army that women were an effective and valuable resource as pilots of military planes.[2]

Aviation was wildly popular in the 1920s and 1930s. The decades are known as the "Golden Age of Aviation." This was the era of Charles Lindbergh and Amelia Earhart. More people went to watch air races and air shows than saw professional and collegiate football and baseball combined. People were intensely interested about airplanes—and women were no exception. In 1929, Amelia Earhart and ninety-eight other women pilots gathered to create the all-women pilots organization, the Ninety-Nines, to promote women flying and aviation in general. The organization still exists today. The women who became WASP during World War II grew up in this era when everyone talked about and loved airplanes, and it inspired them to become pilots themselves.[3]

While women pilots were well-known in the 1930s, they still did not work as pilots in the fledgling airline industry. But they were active in the air show and air racing circuit. One of the women who dominated the racing scene was Jacqueline Cochran. Cochran was born to a poor working family in Florida in 1908, but she was smart, ambitious, and determined to make something of herself. She married young, but when her son was tragically killed in 1925, she left her philandering husband, changed her name from Bessie Mae to Jacqueline, and reinvented herself. She became a pilot in 1932 to help promote her cosmetics business, "Wings to Beauty, Jacqueline Cochran Cosmetics" and a legend was born. She went on to win major aviation awards throughout her lifetime, and even became the first woman, and only second person, to break the speed of sound in 1953. A great advantage to the awards she was winning and the fact that she was now married to Floyd Odlum, one of the richest men in the world, was that she had the opportunity to spend some time in the White House and got to know First Lady Eleanor Roosevelt.[4]

As war began in Europe in September 1939, Cochran saw both a need and an opportunity. She wrote to Eleanor Roosevelt and proposed a plan. The United States, Cochran argued, would undoubtedly be dragged into the European conflict and needed to be prepared. An obvious shortfall in American preparedness was its lack of pilots. It takes time to train a pilot, often six months, and now was the time to begin training. Cochran believed that even with training, the United States would still be short the number of pilots they would need. In addition to pilots being needed to fly in combat overseas, more pilots would be needed in the continental United States flying newly built planes from factories to points of embarkation and other noncombat jobs. There was an important pool of pilots who could help with that important flying to release men for combat: women. Cochran suggested to Mrs. Roosevelt that women pilots would be a useful tool for the United States and asked for her help promoting the idea in appropriate circles.

Despite their best efforts, the time was just not right. Many Americans were not willing to even consider the idea of their nation being a part of another world war, and they certainly were not willing to consider women as military pilots. The bombing of Pearl Harbor in December 1941 would change everything. Once the United States joined the war, those in charge quickly realized that those advocating preparedness had been right. The nation was short of pilots—to the point of desperation. In September 1942, the US Army Air Forces (USAAF) turned to women for help. Nancy Love, another long-time advocate of women pilots, was tapped by the Ferrying Division of the USAAF to hire a small group of highly qualified women pilots to immediately begin flying planes from factories to training bases and points of embarkation. The group of twenty-eight women, all with over a thousand hours of flight time, were known as the Women's Auxiliary Ferrying Squadron (WAFS). These women flew all over the country, demonstrating their ability to fly the most sophisticated planes of the day. But the USAAF realized they would need even more pilots and turned to Jacqueline Cochran for more help.[5]

Cochran had the idea that women pilots with less flying time could be trained, just as men were, to fly military planes. Working with the Army Air Force's training command, she began the Women's Flying Training Detachment (WFTD). All trainees had to already be pilots. In the beginning they needed 200 hours of flying experience, but by the end of the program the women needed only thirty-five hours, just enough to prove ability. The women also had to be high school graduates (most of them had at least two years of college), pass an army physical exam (the same one that men had to pass), and have two personal letters of recommendation. Initially, applicants had to be between twenty-one and thirty-five years of age. Size mattered, too, with height and weight strictly measured, although a few smaller

to the Florsheim shoe empire, arrived in Houston with two afghan hounds and seven trunks and rejected a room in a private home for an apartment in the posh Warwick Hotel. A few other better-off women found penthouse rooms at the Plaza. Others were able to join together and rent apartments in the area. But while the housing problem was solved, wartime realities caused another problem: how to get the women from their far-flung homes to the airport. The homes and hotels of the women were up to fifteen miles from the Houston airport. Rationing of both gasoline and tires severely limited civilians' ability to get "from point A to point B," and the women pilots were no exception. Aviation Enterprises worked to find the women a way to the airport. They were finally able to hire a driver and acquire a less than ideal vehicle. The bus had most recently been owned by a Tyrolean Orchestra and was still painted white "with red and white striped awnings, decorated profusely with edelweiss." If the landladies were confused by the transportation of their visitors, they did not outwardly fuss. Not too long into the program, the army found trucks with trailers attached to the back and built homemade seats to line the trailer. The women called them "cattle trucks," a good indication of their comfort and quality. But desperate times called for desperate measures, and the women were happy to have a ride at all.[9]

The planes available for the women to train were less than ideal as well. As Aviation Enterprises waited for their contract with the army to be signed so they could have priority acquiring military planes, the women trained with civilian planes, including Stearmans, WACOs, Pipers, and Beechcrafts. But the women in the earliest training classes did not mind as much. These were the very planes they had earned their 200 flight hours of experience flying. They knew how to fly these planes, even if they had to learn to fly them the army way. As the first class of thirty women began to prove they could fly, even if they were women, the second and then third classes were allowed to join them. This expansion resulted in more than a hundred women flying out of Houston's William P. Hobby Airport by February 1943. The challenges in Houston were becoming untenable, however, since housing was inadequate and the space for the women at the airport was inadequate. The weather was a real problem too. It got to the point where the women sang a song, lamenting how little flying they were getting to do:

We get up at six in the morning—regardless of where we have been.
But at quarter of eight—it won't hesitate,
The fog rolls in.
We hurry our eating at lunchtime—get out our chute, check the pin.
But at quarter of two—there is nothing to do,
The fog rolls in.
At dusk, when daylight is waning—'tis then at the end of the day,
You can hear us all sigh—it's too late to fly,
And the fog rolls away.[10]

The situation at Houston became so bad that the Gulf Coast Training Command (GCTC), which was in charge of the women, reported to the USAAF that they would need to reduce their goal of trained women in 1943 from 500 to 396 due to the weather often grounding flight training. But the USAAF had already decided to alter the number of women to be trained. Seeing how well these women were doing and needing to replace male combat losses overseas, the USAAF, instead of their original goal of 500 women pilots to do domestic, noncombat flying, increased its need to 750 in 1943. To reach these new goals, however, something had to change. And quickly. At first the Training Command thought they should open a second flying school for women pilots and began looking for a second site. Believing a school with a student capacity of 300 would be adequate, they first inspected Columbia, Missouri. While the University of Missouri was overtaxed, the local all-women's Stephens College, which had an active aviation program before the war, "was ready and willing to cooperate, and possessed excellent accommodations." Unfortunately for Stephens College, they were the only real bright spot in the report on Columbia. The weather, a major factor in Houston, was also considered unfavorable. But the biggest problem was the existing airport and the terrain that surrounded it. The airport would need to be expanded to accommodate flight training, but the rolling terrain was such that it could happen only at great cost. The all-important auxiliary fields where the women would practice landings and other maneuvers "would be difficult to obtain and expensive to repair." Not wanting to take on new problems or unnecessary expenses, the Flying Training Command rejected Columbia, Missouri, as a possible site for training women pilots and kept searching for someplace that would work and be available quickly.[11]

Troubles to the north presented an opportunity for the women's training program. A flight training school was already established at the airport near Sweetwater, Texas, about 200 miles west of Fort Worth. The contractor, Plosser-Prince Air Academy (named for its proprietors, Joe B. Plosser and Charles A. Prince) had been teaching male pilots from the United Kingdom and the United States since the previous August. But in late January 1943, just as the situation in Houston was becoming untenable, Plosser-Prince found itself under indictment by a federal grand jury for fraudulent claims for payment from the government. The Central Flying Training Command (CFTC) proactively decided that while they had not yet been found guilty, there must be some validity to the claims against Plosser-Prince. To avoid negative publicity, the Command canceled its contract with them. The Command quickly decided Sweetwater would be home to the second school for the women and ordered the new class (designated 43-W-4) to be split, with half going to Houston and half to Sweetwater. With plans for them to arrive in Sweetwater on February 21, 1943, Command began its search for a new civilian contractor to run the program. In war, contracts with the government were life and death for businesses large and small. The federal government took firm control over the economy using incentives for companies such as cost-plus contracts while at the same time firmly controlling every aspect of supplies—everything from gasoline and steel to silk and sugar. In aviation, an industry that had been growing throughout the golden age of aviation in the decades before the war, a government contract was particularly important to survival. Planes, oil, gasoline, and even pilots were all controlled by the government. Protesting they had been framed by a subcontractor who had been convicted and was looking to lessen his own prison time, Plosser-Prince Air Academy would not take their dismissal quietly.[12]

Plosser and Prince tried to regain their contract with the CFTC throughout 1943 and 1944. In July 1943, they wrote to the Command blaming the contractor who built the buildings for the flight school in Sweetwater, Victor Nelson, for their troubles. Nelson and his auditor, Robert Young, were both found guilty of fraudulent claims. Nelson and Young testified they were just doing what Plosser and Prince instructed. Plosser and Prince both testified under oath refuting the claim. Nelson and Young were also convicted of fraud at a glider school in Lamesa, Texas, thus weakening their credibility.[13]

Poor Plosser and Prince really got the run-around on all of this. Despite their January 28 decision to abandon their contract to train the male cadets due to the indictments against them, the Gulf Coast Training Command sent the Plosser-Prince Air Academy a new letter of intent on February 8, asking them to run the women's training program in Sweetwater and began negotiating a new contract. It was clearly a case of one hand not knowing what the other was doing. Thus, when the women of class 43-W-4 arrived in Sweetwater on February 21, it was actually the Plosser-Prince Air Academy running the training, not Aviation Enterprises, which was still in Houston. Then on March 10, the Command decided not to give them the contract, as they did not want to prejudice the government case against them one way or the other. At the same time, the Command decided to have only one school for the women at Sweetwater. The closing of operations in Houston meant they needed only one contractor, thus allowing them to offer the Sweetwater contract to Aviation Enterprises.[14]

The historical record only hints at Jacqueline Cochran's involvement in all of this. It is obvious from her deep involvement in every other stage of the women's program that she would have had much to say about all of this. All that has been found to this point is a quote from a telegram in the CFTC official history. Apparently General Brant of the GCTC wrote to Cochran that "everything is fixed up." Plosser-Prince's contract, or really their letter of intent, was officially canceled as of April 3, 1943, and Aviation Enterprises took over on April 4. To their credit, Plosser-Prince transferred authority over operations "without any hours lost in flying time" and "without change in personnel." The biggest change the women saw was that all of the male cadets left Sweetwater by April 6. There is little evidence they noticed any other difference. The acquittal of Joe Plosser and Charles Prince just three weeks later brought them no mercy. The Command still had their doubts about the two men and were happy with Aviation Enterprises, as was Cochran. They were dependable and had "shown considerable interest in this program." Despite the fact that Plosser and Prince continued to advocate for their opportunity to run the program and after further correspondence between the parties, the Command decided to stick with Aviation Enterprises. While imperfect, they were a known entity and it seemed, on the surface at least, the simplest solution. With a site chosen and a contractor in place, the logistical and societal challenges of beginning a new flight school for women began.[15]

Jackie Cochran again tapped Dedie Deaton, who had worked to find housing and organize the women pilots in Houston, to save the day. She spent weeks moving between Houston and Sweetwater, hurriedly readying the new facilities for the incoming fourth class while still in charge of the women in Houston. The "fly in the ointment" of the Sweetwater plan was the fact that the male cadets who were training in Sweetwater would still be there when the women arrived. Deaton, whose grandfather was a proponent of co-education, optimistically believed there would be no problems. Jackie hoped she was right. Deaton got help managing the women in Houston, freeing her to spend more time in Sweetwater. The experience was vastly different than her experience just three months earlier as she scrambled to ready places for the first class. This time she was based at an established army airfield that already had barracks, a ready room, and a mess hall. It also had men in those spaces. But while she did not plan to completely segregate the new women from the male cadets, she had learned her lessons from her early days in Houston. The independent women of the first classes at Houston had rejected much of Deaton's authority, often ignoring her directives and focusing on flying without bothering to follow her rules. After all, even though they were working with the US Army Air Forces, they were technically civilians, and the first classes of trainees chaffed under attempts to treat them otherwise. The challenges of Houston made Deaton determined that the Sweetwater experience was going to be different. The women who arrived in Sweetwater would have nicer amenities, but they would also have military-style discipline from the very beginning. They would get up at six in the morning. They would sweep out their barracks and make their beds military-style. They would arrive on the flight line at quarter after seven, earning demerits for tardiness. Like their male counterparts, they still had to march and do calisthenics. The new 318th Army Air Forces Flying Training Detachment (AAFTD) would behave as though they were really in the military, even if they were technically the same civilians as Houston's 319th.[16]

The fourth class of women pilot trainees was split, with half going to the established training program in Houston and half going to

Avenger Field near Sweetwater, Texas. They were happy to finally have a chance to fly those planes for their country. What they found when they arrived at Sweetwater was men—a lot of them. Avenger Field was being used to train British and American pilots before the women arrived, and the final classes were finishing up before it would become an all-women's base. The men's and women's barracks were just a few short feet away from each other. Aviation Enterprises tried to protect the women's privacy by blacking out the windows on their barracks, but in a time of no air-conditioning, the Texas heat soon meant the windows were open. The women simply ducked low as they made their way from the showers to their lockers, hoping the men could not see them.[17]

Flying was what the women cared about the most, but many welcomed having young men who also loved planes in the same mess hall. The men were supposed to sit at one end of the hall while they ate and the women the other, but they all tended to arrive looking their best and spent much of their meal-time trying to impress and entertain the women. Deaton watched the co-ed group closely, ever wary of a scandal. She did, however, permit movies on Friday and "dates" for dinner on Saturday and Sunday. One night not long after the fourth class arrived in February, the cadets put on a show for the women. Some of the men carried on with the slapstick humor of the day, and one redheaded baritone sang "Glory Road" with such skill that WASP trainee Madge Rutherford was convinced he could have earned a place singing at the Met (Metropolitan Opera in New York) if it were not for the war. Yet another talented cadet pulled out his violin and wooed the women with a Strauss waltz. It was a pleasant distraction from training and the war for both sets of pilots. Soon enough, the men finished their training and were shipped out, leaving Avenger Field to the women pilots.[18]

Jacqueline Cochran was worried about more than the flying that the WASP trainees were doing. She desperately worried about their reputations—even after the male pilots left Avenger Field. Cochran was well aware of the ongoing slander campaign against women in the military, particularly those in the Women's Army Corps. These women were derided as everything from prostitutes employed to "satisfy" men in the military to lesbians doing the "mannish" job of being in the military. Whatever their sexual preference, women who joined the military in World War II were volunteering to serve their country in its greatest time of need. But they were publicly being shamed for their patriotism.

Cochran, already fighting for the opportunity for women to serve as pilots for the AAF, understood any indiscretion, no matter how small, would allow critics of the WASP to pounce and perhaps curtail, if not totally end, her efforts.[19]

When prostitutes calling themselves "WASPs" set up shop in a local hotel, Cochran pressured local officials to shut down their operations. She limited off-base passes for the women and rarely issued overnight ones. In a public relations campaign, Cochran had her trainees build relationships with the local community, encouraging "Sunday Hospitality Day" where after church service the women spent much of the day with a family eating and socializing. Fraternization with the local community was greatly encouraged, where fraternization with fellow male military personnel was not. For example, when word got out that there was an airfield full of "girl pilots," scores of men training across Texas claimed to have mysterious trouble with their planes just as they were nearing Avenger Field, having "forced landing" just to see if the rumors were true. One story had a male pilot flying on one magneto (a small, electrical generator in a plane's engine that fired the spark plugs) so "he could declare a real emergency over Sweetwater." In response, Cochran implemented measures to segregate the trainees from the men, determined to protect the women's reputations. Soon, upon her urging, the USAAF prohibited unscheduled landings at Avenger Field under the premise that it was simply too disruptive to training. This move effectively isolated the women from peering men's eyes. As a result, Avenger Field acquired a new nickname: "Cochran's Convent."[20]

As the room opened up from the departing men, the Training Command decided they could close the women's training in Houston and concentrate all of the women at Avenger Field. Dry, windy, and hot was much better for flying than foggy. And there was plenty of room to expand. The USAAF began to build more barracks, put in real sidewalks, and even built a gymnasium so the women could do their calisthenics whatever the weather. As they had more space, they began to expand the program, admitting even more women into training. The age the women could come into the program was lowered to eighteen and a half, as they realized younger pilots were easier to train (just as military officials discovered with male pilots). Since there were fewer women with extensive flight experience available, they lowered the minimum flight hours before being eligible to only 35 instead of the earlier 200. The training for the women also expanded. It was patterned after the same training male pilots in the USAAF were receiving. By 1944, the women trained for twenty-seven weeks, divided into three distinct phases of nine weeks each. They flew at least 210 hours during training. Flight instruction involved everything a pilot would need, including stalls, spins, landings, and takeoffs. Their ground school expanded as the war went on as well. They took some 309 hours of classes, including math, physics, navigation, aerodynamics, and Morse code. The hours included 42 hours of training on engines and propellers and 50 hours on weather. "Every day we have the same routine," one cadet pilot described her training and schedule in Sweetwater, "mess, inspection, ground school, drill or calisthenics, mess, flight line, mess, then study until 10 at night. . . . [W]hat a wonderful training I'm getting." These women also took 12 hours on military forms and procedures, as once they graduated from training they would be flying as civilian pilots for the USAAF and needed to know how to follow military protocol despite their civilian status.[21]

When the women graduated from their training, they earned a set of silver wings they wore proudly on their new blue uniforms. The army wore tan uniforms during World War II, but Jacqueline Cochran knew that General Henry H. "Hap" Arnold, head of the Army Air Forces, hoped that there would be an independent Air Force after the war (the United States Air Force began in 1947) and that he hoped the uniform of that branch would be blue. Cochran designed the WASP uniform in blue, knowing he would approve of them, thus making the WASP the first American pilots flying military planes to wear the blue.

Upon graduation, the women were sent to 120 different bases across the United States. Their initial job was that of ferry pilot. The ferry pilots were based at Wilmington, Delaware; Long Beach, California; Romulus, Michigan; and Dallas, Texas. The pilots out of Love Field in Dallas spent much of their time flying the planes that were built in the Dallas–Fort Worth area, including the P-51 Mustang and B-24 Liberator. They would take the planes straight from the factories to training bases or, most often, to points of embarkation on the coasts. The WASP served at numerous other bases across Texas as well. In fact, there were twenty-five bases in Texas where the WASP served as pilots. The women at Biggs Army Airfield in El Paso, Texas, flew a variety of different planes on simulated strafing missions (they trained the men on the ground to put on gas masks quickly and how to hide from incoming planes), radar missions, and searchlight tracking missions, all to teach the men on the ground how to find aircraft in preparation for heading overseas. The WASP test-piloted planes, both those newly manufactured and those recently repaired; delivered planes designated scrap to where they would be dismantled; and towed targets for live-action target practice. Nell Stevenson remembers:

> [W]hen we were towing targets, they shot at the targets, and they shot real bullets at the targets. . . . And sometimes they hit the targets, and sometimes they came pretty close to the airplanes. We also towed targets at night, and they were supposed to catch the target in their search light and shoot at the target. Sometimes they would catch the plane in the search light and you would see a flak breaking pretty close to you, and when that happened we would usually abort the mission and roll in our target and go back to base, and tell them we'd come back when they learned to shoot at the right thing.[22]

They further gave male cadets instruction on flying by instrument, tested radar equipment, and ferried planes and, at times, personnel. By their deactivation in December 1944, in fact, the WASP ferried 12,650 planes (77 different types, including the B-17) and had flown over sixty million miles. Flying in this wide variety of duties, the women pilots across Texas and the nation worked to relieve male pilots from domestic flying so they could get to combat quicker, something the United States desperately needed.[23]

While most of the work the WASP did was similar to work male pilots were doing domestically, there was one utilization that was unique to them as women. They were used to shame men into flying. During the war, there were a number of planes with problems that gave them bad reputations among pilots. The Martin B-26 Marauder, a twin-engine medium bomber, was dubbed the "widowmaker" by pilots in part because it had numerous accidents on takeoff and landing early in the war. Another plane that acquired a poor reputation was Boeing's new "B-29 Superfortress." The B-29 was a state-of-the-art new four-engine plane that took its first flight in September 1942. After a tragic crash by the Boeing test pilots, American pilots began to refuse to fly the plane. Colonel Paul Tibbets (who would go on to pilot the *Enola Gay* to drop the atomic bomb on Hiroshima) was in charge of getting pilots trained in the new plane, as it was vital to the war in the Pacific. When Tibbets realized women were flying for the USAAF, he chose two of them, Dora Dougherty and Didi Moorman, to prove to the men that the plane was so easy to fly "even a woman could do it," counting on the sexism of the men to shame them into flying. Tibbets himself thought the women were terrific pilots and thought it was a "pretty good joke" on the men. He took Dougherty and Moorman to airfields where the male pilots were refusing to fly the B-29. The two demonstrated the plane to them, showing them the procedures necessary to fly it safely. It worked. The men gained confidence in the plane, and it went on to be one of the decisive weapons in the war in the Pacific.[24]

While the women loved the opportunity to fly for their country, there were serious risks inherent to the work. Consider the experience of Nell Stevenson from West Texas. While training in Houston, Stevenson noticed her plane violently shaking to the point she feared being tossed from the cockpit. Soon enough, the engine was on fire. Radioing the tower about her situation, she received the instruction to climb to 2,000 feet and bail out. After a fleeting thought, she dismissed it out of hand. "I'm not bailing out," she responded. "I'm bringing it in. Will you clear the field?" This decision created much concern in the tower. "You're what?" the tower instructor incredulously responded. Realizing her determination, he informed her she was clear to land and reminded her when she landed to get out of the plane as soon as possible. Successfully landing and scrambling out of the plane with it still rolling, Stevenson later discovered that her fate rested on one bolt. "You know what," a mechanic who examined the engine after the fire had been extinguished told her, "there's only one bolt holding that engine in. If that bolt had come out, you'd been a goner. You wouldn't have been able to bail out." On another occasion ferrying a B-25 bomber to Lubbock, Texas, Stevenson nearly crashed when low fuel was compounded by horrible Texas weather and exacerbated by zero visibility on approach that almost resulted in her colliding with trees. Stevenson was lucky enough to survive her close calls, but not all were. Thirty-eight women died while flying for the WASP.[25]

The army wanted the WASP to officially be part of the military, rather than working as part of the civil service. In June 1944, a vote came before the US House of Representatives to make it happen. A number of factors, however, worked against this action. New technologies were helping shift the tide of the war. Extended fuel tanks on the American pursuit plane, the P-51 Mustang, meant the plane could escort American bombers farther into their attacks on Germany, thus reducing the losses of American airmen and the need for pilots. A planned invasion of Japan increased the need for ground troops. Thus, the army reduced its pilot training programs, releasing a number of male flight instructors, making them eligible to be drafted into the "walking-man's Army." The men saw the WASP, *women*, flying military planes and argued *they* should have the chance to do the jobs the WASP were doing instead because they were men. They launched a loud and rude campaign against the women, earning the support of some members of Congress who doubted whether women pilots were ever necessary. In this toxic environment, the vote was taken just days after the Allies had invaded France, when many optimistically hoped the war would soon be over, leading them to believe women pilots would be surplus personnel. The WASP lost their chance to officially be a part of the military by only nineteen votes.

As the Allies moved toward Germany, the emergency of the war seemed to be lessening, and thus the need for women to relieve men for combat duty was not as urgent. The army decided it could get their domestic flying done with the men pilots they had and so disbanded the WASP on December 20, 1944, sending them home from their work as pilots just as so many women would be sent home from their work in the factories as soon as men were available. The WASP did not receive any recognition or benefit from the GI Bill after the war. In fact, the work they did was forgotten by most people. Then in the 1970s, when the military decided to once again allow women to fly military planes (no women were allowed to fly for the military from 1944 to 1973), the women of the WASP realized they had been forgotten and decided to do something about it. They rallied together and spent several years pushing for recognition. Finally, after a long grass-roots fight, their work during World War II was recognized as military service and they were allowed to be called veterans. The women became eligible for medical care from the Veterans Administration and were allowed to have a flag on their coffins when they died. In 2009, President Barack

Obama signed legislation recognizing the WASP for their service during the war by awarding them the Congressional Gold Medal. In 2016, Congress voted to allow the women to be interred in Arlington National Cemetery.[26]

Of all the military branches, women enlistments were the highest in the army. Initially the Women's Army Auxiliary Corps (WAAC), it rebranded by dropping the additional *A* and going by Women's Auxiliary Corps (WAC) in 1943. In total, 150,000 served in the organization during the war. General Douglas MacArthur, in fact, acknowledged their abilities and his appreciation when he called them "my best soldiers." He further added that, compared to male soldiers, they worked hard, complained less, and were more disciplined. The labor shortage necessitated the need for women. For each WAC assigned to do essentially a clerical job, there was a man freed for service somewhere else. But necessity intervened, and WAC did more than administrative and clerical work. When established, the WAC were designated "for the purpose of making available to the national defense the knowledge, skill, and special training of women of the nation." Thus, their responsibilities expanded to include lab work, mechanical repair, and communication operations. A few even constructed and operated technical equipment at atomic facilities in the Manhattan Project. These women, however, were at the army's whim and found themselves doing things they believed an insufficient use of their abilities and unnecessary for the war effort. In addition, many never reconciled themselves to female soldiers, believing the social ramifications more dire than any wartime need. Many WAC experienced sneers and a nasty rumor campaign about alleged promiscuity. Thus, many women left the organization and the army struggled with low morale within the ranks of WAC.[27]

Prominent Texan socialite and wife of former governor of Texas William Hobby, Oveta Culp Hobby, headed the organization. Hobby's position raised some concerns about her Southern roots and her attitudes toward African American women. Four thousand black women served in the WAC during the war. To ease concerns, Mary McLeod Bethune was appointed as Hobby's assistant. Bethune, a black woman and an icon in the struggle for equality, worked diligently to enlist African American officers. In total 4,000 black women served in the segregated organization. From Houston, for instance, Elizabeth "Tex" Williams, a black woman, served as a WAC photographer. She often flew on maneuvers, filming combat techniques. She remained in the army until 1970. The officer ranks were also open to Hispanic women. Dorothy Ann Veach from San Antonio was one of the first Texas women to enlist in the organization. By war's end, she became an officer. One prominent WAC was Isabella Martin Henry. From San Antonio, Mary (Valfre) Castro was the first Hispanic WAC from the city. She was trained at radio school in Missouri. During the war, Castro, although trained to transcribe encoded radio messages, was assigned as a drill sergeant for WAC recruits. Born in Waco, Henry received a bachelor's degree from the University of Texas. A short time later, she received a master's degree in sociology at Texas State College for Women in Denton, Texas (today Texas Woman's University). She entered the WAC in 1942, serving the war effort in distinguished fashion attested to by several commendations from the army. Henry retired from the army in 1961. [28]

Elsie Schaffer Martinez joined the WAC in 1943. Following her training, she was assigned to a base in Pueblo, Colorado, developing top-secret reconnaissance photographs and drafting maps from those photographs. Attaining the rank of corporal, she was discharged from the military in 1945. She returned to civilian life, married, and had children. But she remained thoughtful of those who served, volunteering at the Veterans Clinic in Laredo, where she received a commendation for her work. Two years too young to join the WAC on her own (a woman had to be twenty-one to join without parental consent), Maria Sally Salazar headed for San Antonio under the ruse of visiting her sister. On her was her older sister's birth certificate. Her mother soon discovered her ploy but only after she had been accepted. Fearing legal repercussions, her parents decided against reporting the matter to the military. Salazar was assigned overseas, serving in New Guinea and the Philippines, even helping with the invasion of the latter. She recalled that the army used her anywhere needed, but "mostly in the medical field." Battling stress of the sights of war and a poor diet, Salazar fell severely ill, finishing the war in a Manila hospital battling malaria, hepatitis, and amoebic dysentery, the latter two she struggled with for decades after the war. Although struggling physically with the war's aftermath, she never regretted her service. "To me it was an experience I would not change for anything in the world," she proudly stated, "because not just anybody can have that. And my nightmares are with me, and my dreams are with me." Following her discharge, Salazar, who throughout the war went by her sister's name "Amelia," had to seek legal assistance to clear up the confusion and reestablish her own name and age.[29]

WAC came from and trained throughout the United States. In Texas, one place was Stephen F. Austin State College in Nacogdoches (East Texas). The school's attendance was threateningly low. Male students generally dropped out to enter military service or were drafted, and female students found war production too enticing. Upon entering the war, enrollment at the school dropped to only a couple hundred (mostly women) students, down from a high of 1,000 only months before. Struggling for survival, the school's president decided to turn the campus into a school for the military. President Dr. Paul L. Boynton convinced the army to use the college as an instructional facility for WAC. He closed the deal by highlighting the existing facilities needed by the women's organization. The school already had what was necessary to accommodate (house and feed) large numbers of people, including classrooms, dormitories, office equipment, and food facilities. After basic training in Des Moines, Iowa, the first WAC arrived in Nacogdoches in 1943. Their arrival was anything but inconspicuous. Disembarking from the train, dressed in full uniform and in formation, the WAC marched from the depot to the campus amid the initially confused yet proud and welcoming stares of East Texans not sure what to make of these newcomers. The traditional and conservative Nacogdochians soon embraced these female guests, treating them as adoptive daughters. Townsfolk, perhaps remembering their sons and daughters away in service and how communities treated them, welcomed the WAC into the community by organizing a USO club that became awkward when the women were left to dance with themselves because no one asked them to dance. Besides the typical culture complaints about Southern fried food and the "torrid climate," the women's experience was all-around positive before they departed for Seattle, Washington.[30]

Another possibility for women to serve was joining the US Navy. The Women Accepted for Volunteer Emergency Service (WAVES) was created in mid-1942. This was not new to the navy. In World War I, it enrolled 12,000 "Yeomanettes." Initially tasked with clerical work, these women were acting as translators, X-ray technicians, fingerprint experts, and recruiting agents by war's end. Like its predecessor, WAVES' primary duty was clerical, yet not exclusively. These women also became cryptanalysts, signal workers and transmitters, and parachute technicians. Elena Pimentel Guerra from San Antonio was a child of Mexican immigrants. Called "Helen" by her friends, she worked in Naval Intelligence, monitoring Spanish international telegrams (a neutral country sympathetic to Nazi Germany) and long-distance phone calls. Moreover, since she was bilingual, she translated all incoming and outgoing correspondence from the two Latin countries. A few, however, even became instructors for the navy, instructing pilots to fly by instrument and training naval gunners on use of the electrically operated .50-cal machine-gun turrets. Unlike the other branches, such as the WAC, the navy initially resisted black women entry into the WAVES, noting the problems with integration. This was a rational approach due to an irrational policy. The navy, like the army, eventually saw the benefit in women as replacement for men to be sent to the fighting fronts. Their presence freed up a "fighting man." Since almost all black men in its ranks were messmen, naturally, the navy reasoned no practical need for black women. President Franklin D. Roosevelt, however, in late 1944, ordered the navy to incorporate African American women into the WAVES. Although less than 100 actually served in the last year of the war out of a total 84,000 throughout the war, there was one benefit black women serving in the WAVES experienced that their counterparts in the WAC did not. From the very start, they were integrated into existing units alongside white women.[31]

Women also had the opportunity to be marines. The US Marines were the last branch to accept women, which gave the organization the benefit of duly noting and avoiding the problems made by the army with the WAC. Instead of an auxiliary organization, this one would be "in" the navy. Authorized in the summer of 1942, at the same time as the WAVES, the marines hesitated at the thought of an all-female unit. Finally bowing to pressure from Congress and the high brass in the navy, the marines initiated the creation of the United States Marine Corps Women's Reserve (WR)—the marines simply referred to them as women marines or marine women (lowercase designation until 1948 and gendered-specified into the 1970s). To head the WR was Major Ruth Cheney Streeter, prominent civic from New Jersey who initially desired to join the WASP but was rejected five times due to her age (she was forty-seven). Unlike its counterparts in the army, navy, and Coast Guard, the Women's Reserve did not have a snappy nickname. The public bombarded the marines with what they believed the unit should be called: MARS (most likely because of the Coast Guard's SPARS), Femarines, Dainty Devil-Dogs, Glamarines, Women's Leather-neck Aides, and Sub-Marines. "Oh, the men had nicknames for us," laughingly recalled Janie "Tex" Sheppard, a Midlothian native (south of Fort Worth) who left a good-paying manufacturing job constructing B-24s to join the marines. "They called us BAMs, for broad-ass Marines, so we called them HAMs, half-ass Marines. Only the marines could get away with it, though. No one else. If navy men tried, we called them flat-chested WAVES. That shut them up most of the time." In the end, the unit went by "Women's Reserve." It was closed to black and Japanese American women. These women went through three-and-a-half to five-week training sessions, including physical examination, physical training, map reading, safeguarding military information, and customs, courtesies, and history of the Marine Corps (later instructions on the use of weapons was incorporated). Initially, training occurred at college campuses in the Northeast (Mount Holyoke and Hunter College) in cooperation with WAVES and SPARS, but the Marine Corps believed it beneficial to relocate to Camp Lejeune, North Carolina, not only because it could accommodate the numbers but it was also where each marine experienced the Corps' esprit de corps. By war's end, 21,597 women served in the WR, with approximately a thousand having transferred from the WAVES. It was perhaps the unit with the most stringent qualifications for female applicants. Female officer candidates had to be between twenty and forty-nine, with either a college degree of a combination of college/work experience. For non-officers, women had to be aged twenty to thirty-five, with at least two years of high school. They eventually could be sent to thirty specialist schools, which qualified them to perform anything from parachute rigger to aerographer,[32] from control tower operator to aerial gunnery instructor, and from aircraft instruments technician to motion picture operator/technician.[33]

Despite how they acquitted themselves in positions previously believed beyond their capabilities, women never amounted to more than a small percentage of the armed forces during the war. They represented only about 2 percent of its personnel. The military, let alone the country's civilian population, was never comfortable with such a radical departure from established gender norms. Even when employed within the military, these women were positioned in work that was "traditional women's work" in civilian life. The percentage of women filling clerical posts in the US military, in fact, surpassed the number in civilian life. In addition, there were preordained limits on their service. Female officers could not give orders to any male personnel, and there existed a ceiling on promotions. The military resisted taking married women, and for the few in service, their families were denied dependency allowances. Various "transgressions" such as pregnancy and menopause resulted in discharge from service. For the vast number of Americans, the only acceptable role in the armed forces for women was a role they had filled in many wars in the past. Nursing, according to many, was necessary in war yet not threatening to societal norms. It highlighted women's nurturing and compassionate nature. Women could contribute to the war effort without sacrificing their femininity.[34]

Notes

1. Katherine Sharp Landdeck is Associate Professor of History at Texas Woman's University (TWU) in Denton, Texas. The leading expert on the Women Airforce Service Pilots (WASP), Landdeck focuses her work in public history and has worked as both historical consultant and producer on numerous documentaries and helped design an award-winning Tournament of Roses Parade float (essentially a moving, flower-covered exhibit) on the WASP in 2014. She also works as an advisor to Congress, the Smithsonian Air and Space Museum, the National World War II Museum, and the Commemorative Air Force. Landdeck has a forthcoming book published by Crown Publishing Group titled *The Women with Silver Wings: The Inspiring True Story of the Women Airforce Service Pilots of World War II*.

2. Judith N. McArthur and Harold L. Smith, eds., *Texas through Women's Eyes: The Twentieth-Century Experience* (Austin: University of Texas Press, 2010), 92–97. For those interested in further reading about the WASP, see Sally Van Wagenen Keil, *Those Wonderful Women in Their Flying Machines: The Unknown Heroines of World War II* (Rhinebeck, NY: Four Directions Press, 1979); Anne Noggle, *For God, Country and the Thrill of It: Women Airforce Service Pilots During WWII* (College Station: Texas A&M University Press, 1990); Molly Merriman, *Clipped Wings: The Rise and Fall of the Women Airforce Service Pilots (WASPs) of World War II* (New York: New York University Press, 1998); Sarah Byrn Rickman, *WASP of the*

Ferry Command: Women Pilots, Uncommon Deeds (Denton: University of North Texas Press, 2016); Marianne Verges, *On Silver Wings: The Women Airforce Service Pilots of World War II, 1942–1944* (New York: Ballentine Books, 1991); James W. Ure, *Seized by the Sun: The Life and Disappearance of World War II Pilot Gertrude Tompkins* (Chicago: Chicago Review Press Incorporated, 2017); Sarah Byrn Rickman, *The Originals: The Women's Auxiliary Ferrying Squadron of World War II* (Sarasota, FL: Disc Books Inc, 2001); Amy Strebe, *Flying for Her Country: The American and Soviet Women Military Pilots of World War II* (Westport, CT: Greenwood Publishing Group, 2007); Harry F. Snapp, "Pioneering Women in West Texas Skies: Women Airforce Service Pilots of World War II," *West Texas Historical Association Year Book* 70 (1994); Jean Hascall Cole, *Women Pilots of World War II* (Salt Lake City: University of Utah Press, 1992); Ann B. Carl, *A WASP Among Eagles: A Woman Military Test Pilot in World War II* (Washington, DC: Smithsonian Books, 2010); William M. Miller, *To Live and Die a WASP: 38 Women Pilots Who Died in WWII* (n.c.: CreateSpace Independent Publishing Platform, 2016); Amy Nathan, *Yankee Doodle Gals: Women Pilots of World War II* (Washington, DC: National Geographic Society, 2001); Byrd Howell Granger, *On Final Approach: The Women Airforce Service Pilots of World War II* (Scottsdale, AZ: Falconer Publishing, 1991); Marie Mountain Clark, *Dear Mother and Daddy: World War II Letters Home from a WASP* (Livonia, MI: First Page Publications, 2005); Leslie Haynsworth and David Toomey, *Amelia Earhart's Daughters* (New York: William Morrow and Company, 1998); Vera S. Williams, *WASPs: Women Airforce Service Pilots of World War II* (St. Paul, MN: Motorbooks International, 1994); Helena Schrader, *Sisters in Arms: British and American Women Pilots during World War II* (Barnsley, South Yorkshire, UK: Pen and Sword Books, 2006); Marion Stegeman Hodgson, *Winning My Wings: A Woman Airforce Service Pilot in World War II* (Annapolis, MD: Naval Institute Press, 1996); Nancy Robison, "*'We Love to Fly': Women Airforce Service Pilots* (n.c.: CreateSpace Independent Publishing Platform, 2013); David A. Stallman, *Women in the Wild Blue: Target Towing WASP at Camp Davis* (Sugar Creek, OH: Carlisle Printing, 2011); Jaqueline Cochran, *Jackie Cochran: An Autobiography of the Greatest Woman Pilot in Aviation History* (New York: Bantam Books, 1987); Jacqueline Cochran, *The Stars at Noon* (Boston: Little, Brown 1954); and Sarah Byrn Rickman, *Nancy Batson Crews: Alabama's First Lady of Flight* (Tuscaloosa: University of Alabama Press, 2009).

3. See Joseph J. Corn, *The Winged Gospel: America's Romance with Aviation* (Baltimore: Johns Hopkins University Press, 2002). For more on the history of aviation in the Lone Star State, see Barbara Ganson, *Texas Takes Wing: A Century of Flight in the Lone Star State* (Austin: University of Texas Press, 2014).

4. For more on Jacqueline Cochran, see Sherwood Inkley, "Women's Airforce Service Pilots," *New Handbook of Texas Online*, accessed June 12, 2021, https://tshaonline.org/handbook/online/articles/qpw01; Doris L. Rich, *Jackie Cochran: Pilot in the Fastest Lane* (Florida: University Press of Florida, 2007); Cochran, *The Stars at Noon*; Carl, *A Wasp Among Eagles*; and "History" and "Training" Official Archive of Women's Airforce Service Pilots, Texas Woman's University, accessed

June 12, 2021, https://twu.edu/library/womans-collection/collections/women-air-force-service-pilots-official-archive/history/.

5. Jacqueline Cochran, Letter to Eleanor Roosevelt, September 1939, Box 6, Subseries 4: 1939 Files, Jacqueline Cochran Papers, Dwight D. Eisenhower Presidential Library, Abilene, Kansas. It is important to note that Jacqueline Cochran was not the first or only woman who saw the chance to utilize women pilots in case of war. Nancy Love, Phoebe Omelie, and others worked toward similar goals. For Cochran's struggle to awake the nation to the need for pilots, male and female, see Joseph J. Corn, "Making Flying 'Thinkable': Women Pilots and the Selling of Aviation, 1927–1940," *American Quarterly* 31 (Autumn 1979); Dackri D. Davis, "Navigating Discrimination: A Historical Examination of Womens' Experiences of Discrimination and Triumph within the United States Military and Higher Educational Institutions" (PhD diss., Georgia State University, 2014); Cochran, *The Stars at Noon*; Keil, *These Wonderful Women in Their Flying Machines*; and P. O'Connell Pearson, *Fly Girls: The Daring American Women Pilots Who Helped Win WWII* (New York: Simon & Schuster Books for Young Readers, 2018).

6. Carl, *A Wasp Among Eagles*, 39; Sherwood Inkley, "Women's Airforce Service Pilots"; Cochran, *The Stars at Noon*, 120–21, 124, 128; Carl, *A Wasp Among Eagles*, 39; "History" and "Training" Official Archive of Women's Airforce Service Pilots. Jaqueline Cochran's acerbic dealings with military officials is in Davis, "Navigating Discrimination."

7. For the decision to train in Texas, see Thomas E. Alexander, *The Wings of Change: The Army Air Force Experience in Texas during World War II* (College Station: Texas A&M University Press, 2003). For the initial training in Houston, see Leni "Dedie" Deaton, "Supplementary History of the Women's Airforce Service Pilot Training Program at 319th Army Air Forces Flying Training Detachment, Municipal Airport, Houston, Texas, 318th Army Air Forces Flying Training Detachment, Later Designated 2563rd Army Air Forces Base Unit, Avenger Field, Sweetwater, Texas," in Dora Strother collection at Texas Woman's University (TWU).

8. These quotes are Deaton's recollections of her conversation with Jacqueline Cochran. Leoti "Dedie" Deaton, Chief Establishment Officer, Women Airforce Service Pilots. Oral history interview with Ziggy Hunter, March 18, 1975. Edited by Dawn Letson and Nancy M. Durr and available in Woman's Collection at TWU. Joel Draut, "A Glimpse of Houston during World War II," accessed June 12, 2021, https://houstonhistorymagazine.org/wp-content/uploads/2012/10/a-glimpse-of-houston.pdf; Robert H. Peebles, "Shipbuilding," *Handbook of Texas Online*, accessed June 12, 2021, https://tshaonline.org/handbook/online/articles/ets03. For more on the industries in Texas during the war, see Houston Faust Mount's essay on the oil industry or Zachary Montz's essay concerning Texas labor.

9. Leni "Dedie" Deaton, "Supplementary History of the Women's Airforce Service Pilot Training Program."

10. Dora Dougherty Strother McKeown, Unpublished Memoir, Dora Strother collection, 28.

11. *History of WASP Program: Army Air Forces Central Flying Training Command*,

Historical Section, A-2, Army Air Forces Central Flying Command, Randolph Field, TX, 20 January 1945, 24 (hereafter *History of WASP Program*).

12. Letter dated January 22, 1943, as quoted in *History of WASP Program*, 28; *History of WASP Program*, 28–38.

13. *History of WASP Program*, 28–38.

14. Although the case against the pair was circumstantial, in June 1944, the Central Flying Training Command essentially said they would not reinstate Plosser-Prince because they legally did not have to, and Aviation Enterprises was doing a fine job. They recommended Plosser-Prince Air Academy be given preference if other contracts became available. For this, see *History of WASP Program*, 28–38.

15. *History of WASP Program*, 28–38.

16. Doris B. Tanner, *Arnold, Cochran, Deaton: Women Airforce Service Pilots, WWII*, self-published history by WASP Doris Tanner of class 44-W-4, in author's possession and available at TWU; Dora letter home, March 6, 1943; Cochran, *The Stars at Noon*, 127; Sally Van Wagenen Keil, *These Wonderful Women in Their Flying Machines: The Unknown Heroines of World War II* (Rawson, NY: Four Directions Press, 1979), 257–58; and Pearson, *Fly Girls*, 126–27.

17. Doris Brinker Tanner, *The Sweetwater Experience and Leni Leoti*, copy available at TWU; Doris Brinker Tanner and "Dedie" Leoti Deaton, oral history, 1982, transcript in author's possession.

18. Tanner, *The Sweetwater Experience*; Madge Rutherford Minton, Letters home, February 27, 1943.

19. See Leisa D. Meyer's excellent work, *Creating G.I. Jane: Sexuality and Power in the Women's Army Corps during World War II* (New York: Columbia University Press, 1996).

20. Katherine Sharp Landdeck, "WASP of World War II," podcast with *Stuff You Missed in History Class*, https://www.missedinhistory.com/podcasts/wasp-of-wwii-with-dr-katherine-sharp-landdeck-part-1.htm; Dawn Letson, "Girl Pilots of Avenger Field: Sweetwater's Romance with the WASP of World War II," *Sound Historian: Journal of the Texas Oral History Association* 13 (2011), 35–36.

21. Judy Barrett Litoff and David C. Smith, *We're in This War, Too: World War II Letters from American Women in Uniform* (New York: Oxford University Press, 1994), 114; *History of WASP Program*, 54–58;

22. McArthur and Smith, *Texas through Women's Eyes: The Twentieth-Century Experience* (Austin: University of Texas Press, 2010), 136; Keil, *These Wonderful Women in Their Flying Machine*, 249. WASP served at the following Texas bases: Aloe Army Airfield (Victoria, TX); Biggs Army Airfield (El Paso, TX); Blackland Army Airfield (Waco, TX); Bryan Army Air Base (Bryan, TX); Childress Army Airfield (Childress, TX); Dalhart Army Airfield (Dalhart, TX); Eagle Pass Army Air Base (Eagle Pass, TX); Ellington Army Airfield (Houston, TX); Foster Army Airfield (Victoria, TX); Goodfellow Army Airfield (San Angelo, TX); Harlingen Army Airfield (Harlingen, TX); Hondo Army Airfield (Hondo, TX); Kelly Army Air Base (San Antonio, TX); Laredo Army Air Base (Laredo, TX); Love Field (Dallas, TX); Lubbock Army Air Base (Lubbock, TX); Majors Army Airfield (Greenville, TX);

Marfa Army Air Base (Marfa, TX); Moore Army Air Base (Mission, TX); Pecos Army Air Base (Pecos, TX); Perrin Army Air Base (Sherman, TX); Randolph Army Air Base (San Antonio, TX); San Marcos Army Air Base (San Marcos, TX); South Plains Army Air Base (Lubbock, TX); and Waco Army Airfield, (Waco, TX). This information can be found at https://www.pbs.org/wgbh/americanexperience/features/flygirls-wasp-and-b-29/ http://www.wingsacrossamerica.us/wasp/resources/texas.htm.

23. Cochran, *The Stars at Noon*, 127; "Women Fly the B-29," American Experience, accessed June 12, 2021, https://www.pbs.org/wgbh/americanexperience/features/flygirls-wasp-and-b-29/; Keil, *These Wonderful Women in Their Flying Machines*, 257–58; Pearson, *Fly Girls*, 126–27; Letson, "Girl Pilots of Avenger Field," 39; Ganson, *Texas Takes Wing*, 119; "History" and "Training" Official Archive of Women Airforce Service Pilots. For the lone WASP never accounted for, at least the recovery of her body, see James W. Ure, *Seized by the Sun: The Life and Disappearance of World War II Pilot Gertrude Tompkins* (Chicago: Chicago Review Press Incorporated, 2017).

24. Paul Tibbets, Dora Dougherty Strother, and Didi Moorman, Oral histories with author, 1997.

25. Cindy Weigand, *Texas Women in World War II* (Lanham, MD: Republic of Texas Press, 2003), 187–88, 193.

26. The first WASP pilot was buried in Arlington National Cemetery with military honors as early as 2002. The secretary of the army, however, who believed these women should not have been buried in the cemetery, reversed the policy, citing the superintendent of the cemetery lacked the authority to grant burial to the female pilots. Thus, until Congress intervened, further burials were barred. The history of the women leading up to the exclusion at Arlington National Cemetery can be found in Katherine Sharp Landdeck, "The Women Excluded from Arlington National Cemetery," *Atlantic*, January 15, 2016. Full details of the struggle to be buried in Arlington National Cemetery can be found in Katherine Sharp Landdeck, "A Woman Pilot Receives the Military Funeral the Army Denied Her," *Atlantic*, September 8, 2016; Leo Shane, III, "Female WWII Pilots Now Allowed Burial at Arlington," *Military Times*, May 20, 2016; and *Washington Post*, September 7, 2016.

27. Mattie E. Treadwell, "The Women's Army Corps," in *United States Army in World War II, Special Studies*, rev. ed. (1954; repr., Washington, DC: Office of the Chief of Military History, Department of the Army, CMH Pub. 11–8, 1991), 460, "Women's Army Corps (WACs)," *Atomic Heritage Foundation*, April 27, 2018, https://www.atomicheritage.org/history/womens-army-corps-wac; D'Ann Campbell, *Women at War with America: Private Lives in a Patriotic Era* (Cambridge, MA: Harvard University Press, 1984), 35, 37. The premier work on Texas women who served in all branches during the war is Weigand, *Texas Women in World War II*. For a more detailed examination of the WACs, see Judith A. Bellafaire, "The Women's Army Corps: A Commemoration of World War II Service." This can be found at the Center for Military History Online, https://history.army.mil/brochures/

WAC/WAC.HTM. For the rumor campaign against the WAC, and in party against all female military units, see Leisa D. Meyer, *Creating GI Jane: Sexuality and Power in the Women's Army Corps during World War II* (New York: Columbia University Press, 1998). Other works are Bettie J. Morden, *The Women's Army Corps, 1945* (Washington, DC: US Government Printing Office, 1990); Melanie Anne Veach Kirkland, "Daughters of Athena: American Women in the Military during World War II" (master's thesis, Texas Tech University, 2004); Mollie Weinstein Shaffer, *Mollie's War: The Letters of a World War II WAC in Europe* (Jefferson, NC: MacFarland & Company, 2016); Vera S. Williams, *WACS: Women's Army Corps* (Osceola, WI: Motorbooks International, 1997); and Ethel A. Starbird, *When Women First Wore Army Shoes: A First-Person Account of Service as a Member of the Women's Army Corps during WWII* (Bloomington, IN: iUniverse, 2010).

28. John W. Jeffries, *Wartime America: The World War II Home Front*, 2nd ed. (New York: Rowman & Littlefield, 2018), 76. Dorothy Ann Veach's story can be found in Mary Mills Heidbrink, "Veach Served in the Women's Army Corps during World War II," *mySA.com*, September 6, 2017, https://www.mysanantonio.com/sa-obituaries/article/Veach-served-in-the-Women-s-Army-Corps-during-12162636.php. The information on Mary (Valfre) Castro is in Judith Bellafaire, "The Contributions of Hispanic Servicewomen," the *Women's Memorial*, accessed June 12, 2021, https://www.womensmemorial.org/hispanic-servicewomen. Oveta Culp Hobby's biography can be found in Kelli Cardenas Walsh, "Oveta Culp Hobby: A Transformational Leader from the Texas Legislature to Washington, DC" (PhD diss., University of South Carolina, 2006); and Robert Pando, "Oveta Culp Hobby: A Study of Power and Control" (PhD diss., Florida State University, 2008). The biography for Isabella Martin Henry can be found in Isabella M. Henry Papers, the Texas Collection, Baylor University, Waco, Texas. The information about Elizabeth "Tex" William and black women in the WAC is in Cheryl Mullenbach, *Double Victory: How African American Women Broke Race and Gender Barriers to Help Win World War II* (Chicago: Chicago Review Press, 2013), 90–111, 123; Bruce A. Glasrud and Merline Pitre, eds., *Black Women in Texas History* (College Station: Texas A&M University Press, 2008), 140; Jeanne Holm, *Women in the Military: An Unfinished Revolution* (Novato, CA: Presidio Press, 1992), 77–78, 80, 91; Ruthe Winegarten and Sharon Kahn, *Brave Black Women: From Slavery to the Space Shuttle* (Austin: University of Texas Press, 1997), 75. For the experiences of an all-black WAC unit, see Brenda L. Moore, *To Serve My Country, to Serve My Race: The Story of the Only African-American WACs Stationed Overseas during World War II* (New York: New York University Press, 1996); Jesse L. Johnson, *Black Women in the Armed Forces, 1941–1974* (Hampton, VA: Hampton Institute, 1974). More detail on the Women's Army Corps in World War II can be found in Mattie E. Treadwell, "The Women s Army Corps," in *United States Army in World War II, Special Studies*, rev. ed. (1954; repr., Washington, DC: Office of the Chief of Military History, Department of the Army, CMH Pub. 11–8, 1991); Bettie J. Morden's *The Women s Army Corps, 1945–1978* (Washington, DC: US

Government Printing Office, 1989); the Women's Army Corps Veterans Association, *Daughters of Pallas Athene: Cameo Recollections of Women's Army Corps Veterans* (Independence, MO: Print America, 1983); Margaret Flint, *Dress Right, Dress: The Autobiography of a WAC* (New York: Dodd, Mead & Company, 1943); Martha S. Putney, *When the Nation Was in Need: Blacks in the Women's Army Corps during World War II* (Matuchen, NJ: Scarecrow Press, 1992); Ethel A. Starbird, *When Women First Wore Army Shoes: A First-Person Account of Service as a Member of the Women's Army Corps during WWII* (Bloomington, IN: iUniverse, 2010); and Anne Bosanko Green, *One Woman's War: Letters Home from the Women's Army Corps, 1944–1946* (St. Paul: Minnesota Historical Society Press, 1989). For the experiences of a female black officer in the WAC, see Charity Adams Earley, *One Woman's Army: A Black Officer Remembers the WAC* (College Station: Texas A&M University Press, 1989). A more detailed examination of the contribution of black Texas women to the war effort is in the essay authored by Christopher B. Bean, Bernadette Pruitt, and Michael Hurd.

29. Maggie Rivas-Rodriguez et al., *A Legacy Greater Than Words: Stories of US Latinos & Latinas of the WWII Generation* (Austin: US Latino & Latina WWII Oral History Project, 2006), 188–89.

30. Clarice F. Pollard, *Laugh, Cry and Remember: The Journal of a G.I. Lady* (Phoenix, AZ: Journey's Press, 1998), 53–68; Archie P. Macdonald, "WAC's," *TexasEscapes.com*, accessed June 12, 2021, http://www.texasescapes.com/AllThingsHistorical/WACs-Womens-Army-Corps-AM902.htm. More on the WAC's time at Stephen F. Austin is in "Army Administration School: Women's Army Corps, 1943–1944," East Texas Research Center, Ralph W. Steen Library, Stephen F. Austin State University, Nacogdoches, Texas.

31. Susan M. Hartmann, *The Home Front and Beyond: American Women in the 1940s* (Boston: Twayne Publishers, 1982), 41; Judy Barrett Litoff and David C. Smith, *American Women in a World at War: Contemporary Accounts from World War II* (Wilmington, DE: SR Books, 1997), 51–53; Rivas-Rodriguez et al., *A Legacy Greater Than Words*, 214. Fantastic resource concerning women who served in the WAVES is the US Naval Institutes WAVES oral histories, accessed June 12, 2021, https://www.usni.org/heritage/the-waves; Nancy Wilson Ross, *The WAVES: The Story of the Girls in Blue* (New York: Henry Holt and Company, 1943).

32. Aerographer's mates collect, record, and analyze meteorological and oceanographic data.

33. Weigand, *Texas Women in World War II*, 166–67; McArthur and Smith, *Texas through Women's Eyes*, 95; Colonel Mary V. Stremlow, *Free a Marine to Fight: Women Marines in World War II* (Washington, DC: History and Museums Division, Headquarters, US Marine Corps, 1994), 1–3, 5, 9–11, 14–15. For Ruth Cheney Streeter's story during the war, see John T. Mason, *The Atlantic War Remembered: An Oral History Collection* (Annapolis, MD: Naval Institute Press, 1990).

34. Campbell, *Women at War with America*, 53; Michael C. C. Adams, *The Best War Ever: America and World War II* (Baltimore: Johns Hopkins University Press, 1994), 85.

4

Tejanos
On Two Battlegrounds

Arnoldo De León[1]

From what we know about US mobilization following the Japanese attack on Pearl Harbor, Spanish-speaking *colonias* (ethnic neighborhoods) promptly rallied to the war effort. Tejanos responded, like so many other Americans, to the government's call for readiness. They displayed a commitment to national defense both on the battlefield and on the home front.[2]

The Tejano Community and War

The number of Hispanic men and women who actively engaged in military service during the war remains speculative. Many scholars believe between 500,000 and 1 million Hispanics saw military duty. Of these, according to historian Zaragosa Vargas, more than "250,000 Tejanos served in the armed forces, representing 57 percent of the nation's Spanish-speaking servicemen and women." Approximately 15,000 foreign-born Mexicans (most of them living in Texas) saw war duty. They were enlisted under a 1943 agreement with Mexico in which Mexican citizens living in the United States could be conscripted. Close to 1,500 of these men became war casualties.[3]

There existed a multitude of motivations behind Tejano patriotism. Certainly commitment to the nation's defense and the opportunity to prove their patriotism mattered, but Tejanos also sought to uphold the dignity of self, family, and community. Many joined to win respect for their people (*la raza*). For some, as the lyrics in the song "*Soldado Razo*" noted, military exploits afforded the chance to display their inherent valor. There volunteered those who wished to elude poverty and escape discrimination and being regarded as unworthy citizens. Mexico-born Tejanos, for their part, perceived an opening for possible naturalization. Still others had no choice on obligations. Since so many worked in sectors of the economy that failed to qualify them for deferments, draft boards more regularly called them. Whatever their reason for their deployment, Tejanos readily registered for duty. Not infrequently, families saw one or two of their sons off to war and in some cases as many as five or six.[4]

Tejanos learned much more than becoming model GIs during their first weeks in the military. Boot camp also taught them that not all Anglos despised them, as they had come to deduce from their home experience. The military permitted ethnic Mexicans to train and fight alongside whites, while mandating the segregation of African American combatants. Socially white Americans considered Mexicans as non-Caucasian. Yet the legal system regarded them as white. Tejanos thus benefited from integration. From some Anglos and other GIs, indeed, they received help in understanding rules of comportment, dealing with military protocol, translating words or messages they did not understand, and much more. Hispanics discovered, moreover, a more egalitarian attitude in the military. Drill sergeants, to be sure, made no distinction in their vilification. Boot camp's emphasis on patriotism, furthermore, led Tejanos to quickly accept the purpose of war and their need to fight. Their assignments after boot camp to different bases for specialized schooling familiarized Tejanos with places besides the realm of the segregated *barrio* (enclave) or the cotton fields they worked seasonally. The military universe could not help but to broaden their world views as it embraced the cultural lives of (aside from Anglos) the multitude of ethnicities throughout the United States.[5]

The complete story (it can never be told) of the contributions that Tejanos (and Mexican Americans in general) made to the war remains to be written. Presently, sources allow broad sketches of Tejano draftees and volunteers. *Soldados* (soldiers) came from every section of the Lone Star State, although it appears a disproportionate number had South Texas roots. At the more local level, soldiers left settings that ranged anywhere from the large urban centers to, as Los Angeles recruit Raúl Morín put it, "the backwoods, and the hills." Some called San Antonio, Houston, and Austin home, but because Texas as of 1941 still remained largely rural, servicemen typically hailed from smaller towns like Laredo, Corpus Christi, El Paso, San Angelo, and Del Rio. Those responding to duty came from rural communities such as Realitos, Bishop, San Benito, La Joya, and Falfurrias in South Texas or Sanderson, Melvin, Sonora, Marfa, and Alpine in West Texas.[6]

Men and women entering the armed forces packed with them the culture daily nourished and elaborated in out-of-the-way farms and ranches or segregated barrios. Common among almost all was the Spanish language—and its variant strains. Long present within Mexican American communities were competently bilingual personalities. They probably merged the two languages, communicating in a lexicon popularly known as "Tex-Mex." Spanish-dominant soldiers relying on broken English blended the two languages, utilizing a form of "Spanglish." The foreign-born comfortably used a standardized Spanish, perhaps intermixed with English phrases and words. Diversity nonetheless demarcated the large contingent of soldiers. There was, for one, a small yet discernible group constituted of high school and even college graduates. This cohort of Tejanos knew some of life's comforts and were more assimilated, holding in civilian life white-collar positions (e.g., as entrepreneurs and journalists) and professional careers (e.g., as lawyers and doctors) or belonging to the League of United Latin American Citizens (LULAC), the leading activist civic organization of the day. When war broke out, LULAC urged Tejanos to volunteer for duty. Many LULACers did in fact enlist, to the point that membership in local councils dropped significantly. There also existed a large complement of second-generation Tejanos, whose parents had fled to the United States to escape the turmoil of the Mexican Revolution. Foreign-born Tejanos made up a third perceptible component. This coterie of individuals, however, had been in the United States for a number of years and had acquired working skills better than fellow countrymen still struggling as unskilled laborers.[7]

Mexican American soldiers differed in stages of Americanization, and perhaps even class standing. A cut above most would have been the more acculturated and bilingual. But most Tejanos probably were no more than commoners—*la plebe*. These commoners differed from their more Americanized Tejanos in their upbringing amid dire poverty, in their consignment to arduous labor, and in their lack of proper education. Perhaps due to the racial attitudes of the time, many in this stratum had only peripheral association with whites (perhaps in interaction on the job). Part of this crust, but urban-bred, was a small contingent of *pachucos* (youthful rebels who shunned conventionality; oftentimes they belonged to barrio gangs). They took pride in being streetwise and commanding a slang called *caló*. But whatever their social differences, Tejano soldiers maintained "*lo mexicano*," the culture forged and distilled in segregated zones.[8]

Tejanos experienced the war differently. They served in all of the military branches, but overwhelmingly in the army. As Morín observed: "Most of the Mexican Americans who were being drafted then were assigned to the Army and put in the Infantry. The saying was, "'Mexicans, Oakies, Polacks, and Wops. That's all you see in the infantry.'" The story of the fighting prowess of Tejanos would be incomplete if their martial contributions were overlooked. Certainly to be remembered would be the exploits in the Italian campaign of the 36th Division 141st Regiment, Company E, made up mostly of Tejanos from the El Paso and the Far West Texas area. The Division fought daringly at Salerno, Italy (September 1943), where at least two West Texans, Manuel S. Gonzales and Ramón G. Gutiérrez, won commendations for gallantry. Upon landing onshore, Gonzales, of Fort Davis, advanced upon and destroyed a German 88 mm artillery gun and crew. With grenades in hand, he eliminated several machine-gun nests and subsequently a mortar. Gutiérrez (from Del Rio, although he enlisted in Sonora) also gained distinction for meritorious action at the Salerno beach. Although wounded, Gutiérrez defiantly advanced toward an enemy machine-gun pit to silence it. But then, ordered on a suicidal mission to cross the Rapido River into German-held ground, the unit met with disaster. Replenished soon after, Company E continued toward Rome, ultimately fighting into Germany. In addition, Tejanos waded ashore at Normandy in June 1944 during the D-Day landings and marched and fought their way into Germany as the Allies ultimately defeated Nazi Germany.[9]

Tejanos contributed to battle in numerous capacities, executing their duties with purpose and valor. Richard G. Candelaria from El Paso was a fighter pilot in Europe. He flew P-51s, escorting bombers. "I wanted to be a fighter pilot," he declared. "That was my one wish." Having shot down six enemy planes, he earned the title "Fighter Ace." Jesús L. Armendáriz from El Paso served as a medic in the 1st Infantry Division ("the Big Red One"), treating the wounded from North Africa to the liberation of Rome. From San Benito, Texas, Guadalupe Conde served as a cook with the 36th Infantry Division. In fact, he was the only Tejano in his unit, refusing transfer to the all-Hispanic Company E. During the invasion of Italy (Salerno), Conde assisted the invasion force by running water, blankets, ammunition, and C rations to the invasion force. Afterward, he collected the dog tags off the dead. Rudulfo "Rudy" Acosta was a gunner on B-17s and B-24s. Uncertain about serving in the infantry, Acosta was relieved to be placed initially with the Signal Corps, then subsequently selected for training in gunnery school. "I remembered the old movies you see with the guy [in the infantry] sloshing through the mud and foxholes," he recalled. "That's not for me." He admitted his experience in the army and thirty-six missions flown "aged [him] 10 years in knowledge." Guadalupe Garza was drafted into the army and trained in the field artillery. Following an assignment in North Africa, he came ashore during the invasion of Sicily. He and a fellow soldier unwittingly came ashore behind German lines. They evaded capture for seven days, surviving only on grapes before reaching their unit. Ladislao L. C. Castro was from Austin. He enlisted in the Army Air Corps in late 1942, ultimately assigned to the crew of a B-24 Liberator as an aerial gunner. Having participated in twenty-one missions, Castro's fate turned when on his final mission over Germany the plane was hit by anti-aircraft fire. The damaged bomber made it as far as occupied France before finally being shot down. The crew, including a wounded Castro (shot in the leg), safely bailed out. Unable to deploy his parachute at a safe altitude, Castro hit the ground very hard, breaking his leg. He hid himself in a haystack as German patrols captured his crew and searched unsuccessfully for him. He remained in hiding in Amiens (northern France) with assistance from the French underground until Canadian forces liberated the city following the Normandy invasion.[10]

Drafted in 1943 into the army, Raúl Mata Martínez from Cementville (near San Antonio) recalled his fear about combat. Although never completely overcoming his fear, he did not let it paralyze him from performing his duty. Martinez became a skilled shot as a machine-gun specialist. “I learned to shoot from the hip running without aiming,” he bragged. He saw action in North Africa, Sicily, Italy, France, and into Germany and was part of the occupation of Austria. One of his most memorable moments was his initial excitement of buying some dried meat from a street vendor in North Africa. It was not until he’d already eaten much of it that he learned it was dog meat. “Well, now it’s too late,” he resignedly acknowledged. “We already had some in our stomachs.” Eduardo Botello embodied perseverance in the war. Raised in Laredo, he was drafted in 1943. Only one of two Hispanics in the 79th Infantry Division, he experienced the typical racial slights but appeared unfazed by it, remarking his treatment was “just like any other soldier.” He came ashore at Utah Beach in France, narrowly surviving a collapsing house. Wounded three times during the war, his last was the most serious. Having waded ashore and crossed the countryside of France into Germany, Botello was wounded when a mortar shell exploded nearby, concussing him. “I had blood coming out of my ears, mouth and nose,” he described. Following the war, he worked for the US Customs for four decades along the Texas-Mexico border.[11]

Their saga in the Pacific theater calls further attention to the heroism of the Tejano serviceman. Tejanos were part of the US command that fought bravely at Bataan and Corregidor (the Philippines), who gamely helped repel Japanese fleets in the Battles of Midway and the Coral Sea, and then bolstered fellow Marine Corps fighters in capturing Guadalcanal, Iwo Jima, Okinawa, and other Japanese-occupied islands. A native of Austin, Candelario Hernández enlisted in the army. Serving in the 32nd Infantry Division, he was shipped to the Southwest Pacific, seeing action in New Guinea. There he barely survived a bout with malaria and defending the Driniumor River against the Japanese. Carlos Quintana entered service before Pearl Harbor. With US entry, he joined the 165th Infantry Regiment, protecting the Hawaiian Islands after the December 7, 1941, attack on Pearl Harbor. By war’s end, Quintana participated in three battles in the Pacific (Gilbert Islands, Marshall Islands, and Saipan). It was in the latter that a Japanese mortar exploded near him, sending shrapnel into his tongue and severing a major artery in his mouth. The injury impeded his ability to speak for the next six years.[12]

By any standard, Tejanos displayed resolve in the face of the enemy. Private first class in the 32nd Infantry Regiment, Rodolfo Mireles of Benavides, Texas, for example, accompanied General Douglas MacArthur's forces in recapturing the Philippines. His unit then landed in Okinawa, where Mireles was killed in action on April 10, 1945. Initially buried on the island, the government later recovered his remains and reinterred him in Benavides in March 1949. As did Mireles, Tejanos in World War II received numerous distinguished medals and citations, among them five Congressional Medals of Honor and many Distinguished Service Crosses (a commendation ranking second only to the Congressional Medal of Honor), the Distinguished Flying Cross, Air Medals, Oak Leaf Clusters, Silver Stars, Bronze Stars, Battle Stars, and, expectedly, Purple Hearts.[13]

Tejanas also aided the war effort, both as civilians and as soldiers. On the home front, they assisted as nurses as hospitals faced a shortage of medical personnel. Some filled openings in the civil service sector and other white-collar vocations, working as secretaries, translators, and mail censors. Tejanas also found a demand for their labor in the war industry. In San Antonio, many met the need for aircraft mechanics at local Kelly Field. Mexican American women also volunteered for military service in designated female units such as the Women's Army Corps (converted in 1943 from the Women's Army Auxiliary Corps, or WAAC) and in the Army Nurse Corps. Those who opted for nursing duties received assignments to numerous stations, some stateside but others on the war front. Mexican American nurses, indeed, served in both the Pacific and European theaters. As with their male counterparts, servicewomen gained new experiences. Many came to view Anglos as comrades in arms and not always the stereotypical racist; indeed, some of the women found their soul mates in the military and married them. The war exposed Tejanas to employment opportunities beyond the migrant world. Assignments took them to exciting places outside mundane segregated environs. As military personnel, they found schooling (which remained financially beyond most Mexican American families), which provided an avenue for advancement. The prospect of social mobility was not lost on some Tejanas.[14]

Julia Aguillón, from Laredo, joined the civil defense. This was the civilian organization to coordinate state and federal measures in case of Axis invasion. After her husband was drafted, Josephine Ledesma Walker volunteered to work as an airplane mechanic. She trained at Randolph Field, where she was the only Hispanic woman. Sent to an army base in Big Spring, Texas (northwest of San Angelo in West Texas), she was the only woman assigned to the hangar. Ester Pérez followed a similar path. The Needville native initially worked at Kelly Field when she learned of the call for women to fill in for men being shipped abroad. Despite the reservations of her mother, she signed up for overseas service. Following her training in California, Pérez was ordered to Hawaii as an engine mechanic for combat aircraft. From San Antonio, Rafaela Muñiz Esquivel served with the 242nd General Hospital in France. She noted the war's primitive conditions, remembering how she and her comrades had to burn their curtains for warmth. More distressing, however, was ministering to the never-ending wounded. "They used to bring them [the wounded] by the loads. . . . There was no way that we could really get undressed [to sleep]," she lamented.[15]

Long were the years during which individual families worried about the fate of their sons, husbands, or brothers. Gone to fight were siblings of preteen youngsters, heads of households already with a growing family, recently married men, and many more conscripted under the Selective Training and Service Act passed in 1940. Wives now had to manage by themselves, finding work, raising children, and maintaining a semblance of normalcy. Families prayed daily for their loved ones' safe return, fearing telegrams reporting death or missing in action. Literate family members wrote letters to soldiers wishing them well or bringing them up-to-date on news from home. The wider public contributed to the war effort through patriotic parades, war bond sales, contributions to the Red Cross, blood drives, and a general spirit of community. Young women found gratification in becoming pen pals with Tejano soldiers and apprising them of life on the home front. Others joined United Service Organizations (USO) to lift soldier morale. In San Antonio, a Spanish-language theater not only adopted military and patriotic themes and incorporated them into their stage presentations, but also sponsored benefit drives.[16]

World War II and Life Struggles

There existed within Tejano communities doubts about defending a country that asserted, but did not extend, equality to all. On the eve of the war, poverty gripped much of the Mexican American community. In cities such as San Antonio, Houston, and Dallas, Hispanics faced grim circumstances, barely surviving in quarters neglected by city officials, dealing with disease, hunger, and uncertainty. In parts of rural South Texas, people during the 1930s dwelled in shelters hardly worthy of the designation as hovels. Without adequate health care, these communities contracted diseases such as diphtheria and tuberculosis at near epidemic rates and many children died in infancy. Few school-aged children received an education. Adding to this uncertainty was the possibility of deportation and repatriation drives.[17]

Into the war years, privation, illness, premature death, illiteracy, and general impoverishment beset the broader Tejano community. As in the past, many Hispanics earned dismal wages as migrant farmworkers with the increased demand for foodstuffs. Texas farmers relied heavily upon Hispanic field hands for labor. But so did Midwestern farmers in need of a workforce skilled in picking cherries and strawberries and in harvesting vegetables such as tomatoes, onions, and corn. As a result, Tejanos migrated as far north as Michigan, Wisconsin, and Illinois. Accompanying misery and migratory displacement was discrimination. Prior to World War II, white society, notwithstanding ethnic Mexicans' legal recognition as Caucasian, abided by segregationist customs treating Tejanos as second-class citizens. Anglos also dominated the political system through means of disfranchisement like the poll tax that Tejano voting power was effectively neutralized. These attitudes and wrongdoings continued even during the war. Draft boards, staffed by white men, shamelessly discriminated against Tejanos, prioritizing them before Anglo boys. Soldiers in uniform were often denied service at lunch counters at bus stops, pharmacies, cafés, and dime stores. Such policies even did not spare dignitaries from Mexico traveling in Texas on official business.[18]

Such cases of injustice became increasingly brazen in cities then swelling with rural people seeking jobs created by the war industry. Census data attest to a rural to urban transformation. In 1930, according to governmental statistics, 33.6 percent of the Texas population worked as farm labor. By 1950, the percentage had fallen to 23.2 percent. The trend from farm to city was obvious to contemporaries: One state agency noted that there were 260,000 fewer farm residents in the middle years of the war than had been in 1940. From a citizenry of some 2,911,389 (or 45.4 percent of the total population in 1940), the number of persons in Texas towns and cities grew to 4,834,000 by mid-twentieth century, or 62.7 percent of the total population. Tejanos accompanied this wartime trek, lured from low-paying farm work by the possibility of higher-wage employment defense-related industry. Cities tantalized Tejanos with possibilities of a better life, such as to be found in military installations based in San Antonio. But urban discrimination mirrored the kind prevalent in rural areas. Armed services plant managers did not prioritize Tejanos, assigning them to lesser-paying positions, if at all. They found no solace from racial prejudice in the private industrial sector either. Those fortunate to find work with oil refineries or smelting plants were marginalized in the least-desirable jobs with little promise of promotion. Similar habits infested the blue-collar economy. Male wage earners managed a livelihood as truck drivers, deliverymen, mechanics, construction workers, carpenter helpers, or cooks, but little else. Added to this were dismissive public officials and hostile law enforcement.[19]

Home Front Efforts to Eliminate Injustices

Such conditions as afflicted Tejanos socially and economically did not go unchallenged by Mexican American activists. In fact, agitation on behalf of civil and labor rights accelerated during World War II. The historian Thomas A. Guglielmo offers several reasons why this movement quickened. Participation in the war effort gave legitimacy to any Tejano demands for equality. As Tejanos accepted the fight for democracy against totalitarianism and racism overseas, they championed a parallel struggle against race prejudice at home. Government campaigns to counter Nazi propaganda (one that accentuated American bigotry) proved salutary to communities battling injustices. Mexico assisted in pressuring Texas to grant freedoms to Mexican Americans. Tejano leaders, both from LULAC and like-minded organizations combating inequality, grasped the historical moment to try and defeat undemocratic forces at home. Professor Emilio Zamora and others find the most diligent members of the LULAC team in this fight were Alonso Perales, Carlos Castañeda, M.C. Gonzales, George I. Sánchez, and José de la Luz Sáenz.[20]

Just what perspective did these historical actors have on the matter of white privilege (an issue that injected itself into the wartime movement) for equality? A debate has emerged during recent years as to whether Tejano leaders fought for "Caucasian rights" only or for rights applicable to all minorities. One argument posits that Mexicans during World War II considered themselves as white people and thus waged a struggle for Tejano citizenship that excluded rights for other racial minorities. In addressing this premise, others maintain that evidence indicates otherwise, that both Tejano and African American leaders collaborated for their mutual benefit. This debate may continue for some years to come, but for the moment, it should be assumed that the issue of "color" entered into the thinking of those Tejano leaders who thought of equality in terms of "Caucasian rights" only, and for those who considered dismantling Jim Crow for all.[21]

The historical moment in Texas did appear fortuitous for proponents of egalitarianism. Moreover, Mexico pledged to press its own diplomatic campaign to end discrimination in the state. Mexico's promise synchronized with the Tejanos' undeterred offensive for social improvement. Among the many inequities attacked was the dismal state of Mexican American schools. University of Texas Professor George I. Sánchez, serving as LULAC president in 1941–42, assumed leadership on the matter. He faulted the Texas educational system for being inattentive to the concerns of Hispanic children. So-called Mexican schools were too often dilapidated and overcrowded. In exasperation, Sánchez noted in 1942 that in keeping with wartime good neighborliness, Texas paid more attention to schooling in Latin America than it did to Hispanics in the United States. The World War II cohort of leaders also aggressively targeted the entrenched system of public segregation. The practice was especially galling at a time when Texans should have been moved by the spirit of friendliness and cooperation. LULAC lobbied the state legislature for a civil rights statute outlawing discrimination against Tejanos in public accommodations.

In pursuing such a law, LULAC personnel spoke at public hearings, gave press interviews, and lobbied sympathetic legislators.[22]

Not confining themselves to the issue of civil liberties, LULACers also focused on Tejano labor rights. The organization seemed to be the logical envoy for Mexican American labor grievances since governmental officials considered it nonthreatening. Further, LULACers held themselves up (as indeed they had since founding their organization) as true and loyal Americans. Of concern were the working conditions in industry and the fields. To be sure, LULAC was not alone in this campaign. Other groups expressed sympathy for workers. Also assisting in the labor rights struggle were Mexican consuls, Mexican American journalists, local *mutualista* (mutual aid) groups, and labor unions. But LULAC remained in the forefront of guaranteeing labor rights for Tejanos, artfully applying to its mission the wartime emphasis on justice and democracy. In its quest for dramatizing their struggle and achieving improvements for Tejanos, LULAC followed a multi-front course. It first coordinated its efforts with officials in Mexico. It then appealed to the general public for cooperation in the spirit of the Good Neighbor Policy (the US strategy for advancing healthy hemispheric relations with Latin America). Further, LULACers solicited federal assistance from the Fair Employment Practices Committee (FEPC), although for unexplained reasons, Hispanics tended not to register complaints with the organization in nearly the numbers of their African American counterparts. The FEPC had been established by President Franklin D. Roosevelt with Executive Order 8802 even before the 1941 attack on Pearl Harbor, and it held the responsibility of enforcing federal policies of nondiscrimination in defense plants, in government hiring practices, and in relations to labor unions. Among LULACers most active in this effort to have the FEPC dramatize workplace complaints in wartime industries were the aforementioned Gonzales, Castañeda, Perales, and Sánchez.[23]

Castañeda began serving as an FEPC field examiner in the summer of 1943. A professor of history at the University of Texas at that time, Castañeda seemed a good candidate for appointment to that FEPC office given his established recognition as an empathetic spokesperson for Mexican American causes. Stationed in Dallas, Castañeda successfully used his network of ties with fellow LULACers to get Mexican

American workers in Texas and other Southwest states to register their grievances with the agency. Like his contemporaries, Castañeda would persist after the war in his goal of achieving labor and civil rights for Tejanos. The government of Mexico and its consular offices in Texas were determined co-agents alongside Tejano activists to abolish racial discrimination and segregation. Mexico's activism on behalf of those Mexicans (*en el estranjero*, Mexicans living in the United States) was encouraged by its status as the United States' most trusted partner in Latin America to safeguard the continent from the Axis powers. Mexico's bold determination for Tejano rights rested, in part, in discerning if the United States was genuinely committed to enforcing the principles behind the Good Neighbor Policy.[24]

Mexico thus pressured the Texas government to confer constitutional rights upon Tejanos. Discrimination seemed so apparent (a conclusion drawn from reports by consuls, private citizens from Mexico touring the state, and grievances made by Mexican American citizens) that Mexican officials (in alliance with LULACers) pushed for a civil rights law. To achieve this, Mexican officials declared that not until Texas lifted its practice of public indiscretions would they allow the 1942 Bracero Program (the wartime arrangement by which laborers from Mexico could work seasonally in the United States) to be permitted in the state. Desperate for field laborers, farmers began lobbying to have discrimination against Mexican nationals outlawed, a concession from the state in the Caucasian Race Resolution (discussed below). Still, it would not be until 1947 that Mexico rescinded its embargo on laborers (*braceros*) to Texas. By then, the embargo was only on paper because the state's labor need enticed many Mexican citizens to cross into Texas illegally. Diplomatic force from Mexico and LULAC (in addition to pressure from cotton growers) had, in the meantime, moved the Texas legislature in June 1943 to ratify the aforementioned Caucasian Race Resolution. The edict outlawed discrimination against Mexican nationals in public places. Mexico made little of the enactment, however, recognizing it to be not much more than a meaningless ploy to acquire a supply of *braceros*. When LULAC tested the resolution, in fact, a Texas court declared it not to be a law but only a declaration and thus legally unenforceable. Mexico of course lamented the state's less-than-genuine efforts against discrimination.[25]

Then in August 1943, Governor Coke R. Stevenson established the Good Neighbor Commission (GNC). Governor Stevenson was more opposed to African Americans in his racial hierarchy and so was quite a bit more responsive to the complaints of Hispanics. "Meskins is pretty good folks," the governor answered to a state department official's request for the GNC. "If it was niggers, it'd be different." The governor charged the body with investigating problems of discrimination in the state, offering measures for solving them and prescribing proper enforcement procedures. While some LULACers such as Alonso Perales were optimistic, Mexican officials (as did several LULACers) suspected the GNC as another display (along with the Caucasian Race Resolution) of feigned Texas neighborliness and not an agency seriously committed to racial equality for Hispanics. For Mexico, the GNC's approach to race relations (which involved education programs instead of viable steps to outlaw discrimination) was too deliberate and diluted to seriously carry out the spirit of the Good Neighbor Policy. Reactionary conservative forces within the GNC, Mexican officials further detected, undermined the campaign. So discouraged were Mexican officials with the designs by white Texans to deal with race relations that it abandoned any hope of solving the discrimination problem in Texas after the war.[26]

The War's Effects

Some scholars have viewed World War II as an epic moment prompting Mexican Americans to agitate for equality. In truth, segments within Tejano society ante-dating the war regarded themselves as dutiful Americans deserving of protections under the US Constitution. But then, the government's call to arms confirmed for a great many Tejanos the conviction that Hispanics were bona fide American citizens. The war had particular impact on returning GIs expecting treatment equal to that of their fellow Americans. To the lament of many, however, Anglo Texans resisted Mexican American equality. Segregation remained, mistreatment of Tejanos by law enforcement persisted, and poll tax requirements curtailed Tejano voting clout.[27]

After the war, Tejanos confidently hastened their struggle for constitutional guarantees. Wartime leaders, among them Perales, Castañeda,

Sánchez, and Gonzales, remained in the fight, but many women of the war and postwar eras, heartened by the war message of egalitarianism, joined them. This postwar struggle for equal rights yielded results in the courtroom. In *Delgado v. Bastrop* (1948), LULAC convinced a district court to overturn the entrenched practice of segregating Mexican American students on school campuses. In *Hernández v. Texas* (1954), civil rights leaders convinced the Supreme Court to recognize Mexican Americans as a "class apart" and thus deserving of equal status with "white" Americans. Supportive in these (and other) cases was a postwar organization that adopted the name of the American GI Forum (AGIF). Organized by World War II veteran Dr. Héctor P. García of Corpus Christi, the Forum initially sought to expedite government medical benefits for returning Tejano veterans. Thrust into the limelight in 1949 by the Longoria episode in which the funeral home at Three Rivers, Texas (a community south of San Antonio), forbade a wake for the slain soldier Félix Longoria, the AGIF would go on to become a strong voice for Tejano rights for years to come.[28]

In its persistent campaign for labor rights in the postwar years, LULAC and other activists continued without the assistance of erstwhile wartime allies. The GNC hobbled along only as a painful reminder of lost opportunity. Mexico after the war no longer held a serious interest in the matter of civil rights for Mexican Americans. Furthermore, the FEPC ceased functioning when Congress defunded it in 1946. Nonetheless, LULAC, as well as the AGIF, targeted institutional barriers impeding improvement in Tejano working conditions, among them the Bracero Program, which Mexico opened to Texas farmers in 1947. Protecting the large agricultural force of Tejanos against competition from *braceros*, LULAC argued the immigrants had an adverse effect on the domestic labor force by lowering wages and exacerbating poverty for Tejano citizens, thus forcing them *pal norte* (to the Midwest). A cadre of women who answered the call to arms in the war similarly displayed a civic consciousness after 1945 and in the process challenged domesticity norms. As public servants working in municipal departments, other women used their employment position after the war to serve less privileged Tejanos. They offered health assistance where necessary, acted as intermediaries between the public and city bureaucrats, or coordinated work with police departments to curb delinquency. Still others, as employees of government agencies such as the Veterans Administration, helped returning veterans to readjust to society.[29]

The war not only pressed Tejanos to protest for equality, but induced them to embrace the cultural and ideological ethos of the nation. Being exposed to new ways of life domestically, residing in urban areas, and working in the defense industry and on overseas assignments and battlefields collectively accelerated their Americanization. Assimilation affected Tejanos, this argument contends, who more confidently identified with US mainstream values and norms. According to a counter school of thought, however, the war and attendant geographic and demographic change did not drastically change cultural ways. For one, many self-assured and loyal US citizens did not jettison the heritage they inherited from their parents. The majority of Tejanos continued living in semi-autonomous colonias that sustained "*lo mexicano*." Furthermore, throughout Texas, both in urban and rural communities, there existed a large cohort of first-generation immigrants with strong cultural ties to Mexico. Some citizens were sentimental, rejecting a US culture that abetted discrimination. Even as discrimination flourished during the war in the agricultural sector, in wartime plants, and in industrial yards, Mexican Americans progressed, although the historian Emilio Zamora observes that they did not see an uplifting equal to that of Anglos and African Americans. Still, their employment experiences in the war and the rural to urban shift augured newer prospects for upward mobility.[30]

Although wartime opportunities slowly dissipated, the developing postwar economy in the cities nonetheless generated slightly better wages than before. The boom in cotton production in the late 1940s offered pickers benefits against lingering deprivation. Increased economic opportunities affected Tejano society, delineating communities along class lines. A sampling from the Latinos and Latinas in the World War II Project of occupations held by World War II veterans shows this stratification. While some ex-GIs returned to "traditional" jobs such as truck drivers, construction workers, custodians, sheep shearers, and various general trades, others developed careers in management and carved out successes as business owners, engineers, accountants, educators, and white-collar professionals.[31]

The decade following the end of World War II was as transformative for Tejano communities as for the Lone Star State. Texas in the postwar era gravitated toward national Americanization, similar to other Southern states that adopted the ethos of the country at large. It diversified its economy, complementing farming and ranching with increased oil and gas production and integrating itself into the national orbit by accepting federal monies in the expanding military industrial complex. It transitioned politically also. Fresh liberal voices surfaced (Lyndon B. Johnson, Ralph Yarborough, and Henry B. González) as the old segregationist structure crumbled before the relentless forces for racial equality. The state modernized and left behind the old parochialism. Information on the latest national and international developments came into homes via radio and television, as did reports on the latest fashion trends, fads, and music styles. World War II urbanizing movements continued, accompanied by an explosive building of new banks, department stores, fast-food chains, hospitals, legal offices, and theaters that together brought a cosmopolitan quality to the cityscape. Texans partnered in the prosperity of midcentury America, and the boom nurtured a class of middling status (left behind, of course, were thousands seeking escape from a vast pool of semi-skilled and unskilled laborers). Certainly, the new age augured better possibilities for many, but old ways died hard in Texas, and so ethnic organizations and Tejanos with new approaches and experiences gained from living in the postwar milieu would carry on the civil rights struggles—and comply with obligations to the nation's defense.[32]

Notes

1. Arnoldo De León is the Distinguished Professor of History Emeritus at Angelo State University in San Angelo, Texas. A noted student of Tejano history, De León has published many books and articles concerning Hispanic Texas.

2. Relevant works on Tejanos and World War II include Maggie Rivas-Rodríguez et al., *A Legacy Greater Than Words: Stories of US Latinos & Latinas of the WWII Generation* (Austin: US Latino & Latina WWII Oral History Project, 2006); Maggie Rivas-Rodríguez, ed., *Mexican Americans in World War II* (Austin: University of Texas Press, 2005); Maggie Rivas-Rodríguez and Emilio Zamora, eds., *Beyond the Latino World War II Hero: The Social and Political Legacy of a Generation* (Austin: University of Texas Press, 2009); Maggie Rivas-Rodríguez and B. V. Olguín, eds., *Latina/os and World War II: Mobility, Agency, and Ideology* (Austin: University of Texas Press, 2014); Emilio Zamora, *Claiming Rights and Righting*

Wrongs in Texas: Mexican Workers and Job Politics during World War II (College Station: Texas A&M University Press, 2009); Richard Griswold del Castillo, ed., *World War II and Mexican American Civil Rights* (Austin: University of Texas Press, 2008); Thomas A. Guglielmo, "Fighting for Caucasian Rights: Mexicans, Mexican Americans, and the Transnational Struggle for Civil Rights in World War II Texas," *Journal of American History* 92 (March 2006); Arnoldo De León, "Wartime USA: West Texas Tejanos in World War II and Korea," in *Tejano West Texas* (College Station: Texas A&M University Press, 2015); Raúl Morín, *Among the Valiant: Mexican-Americans in WW II and Korea* (Alhambra, CA: Borden Publishing Company, 1966); William L. Adams, *Valley Vets: An Oral History of World War II Veterans of the Lower Rio Grande Valley* (Austin: Eakin Press, 1999); Dave Gutiérrez, *Patriots from the Barrio: The True WWII Story of the Men Who Served in the US Army's All Mexican American Combat Unit, the 36th Division 141st Regiment, 2nd Battalion, Company E* (Bloomington, IN: XLIBRIS, 2014); and Alex Mendoza, "'I Know of No Other Country': Tejanos and the American Wars of the Twentieth Century," *Military History of the West* 41 (2011).

3. Zaragosa Vargas, *Labor Rights Are Civil Rights: Mexican American Workers in 20th Century America* (Princeton, NJ: Princeton University Press, 2005), 210; Emilio Zamora, "Mexican Nationals in US Military: Diplomacy and Battlefield Sacrifice," in *Beyond the Latino World War II Hero*, eds., Rivas-Rodríguez and Zamora, 90, 91, 94, 96, 98–99. Alex Mendoza in "'I Know No Other Country,'" 38, offers an estimate of 100,000 Tejanos who saw duty. Providing approximations for all US Hispanic personnel who served are Karl Eschback and Maggie Rivas-Rodríguez, "Navigating Bureaucratic Imprecision in the Search for an Accurate Count of Latino/a Military Service in World War II," in *Latina/os and World War II*, eds. Rivas-Rodríguez and Olguín, xvi; and Neil Foley, *Mexicans in the Making of America* (Cambridge, MA: The Belknap Press of Harvard University Press, 2014), 97, 102–103.

4. Griswold del Castillo, ed., *World War II and Mexican American Civil Rights*, 50–51; Mendoza, "'I Know No Other Country,'" 39, 41; Vargas, *Labor Rights Are Civil Rights*, 203, 208; De León, "Wartime USA," 128; Rivas-Rodríguez et al., *A Legacy Greater Than Words*, Chapter 5.

5. Luis Alvarez, "Transnational Latino Soldiering: Military Service and Ethnic Politics during World War II," in *Latina/os and World War II: Mobility, Agency, and Ideology*, eds. Rivas-Rodríguez and Olguín, 78–80; Morín, *Among the Valiant*, 29, 88. The training camp experience of Tejanos during World War I is covered in José A. Ramírez, *To the Line of Fire: Mexican Texans and World War I* (College Station: Texas A&M University Press, 2009), Chapter 5.

6. Morín, *Among the Valiant*, 27. Conclusions regarding local origins of these individuals are drawn from a sampling of interviews contained in Rivas-Rodríguez et al., *A Legacy Greater Than Words*; De León, "Wartime USA," 128, 135–38; and Adams, *Valley Vets*.

7. Morín, *Among the Valiant*, 28–33; Craig A. Kaplowitz, *LULAC: Mexican Americans and National Policy* (College Station: Texas A&M University Press,

2005), 39; Zamora, "Mexican Nationals in US Military," 98, 104. For more details concerning LULAC, see Cynthia E. Orozco, "Regionalism, Politics, and Gender in Southwest History: The League of United Latin American Citizens' Expansion into New Mexico from Texas 1929–1945," *Western Historical Quarterly* 29 (Winter 1998); Benjamin Márquez, "The Politics of Race and Assimilation: The League of United Latin American Citizens, 1929–1940," *Western Political Quarterly* 43 (1989); Benjamin Márquez, *LULAC: The Evolution of a Mexican American Political Organization* (Austin: University of Texas Press, 1993); Mario T. Garcia, *Mexican Americans: Leadership, Ideology, and Identity, 1930–1960* (New Haven, CT: Yale University Press, 1989); and Edward D. Garza, "LULAC: League of United Latin American Citizens" (master's thesis, Southwest Texas State Teachers College, 1951).

8. Morín, *Among the Valiant*, 27–33; De León, "Wartime USA," 130–131. For an expansion of the reaction to pachucos, see Elizabeth R. Escobedo, "The Pachuca Panic: Sexual and Cultural Battleground in World War II," *Western Historical Quarterly* 38 (Summer 2007); and Catherine S. Ramírez, *The Woman in the Zoot Suit: Gender, Nationalism, and the Cultural Politics of Memory* (Durham, NC: Duke University Press, 2009).

9. Morín, *Among the Valiant*, 84. For other works highlighting the military exploits of Hispanics, see Marc Wilson, *Hero Street, USA: The Story of Little Mexico's Fallen Soldiers* (Norman: University of Oklahoma Press, 2009); and Carlos Harrison, *The Ghosts of Hero Street: How One Small Mexican-American Community Gave So Much in World War II and Korea* (New York: Berkeley Publishing Group, 2014). For a more detailed discussion of what Tejanos in the 36th Infantry Division in World War II experienced during the war and the controversial Rapido River crossing, see Robert L. Wagner, "Rapido River Controversy: A Review," *East Texas Historical Journal* 28 (1990); Robert L. Wagner, *The Texas Army: A History of the 36th Division in the Italian Campaign* (Buffalo Gap, TX: State House Press, 1991); Martin Blumenson, *Bloody River: The Real Tragedy of the Rapido* (Boston: Houghton Mifflin, 1970); Mark W. Clark, *Calculated Risk* (New York: Harpers and Brothers, 1950); Rick Atkinson, *The Day of Battle: The War in Sicily and Italy, 1943–1944* (New York: Henry Holt and Company, 2007); Jon Mikolashek, *General Mark Clark: Commander of US Fifth Army and Liberator of Rome* (Philadelphia: Casemate, 2013); Martin Blumenson, *Mark Clark: The Last of the Great World War II Commanders* (New York: St. Martin's Press, 1984); Duane Schultz, *Crossing the Rapido: A Tragedy of World War II* (Yardley, PA: Westholme Publishing, 2010); Lee Carraway Smith, *A River Swift and Deadly: The 36th "Texas" Infantry Division at the Rapido River* (Austin: Eakin Press, 1989); Richard Huff, ed., *A Pictorial History of the 36th "Texas" Infantry Division* (Austin: Battery Press, 1979); Samuel S. Ortega and Arnulfo Hernández Jr., *The Men of Company E: Toughest Chicano Soldiers of World War II, Company E of El Paso, Texas, 2nd Battalion, 141st Infantry Regiment, 36th Infantry Division* (n.c: CreateSpace Independent Publishing Platform, 2015); Bruce L. Brager, *The Texas 36th Division: A History* (Austin: Eakin Press, 2000); and Gutiérrez, *Patriots from the Barrio*. Among several other war medals,

Gonzales earned the Distinguished Service Cross and Gutiérrez the Silver Star.

10. Rivas-Rodríguez et. al., *A Legacy Greater than Words*, 11, 13, 16, 25–27.

11. Rivas-Rodríguez et. al., *A Legacy Greater than Words*, 19, 38.

12. Rivas-Rodríguez et. al., *A Legacy Greater than Words*, 99–100.

13. "Private First Class Rodolfo Mireles, 38460504, US Army, January 22, 1925 Killed in Action April 10, 1945 Okinawa, Japan," SCRIBD.com, accessed June 13, 2021, http://www.scribd.com/doc/261653088. This discussion on Tejano fighting men draws from information culled from Morín, *Among the Valiant*, 59, 61–74, 94–98, 202, 206, 237–38, and Chapter 10; Rivas-Rodríguez et al., *A Legacy Greater than Words*; Gutiérrez, *Patriots from the Barrio*; Adams, *Valley Vets*; De León, "Wartime USA," 138; and US Government, *Hispanics in America's Defense* (Washington, DC: Neale Publishing, 1989), 29–30.

14. Joanne Rao Sánchez, "The Latinas of World War II: From Familial Shelter to Expanding Horizons," in *Beyond the Latino World War II Hero*, eds. Rivas-Rodríguez and Zamora, 65, 74–86; Teresa Palomo Acosta and Ruthe Winegarten, *Las Tejanas: 300 Years of History* (Austin: University of Texas Press, 2003), 180–82; De León, "Wartime USA," 132; Zamora, *Claiming Rights and Righting Wrongs in Texas*, 58; and Rivas-Rodríguez et al., *A Legacy Greater Than Words*, 184–86, 189. More on the experience of Hispanic women and Tejanas in World War II are Vicki L. Ruiz, *From Out of the Shadows: Mexican Women in Twentieth-Century America* (New York: Oxford University Press, 2008); and Christine Marín, "Mexican Americans on the Home Front: Community Organizations in Arizona during World War II," *Perspectives in Mexican American Studies* 4 (1993).

15. Rivas-Rodríguez et al., *A Legacy Greater than Words*, 184, 213, 215–16.

16. Rivas-Rodríguez et al., *A Legacy Greater than Words*, 223, and Chapter 7: "Everyday Lives of Latinos and Latinas during World War II"; Sánchez, "The Latinas of WWII," 63; Zaragosa Vargas, *Crucible of Struggle: A History of Mexican Americans from Colonial Times to the Present Era* (New York: Oxford University Press, 2011), 262; Peter C. Haney, "*Capitán, ¿a que huele la sangre?*: Mexicana/o Vaudeville and Militarized Citizenship during World War II," in *Latina/os and World War II*, eds. Rivas-Rodríguez and Olguín, 143, 145.

17. Griswold del Castillo, ed., *World War II and Mexican American Civil Rights*, 9–15; Arnoldo De León, *Mexican Americans in Texas: A Brief History*, 3rd ed. (Wheeling, IL: Harlan Davidson, 2009), 106–7.

18. Vargas, *Labor Rights Are Civil Rights*, 207, 209–10; Zamora, *Claiming Rights and Righting Wrongs in Texas*, 35, 101–11; Griswold del Castillo, ed., *World War II and Mexican American Civil Rights*, 11; Dionisio Valdes, "The Mexican American Dream and World War II: A View from the Midwest," in *Mexican Americans & World War II*, ed. Rivas-Rodríguez, 123; Vargas, *Crucible of Struggle*, 246. Studies that further discuss the discrimination in politics and the Tejano response are Cynthia E. Orozco, *No Mexicans, Women, or Dogs Allowed: The Rise of the Mexican American Civil Rights Movement* (Austin: University of Texas Press, 2009); and David Montejano, *Anglos and Mexicans in the Making of Texas, 1836–1986* (Austin:

University of Texas Press, 1987). Comparisons with the experiences of Hispanic farmhands during the war in other states can be found in Matt García, *A World of Its Own: Race, Color, and Citrus in the Making of Greater Los Angeles, 1900–1970* (Chapel Hill: University of North Carolina Press, 2001).

19. Montejano, *Anglos and Mexicans*, 264, 272–73, 297–98; Foley, *Mexicans in the Making of America*, 83; Richard A. García, *Rise of the Mexican American Middle Class: San Antonio, 1920–1941* (College Station: Texas A&M University Press, 1991), 302; Zamora, *Claiming Rights and Righting Wrongs in Texas*, 29, 54–55, 158–59, 179, 182–83; Vargas, *Labor Rights are Civil Rights*, 203–04, 207, 211; Rivas-Rodríguez et al., *A Legacy Greater than Words*, xxvii–viii. For similar experiences and challenges for Hispanics outside of Texas in the urban areas during the war, see Edward J. Escobar, *Race, Police, and the Making of a Political Identity: Mexican Americans and the Los Angeles Police Department, 1900–1945* (Berkeley: University of California Press, 1999); Albert Camarillo, "Navigating Segregated Life in America's Racial Borderlands, 1910s–1950s," *Journal of American History* 100 (December 2013); Jamie L. Bronstein, *Two Nations, Indivisible: A History of Inequality in America* (Santa Barbara, CA: Praeger, 2016); Bradford Luckingham, *Minorities in Phoenix: A Profile of Mexican American, Chinese American, and African American Communities, 1860–1992* (Tucson: University of Arizona Press, 1994); Luis Alvarez, *The Power of the Zoot: Youth Culture and Resistance during World War II* (Berkeley: University of California Press, 2008); Mauricio Mazón, *The Zoot-Suit Riots: The Psychology of Symbolic Annihilation* (Austin: University of Texas Press, 1984); Mark A. Weitz, *The Sleepy Lagoon Murder Case: Race Discrimination and Mexican-American Rights* (Lawrence: University of Kansas Press, 2010); Solomon James Jones, "The Government Riots of Los Angeles 1943" (master's thesis, University of California, Los Angeles, 1969); and Eduardo Obregón Pagán, *Murder at the Sleepy Lagoon: Zoot Suits, Race, and Riot in Wartime Los Angeles* (Chapel Hill: University of North Carolina Press, 2003).

20. Guglielmo, "Fighting for Caucasian Rights," 1216–18; Zamora, *Claiming Rights and Righting Wrongs in Texas*, 17, 68–73, 119, 211; Carlos Kevin Blanton, *George I. Sánchez: The Long Fight for Mexican American Integration* (New Haven, CT: Yale University Press, 2014), 79, 87–90; Benjamin Márquez, "In Defense of My People: Alonso S. Perales and the Moral Construction of Citizenship," in *In Defense of My People: Alonso S. Perales and the Development of Mexican-American Public Intellectuals*, ed. Michael A. Olivas (Houston: Arte Público Press, 2012), 39–40.

21. Guglielmo, "Fighting for Caucasian Rights," 1213–14, 1234–37; Zamora, *Claiming Rights and Righting Wrongs in Texas*, 9–11, 96, 215–16; Neil Foley, "Becoming Hispanic: Mexican Americans and the Faustina Pact with Whiteness," in *Reflexionies 1997: New Directions in Mexican American Studies*, ed. Neil Foley (Austin: CMAS Books, University of Texas Press, 1998), 53–70; Nancy Foner and George M. Frederickson, eds. *Not Just Black and White: Historical and Contemporary Perspectives on Immigration, Race, and Ethnicity in the United States* (New

York: Russell Sage Foundation, 2004); George A. Martínez, "The Legal Construction of Race: Mexican-Americans and Whiteness," *Harvard Latino Law Review* 2 (Fall 1997); Blanton, *George I.* Sánchez, 92, 183; Michael Phillips, "Why Is Big Tex Still a White Cowboy?" in *Beyond Texas through Time: Breaking Away from Past Interpretation*, eds. Walter Buenger and Arnoldo De León (College Station: Texas A&M University Press, 2011), 132–37; and *ibid.*; Blanton, "Deconstructing Texas," 191–92. For further illumination of the struggle for Hispanics to be designated as not white, and with a separate, legal identity, see Anthony Quiroz, *Claiming Citizenship: Mexican Americans in Victoria, Texas* (College Station: Texas A&M University Press, 2005); Patrick D. Lukens, *A Quiet Victory for Latino Rights: FDR and the Controversy over "Whiteness"* (Tucson: University of Arizona Press, 2012); and Guadalupe San Miguel Jr., *Brown, not White: School Integration and the Chicano Movement in Houston* (Houston, TX: Center for Mexican American Studies, University of Houston Press, 2001).

22. Zamora, *Claiming Rights and Righting Wrongs in Texas*, 8, 80–81, 98–99, 101, 117; Guadalupe San Miguel Jr., *"Let All of Them Take Heed": Mexican Americans and the Campaign for Educational Equality in Texas, 1910–1981* (Austin: University of Texas Press, 1987), 95–99; Guglielmo, "Fighting for Caucasian Rights," 1221–22, 1226–29.

23. Zamora, *Claiming Rights and Righting Wrongs in Texas*, 2, 18, 98, 119–20, 122–23, 125–27, 181, 185, 205, 211–12. For the differences in complaints by African Americans and Hispanics, see Elizabeth R. Escobedo, *From Coveralls to Zoot Suits: The Lives of Mexican American Women on the World War II Home Front* (Chapel Hill: University of North Carolina Press, 2013). A comprehensive and generally favorable assessment of the Committee is Merl Elwyn Reed, *Seedtime for the Modern Civil Rights Movement: The President's Committee on Fair Employment Practice, 1941–1946* (Baton Rouge: Louisiana State University Press, 1991). Other works on the Committee include Herbert Garfinkel, *When Negroes March: The March on Washington Movement in the Organizational Policies for FEPC* (Glencoe, IL: Free Press, 1959); Andrew E. Kersten, *Race, Jobs, and the War: The FEPC in the Midwest, 1941–1946* (Urbana: University of Illinois Press, 2007); Louis C. Kesselman, *The Social Politics of FEPC: A Study in Reform Pressure Movements* (Chapel Hill: University of North Carolina Press, 1948); Clete Daniel, *Chicano Workers and the Politics of Fairness: The FEPC in the Southwest, 1941–1945* (Austin: University of Texas Press, 1991); William J. Collins, "Race, Roosevelt, and Wartime Production: Fair Employment in World War II Labor Markets," *American Economic Review* 91 (March 2001); and Louis Ruchames, *Race, Jobs, and Politics: The Story of FEPC* (Westport, CT: Negro Universities Press, 1953). Local studies concerning the FEPC in Texas include Ernest Obadele-Starks, *Black Unionism in the Industrial South* (College Station: Texas A&M University Press, 2000); Michael R. Botson Jr., *Labor, Civil Rights, and the Hughes Tool Company* (College Station: Texas A&M University Press, 2005); Emilio Zamora, "The Failed Promise of Wartime Opportunity for Mexicans in the Texas Oil Industry," *Southwestern Historical Quarterly*

95 (January 1992); Charles D. Thompson Jr. and Melinda F. Wiggins, eds., *The Human Cost of Food: Farmworkers' Lives, Labor, and Advocacy* (Austin: University of Texas Press, 2002); and Joseph Abel, "African Americans, Labor Unions, and the Struggle for Fair Employment in the Aircraft Manufacturing Industry of Texas, 1941–1945," *Journal of Southern History* 77 (August 2011). Local studies of the FEPC in similar Southern contexts include Alex Lichtenstein, "Exclusion, Fair Employment, or Interracial Unionism: Race Relations in Florida's Shipyards during World War II," in *Labor in the Modern South*, ed. Glen T. Eskew (Athens: University of Georgia Press, 2011); and Bruce Nelson, "Organized Labor and the Struggle for Black Equality in Mobile during World War II," *Journal of American History* 80 (December 1993). Those interested in examining the limits of reform during the war can see Alan Brinkley, *The End of Reform: New Deal Liberalism in Recession and War* (New York: Vintage Books, 1995); and Wendy L. Wall, *Inventing the "American Way": The Politics of Consensus from the New Deal to the Civil Rights Movement* (New York: Oxford University Press, 2008).

24. Zamora, *Claiming Rights and Righting Wrongs in Texas*, 2, 15, 66, 89, 134, 162–63, 216–18; Marianne M. Bueno, "'Intellectually He Was Courageous; in Public Action He Was Cautious and Prudent': A Reassessment of Carlos E. Castañeda's Wartime Service," in *Latinas/os and World War II*, eds. Rivas-Rodríguez and Olguín, 95–112; Félix D. Almaráz, *Knight without Armor: Carlos Eduardo Castañeda, 1896–1958* (College Station: Texas A&M University Press, 1999), 216–65. Almaráz further covers Castañeda's life in "Carlos Eduardo Castañeda, Mexican-American Historian: The Formative Years, 1896–1927," *Pacific Historical Review* 42 (August 1973): 319–34; and Felix D. Almaráz Jr., "The Making of a Boltonian: Carlos E. Castañeda of Texas—The Early Years," *Red River Valley Historical Review* 1 (Winter 1974): 329–50. For the relationship and cooperation between the US and Mexico, see Guglielmo, "Fighting for Caucasian Rights"; and Foley, *Mexicans in the Making of America.*

25. Zamora, *Claiming Rights and Righting Wrongs in Texas*, 16, 68–73, 80–82, 88–89, 101, 111–12; Foley, *Mexicans in the Making of America*, 75–84, 87–89; San Miguel, "*Let All of Them Take Heed*," 93. For more on the Caucasian Race Resolution, see Matt S. Meier and Feliciano Ribera, *Mexican Americans, American Mexicans: From Conquistadors to Chicanos* (New York: Hill and Wang, 1993). Some insight into the Bracero program can be found in Ana Elizabeth Rosas, "Breaking the Silence: Mexican Children and Women's Confrontation of *Bracero* Family Separation, 1942–1964," *Gender and History* 23 (August 2011); John Weber, *From the South Texas to the Nation: The Exploitation of Mexican Labor in the Twentieth Century* (Chapel Hill: North Carolina University Press, 2015); Barbara Driscoll De Alvarado, *The Tracks North: The Railroad Bracero Program of World War II* (Austin: Center for Mexican American Studies and the University of Texas Press, 1999); Don Mitchell, *They Saved the Crops: Labor, Landscape, and the Struggle Over Industrial Farming in Bracero-Era California* (Athens: University of Georgia Press, 2012); Ronald Takaki, *Double Victory: A Multicultural History of America in World War II* (New York: Back Bay Books, 2000); Erasmo Gamboa and Kevin Leonard,

Mexican Labor and World War II: Braceros in the Pacific Northwest, 1942–1947 (Seattle: University of Washington Press, 2000); Michael Snodgrass, "The Bracero Program, 1942–1964," in *Beyond the Border: The History of Mexican-US Migration*, ed. Mark Overmyer-Velásquez (New York: Oxford University Press, 2011); Otey M. Scruggs, "Texas and the Bracero Program, 1942–1947," *Pacific Historical Review* 32 (August 1963); Richard B. Craig, *The Bracero Program: Interest Groups and Foreign Policy* (Austin: University of Texas Press, 1971); HannaLore Hein, "The Mexican Invasion . . . by Invitation Only: A Critical Look at the Legacy and Consequences of the Bracero Program, 1942–1964" (undergraduate honors thesis, University of Colorado, 2011); and Ana Elizabeth Rosas, *Abrazando el Espíritu: Bracero Families Confront the US-Mexico Border* (Oakland: University of California Press, 2014). For additional work on the cooperation between the United States and Latin American countries during the war years, see John Granato II, "Dennis Chavez and the Inter-American Ideal, 1936–1962" (master's thesis, University of New Mexico, 2012); and Roy Luján, "Dennis Chavez and the National Agenda: 1933–1946," *New Mexico Historical Review* 74 (January 1999).

26. George N. Green, *The Establishment in Texas Politics: The Primitive Years, 1938–1957* (Westport, CT: Greenwood Press, 1979), 81; San Miguel, "*Let All of Them Take Heed*," 93–94; Zamora, *Claiming Rights and Righting Wrongs in Texas*, 81, 84, 94, 118–19; Márquez, "In Defense of My People," 40–41. For more detailed studies of the Good Neighbor Commission and the Good Neighbor Policy as a whole, see George N. Green, "The Good Neighbor Commission and Texas Mexicans," in *Ethnic Minorities in Gulf Coast Society*, eds. Jerrell Shofner and Linda Ellsworth (Pensacola, FL: Gulf Coast History Conference, 1979); Pauline Rochester Kibbe, *Latin Americans in Texas* (Albuquerque: University of New Mexico Press, 1946); Harold E. Davies, "Practicing the Good-Neighbor Policy," *Journal of Higher Education* 17 (1946); Nellie Kingrea, *History of the First Ten Years of the Texas Good Neighbor Commission* (Fort Worth: Texas Christian University Press, 1954); Robert Dallek, *Franklin D. Roosevelt and American Foreign Policy, 1932–1945* (New York: Oxford University Press, 1995); Mary E. Stuckey, *The Good Neighbor: Franklin D. Roosevelt and the Rhetoric of American Power* (East Lansing: Michigan State University Press, 2013); Irwin F. Gellman, *Good Neighbor Diplomacy: United States Policies in Latin America, 1933–1945* (Baltimore: Johns Hopkins University Press, 1979); Bryce Wood, *The Making of the Good Neighbor Policy* (New York: Columbia University Press, 1961); Fredrick B. Pike, *FDR's Good Neighbor Policy: Sixty Years of Generally Gentle Chaos* (Austin: University of Texas Press, 1995); and George Little, "A Study of the Texas Good Neighbor Commission" (master's thesis, University of Houston, 1953). The best works on Coke R. Stevenson are Booth Mooney, *Mister Texas: The Story of Coke Stevenson* (Dallas: Texas Printing House, 1947), and Green, *The Establishment in Texas Politics*.

27. Manuel Peña, *The Texas-Mexican Conjunto: History of a Working Class Music* (Austin: University of Texas Press, 1985), 5, 116; Griswold del Castillo, ed., *World War II and Mexican American Civil Rights*, 1, 4; Rivas-Rodríguez et al., *A Legacy Greater than Words*, xxviii, 257; De León, *Mexican Americans in Texas*, 126.

28. Kaplowitz, *LULAC*, 39; De León, *Mexican Americans in Texas*, 128; San Miguel, "*Let All of Them Take Heed*," 123–26; Carl Allsup, *The American G.I. Forum: Origins and Evolution* (Austin: Center for Mexican American Studies and the University of Texas Press, 1982), 33–35, 73–77, 84–85; Patrick J. Carroll, *Felix Longoria's Wake: Bereavement, Racism, and the Rise of Mexican American Activism* (Austin: University of Texas Press, 2003), 173–75. Further works on the American GI Forum in the postwar years is Henry A. J. Ramos, *The American G.I. Forum: In Pursuit of the Dream, 1948–1983* (Houston: Arte Publico Press, 1998); and Steven Rosales, "Fighting the Peace at Home: Mexican American Veterans and the 1944 GI Bill of Rights," *Pacific Historical Review* 80 (November 2011).

29. Zamora, *Claiming Rights and Righting Wrongs in Texas*, 94–95, 118; Ignacio García, *Hector P. García: In Relentless Pursuit of Justice* (Houston: Arte Público Press, 2002), 157–62; Rivas-Rodríguez et al., *A Legacy Greater than Words*, 229, 262, 268–69, 283, 290, 307; De León, *Mexican Americans in Texas*, 128.

30. Zamora, *Claiming Rights and Righting Wrongs in Texas*, 1, 205–6. For arguments on assimilation, see Peña, *The Texas Mexican Conjunto*, 116–18; García, *Rise of the Mexican American Middle Class*, 303. For arguments that it did not have such an impact on Tejano cultural identity, see David Gutiérrez, *Walls and Mirrors: Mexican Americans, Mexican Immigrants, and the Politics of Ethnicity* (Berkeley: University of California Press, 1995), 146–47.

31. Peña, *The Texas Mexican Conjunto*, 5, 116–17. For the myriad of jobs that Tejano GIs returned to following their service, see Rivas-Rodríguez et al., *A Legacy Greater than Words*.

32. For a few works examining the actions of Hispanics in the postwar era, especially their struggle against segregation, marginalization, and poverty, see Lilia Hernández, *Brown in the Windy City: Mexicans and Puerto Ricans in Postwar Chicago* (Chicago: University of Chicago Press, 2012); Felipe Hinojosa, "*¡Medicina Sí Muerte No!*: Race, Public Health, and the Long War on Poverty in Mathis, Texas, 1948–1971," *Western Historical Quarterly* 44 (Winter 2013); Benjamin Márquez, *Democratizing Texas Politics: Race, Identity, and Mexican American Empowerment, 1945–2002* (Austin: University of Texas Press, 2014); Leslie V. Tischauser, *The Changing Nature of Racial and Ethnic Conflict in United States History: 1492 to the Present* (Lanham, MD: University Press of America, 2002); Brian D. Behnken, *Fighting Their Own Battles: Mexican Americans, African Americans, and Their Struggle for Civil Rights in Texas* (Chapel Hill: University of North Carolina Press, 2011); and Marc Simon Rodríguez, *The Tejano Diaspora: Mexican Americanism and Ethnic Politics in Texas and Wisconsin* (Chapel Hill: University of North Carolina Press, 2011).

5

Opportunity and Organized Labor in Wartime Texas, 1939–45

Zachary Montz [1]

In the opening days of the Second World War, President Franklin D. Roosevelt made clear to the world his plan for American victory. The United States, he announced, would defeat the Axis powers not just by military ability, but also with "crushing superiority of equipment." Roosevelt's desire to fight and win a fully mechanized war would require a total mobilization of American industry and labor. To build and fuel this unprecedented war machine, Washington had to look beyond the industrial Northeast. Texas, with ample resources, an established petroleum industry, and advantageous location against enemy attack, attracted the attention of industrial planners. The federal government poured more than seven billion dollars into the state in the first years of the war to build aircraft plants in Dallas and Fort Worth; shipyards in Orange, Beaumont, Houston, and Galveston; and steel mills in Houston and East Texas. Of the top forty metropolitan areas receiving the largest shares of defense supply contracts, only three were in the South. Those three were actually all in Texas: Houston, Fort Worth, and Beaumont. The state, in fact, led the region in aircraft production and shipbuilding, which accounted for approximately two-thirds of the region's defense contracts. Refineries all along the Gulf Coast were expanded to meet the army's near-insatiable need for gasoline, distilling units were added to produce 100-octane aircraft fuel and precursor chemicals, and new technologically advanced synthetic rubber plants were quickly erected.[2]

The war was a boon to Texas industry, which grew more from 1941 to 1945 than in any other period in its history. This growth spurred major changes in the state's workforce, as men and women rallied to meet Roosevelt's ambitious production goals. At its peak, the Todd Shipyards on the Houston Ship Channel employed 40,000 men and women building cargo vessels, while 20,000 employees at the nearby Brown Shipbuilding Company built destroyer escorts and Liberty ships. The sprawling North American Aviation plant in Grand Prairie (between Dallas and Fort Worth) had more than 39,000 Texans assembling warplanes at its production peak in 1944. And refinery workforces more than doubled, with the state's largest facility, the Humble refinery at Baytown, counting almost 9,000 employees in the last year of the war. For Texans on the home front, war work represented both a patriotic duty and an opportunity to leave behind a decade of economic depression. The lure of well-paying employment in war plants was especially strong for rural Texans, whose exodus from farms and small towns into industrial cities caused some rural counties to lose more than 30 percent of their population from 1940 to 1943. Women, too, entered a new world during the war, as they responded to a steady stream of radio spots and newspaper advertisements urging them to take up rivet guns and welding torches.[3]

The fight against fascism was carried out in defense of freedom and democracy. In war work, Americans would find what Roosevelt called "freedom from want," a liberation from poverty's political and social instability. Wartime Americans also pursued freedom and democracy by joining labor unions. With the promise of increased agency for workers, unions grew significantly during the war. This was no less true in Texas, where the new economic and institutional landscape of the war years helped the state's struggling labor movement rise to prominence. Labor unions in Texas' largest industries built support among new workers, women, and minorities during the war to become a lasting part of the state's postwar economy. In the process, the war also spurred African Americans and Tejanos to challenge the Jim Crow system that governed work and opportunity in the state. Minority workers' fight against economic discrimination and the growth of labor unions during the war were related developments. Many unions in Texas, as in the broader United States, were restricted to whites. But the unions that grew the most in wartime Texas (and that are the subject of this essay) were organized on an interracial basis. During the war, these unions looked to minority workers for support. Those same minorities looked to labor to assist in combating discrimination, thus making them among the most committed unionists. But labor's legacy of fairly representing the interests of minority members was, at best, mixed. Unionization brought real material gains to minority workers, but labor was just as likely to be an impediment to equality as it was to be an aid. In 1942, a federal official considering discrimination faced by black Texas oil workers opined that, in this war against "Hitler and his Master Race," safeguarding equal rights in employment was a "test of our sincerity in the cause for which we are fighting" and central to "the promise of American democracy regardless of color." If this was the case, Texas labor largely failed.[4]

Texas Labor before the War

The swell of industrial employment during the war produced significant growth in the state's labor unions. Industrialists had long touted the open shop in Texas as guaranteeing "freedom from serious friction in the labor world." In the 1920s and the first half of the Depression, Texas employers enjoyed a free hand with their workers. Most low-wage laborers, a group that disproportionately included minorities and women, lacked effective union representation. Workers for some of the state's largest industrial employers belonged to "independent" unions unaffiliated with any national labor body. These were dubbed "company unions" by critics for their close connection to management and general deference to corporate prerogative. While there was a good deal of truth to business boosters' depiction of an open-shop Texas, the state was hardly a union desert. In the late 1930s, the railroad brotherhoods counted more than 15,000 members, while more than 200,000 Texans belonged to craft unions affiliated with the American Federation of Labor (AFL), representing workers in the building trades, in skilled crafts like welding and boilermaking, and other professions as varied as baking and barbering.[5]

However, it was the new unions in large industry that challenged Texas employers in the 1930s. Largely squashed in the 1920s, unionist sentiment revitalized in the early 1930s when frustrated and anxious oil workers revived the moribund oil workers union. These efforts were assisted by federal legislation. Passed in 1935, the National Labor Relations Act, more commonly known as the Wagner Act, was the most pro-union bill in American history. Among other things, the act permitted collective bargaining, a practice where unions negotiate as a whole with their employer instead of individually, thus greatly strengthening their bargaining power. Central to its mission was the creation of the National Labor Relations Board (NLRB). The law charged this five-man organization with ensuring employees' right to organize and protecting against unfair labor practices by employers, including interfering with the creation of a union. By 1936, therefore, oil workers had established growing union locals at most of the major oil refineries and could point to a new union contract with the Sinclair refinery in Houston as a sign of its success. That year, the Oil Workers International Union (OWIU) dropped its affiliation with the craft-focused AFL and joined the Congress of Industrial Organizations (CIO), a newly formed body of labor unions that were dedicated to organizing entire industries, rather than only workers who performed certain jobs or crafts. The most prominent of these "industrial unions" in the late 1930s in Texas were the OWIU and the United Steelworkers of America (USWA). They formed the heart of the Texas State Industrial Union Council, the state's coordinating body of industrial unions. Although the OWIU and the USWA both had their origins in earlier organizations representing white, skilled, and relatively well-paid men, the two unions embraced the CIO's commitment to bridging the traditional racial and craft divisions of industrial workforces. That philosophy was reflected in the early efforts of the Texas CIO in the late 1930s to organize industries as varied as smelters and packinghouses, pecan shelling plants and cotton mills, railroad tie lumberyards, and docks and ships, regardless of race or sex.[6]

Their organizing campaigns produced mixed results. In a major triumph, OWIU Local 367 gained union recognition at the giant Shell refinery in Pasadena (south of Houston) by winning a representation election supervised by the NLRB. However, compared to successes in the North (where CIO unions organized key industries like rubber, steel, and automobile manufacturing), labor's victories in Texas were scarce. Such efforts met fierce resistance from industrialists committed to the "open shop" system in which companies would negotiate the terms of employment with individual employees, company unions, or with small unions representing groups of workers, but never with a single powerful union claiming the right to bargain exclusively on behalf of all workers. The determination to thwart unions was at times astounding in its scope. When OWIU Local 333 planned a strike to force Humble Oil to recognize its union, managers at the company's Baytown refinery assembled an armed private force to bring in replacement workers, going so far as to construct an airstrip on the plant's sprawling grounds to ensure uninterrupted deliveries of men and supplies during any work stoppage. Such opposition proved successful; in fact, prior to Pearl Harbor, only two of the state's major oil refineries in Texas operated under union contracts. Other CIO unions suffered similar defeats. At Houston's Hughes Tool Company, for example, officials of the Independent Metalworkers Union (IMW), a segregated company union that existed in various forms at Hughes since the 1920s, threatened supports and accused USWA organizers of being Communist "dupes" intent on bringing about racial equality. In a 1941 representation election, Hughes workers opted to stay in the IMW, rejecting the USWA by large margins. The union breakthrough in Texas would have to await the changes ushered in by the Second World War.[7]

Labor Organizing in Wartime Texas

With US mobilization, opponents attacked organized labor as a threat to war production. Texas governor W. Lee "Pappy" O'Daniel warned an "imported racketeering, fifth column, radical, violence-producing element" targeted the state's "essential industries." The president of the Texas Association of Manufacturers feared that "sinister influences . . . so prevalent in the North" would use the war to impose CIO unionism on "the better class of labor in this section of the country." Ex-congressman Joe Henry Eagle, trying to regain his seat from Houston's more labor-friendly representative Albert Thomas, alleged subversion, warning of a plot from "communists [who] have drawn plans of every pipe running to the Baytown refinery." In a national radio broadcast at the dedication of the new North American Aviation plant in Grand Prairie, Governor O'Daniel declared Texas ready to defeat the labor threat. "Let any wild-eyed labor agitators . . . from distant states or foreign countries come to Texas and attempt . . . to slow down or stop work at this airplane factory or any other industry," he taunted, "and they will have plenty of time to rue their folly while they pick cotton on our Texas prison farms."[8]

Despite the anti-union bluster, certain developments in the war years tilted organizing battles in labor's favor. Tight labor markets boosted worker bargaining power and undermined management threats against union activists. As employers filled vacancies, unions could draw from new employees untainted by years of exposure to anti-union propaganda from supervisors. And, while business-aligned Texas politicians attacked unions, it would be the federal government that exerted the most influence over labor relations in major Texas industries. After a decade of labor turmoil, Uncle Sam needed peace between labor and management to ensure uninterrupted military production. To achieve this, the Roosevelt administration exacted a no-strike pledge from labor unions and imposed a cap on wage growth. In return, the government compelled employers to negotiate with unions and implemented so-called labor security measures that nudged new workers into unions and kept them on the membership rolls for the duration of the war. The task of overseeing the terms of the labor peace was left to the War Labor Board (WLB), an executive agency with considerable power to force binding arbitration and impose contract terms. Some labor leaders cried foul, but for Texas unions the government's war labor policies represented a significant and favorable shift in power. While Texas employers had previously resisted even recognizing unions, the Roosevelt administration acknowledged labor as essential partners in the war effort.[9]

Texas labor activists jumped at Roosevelt's call for labor patriotism and production. Among the largest and most successful efforts was the attempt to unionize the state's oil refineries. In 1941, Shell refinery worker and Local 367 leader John Crossland convinced the national OWIU to back an aggressive organizing campaign in Texas. The Gulf Coast oil industry was the focus of Washington's investment in greater refining capacity, in part because facilities on the Pacific and Atlantic coasts were thought more vulnerable to attack. The pairing of Uncle Sam's dollars with the government's more favorable union policies created an opportunity for Texas refinery workers to form strong unions capable of bargaining with recalcitrant employers. The oil workers began their organizing drive in February 1942 in Texas City, home to the large Pan-American refinery and the much smaller

Southport Petroleum plant. The union was met by red-baiting and charges of disloyalty from the local Chamber of Commerce and leaders of the Pan-American company union, but the attitude inside the refineries and in the surrounding working-class neighborhoods was more receptive. Managers at Southport had long insisted they would never negotiate with a union, a tactic that often discouraged workers to unionize in the first place. What was the point of risking management retaliation if the union would never be able to produce a deal with the company? In 1938, an OWIU drive at Southport failed when union members withdrew their request for a representation election rather than turn over membership lists to the company. But with the war came the promise that the WLB would force recalcitrant employers to come to terms with unions. The new landscape of federal labor policy made all the difference at Southport. Within a month of the OWIU's arrival in Texas City, Southport workers overwhelmingly voted to join the union and appealed successfully to the WLB to force the company into binding arbitration over a new contract.[10]

Strong labor unions offered workers a way to counter the arbitrary power of foremen, representation in grievance proceedings, seniority systems that created predictable and fair systems of promotion and layoffs, and the power to negotiate for better working conditions and wages. In wartime labor organizing campaigns, union values were married with patriotic ones. As the OWIU worked to build support at the Pan-American refinery, for example, it threw a large "Oil for Victory" rally to showcase strong patriotic support for the union. Beginning in La Marque (near Galveston), black and white members of Local 449 marched up Texas Avenue past the refinery and into downtown Texas City (adjacent to La Marque), where they were joined by other unionists, the Central High School band, firefighters, and the pro-unionist mayor. The parade ended at city hall, emblazoned with a sixty-foot banner reading "BOIL HITLER IN TEXAS OIL—CIO." The crowd heard the mayor, OWIU president O. A. Knight, and George Roberts of the War Production Board (a federal agency that supervised war production), praising the union and its members for their contribution to the national war effort. Two weeks later, the union scored its second election victory in Texas City, an auspicious start for a campaign that in the next two years would bring all but one of the state's major refineries into the OWIU.[11]

In wartime organizing campaigns, unionism and Americanism marched hand in hand. Indeed, to labor-backers, the war against the Axis powers gave additional meaning to longstanding labor ideals about worker rights to protest and assemble, workplace due process, democratic decision-making, and resistance to management "autocracy." As an OWIU flyer distributed at Humble's Baytown refinery argued, unionizing meant maintaining "Americans standards" for "Humble workers and the sons of Humble workers upon their return from war," and to see to it that "nobody here in America is able to impose the kind of Hitlerism they are fighting against" abroad. Union efforts to force employers to comply with government orders became, in the context of the war, acts of patriotism. When Humble executives classified new hires as "temporary" employees to circumvent Selective Service Act requirements that workers sent overseas be given priority in hiring after their return, the OWIU accused the company of trying to "sabotage our Commander-in-Chief" on labor matters. Of course, from the employer's perspective, it was the demands of labor that threatened war production. The Southern Aircraft Company in Dallas labeled CIO organizers "Hitler's Children," and encouraged workers to show that they were "not a traitor" by "vot[ing] against the CIO." At the Continental Motors plant in Garland, the company's Non-Union Committee blamed an organizing effort by the Autoworkers union for producing "much unrest and dissatisfaction" that threatened to halt worker "efforts to put an end to [the war] at the earliest date possible." A "vote against the CIO," the company urged, was a "vote for Victory and Freedom."[12]

Ultimately, employer efforts to thwart union drives were most successful at plants with long-established company unions and long histories of management retaliation. Baytown refinery supervisors warned workers the CIO "ain't going to get you nowhere," a point reinforced by threatening to fire union supporters and assigning them to the hardest jobs. One gang pusher warned his crew that if they joined the CIO, "you will be in the Army next." This is exactly what happened to outspoken CIO supporter Hervie Bradley, who was fired on the pretext of eating a sandwich without authorization. His exemption gone, Bradley was soon drafted. On the other hand, Baytown foremen assigned workers who kept their "mouth quiet" to work "light job[s]" in the warehouse, where the clerk would "fix them up" with a membership in the Employee

Federation. When Baytown workers voted on union representation in 1943, they opted for the long-established Employee Federation over the OWIU by a two-to-one margin. It was the most significant defeat for Texas unions during the war.[13]

Elsewhere, organizers found success taking on established company unions by focusing on new employees. The success of the steelworkers union at the Hughes Tool Company provides a good example of the fertile ground created by the rapid wartime expansion of the workforce. In 1941, with mobilization just beginning, the USWA lost an election challenge to the IMW, the plant's long-established segregated company union. At the time, Hughes employed 3,600 people in its oil tools plant in Houston's East End. Over the next year, Hughes added new facilities to manufacture airplane struts and gun barrels and hired thousands of workers. At its peak of operations in 1945, the company's three divisions employed a total of 9,100 employees. The USWA focused its efforts on the hundreds of workers being added to the payroll each month. In the strut plant, the union obtained commitments with the simple strategy of asking new members to organize their friends. At the main plant, it looked outside of the traditional union base in the production divisions to organize cafeteria workers, newly hired "janitresses and matrons," and drivers who shuttled parts, blueprints, and workers between the different Hughes facilities. The strategy worked. In a December 1942 representation election, the USWA barely bested the IMW. The union cards submitted to the NLRB before the election help explain the USWA's ability to reverse its earlier election loss. While many IMW supporters were longer-term employees who joined Hughes well before the war, a majority of the cards submitted by the USWA came from the growing population of new employees who had little attachment to the company, its acrimonious labor history, or its company union.[14]

In plants built during the war, organizers found their task much easier. There, workers showed overwhelming support for unions from both the AFL and CIO. Workers at Humble Oil's new butadiene (an important component for the production of synthetic rubber) plant in Ingleside, a hundred miles south of the Baytown refinery, broke with company tradition by voting in the OWIU in 1943. Corporate opposition to the union was fierce (the federal government had to step in and operate the plant in 1944 when managers refused to deal with the union) but with no established employee federation, workers made an easy choice to organize under the oil worker banner. Similar victories occurred out at other war-built plants. When the Sheffield primary steel mill opened on the Houston Ship Channel in 1942, workers delivered a resounding endorsement for USWA representation. In Grand Prairie, workers at the gigantic North American Aviation plant voted in the United Auto Workers (UAW) while in Fort Worth, and more than 90 percent of workers at the Consolidated Vultee plant defied management in support of the International Association of Machinists (IAM), an AFL union with a history of representing workers in the West Coast aircraft assembly industry.[15]

Opportunity and Discrimination in War Work

As men went overseas, women stepped into jobs formerly held exclusively by men. This, although seen as necessary for war production, did not happen without anxiety about blurring the proper place for women in society. To limit any permanent disruption, unions as well as management often segregated workers by sex and, of course, let it be known to the female worker her position was part of the war effort and not to be expected beyond. This was particularly the case in the aircraft industry in North Texas, where enormous orders created a near insatiable demand for labor. More than 30 percent of new hires in the first year of production at the North American plant were women. At Consolidated Vultee, the female percentage of the workforce neared 40 percent by war's end. Thus, in order to produce planes, women in aircraft plants worked in skilled and unskilled tasks alongside men operating presses, drills, and rivet guns, and running wire and painting. Their experience in aircraft plants was hardly unique. Anywhere there was war work, there were women. In oil refineries, women worked as janitors, timekeepers, clerks, electricians, carpenters, and chemists in the laboratory. Women in the shipyards worked as metal cutters and welders, made wooden templates, and performed a lot of the drafting necessary to take the ship from planning to reality.[16]

War work provided white women with patriotic as well as economic opportunities. In a sign of the importance of women's support to organized labor during the war, union contracts often included clauses guaranteeing equal pay. Black women, on the other hand, were denied, if hired at all, such guarantees and relegated to the lowest-paying positions in segregated cafeterias. Black men also found themselves blocked from war jobs. Despite government training programs for African Americans, aircraft manufacturers initially refused to hire them. Labor unions in that industry, at times, contributed to the problem. The IAM union at Consolidated Vultee, for example, excluded blacks entirely, locking them out of production work and consigning the few hired to jobs in janitorial and maintenance positions.[17]

Even where black workers had long been part of the workforce, they faced job discrimination. The central organizing principle of industrial employment in Texas was the distinction between "production," "operating," or "mechanical" work, all of which was restricted to white employees, and labor or maintenance jobs, which were filled largely by minority workers. White production workers began careers as apprentices or helpers and rose along defined lines of progression, or "job ladders," to become semi-skilled and then skilled operators or craftsmen. Minority workers in similar jobs could gain seniority and be promoted but could never progress in a similar manner to whites. In some places, white employees did work in labor divisions, often supervising groups of minority employees. This segregation was not about physical separation. Minorities worked in the same places as whites, and senior minority laborers often performed similar tasks as white workers in higher divisions. What defined industrial segregation was the segregation of opportunity. No matter how senior or how skilled a minority worker, his ceiling was already set.[18]

Many of the most highly skilled workers in refineries, oil tools factories, and other industries crucial to the war effort were exempted from military service. Nonetheless, plant expansion and conscription produced severe shortages in the semi-skilled ranks. For minority workers, this seemed a logical time to begin opening production jobs to experienced minority laborers. At Hughes Tool, for example, African Americans urged the company to fill vacant welder, lathe-operator, and machinist positions with senior black workers, many of whom had considerable job knowledge gained from years of service as helpers and assistants to white skilled workers. But the policies of the federal government and corporate management inhibited such upgrading. The regional office of the War Manpower Commission encouraged Texas employers to hire white women to fill jobs from which "the colored worker in the area is generally restricted." The employment of white women during the war also advanced the interest of company managers by preserving the color line. At the company's new aircraft strut plant, for example, an aggressive program to recruit and train female workers was implemented, thus precluding experienced black workers from the main plant. The effort showed in the strut plant's employment figures. In the first year of operation, the company hired 361 women, 22 percent of the plant's total workforce. Black employees, barred from certain positions, held only 16 percent of the jobs. In the eyes of many industrial employers, women war workers were placeholders, able to meet a voracious but temporary demand for labor without upsetting the long-standing systems of racial discrimination.[19]

Labor Organizing and Minority Workers

With Texas employers firmly committed to Jim Crow, black and Hispanic workers looked to the labor movement for redress. Consider the industrial unions of the CIO, which were committed in principle to a model of interracial organizing. As labor unions sought to establish worker control over systems of hiring, promotion, and discipline, minority workers hoped they would represent the interests of *all* their workers, regardless of race. Labor rights had special meaning to minority workers in an era when discrimination created a bifurcated society. The rights established by the Wagner Act and union contracts were, for minority workers in the South, the only rights that powerful whites were bound to respect. Carter Wesley, the black editor of the *Houston Informer*, had been making this very case to black workers since the first appearance of CIO organizers in the city in 1937. Wesley urged African American workers into unions but knew their limitations. The "CIO . . . in Texas is taking in the same prejudiced workers who have fought Negroes all their lives," he acknowledged, but they would have to respect the interests of their black co-unionists because they "need Negroes" in representation elections "to sew-up and keep the shops." Richard Grovey, head of the Houston black barbers union and a well-known local civil rights activist, was likewise an advocate of black labor movement participation, urging workers in public meetings to "join the CIO . . . and demand the right to enjoy the blessings, economic and political, inherent in this democratic setup."[20]

White labor activists seemed to validate the optimism of black union backers. Speaking to an audience at the Houston chapter of the National Association for the Advancement of Colored People (NAACP), CIO organizer Roy Sessions made bold promises (touting, for example, interracial unionism could bring about a "Second Emancipation") but also offered a pragmatic case for black unionism, pointing to the "higher wages paid to Negro workers in the two oil refineries organized under the CIO here" and to the CIO's policy of prioritizing wage increases for the lowest-paid workers. In 1941, white steelworker organizers assured black workers "we of the CIO know that unless we organize our colored co-employees the employers shall always be able to create friction between white and colored in order to lower the standard of living of all of us. It is, therefore, not only a Christian Act to help and associate all workers regardless of color and creed, but it is good sound business protection for all workers." With representation elections often close affairs, organizers saw strong support from minority workers as indispensable.[21]

The organization of black and Tejano workers was given particular importance by the leaders of the oil workers' campaign, many of whom had experience building interracial unions in hostile environments. Lead organizer Clyde Johnson came from the ranks of labor radicals who saw the union movement in principled terms of class struggle and racial justice. He had been the Alabama Communist Party's chief labor organizer in the mid-1930s and head of the interracial Alabama Share Croppers Union. For his actions, the police nearly beat him to death. In his inaugural OWIU campaigns in Texas City, Johnson worked to build black support at the Pan-American refinery, where they made up roughly 13 percent of the 957 hourly employees. The OWIU pledged to fight for equal pay for equal work, to open bidding on all jobs to black applicants, and to give whites and blacks equal seniority rights. Johnson presented his "revolutionary program" as benefiting both black laborers and many lower-skilled white workers by opening access to higher-skilled positions monopolized by members of the refinery's AFL craft unions. Strong support from black workers helped bring about victories for the OWIU at the Southport and Pan-American refineries in Texas City. In contentious contract negotiations with both companies, the union made good on its promise. It asked the WLB to eliminate the separate racial classifications in the refinery's labor division and bring black workers up to the existing "white" pay scale there. The WLB sided with the union, setting a new "equal pay for equal work" standard in OWIU contracts and affirming the OWIU's strategy to make organizing minority workers a top priority.[22]

In hindsight, the organizing campaigns in Texas City would be notable for their lack of racial animosity. If outreach to minority workers increased support for the OWIU, it could also be used by opponents to bludgeon the CIO. In its unsuccessful, yearlong struggle to organize the Humble Oil Baytown refinery, OWIU organizers faced a constant barrage of race-baiting attacks from the employee dedera-tion and the company, which gave a no-show job to a local newspaper editor to serve as a full-time propagandist inside the plant gates. When the union had initial success organizing the refinery's 450 black and Hispanic laborers with its pledge for equal wages, it was accused of carrying on a "secret campaign" promising to end "all forms of racial segregation" at the expense of "the White workers in Baytown." Supervisors urged "thousands of Texas country boys here in Baytown" to stop the CIO from coming "into our Southern State of Texas, brandishing a torch of racial hatred" against whites. "The place to check them is HERE and NOW. Tomorrow may be too late." By raising the specter of integration, company warnings about the CIO's program of "absolute equality on the job" offended many white workers and put the union on the defense. "If anyone starts the anti-Negro stuff," organizers instructed union members, "ask what the CIO has said to Negroes. The answer is equal pay for equal work." Organizers like Clyde Johnson, deeply committed to racial equality, preferred desegregation of the skilled jobs, but he was careful to strike a balance between the aspirations of racial minorities and expectations and tolerance of white workers. Johnson's plan to calm the racial fears of white workers through incremental steps failed. Subject to more than a year of race-baiting propaganda, the majority of white Baytown workers remained with the segregated employee federation.[23]

Elsewhere, interracial CIO unions arranged white workers opposed to integrating the job ranks so that they did not have to directly work among African Americans. In preparation for a 1942 representation election at Hughes Tool, the USWA union there split into two segregated units, white Local 1742 and black Local 2457. For true believers in the CIO's biracial mission like black organizer Richard Grovey, segregating the union was a lamentable development, but one that was made necessary by the presence of white workers unwilling "to concede to the Negro his full share." Segregated CIO unionism was based on a recognition that union activists could not quickly build interracial solidarity in a workforce that had long been segregated. Some have argued that segregated locals may have provided some benefits to black unionists. Indeed, at Hughes, both black and white unionists had supported the move to split the union. In an integrated CIO union, black workers would likely be a permanent minority faction in union decision-making. Remaining local ensured black leaders could give voice to black interests, and Local 1742 and 2457 were both represented on contract and grievance committees, giving black union leaders the ability to block union decisions that might push black workers out of jobs or cut them out of pay increases.[24]

Segregated CIO unionism was also crucial to the success of the OWIU in Port Arthur (southeast of Beaumont). There, leaders of black Local 254, convinced that white racism prevented true interracial unionism, insisted on keeping a segregated setup established in the 1930s, going so far as to withhold support for the OWIU in a 1938 representation election at Gulf Oil where black workers feared the members of white Local 23 would take full control of the representation process. In 1943, white organizers in Local 254 focused on support from the refinery's 1,000 black employees, canvassing Port Arthur's black neighborhoods for support. White organizer F. H. Mitchell was beaten by racist Port Arthur police chief H. F. Baker, who declared "there will be no God Damn CIO" in his town. But such intimidation and warnings from the company that "the CIO Promises Negroes Equality with Whites," may have backfired, as the oil workers won their representation election with 60 percent of the vote. A majority of white workers voted against the OWIU, but the union prevailed due to the black block voting.[25]

Union Activism and Union Discrimination

Minority unionists, whether in segregated or integrated locals, were essential to the success of unions in Texas industry. How far did unions go to ensure the success of minority workers? During the war, most unions representing workers in large industries followed the "equal pay" precedent set by the WLB and the OWIU in 1942. In plants where minority and white workers performed similar work, but with discriminatory wage scales, this new standard for union contracts benefited minority workers. But the impact of equal wage rules was negligible where companies assigned low-paid "common labor" roles exclusively to minorities, with higher classifications of work reserved for whites. In these instances, minority workers could benefit from union representation of grievances challenging the common management tactic of down-classifying the work done by minority employees. In situations where the union could demonstrate that minority workers performed work equivalent to that done by differently classified whites, successful grievances could bring senior minority workers up to "white" pay rates, even if they could not be upgraded into production divisions.

Equal pay and grievance representation were significant steps forward for black and Mexican American union members. Texas unions adopted these practices in 1942 and 1943, as union locals first gained representation rights (not coincidentally, in elections where they counted on minority support). But job segregation remained untouched. With the notable exception of the smelter unions in El Paso, which had overwhelmingly Hispanic memberships, most Texas industrial unions were majority white, leaving union leaders to fear integration's effect on white workers' attitudes, thus costing the unions their workplace majorities and exclusive bargaining rights. Leaders of the black USWA local at Hughes Tool, for example, were concerned enough about an anti-union backlash that they agreed to delay the union's joint proposal to promote desegregated labor division. When the combined leadership of the black and white USWA locals filed a brief in early 1945 asking the WLB to strike out all discriminatory provisions in the union's contract with Hughes, the blowback came not just from white workers but also from management. Hughes supervisors threatened a wildcat strike if the WLB acceded to the union's desegregation request. The federal government, now faced with the prospect of a drill bit shortage, backed down, shelving desegregation attempts at the company. At Hughes, black workers' attempts to pursue equal opportunity through their union had devastating consequences. In 1946, Hughes's white workers turned decisively against the USWA, throwing it out of the plant in favor of the company union, which colluded with management over the next two decades to keep the company's Jim Crow policies in place.[26]

The fragility of the USWA majority at Hughes Tool was a major contributor to the union's inability to push its plan to upgrade black workers. But security was no guarantee that a union would advance the interests of their minority members. OWIU unions at the Sinclair refinery in Houston and Shell in Pasadena, both of which were firmly in place by the late 1930s, had little reason to appeal to minority members, and neither union made any effort to guarantee equal pay or alter any discriminatory provisions in the contracts they had signed before the war. Many of the AFL unions in shipyards had racial bars to membership and opposed any efforts to upgrade minority workers into skilled positions. When minority workers saw little chance in combating discrimination through union action, they found redress: the Fair Employment Practices Committee (FEPC). Created in 1941 by President Roosevelt via Executive Order 8802, in large part to head off black protest, the FEPC was given the authority to respond to complaints, investigate discriminatory conditions in industry, and order war contractors to remedy discriminatory practices. Although strengthened in 1943, the FEPC lacked the power to unilaterally impose contract changes, instead negotiating with unions and employers to find common ground. While a general historical consensus holds that the FEPC, despite the dogged efforts of its staff, was unable to overcome its limitations to effect lasting racial change, local studies of the FEPC in Texas show that the outcome of cases depended largely on the interests and attitudes of employers, local union leaders, and rank-and-file workers.[27]

Employers and unions often blocked FEPC efforts. In the railroad industry, for example, corporate executives and the all-white railroad brotherhoods both denied that any discrimination existed, leaving the FEPC to face a unified union-management front it was incapable of dividing. The agency faced a particularly difficult situation in Texas shipyards. In June 1943, violence erupted in Beaumont when a white wife of a Pennsylvania Shipyard worker accused an African American man of rape. This sent thousands of whites into black neighborhoods, where they ransacked homes and assaulted residents. It took 1,800 state guardsmen to quell the riot. Some observers faulted the boilermakers union for stirring up racial tension. After the riot, Texas shipyard unions stonewalled FEPC investigators by simply refusing to appear at hearing. Shipyard employers, for their part, admitted to discriminatory practices but pointed to union hostility and the riot as justification for not hiring minority workers into skilled positions. Some labor unions, with prodding from the FEPC, began to better represent minority workers. Unions in the aircraft industry, eager to constrain the arbitrary authority of managers, used grievance procedures to resolve FEPC complaints filed by minority workers. At the North American plant, the UAW and the FEPC went further, pushing the company to increase its hiring of minority workers into semi-skilled positions; by mid-1944, the plant had 2,300 black employees, including some working as assemblers, riveters, and inspectors. Even the racially exclusive IAM union at Consolidated Vultee took some measures to help minorities by demanding the company correctly classify and compensate work performed by African Americans. Production positions at the plant, however, remained all white, in accordance with the desires of both union and management.[28]

At the state and national level, the unions of the CIO were in full support of the FEPC's efforts to remedy discrimination, but power lay at the local level. Consider the FEPC's biggest case in Texas that involved the OWIU Local 367 at the Pasadena Shell refinery. The case began in early 1943, when thirty-four Mexican American workers asked Local 367 to represent them in challenges with Shell's discriminatory practices. When the union refused, the men dropped their union memberships and appealed to the Mexican consul in Houston, who forwarded their charges on to the FEPC. The complaints began a two-year investigation into refinery discrimination by Carlos Castañeda, a University of Texas historian and regional director of the FEPC. Castañeda's study led him to focus on Shell, where the contract with Local 367 (in place since 1938) continued to racially discriminate in wages and job placement. In late 1944, the FEPC proposed upgrading a handful of Hispanic workers, a decision driven both by pressure from the Mexican government to protect the rights of Mexican nationals in Texas, and by the director's mistaken belief that discrimination against that group was less intense than against blacks. Both the unions and the company refused to implement the FEPC's plan.[29]

Frustrated, the FEPC tried in March 1945 to implement its upgrading policy unilaterally. Over the span of two weeks, the FEPC eased its plan into action, first promoting two Tejano workers into the automotive division, and then moving seven African Americans into entry-level positions in various production divisions. The response was protest. White workers walked off the job, threatening a full shutdown unless the promotions were rescinded. Efforts by state and national OWIU leaders to enforce the official nondiscrimination policy of the union failed, as rank-and-file workers ousted integration supporters from the union local's leadership and formed their own pro-segregation committee to negotiate with the FEPC. Faced with such a response, the FEPC backed down, agreeing to a compromise proposal to create a fully segregated line of promotion for minority workers in a production area of the plant separate from whites. The plan met with some approval from blacks, who judged it the only possible way to gain promotions but was rejected by Hispanics who wanted nothing less than full integration (discrimination against Tejanos, although overt, was not nearly as intense as against black Texans, yet noticeably pervasive). In the end, the split between the two groups did not matter. The FEPC closed the case before the war ended, and the segregated upgrading scheme quietly died. In its last major action in Texas, the FEPC showed that neither it, nor CIO union leaders, could effectively overcome resistance to racial equality.[30]

As war production wound down, employment in Texas' defense plants dropped precipitously and layoffs skyrocketed. Shipyards shuttered and aircraft plants closed their doors permanently. Layoffs had a disproportionate impact on black workers, who were the first to go under "last hired, first fired" seniority rules. Even for laid-off defense workers, however, wartime gains were "ephemeral yet undeniable." Working Texans in 1945 had obtained a measure of economic security unknown to many of them before the war. While payrolls and union rolls both dropped during the postwar demobilization, organized labor's wartime gains would not be undone. Counting about 20,000 members before the war, the unions of the CIO in Texas entered 1946 with three times that amount. Such efforts, in fact, contributed to a national increase of black union membership. By war's end, 700,000 African Americans were union labor. The UAW retained its presence in North Texas, organizing the postwar aircraft manufacturers in the mothballed North American plant in 1946, and auto and aerospace firms moved into the region in the subsequent decade. The USWA remained in steel mills in Houston and East Texas, and although the local at Hughes Tool collapsed in 1946, workers at other large oil tools firms were organized under the union banner. After its successful wartime organizing push, the OWIU emerged from the war the most powerful union in Texas, winning strikes in the late 1940s and early 1950s that produced economic benefits for members. Although prewar Texas working men were less organized and lower paid than their Northern counterparts, they emerged from the war every bit his equal.[31]

For minority workers in Texas, the wartime record was decidedly mixed. Equal pay meant larger paychecks, and the rounds of nationwide straight wage increases obtained by CIO unions after the war meant proportionately larger percentage increases for all workers in the lower ranks. Such gains, however, failed to break down barriers to equal opportunity still facing minority workers. At war's end, black Texans in the NAACP campaigned to make the FEPC permanent, hoping governmental pressure would give minority workers a formidable tool against racism. The state's top labor leaders joined the call. Knowing their locals would inevitably have to confront the issue of job segregation, union officials hoped to place the onus of integration on the government, rather than on union locals since white opposition was so intense. But the FEPC died at the hands of Southern congressmen in early 1946, leaving the problem of discrimination to labor. Union leaders in the next decades would have to face a central shortcoming of labor's otherwise successful rise during the war: Organizers had built interracial worker coalitions capable of winning representation elections but failed to produce the sort of interracial solidarity to effect meaningful change. During the war, Texas minorities hoped they could pursue both substantive gain and equal opportunity through their unions, but the promise of unionism had proven largely illusory. In postwar Texas, they would discover organized labor to be as much an obstacle as an ally in their progress.[32]

Notes

1. Zachary Montz specializes in labor and civil rights history. A member of the Sam Houston State University faculty as a Lecturer of History, Montz is currently revising his dissertation for publication.

2. The quote can be found in Annual Budget Message to Congress, January 5, 1942, in Franklin D. Roosevelt, *The Public Papers and Addresses of Franklin D. Roosevelt 1942 Volume, The Tide Turns: Compiled with Special Material and Explanatory Notes by Samuel I. Rosenman* (New York: Harper & Brothers Publishers 1950),

7; Daniel Kryder, *Divided Arsenal: Race and the American State during World War II* (Cambridge, UK: Cambridge University Press), 206–07. For works examining the initial mobilization, see Joseph A Pratt, *The Growth of a Refining Region* (Greenwich, CT: Jai Press, 1980); Catherine Lutz, *Homefront: A Military City and the American Twentieth Century* (Boston: Beacon Press, 2001); Mark Harrison, ed., *The Economics of World War II: Six Great Powers in Industrial Comparison* (New York: Cambridge University Press, 1998); Harold G. Vatter, *The US Economy in World War II* (New York: Columbia University Press, 1985); Alan S. Milward, *War, Economy, and Society, 1939–1945* (Berkeley: University of California Press, 1977); Donald M. Nelson, *Arsenal of Democracy: The Story of American War Production* (New York: Harcourt, Brace, and Company, 1946); A. J. Baime, *The Arsenal of Democracy: FDR, Detroit, and an Epic Quest to Arm an America at War* (New York: Houghton Mifflin Harcourt, 2014); Irving Brinton Holley Jr., *Buying Aircraft: Material Procurement for the Army Air Forces* (Washington, DC: Government Printing Office, 1964); James T. Sparrow, *Warfare State: World War II America and the Age of Big Government* (New York: Oxford University Press, 2011); Norman Beasley, *Knudsen: A Biography* (New York: McGraw-Hill Book Company, 1947); Paul Kennedy, *Engineers of Victory: The Problem Solvers Who Turned the Tide in the Second World War* (New York: Random House, 2013); Arthur Herman, *Freedom's Forge: How American Business Produced Victory in World War II* (New York: Random House, 2012); Robert Higgs, "Wartime Prosperity? A Reassessment of the US Economy in the 1940s," *Journal of Economic History* 52 (March 1992); Paul A. C. Koistinen, *Arsenal of World War II: The Political Economy of American Warfare, 1940–1945* (Lawrence: University Press of Kansas, 2004); Gerald D. Nash, *The American West Transformed: The Impact of the Second World War* (Lincoln: University of Nebraska Press, 1990); Gregory Hooks, *Forging the Military-Industrial Complex: World War II's Battle of the Potomac* (Urbana: University of Illinois Press, 1991); Joseph Abel, "African Americans, Labor Unions, and the Struggle for Fair Employment in the Aircraft Manufacturing Industry of Texas, 1941–1945," *Journal of Southern History* 77 (August 2011); Bruce J. Schulman, *From Cotton Belt to Sunbelt: Federal Policy, Economic Development and the Transformation of the South, 1938–1980* (New York: Oxford University Press, 1991); Ralph Wooster, "East Texas in World War II," *East Texas Historical Journal* 45 (September 2007); and Henrietta M. Larson and Kenneth Porter, *History of Humble Oil & Refining Company* (New York: Arno Press, 1959).

3. On Roosevelt's ambitious production schedule, see, in addition to the works above, David M. Kennedy, *Freedom from Fear: The American People in Depression and War, 1929–1945* (New York: Oxford University Press, 1999); Elizabeth Borgwardt, *A New Deal for the World: America's Vision for Human Rights* (Cambridge, MA: Harvard University Press, 2005); Halford R. Ryan, *Franklin D. Roosevelt's Rhetorical Presidency* (New York: Greenwood Press, 1988); and State of the Union Address, January 6, 1941, in Franklin D. Roosevelt, *The Public Papers and Addresses of Franklin D. Roosevelt, 1941 Volume, The Call to Battle Stations:*

Compiled with Special Material and Explanatory Notes by Samuel I. Rosenman (New York: Harper & Brothers Publishers, 1950). On Roosevelt's notion of the economic rights at stake in the war, see Cass Sunstein, *The Second Bill of Rights: FDR's Unfinished Revolution—And Why We Need It More than Ever* (New York: Basic Books, 2004). For the importance of the Houston Shipyard not only to the rise of Houston and the Gulf Coast region, but also to the Lone Star State's and the country's war mobilization, see Gerald J. Fischer, *A Statistical Summary of Shipbuilding Under the US Maritime Commission during World War II* (Washington, DC: Government Printing Office, 1949); Craig Hlavaty, "How Texas reacted to and benefitted from World War II," *Houston Chronicle*, November 10, 2017; Andrew W. Hall, "Blue-Water Ships, Brown-Water Bayou: Wartime Construction, 1941–1945," *Houston History Magazine* 12 (October 31, 2014); and Frederic C. Lane, *Ships for Victory: A History of Shipbuilding under the US Maritime Commission in World War II* (Baltimore: Johns Hopkins University Press, 1951). Studies of the ships constructed in the various shipbuilding companies in Houston are L. A. Sawyer, *Liberty Ships: The History of the Emergency Type Cargo Ships Constructed in the United States during the Second World War* (Cambridge, MD: Cornell Maritime, 1970); Peter Elphick, *Liberty: The Ships That Won the War* (Annapolis, MD: Naval Institute Press, 2006); Greg H. Williams, *The Liberty Ships of World War II: A Record of the 2,710 Vessels and Their Builders, Operators, and Namesakes, with a History of the Jeremiah O'Brien* (Jefferson, NC: McFarland and Company, 2014); and John G. Bunker, *Liberty Ships: The Ugly Ducklings of World War II* (Annapolis, MD: Naval Institute Press, 1973).

4. The quotation can be found in Frank P. Graham, opinion in National War Labor Board Case No. 771 (2898-CS-D), in the Matter of Southport Petroleum Company (Texas City, Texas) and Oil Workers' International Union, Local 449, CIO, June 5, 1943. Roosevelt's speech concerning "freedom from want" is in State of the Union Address, January 6, 1941, in Franklin D. Roosevelt, *The Public Papers and Addresses of Franklin D. Roosevelt 1941 Volume, Humanity on the Defensive: Compiled with Special Material and Explanatory Notes by Samuel I. Rosenman* (New York: Harper & Brothers Publishers, 1950). Works that stress the positive relationship between labor and civil rights struggles include Michael K. Honey, *Southern Labor and Black Civil Rights: Organizing Memphis Workers* (Urbana: University of Illinois Press, 1993); Robert Korstad, *Civil Rights Unionism: Tobacco Workers and the Struggle for Democracy in the Mid-Twentieth-Century South* (Chapel Hill: University of North Carolina Press, 2003). The failure of Congress of Industrial Organizations unions to live up to its professional antidiscrimination policies is emphasized in Bruce Nelson, "'CIO Meant One Thing for the Whites and Another Thing for Us': Steelworkers and Civil Rights, 1936–1974," in *Southern Labor in Transition, 1940–1995*, ed. Robert H. Zieger (Knoxville: University of Tennessee Press, 1997); Paul D. Moreno, *Black Americans and Organized Labor: A New History* (Baton Rouge: Louisiana State University Press, 2008); and Herbert Hill, *Black Labor and the American Legal System: Race, Work, and the Law* (Madison: University of Wisconsin Press, 1977).

5. The quotation is from David Botter, "Labor Looks at Texas," *Southwest Review* XXXI (Spring 1946), 112–13, 115. In conjunction with the works listed throughout this essay, further works chronicling labor/union history in Texas before the war are F. Ray Marshall, "Some Reflections on Labor History," *Southwestern Historical Quarterly* 75 (October 1971); Maximilian Krochmal, "Labor, Civil Rights, and the Struggle for Democracy in Mid-Twentieth Century Texas" (PhD diss., Duke University, 2013); Emilio Zamora, *The World of the Mexican Worker in Texas* (College Station: Texas A&M University Press, 1993); Gregg Andrews, "Unionizing the Trinity Portland Cement Company in Dallas, Texas, 1934–1939," *Southwestern Historical Quarterly* 111 (July 2007); Joseph P. Goldberg, *The Maritime Story: A Study of Labor-Management Relations* (Cambridge, MA: Harvard University Press, 1958); Ruth Alice Allen, *Chapters in the History of Organized Labor in Texas* (Austin: University of Texas Publication, 1941); Michael R. Botson Jr., "Jim Crow Wearing Steel-Toed Shoes and Safety Glasses: Dual Unionism at the Hughes Tool Company, 1918–1942," *Houston Review* 16 (1994); Grady Lee Mullenix, "History of the Texas State Federation of Labor" (PhD diss., University of Texas, 1955); and the Labor Movement in Texas Collection, 1845–1954, Dolph Briscoe Center for American History, University of Texas. The attitudes of industrialists to the open shop in Texas is best expressed in *Houston* [Chamber of Commerce journal] October 1938. Important exceptions to this trend include the black longshoremen's unions in Houston and Galveston and black railroad unions (see Rebecca Anne Montes, "Working for American Rights: Black, White and Mexican American Dockworkers in Texas during the Great Depression" (PhD diss., University of Texas, 2005); and Eric Arnesen, *Brotherhoods of Color: Black Railroad Workers and the Struggle for Equality* (Cambridge, MA: Harvard University Press, 2001). The premier work on the American Federation of Labor during World War II is Andrew E. Kersten's, *Labor's Home Front: The American Federation of Labor during World War II* (New York: New York University Press, 2009).

6. See Ray Davidson, *Challenging the Giants: A History of the Oil, Chemical and Atomic Workers International Union* (Denver, CO: Oil, Chemical and Atomic Workers International Union, 1988); and Murray Polakoff, "The Development of the Texas State CIO Council" (PhD diss., Columbia University, 1955). Overviews of early organizing are George N. Green, "Texas State Industrial Union Council," *Handbook of Texas Online*, accessed June 13, 2021, http://www.tshaonline.org/handbook/online/articles/octbg; Rick Halpern, "Interracial Unionism in the Southwest: Fort Worth's Packinghouse Workers, 1937–1954," in *Organized Labor in the Twentieth-Century South*, ed. Robert H. Zieger (Knoxville: University of Tennessee Press, 1991); Harold Shapiro, "The Pecan Shellers of San Antonio," *Southwestern Social Science Quarterly* 32 (March 1951); Frank Arnold, "Humberto Silex: CIO Organizer from Nicaragua," *Southwest Economy and Society* 4 (Fall 1978); and Gilbert Mers, *Working the Waterfront: The Ups and Downs of a Rebel Longshoreman* (Austin: University of Texas Press, 1988). The definitive works examining the CIO's operations during World War II are Nelson Lichenstein, *Labor's War at Home: The CIO in World War II* (Philadelphia: Temple University

Press, 2003); and Clyde Johnson, "CIO Oil Workers' Organizing Campaign in Texas, 1942–1943," in *Essays in Southern Labor History Conference, 1976*, eds. Gary M. Fink and Merl E. Reed (Westport, CT: Greenwood Press, 1976). Other very helpful works are Robert H. Zieger, *The CIO 1933–1935* (Chapel Hill: University of North Carolina Press, 1995); Frances Fox Piven and Richard A. Cloward, *Poor People's Movements: Why They Succeed and How They Fail* (New York: Vintage Books, 1979); Morgan O. Reynolds, *Power and Privilege: Labor Unions in America* (New York; Universe Books, 1984); Irving Bernstein, *The Turbulent Years: A History of the American Workers, 1933–1941* (Chicago: Haymarket Books, 2010); Philip Dray, *There Is Power in a Union: The Epic Story of Labor in America* (New York: Anchor Books, 2010); Howard Kimeldorf, *Reds or Rackets? The Making of Radical and Conservative Unions on the Waterfront* (Berkeley: University of California Press, 1988); Art Preis, *Labor's Giant Step: The First Twenty Years of the CIO: 1936–55* (New York: Pathfinder Press, 1964); and George Lipsitz, *Rainbow at Midnight: Labor and Culture in the 1940s* (Urbana: University of Illinois Press, 1994). Records of the Congress of Industrial Organizations, 1934–1958 can be found at the American Catholic History Research Center and University Archives, Catholic University of American, Washington, DC. Works specifically examining the Wagner Act are Richard C. Cortner, *The Wagner Act Cases* (Knoxville: University of Tennessee Press, 1964); Michael Goldfield, "Worker Insurgency, Radical Organization, and New Deal Labor Legislation," *American Political Science Quarterly Review* 83 (December 1989); G. William Domhoff and Michael J. Webber, *Class and Power in the New Deal: Corporate Moderates, Southern Democrats, and the Liberal-Labor Coalition* (Redwood City, CA: Stanford University Press, 2011); Colin Gordon, *New Deals: Business, Labor, and Politics in America, 1920–1935* (New York: Cambridge University Press, 1994); James A. Gross, *The Reshaping of the National Labor Relations Board: National Labor Policy in Transition, 1937–1947* (Albany: State University of New York Press, 1981); Daniel Nelson, "The Other New Deal and Labor: The Regulatory State and the Unions, 1933–1940," *Journal of Policy History* 13 (January 2001); Holly J. McCammon, "Legal Limits on Labor Militancy: US Labor Law and the Right to Strike since the New Deal," *Social Problems* 37 (May 1990); and Leon. H. Keyserling, "The Wagner Act: Its Origin and Current Significance," *George Washington Law Review* 29 (1960–1961). For a focus on collective bargaining, see Irving Bernstein, *New Deal Collective Bargaining Policy* (Berkeley: University of California Press, 1950).

7. Refer to Davidson, *Challenging the Giants*; John Wooding, Charles Levenstein, and Beth Rosenberg, "The Oil, Chemical and Atomic Workers International Union: Refining Strategies for Labor," *International Journal of Health Services* 27 (1997); Harvey O'Connor, *History of the Oil Workers International Union (CIO)* (Denver, CO: Oil Workers International Union, 1950); and In the Matter of Hughes Tool Company and Independent Metal Workers Union Locals Nos. 1 and 2, 36 N.L.R.B. 904 (1941), accessed June 13, 2031, https://casetext.com/admin-law/hughes-tool-co-10. On the history of IMW locals at Hughes, see Michael R. Botson Jr., *Labor, Civil Rights, and the Hughes Tool Company* (College Station, TX:

Texas A&M University Press, 2005). For the OWIU's efforts at organizing, albeit sympathetic reviews, see Clyde Johnson, "CIO Oil Workers' Organizing Campaign in Texas, 1942–1943," in *Essays in Southern Labor History Conference, 1976*, eds. Gary M. Fink and Merl E. Reed (Westport, CT: Greenwood Press, 1976). For the fears in Texas about the CIO and radicalism, including communism, see Papers of US Representative Martin Dies, Sam Houston Regional Library and Research Center, Texas State Library and Archives Commission, Liberty, Texas, particularly Boxes 4 and 15.

8. The first quotation comes from March 13, 1941, Speech to Texas Legislature, in *Journal of the Senate of Texas, Regular Session, 47th Legislature*, 2 vols. (Austin: A. G. Baldwin & Sons, 1941), 1: 496. The second quotation is in *Texas Industry*, March 1942, p. 16. The third quotation can be found in Ernest Obadele-Starks, *Black Unionism in the Industrial South* (College Station: Texas A&M University Press, 2000), 22. The last quotation is in "Speech on anti-strike, anti-violence bill, April 7, 1941" Radio broadcast files, Box 66, Records of Texas Governor W. Lee O'Daniel, Texas State Library and Archives. For a sampling of business community red-baiting, see "Harris Country Association for Industrial Peace" Newsletters, in Labor Movement in Texas Collection, Box 2E189, Briscoe Center for American History. For the governor's red-baiting, see Polakoff, "The Development of the Texas State CIO Council"; and Seth Shepard McKay, *W. Lee O'Daniel and Texas Politics, 1938–1942* (Lubbock: Texas Tech Press, 1944). Further studies highlighting anti-communism during the war are William Gellerman, *Martin Dies* (New York: De Capo Press, 1972); Martin Dies, *Martin Dies' Story* (New York: Bookmailer, 1963); George N. Green, "Anti-Labor Politics in Texas, 1941–1957," in *American Labor in the Southwest: The First Hundred Years*, ed. James C. Foster (Tucson: University of Arizona Press, 1982); August Raymond Ogden, *The Dies Committee: A Study of the Special House Committee for the Investigation of Un-American Activities, 1938–1944* (Westport, CT: Greenwood Press, 1984); and George N. Green, *The Establishment in Texas Politics: The Primitive Years, 1938–1957* (Westport, CT: Greenwood, 1979). A few works detailing the relationship between unions and communism are Bruce Nelson, *Workers on the Waterfront: Seamen, Longshoremen, and Unionism in the 1930s* (Urbana: University of Illinois Press, 1988).

9. For helpful, yet sympathetic, works on President Franklin D. Roosevelt's attitude toward unions, see David B. Woolner, "FDR's Championing of Labor Unions Key to Prosperous Post-War Economy," Next New Deal: The Blog of the Roosevelt Institute, July 22, 2011, www.rooseveltinstitute.org; and Kenneth S. Davis, *The New Deal Years, 1933–1937* (New York: Random House, 1986). Less favorable views are in Amity Schlaes, *The Forgotten Man: A New History of the Great Depression* (New York: HarperCollins Publishers, 2008); William L. O'Neill, *A Democracy at War: America's Fight at Home & Abroad in World War II* (Cambridge, MA: Harvard University Press, 1993); and Jim Powell, *FDR's Folly: How Roosevelt and His New Deal Prolonged the Great Depression* (New York: Three Rivers Press, 2003). Further information can be found at the website for the Franklin D. Roosevelt Presidential Library and Museum, https://fdrlibrary.org.

10. The quotation is in Ray Davidson, *Challenging the Giants*, 145. See In the Matter of Southport Petroleum Co. and O.W.I.U., Local No. 227, 8 N.L.R.B. 792 (1938); and In the Matter of Southport Petroleum Company of Delaware and O.W.I.U, Local 449, 30 N.L.R.B. 257 (1942). Citations of NLRB records are to published NLRB reporters, which contain trial examiners reports and board findings. They are available on the NLRB website at https://www.nlrb.gov, (accessed June 13, 2021).

11. See Davidson, *Challenging the Giants*. The War Production Board was an agency created by President Roosevelt through executive order that supervised war production. For more on the organization, see Civil Production Administration, *Industrial Mobilization for the War: History of the War Production Board and Production Agencies, 1940–1945*, 1 vol., *Program and Administration* (Washington, DC: Government Printing Organization, 1947); and Bruce Catton, *The War Lords of Washington* (New York: Harcourt, Brace, and Company, 1948).

12. In order, the three quotations are in "Men in Service Say Vote CIO," *CIO Campaigner*, November 20, 1943; "Make It CIO in January," OWIU circular [undated, January 1943] in Sutton J. Boyd, "Appeals Made to Employees to Influence Their Decision Regarding Collective Bargaining" (master's thesis, North Texas State Teachers College, 1948), 78–79; "Hitler's Children," Southern Aircraft Company, 1943; and "Fact Finder for Southern Aircraft Employees," June 1943, in Boyd, "Appeals Made to Employees," 22, 25.

13. Testimony of Baytown workers and supervisors in In the Matter of Humble Oil & Refining Company and O.W.I.U., Local 1002, and Oil Workers Organizing Campaign (CIO), 48 N.L.R.B. 1118, 1124–27, 1134–39 (1943), accessed June 13, 2021, https://www.nlrb.gov. The OWIU received 35.2 percent of the vote; the Employee Federation, 64.8 percent. See In the Matter of Humble Oil & Refining and Local 1002, OWIU (CIO), 54 N.L.R.B. 78 (1943), accessed June 13, 2021, https://www.nlrb.gov. A more detailed look at the struggles experienced by the CIO in its attempts to unionize the Baytown refinery, see Michael R. Botson Jr., "We're Sticking by Our Union: The Battle for Baytown, 1942–1943," *Houston History Magazine* 8 (April 18, 2011); and Michael R. Botson Jr., and Tyler Priest, "Bucking the Odds: Organized Labor in Gulf Coast Oil Refining," *Journal of American History* 99 (2012).

14. For employment figures, see "War Manpower Commission Labor Market Developments Report for the Houston, TX Area," February 1, 1943, Item C-13 "Summary of Employment of Women and Non-Whites." This is located in the Papers of Albert Thomas, Series 1, Box 1, Defense Housing, WRC (strut plant); Final Disposition Report, Case 10-BR-34, HT, FEPC Papers, reel 96FR (strut and main plant); In the Matter of Hughes Tool Co. (Dickson gun plant) and USWA Locals 1742 and 2457, CIO, 53 N.L.R.B. 547, 548, fn. 1 (1943). Peak employment figure from John H. Ohly, *Industrialists in Olive Drab: The Emergency Operation of Private Industries during World War II* (Washington, DC: Center of Military History, US Army, 1999), 358, Appendix EE, item 14. The situation in the strut plant is in Botson Jr., *Labor, Civil Rights, and Hughes Tool Company*. The situation

in the main plant came from In the Matter of Hughes Tool Company and United Steelworkers of America, Local Unions Nos. 1742 and 2457, CIO, 45 N.L.R.B. 821, 823 (1942), accessed June 13, 2021, https://www.nlrb.gov.

For the December election, see In the Matter of Hughes Tool Company and United Steelworkers of America, Local Unions Nos. 1742 and 2457, CIO, 45 N.L.R.B. 821, 823, fn3 (1942), accessed June 13, 2021, https://www.nlrb.gov.

15. The information in the paragraph came from In the Matter of Sheffield Steel Corp. of Texas and USWA, Local 2708, 44 N.L.R.B. 955 (1942); Joseph Abel, "African Americans, Labor Unions, and the Struggle for Fair Employment"; Kirk White, "The Development of IAM District Lodge 776 in Fort Worth, Texas, 1942–1946" (master's thesis, University of North Texas, 1999). For a more detailed look at synthetic rubber production, see American Chemic Society, *United States Synthetic Rubber Program, 1939–1945* (Akron, OH: Division of the History of Chemistry and the Office of Communications, 1998); and Paul Wendt, "The Control of Rubber in World War II," *Southern Economic Journal* 13 (January 1947). The relationship between the CIO and AFL, a history often quite divisive and cantankerous, on the eve of the Second World War is explored in Walter Galenson, *The CIO Challenge to the AFL: A History of the American Labor Movement, 1935–1941* (Cambridge, MA: Harvard University Press, 1960).

16. See Abel, "African Americans, Labor Unions, and the Struggle for Fair Employment"; Ruth Milkman, *Gender at Work: The Dynamics of Job Segregation by Sex during World War II* (Urbana: University of Illinois Press, 1987); Wooster, "East Texas in World War II"; Gary J. Rabalais, "Humble Women at War: The Case of Humble's Baytown Refinery, 1942–1945," *Houston Review of History and Culture* 2 (Spring 2005); and Charlotte A. Holliman, "Beaumont Women during World War II," *Texas Gulf and Historical Record* XXXI (November 1995).

17. Look at George N. Green, "Texas State Industrial Union Council," *Handbook of Texas Online*, accessed June 13, 2021, https://tshaonline.org/handbook/online/articles/octbg; and Abel, "African Americans, Labor Unions, and the Struggle for Fair Employment." In addition to the above-mentioned works, more on black women denied certain jobs due to racial policies is in Philip S. Foner, *Women and the American Labor Movement* (New York: Free Press, 1979); Emily Yellin, *Our Mothers' War: American Women at Home and at the Front during World War II* (New York: Free Press, 2004); Katherine Turk, "'A Fair Chance to Do My Part of Work': Black Women, War Work, and Rights Claims at the Kingsbury Ordnance Plant," *Indiana Magazine of History* 108 (September 2012); Jacqueline Jones, *Labor of Love, Labor of Sorrow: Black Women, Work, and the Family from Slavery to the Present* (New York: Basic Books, 2010); Judith N. McArthur and Harold L. Smith, *Texas through Women's Eyes: The Twentieth-Century Experience* (Austin: University of Texas Press, 2010); and Jacqueline Jones, *American Work: Four Centuries of Black and White Labor* (New York: W. W. Norton and Company, 1998).

18. In addition to the works already cited concerning discrimination by unions against minorities, other useful works are Michael R. Botson Jr., "No Gold Watch for Jim Crow's Retirement: The Abolition of Segregated Unionism at Houston's

Hughes Tool Company," *Southwestern Historical Quarterly* 51 (April 1998); Philip S. Foner, *Organized Labor and the Black Worker, 1619–1981*, 2nd ed. (New York: International Publisher, 1982); Paul Frymer, *Black and Blue: African Americans, the Labor Movement and the Decline of the Democratic Party* (Princeton, NJ: Princeton University Press, 2007); Charles D. Chamberlain, *Victory at Home: Manpower and Race in the American South during World War II* (Athens: University of Georgia Press, 2003); and Bruce A. Glasrud and Gregg Andrews, "Confronting White Supremacy: The African American Left in Texas, 1874–1974," in *The Texas Left: The Radical Roots of Lone Star Liberalism*, eds. David O'Donald Cullen and Kyle Grant Wilkison (College Station: Texas A&M University Press, 2010).

19. See, Botson Jr., *Labor, Civil Rights, and Hughes Tool Company*; and Final Disposition Report, Case 10-BR-34, HT, FEPC Papers, reel 96FR. The War Manpower Commission thought it would be much easier to press employers to use the "ample supply" of female workers than it would be to get them to change their segregation policies. (See "War Manpower Commission Labor Market Developments Report for the Houston, TX Area," February 1, 1943, 3, 6. Papers of Albert Thomas, Series 1, Box 1, Defense Housing, WRC). Further reading on the limits of the War Manpower Commission's, and the government as a whole, ability to effect change regarding the hiring of women includes Deborah Fink, "What Kind of Woman Would Work in Meatpacking, Anyway? World War II and the Road to Fair Employment," *Great Plains Research* 5 (Fall 1995); and William J. Breen, "Women and Work: The Limit of War Manpower Commission Policy in World War II," *Australasian Journal of American Studies* 20 (December 2001). The records for the War Manpower Commission can be found at the National Archives, Record Group 211.

20. This paragraph came from the *Informer*, May 1, 1937, and August 23, 1941; Melinda Chateauvert, *Marching Together: Women of the Brotherhood of Sleeping Car Porters* (Urbana, IL: University of Illinois Press, 1998), 104. The advocacy of Carter Wesley can also be found in Nancy Eckols Bessent, "The Publisher: A Biography of Carter W. Wesley" (master's thesis, University of Texas, 1981). Richard Grovey's story is in Gary M. Lavergne, *Before Brown: Heman Marion Sweatt, Thurgood Marshall, and the Long Road to Justice* (Austin: University of Texas Press, 2010); and Bernadette Pruitt, *The Other Great Migration: The Movement of Rural African Americans to Houston, 1900–1941* (College Station: Texas A&M University Press, 2013).

21. The quotation is from Botson Jr., *Labor, Civil Rights, and Hughes Tool Company*, 116. The rest of the paragraph came from the *Informer*, May 29, 1937. To recruit black workers, unions often built links to community institutions. The UAW, for example, coordinated its efforts with the Dallas Negro Chamber of Commerce. For this, see Abel, "African Americans, Labor Unions, and the Struggle for Fair Employment," 620. In Houston, the most prominent black CIO backers were all affiliated with the city's active NAACP, and branch president Lulu B. White built strong links between the civil rights group and black labor leaders in the city. For this, see Michael Lowery Gillette, "The NAACP in Texas, 1937–1957"

(PhD diss., University of Texas, 1984); Melvin J. Banks, "The Pursuit of Equality: The Movement for First Class Citizenship among Negroes in Texas, 1920–1950" (PhD diss., Syracuse University, 1962); and Merline Pitre, *In Struggle Against Jim Crow: Lulu B. White and the NAACP, 1900–1957* (College Station: Texas A&M University Press, 1999).

22. See Robin D. G. Kelley, "A Lifelong Radical: Clyde L. Johnson, 1908–1994," *Radical History Review* 62 (March 1995); and National War Labor Board Case No. 771 (2898-CS-D). In the Matter of Southport Petroleum Company (Texas City, Texas) and Oil Workers' International Union; Local 449, CIO, June 5, 1943; Clyde Johnson, "CIO Oil Workers' Organizing Campaign," 178. Johnson first came to Texas to assist a strike by San Antonio pecan shellers and remained to organize a biracial union of cotton compress and flour mill workers on the Houston ship channel. On Johnson's involvement with the pecan shellers, see Zaragosa Vargas, *Labor Rights Are Civil Rights: Mexican American Workers in Twentieth-Century America* (Princeton, NJ: Princeton University Press, 2005). Further works on Johnson's activist and organizing actions, especially in Alabama, are Robin D. G. Kelley, *Hammer and Hoe: Alabama Communists during the Great Depression* (Chapel Hill: University of North Carolina Press, 1990); and Lowell K. Dyson, *Red Harvest: The Communist Party and American Farmers* (Lincoln: University of Nebraska Press, 1982).

23. The first and second quotations came from the *Bulletin* #9, October 23, 1942. The third quotation is in Exhibit in In the Matter of Humble Oil & Refining Company and O.W.I.U., Local 1002, and Oil Workers Organizing Campaign (CIO), 48 N.L.R.B. 1118, 1138 (1943). Also, see Baytown OWOC handbill, March 1943, excerpted in Boyd, "Appeals Made to Employees," 79.

24. The quotation is in the *Houston Informer*, October 11, 1941. For additional information, see Botson Jr., *Labor, Civil Rights, and Hughes Tool Company*; and Obadele-Starks, *Black Unionism in the Industrial South*.

25. The first quotation is in O'Connor, *History of the Oil Workers International Union*, 309–15. The next quotation can be found in Handbill quoted Clyde Johnson, "CIO Oil Workers' Organizing Campaign," 182. Additional information is in Davidson, *Challenging the Giants*; Obadele-Starks, *Black Unionism in the Industrial South*; and F. Ray Marshall, "Some Factors Influencing the Upgrading of Negroes in the Southern Petroleum Refining Industry," *Social Forces* 42 (December 1963).

26. See Botson Jr., *Labor, Civil Rights, and Hughes Tool Company*; Obadele-Starks, *Black Unionism in the Industrial South*; and Petition to the NWLB, In the Matter of Hughes Tool Company and USWA Locals 1742 and 2457, February 14, 1945, HT, FEPC Papers, reel 96FR.

27. On black pressure and the origins of the FEPC, see Paula F. Pfeffer, *A. Philip Randolph, Pioneer of the Civil Rights Movement* (Baton Rouge: Louisiana State University Press, 1996); Jervis Anderson, *A Philip Randolph: A Biographical Portrait* (Berkeley: University of California Press, 1986); Daniel S. Davis, *Mr. Black Labor: The Story of A. Phillip Randolph, Father of the Civil Rights Movement* (New York: E. P. Dutton, 1972); Andrew E. Kersten, *A. Philip Randolph: A Life in*

the Vanguard (New York: Rowman and Littlefield Publishers, 2006); and Andrew E. Kersten and Clarence Lang, eds., *Reframing Randolph: Labor, Black Freedom, and the Legacies of A. Philip Randolph* (New York: New York University Press, 2015). A comprehensive and generally favorable assessment of the Committee is Merl Elwyn Reed, *Seedtime for the Modern Civil Rights Movement: The President's Committee on Fair Employment Practice, 1941–1946* (Baton Rouge: Louisiana State University Press, 1991). Other works on the Committee include Herbert Garfinkel, *When Negroes March: The March on Washington Movement in the Organizational Policies for FEPC* (Glencoe, IL: Free Press, 1959); Andrew E. Kersten, *Race, Jobs, and the War: The FEPC in the Midwest, 1941–1946* (Urbana: University of Illinois Press, 2007); Louis C. Kesselman, *The Social Politics of FEPC: A Study in Reform Pressure Movements* (Chapel Hill: University of North Carolina Press, 1948); and Louis Ruchames, *Race, Jobs, and Politics: The Story of FEPC* (Westport, CT: Negro Universities Press, 1953). Local studies in Texas include Obadele-Starks, *Black Unionism in the Industrial South*; Botson Jr., *Labor, Civil Rights, and the Hughes Tool Company*; Emilio Zamora, "The Failed Promise of Wartime Opportunity for Mexicans in the Texas Oil Industry," *Southwestern Historical Quarterly* 95 (January 1992); and Abel, "African Americans, Labor Unions, and the Struggle for Fair Employment." Local studies of the FEPC in similar Southern contexts include Alex Lichtenstein, "Exclusion, Fair Employment, or Interracial Unionism: Race Relations in Florida's Shipyards during World War II," in *Labor in the Modern South*, ed. Glen T. Eskew (Athens: University of Georgia Press, 2011); and Bruce Nelson, "Organized Labor and the Struggle for Black Equality in Mobile during World War II," *Journal of American History* 80 (December 1993). Those interested in examining the limits of reform during the war can see Alan Brinkley, *The End of Reform: New Deal Liberalism in Recession and War* (New York: Vintage Books, 1995); and Wendy L. Wall, *Inventing the "American Way": The Politics of Consensus from the New Deal to the Civil Rights Movement* (New York: Oxford University Press, 2008).

28. See Obadele-Starks, *Black Unionism in the Industrial South*; James A Burran, "Violence in an 'Arsenal of Democracy,'" *East Texas Historical Journal* 14 (Spring 1976); and Abel, "African Americans, Labor Unions, and the Struggle for Fair Employment."

29. See Emilio Zamora, *Claiming Rights and Righting Wrongs in Texas: Mexican Workers and Job Politics during World War II* (College Station: Texas A&M University Press, 2009), 63–96, 158–80; Emilio Zamora, "The Failed Promise of Wartime Opportunity for Mexicans in the Oil Industry," in *Texas Labor History*, eds. Bruce A. Glasrud and James C. Maroney (College Station: Texas A&M University Press, 2013), 341; "Request for Further Action, Shell Oil Refinery, Houston, TX, March 1, 1944," in Denton Watson and Elizabeth Nuxoll, *The Papers of Clarence Mitchell Jr.*, 240–41; "Memorandum on Shell Oil Company, Houston, TX," March 26, 1945; Maslow to Ellinger, August 30, 1944, Shell Oil file (hereinafter, SO), FEPC Papers, Reel 101FR, in Denton Watson and Elizabeth Nuxoll, *The Papers of Clarence Mitchell Jr.*, 487. The state CIO had been on record in support of the FEPC since

its 1942 convention, but divisions on the issues of segregated locals and discrimination were apparent at state gatherings during the war. For these see, Murray Polakoff, "Internal Pressures on the Texas State CIO Council, 1937–1955," *Industrial and Labor Relations Review* 12 (January 1959).

30. See Zamora, *Claiming Rights and Righting Wrongs in Texas*, 176–79; Weekly Report, March 3, 1945, SO, FEPC Papers, reel 101FR; Summary of Shell Oil Case, May 5, 1945, SO, FEPC Papers, reel 21; and Houston *Informer*, May 5 and June 24, 1945.

31. This quotation is from Abel, "African Americans, Labor Unions, and the Struggle for Fair Employment," 597. Information from this paragraph can be found in Rabalais, "Humble Women at War"; Vatter, *The US Economy in World War II*, 127; Botter, "Labor Looks at Texas"; and Green, "Texas State Industrial Union Council." On the success of OWIU strikes after WWII, see Connor, *History of the Oil Workers International Union*; Davidson, *Challenging the Giants*; Myron Hoch, "The Oil Strike of 1945," *Southern Economic Journal* 15 (October 1948); and Gene Bethel, "An Analysis of Collective Bargaining Agreements in the Texas Petroleum Refining Industry, 1945–1950" (master's thesis, University of Texas, 1951). For the experiences for women, both white and black, with demobilization, see Judie Gammage, "Quest for Equality: An Historical Overview of Women's Rights Activism in Texas, 1890–1975" (PhD diss., North Texas State University, 1982); Karen Tucker Anderson, "Last Hired, First Fired: Black Women Workers during World War II," *Journal of American History* 69 (June 1982); Alice Kessler-Harris, *Out to Work: A History of Wage-Earning Women in the United States* (New York: Oxford University Press, 2003); Joanne Meyerowitz, ed., *No June Cleaver: Women and Gender in Postwar America, 1945–1960* (Philadelphia: Temple University Press, 1994); Sheila Tobias and L. Anderson, "What Really Happened to Rosie the Riveter? Demobilization and the Female Labor Force, 1944–1947," in *Women's America*, eds. Linda K. Kerber and Jane De Hart-Mathews (New York: Oxford University Press, 1982); and Claudia Goldin and Claudia Olivetti, "Shocking Labor Supply: A Reassessment of the Role of World War II on Women's Labor Supply," *American Economic Review: Papers and Proceedings* 103 (May 2013).

32. See, Pitre, *In Struggle Against Jim Crow*; and *Houston Informer*, January 13, 1945. The state CIO had been on record in support of the FEPC since its 1942 convention. The tensions inherent in the discrimination issue were apparent at the 1945 gathering, where a resolution opposing segregated "Jim Crow" locals failed to come to a vote. For this, see Polakoff, "Internal Pressures on the Texas State CIO Council." On black workers in Texas fighting union and employer discrimination in the postwar decades, see Botson Jr., *Labor, Civil Rights, and the Hughes Tool Company*; Sophia Z. Lee, "Hotspots in a Cold War: The NAACP's Postwar Workplace Constitutionalism, 1948–1964," *Law and History Review* 26 (June 2008); Hill, *Black Labor and the American Legal System: Race, Work, and the Law*; Kim Moody, *An Injury to All: The Decline of American Unionism* (New York: Verso, 1988); and Zachary Montz, "'Negro Laborers to the Crossroads': Organized Labor and the Traditions of Black Unionism in Houston, Texas, 1935–1964" (PhD diss., University of Texas, 2013).

6

Victory Crude

Texas Oil in World War II

Houston Faust Mount II[1]

For most Americans, mention of the words *World War II* calls to mind violent drama on a titanic scale. Perhaps one thinks first of the larger-than-life figures of Winston Churchill, Franklin D. Roosevelt, Joseph Stalin, George S. Patton, or Erwin Rommel. Or maybe of more anonymous moments that encapsulated the struggle for victory, such as the raising of the US flag on Iwo Jima. Those who served will have their own memories. Those who did not or those from later generations may think of family members and acquaintances who did serve. Some will first remember Pearl Harbor. Some will reflect on the home front and the common effort to support the cause of those fighting in the theaters of war. When one turns to the role of Texas in World War II, one will find the Texans who participated in all of these various aspects of the struggle. But among the images that it will almost certainly not conjure up are those of an oil derrick or the rhythmic nodding of a pump jack. Yet the Texas oil industry played a role in World War II that was essential to the Allied victory. Without Texas oil, many of the most crucial moments of World War II might have had vastly different outcomes. And while it is too strong an assertion to give Texas oil the credit for the Allied victory, it is valuable to reflect upon the pervasive and underappreciated role that it did play.

To begin understanding the role the Texas petroleum industry played in World War II, one must reflect on the transformation of warfare in the first half of the twentieth century. During the nineteenth century, the advent of the railroad had changed the way that war was fought. During the twentieth century, that revolution in transportation would be extended with the development of the internal-combustion engine and its application in ships, automobiles, and airplanes. The potential for "mechanized" warfare had been proven on a limited scale in World War I with the use of Paris taxis as transport, the deployment of the first tanks on the battlefield, and the pioneering of aviation warfare. All of this was a mere foreshadowing of the pervasive use of petroleum-powered weapons in World War II.[2]

A brief survey of key moments in the war will give some sense of the role that petroleum played in the struggle. From the beginning, oil was essential. Hitler's generals ushered in a new kind of warfare with blitzkrieg—lightning war—which was defined by armored columns breaking through enemy lines to be followed by mechanized and conventional infantry support. Like the tanks and troop transports, air support provided by the *Luftwaffe* was dependent upon fossil fuel supplies. It was an approach that proved victorious for Germany in its invasion of Poland and France, and it almost succeeded against the Soviet Union.[3]

If the petroleum-powered internal-combustion engine had created new possibilities in warfare, it also created new problems for strategic planners. Quite simply, national security interests could be dictated by access to oil supplies, which could lead to very difficult decisions when faced with scarcity. The Japanese government faced one such decision in 1941 as increasing sanctions by the United States threatened to cut off oil supplies that were vital to the operation of the Imperial Japanese Navy. Without fuel, the battleships and carriers of the Japanese Empire would be sitting ducks. Rather than renounce its war of conquest in Asia, the leadership opted to gamble everything in an all-out war with the United States. With the United States to be crippled by attacks on Hawaii and the Philippines, alternative petroleum sources could be safely secured by occupation of the Dutch East Indies (today Indonesia). It was a decision that proved to be both fateful and disastrous.[4]

The strategic limitations that oil supplies imposed on Japan were equally problematic for Germany. Expensive synthetic fuel plants provided some resources for Germany, but these proved to be highly vulnerable to Allied bombers. Control of the Ploesti oilfields in

Rumania also contributed to the German war effort, but these resources became an increasingly common target for air attack as the war progressed. For the United States and its allies, the challenges of rolling back the impressive Axis advance across the globe were greatly alleviated by abundant petroleum reserves. Although significant shortages could occur at key moments and logistics posed constant problems, the planners of the Allied campaigns against Germany and Japan could generally count upon the availability of oil resources for the fight. American submarines, powered by diesel fuel, devastated the Japanese tanker fleet, effectively depriving Japan of its access to the petroleum resources that had been one of its major war goals. Allied bombers, fueled by American gasoline, devastated the war machines of Germany, and Japan and made victory possible if not inevitable. Allied tanks and trucks in Europe could similarly count on American gasoline supplies as the fronts advanced toward ultimate victory.[5]

The supply of petroleum was almost as essential to the Allied victory as oxygen. But how important was American oil in general and Texan oil in particular? Here, it is important to recognize that the current situation in the global oil industry is very different from the conditions that prevailed during World War II. When one thinks of oil today, one is likely to think of the Middle East. During the 1930s and early 1940s, production in the Middle East was negligible compared to that of the United States. The statistics starkly illustrate the dominance of American oil. In 1939, as the war began in Europe, global oil production registered at approximately 2.08 billion barrels. Of that total, approximately 1.26 billion barrels were produced in the United States—that represented almost 61 percent of total world production. The strategic significance of this production advantage over the Axis powers can be appreciated by a brief glance at the production statistics for both Germany and Japan at that time—a mere 4.5 *million* and 2.7 *million* barrels, respectively, or 0.3 percent of global production. While Germany and Japan obtained access to some oil reserves by conquest and alliance, the problem of oil loomed for the Axis from the start. The Allies in contrast inhabited a completely different strategic world.[6]

But how much of that American oil was Texan oil? Quite a bit. With 17,350 workers at twelve oil refineries and nearly a dozen new major oil-field discoveries during the war, Texas had the largest oil industry and infrastructure in the country. Of total American production of 1.26 billion barrels in 1939, Texas accounted for over 483 million barrels produced. That is approximately 38 percent of the total production of the United States. Even in global terms, the record is impressive. Texas production amounted to almost one-quarter of all oil produced worldwide in 1939. This is even more remarkable when one considers that oil production was curtailed by regulation during these years to stabilize prices and promote conservation. With the scale and significance of Texas oil in mind, what then was the story of the industry during World War II? What contributions did Texans make in the management of the war effort in terms of mobilization and coordination of oil resources? With what unique problems did industry leaders wrestle, and how successful were they at meeting the goals of wartime need?[7]

To answer these questions, it is useful to first consider the complexity of the oil industry in Texas and the United States as a whole. Although there had been some talk of declaring the oil industry a public utility in the darkest days of the Depression, it remained an economic sector dominated by private actors. The industry could be divided into several different stages, including production, transportation, refining, and marketing. Among the most powerful actors in the industry were "majors" such as the corporate heirs of John D. Rockefeller's Standard Oil. This included companies such as Standard Oil of New Jersey, Standard Oil of New York, Standard Oil of Indiana, and Standard Oil of California. Also among the major companies were some corporations that had Texas pedigrees, including the Texas Company (Texaco) and Gulf Oil. Major oil companies were both domestic and international actors, operating in many states and countries. They tended to be more dominant in "downstream" stages of the industry, especially transportation, refining, and marketing. The production stage of the industry was more likely to include small operators who were locally rooted. In Texas, these "independent" producers were numerous and politically powerful. Because of their number, they were difficult to control and often were the bugbears of state and federal planners who believed they knew better. They could also represent the romantic vision of the oil dream, sometimes in the form of a lone individual taking big risks with limited resources to bring in a new well and strike it rich.[8]

However powerful that dream, all operators, whether major corporations or independent oil companies, lived within the realm of the laws of economics. Before the war, industry participants were motivated by profit. With the attack on Pearl Harbor, there was a new motive—victory—that influenced each actor to varying degrees. Federal and state regulators would attempt to coordinate the industry to meet the needs of the war but on its most essential level, the oil business remained a business. This meant that operators were limited by their own resources and were unlikely to act in ways that ran too strongly against their own economic interests. They also were more than willing to voice objections to policies and regulations that they viewed as counterproductive or unreasonable. In considering the role of Texas oil in the war, it is useful to keep the multitude of these private actors in mind. Although big initiatives by federal and state regulators draw warranted attention, it was ultimately a crowd of private operators that carried out the business of extracting and refining the oil that the war effort required.

The task of coordinating the constellation of private oil companies in World War II fell to a variety of federal and state regulatory bodies. It was not a system that had come about according to a master plan but was rather the result of haphazard political developments that had taken place over the course of the Depression. The Depression of the 1930s had resulted from a financial crisis, but it also coincided with a production crisis in the oil industry. In this case, the problem was overproduction, in large part a result of the discovery of the giant East Texas oil field in 1930. The development of the East Texas field sent prices tumbling. In 1931, the average cost per barrel in the United States fell to 65 cents. In East Texas oilfields, the price of crude oil fell as low as 2 cents per barrel. Compounding the impact of the Depression, overproduction of oil and the inevitable decline of crude oil prices hit the industry hard. As profits vanished, oilmen became increasingly open to the possibility of regulation. It seemed to many that the oil business needed to be saved from itself. And increasingly, oilmen began to speak of a need for conservation to alleviate the price collapse.[9]

In the early days of the Roosevelt administration, Secretary of the Interior Harold Ickes had advocated a strong role for federal regulators in the oil business. Ickes was a longtime progressive politician who believed that federal direction was necessary to avoid excessive waste. A self-proclaimed "curmudgeon," Ickes's outlook and personality was not reassuring to oilmen contemplating the imposition of a federal regulatory regime. His lack of experience and technical expertise in the complex business of finding, producing, transporting, refining, and marketing petroleum was particularly unsettling for the oil companies. For all these reasons, his appeal for the creation of a new office of federal "oil czar" to directly manage national petroleum policy fell flat.[10]

Nonetheless, oilmen were concerned about a possible nationalization of the industry by Ickes and other advocates of regulation. These concerns, in addition to the chaotic situation in oilfields, brought many to the table in drafting a federal oil industry code under aegis of the National Recovery Administration, if only to shape the contemplated regulatory regime. But the Oil Code proved to be short-lived. In June 1935, the Supreme Court pronounced the National Industrial Recovery Act unconstitutional, thus rendering the Oil Code a dead letter.[11]

The death of the Oil Code did not mark the end of Ickes's plans for federal regulation of the industry, but it did increase the urgency for state regulators to address the crisis in the industry. In the Lone Star State, it was the Texas Railroad Commission (TRC) that tried to stabilize oil prices by setting limits to allowable production—*prorationing* in industry terms. Unfortunately for advocates of conservation, litigation by opponents of state regulation in Texas blocked efforts to curtail production in the early 1930s. But after 1934, victory in the courts allowed the Commission to issue effective prorationing orders. This arguably made the TRC the most powerful regulatory body in the US oil industry with the ability to significantly affect the price of oil. Its commissioners would play a major role in coordinating the industry in Texas and beyond during World War II. And among these commissioners, one man played a prominent role in battles with both the industry and rival federal regulators—Colonel Ernest O. Thompson.[12]

As the leading figure on the TRC, Colonel Thompson voiced strident opposition to federal regulation. Born in Wise County, Texas, he moved to Amarillo when he was a young man and subsequently studied law at the University of Texas. Thompson served in the infantry in

World War I and won promotion to the rank of lieutenant colonel for his development of machine-gun tactics. Returning to Amarillo, he practiced law before entering politics, serving as mayor for two terms. In 1932, he was appointed to serve as a commissioner on the TRC by Governor Ross Sterling. Thompson felt sure that state regulatory bodies like the TRC could do a better job of directing the oil industry in Texas than federal agencies could. As talk of federal guidance grew in the early 1930s, Thompson employed rhetoric that drew heavily on Southern support for "states' rights" in his opposition to a federally directed regulatory regime. Secretary of the Interior Ickes was a favorite target of Thompson's ire, and the relationship between these two men with oversight of the petroleum industry in Texas was frosty.[13]

Approaching war clouds led to a multiplication of regulatory bodies rather than a streamlining of the system and complicated efforts to develop a national policy on oil. On May 28, 1941, President Roosevelt chose to confer additional advisory powers on Secretary of the Interior Ickes, naming him petroleum coordinator for National Defense. The powers of the new agency were vague, but Ickes planned to make an inventory of available oil reserves, facilitate pooling of resources, organize advisory committees of industry representatives, and coordinate federal petroleum policies. Significantly, the new office did not include powers to compel the oil companies in its preparation for possible war. Although it may be surprising to those familiar with the more powerful reach of some contemporary federal agencies, this limitation greatly curtailed the ability of the petroleum coordinator to direct the industry. Ickes needed the cooperation of oilmen and of state regulatory boards like the TRC in order to effect policy.[14]

Later, as the nation mobilized for war, Ickes pressed the president for greater authority over the petroleum industry. The result was an executive order issued on December 2, 1942, that rechristened the Office of the Petroleum Coordinator (OPC) as the Petroleum Administration for War (PAW). Ickes took up his new role as petroleum administrator and enjoyed a slight expansion of his purview. He was now empowered to set rules regarding production, transportation, and distribution of oil. Additionally, the order charged PAW with shaping policies aimed at increasing production through conservation, drilling, and consumption control. But as with the OPC, the PAW did not have sole discretion over petroleum policy. The president assigned control over the use of scarce materials used by the industry to the War Production Board. Further, and to the irritation of Ickes, the Office of Price Administration (OPA) would direct price regulation. This meant that the PAW still had to solicit support from these agencies in order to implement its own policies. And of course, state agencies like the TRC continued to regulate independently for their own jurisdictions.[15] So attempts to coordinate the oil industry for war took place within this context of conflicting bureaucracies and conflicting personalities. Even when planners were able to agree, they faced a multitude of contending private companies that had ideas of their own.

It was not a promising situation, and efforts to direct the industry to achieve war aims had decidedly mixed results. In Texas, as elsewhere, one can point to a share of achievements and failures. One challenge in Texas that was partially overcome was the overt hostility that existed between Secretary of the Interior Ickes and Colonel Thompson of the TRC. This was achieved in part by the mediation of an "adopted" Texan geologist and independent oilman, Everette Lee DeGolyer. DeGolyer enjoyed a storied career in the industry. It began with the discovery of what was, at the time, the largest oil well in history, while working in Mexico in 1910. After playing a founding role in a number of independent oil and geophysical exploration companies, he moved to Dallas in 1936. DeGolyer had worked on the federal Oil Code early in the Roosevelt administration and had been frustrated with Thompson's opposition. But over the course of the decade, he warmed to the colonel and the two became friendly.[16]

DeGolyer began working in 1941 as a federal regulator under Ickes, first with his appointment as director of conservation, then later as assistant deputy petroleum coordinator. In fact, his promotion was an important part of an effort to heal a rift that had developed between Ickes and the TRC. Beginning in May 1942, the TRC had exceeded production recommendations made by the OPC by more than 100,000 barrels. As the conflict festered into June, Ickes dispatched DeGolyer to negotiate with Chairman Thompson. After Thompson declared the conference to be "satisfactory," it appeared that the crisis was over. Summarizing the state of affairs, the *Dallas Morning News* headline declared "Dove of Peace About to Light on Rail Board."[17]

If the conflicting personalities of Ickes and Thompson presented challenges to coordinating the industry, the complexity of oilfield operations were even more problematic for planners. Despite the best intentions, many regulations that were imposed to promote conservation of scarce wartime resources impeded the development of oilfields. A good example was federal Conservation Order M-68, issued on December 23, 1941, which made 40-acre spacing for oil wells and 640-acre spacing for gas wells mandatory. The order also prioritized the assignment of scarce materials to "wildcat" wells. These wildcat wells were defined as a well drilled no less than two miles from an existing well. The idea was that materials should not be used to drill unnecessary wells in reservoirs where existing wells could be used to produce the oil. The problem was that surface-acre spacing might not correspond with underlying geology. For instance, a deeper well might stand close by a shallow well on the surface but drain oil from an entirely different reservoir. In other cases, multiple small reservoirs might be drained only by wells that were closely spaced at the surface. These wells would be excluded under the order while scarce materials might be assigned to improbable sites that met the regulatory definition of wildcat wells. It was a case where geological complexity undermined regulatory intent, and the result was inefficient development of oilfields in Texas and elsewhere. Fortunately for the Allies, production was still sufficient to meet the needs for victory.[18]

In addition to the challenges of material scarcity, operators also faced a scarcity in labor. Even before Pearl Harbor, many oil companies were losing workers to growing defense industries. With the advent of war, conscription further culled the number of available workers. The skilled labor required for efficient drilling could not easily be met by the high school students and older workers hired to make up for the losses. As a result, the speed of drilling slowed considerably.[19]

Other federal agencies presented even greater obstacles to plans for expanded development. Among the most problematic was the OPA, which imposed price controls on oil for the benefit of consumers. By keeping the price of oil low, the OPA ensured that there would be little incentive for exploratory drilling, even if oil companies were able to obtain steel for their wells and workers to drill them. In an act of astonishing unity, both Harold Ickes and TRC chairman Ernest O. Thompson supported calls for higher oil prices. No matter, the OPA was mostly intransigent, and for all Ickes's influence in the Roosevelt administration, he was not in a position to dictate policy to another federal agency.[20]

If planning measures backfired in cases such as M-68, there were other instances where regulators were able to work with the industry in more productive ways. Conservation measures undertaken in the East Texas field serve as one such positive example. Geologists estimated that the East Texas field held petroleum reserves figuring in billions of barrels of oil. They also reckoned that one-eighth to one-sixth of the nation's proved reserves lay in this subterranean reservoir. For this reason, conditions in the East Texas field were of special concern to the men working under Ickes.[21]

Shortly after accepting his position under Ickes, DeGolyer turned his attention to the East Texas field. On August 24, 1941, he submitted a memorandum outlining a situation that he saw as increasingly worrisome. At the root of the problem was pressure. Production of oil in the field was sapping underground pressure at an alarming rate. As a petroleum geologist, DeGolyer understood the grave threat that this presented. Oilfield conservation was not simply a matter of avoiding waste after the oil reached the surface. It involved understanding the fluid mechanics that produced the oil in the first place. Some force had to be able to push or pull oil from the ground, or it was just as useless to industry as if burned at the wellhead. In all productive oilfields, some sort of force made it possible to extract oil. In some cases, high subterranean pressure could push crude to the surface without assistance. In other cases, it was necessary to pump it up. But even with the aid of pump jacks, certain minimum pressure was necessary to make production economical. A number of forces at work below the earth could provide this much-needed pressure. Natural gas, pushing down on crude oil from a higher level, could help propel it up through a well. Gas might also exist in solution with petroleum and provide necessary lift, much as carbonation in a soda can force liquid out of an agitated bottle. Finally, subterranean water, pressing from below or laterally against the crude oil, could provide the force that would bring oil to the surface—and this was the case in the East Texas field.[22]

That pressure was falling precipitously in 1941, and petroleum engineers had a good idea why this was the case. Throughout the field, oil wells were producing water mixed together with the crude oil. This was a nuisance for many operators, but few made any effort to return the water to the reservoir. The result was that pressure continued to fall, and as a result, companies would ultimately extract less oil from the field. That is, unless something was done about it. There was little that oilmen could do to stop the production of water with the oil. Yet, once it had made its way to the surface, it was possible to separate the crude from the unwanted water and reinject the water into the reservoir. This involved a complicated process that had not quite been perfected yet. But if properly implemented, reinjection would have the effect of maintaining pressure within the oilfield, thus preventing "underground waste" and ensuring greater ultimate recovery of petroleum.[23]

Everette Lee DeGolyer was not alone in his concern regarding the East Texas field. In fact, Ernest O. Thompson and the TRC were already considering the matter. The Commission and a number of oilmen agreed that water injection was essential. In order to implement the plan, federal, state, and local interests supported the formation of the East Texas Salt Water Disposal Company. The name was somewhat misleading. The company in question would be responsible for "disposing" of water produced by oil wells by reinjecting it into the reservoir.[24]

Despite the national importance of the East Texas field, state and federal regulators had only limited power to implement the plan. The plan went forward, but there was resistance, and some major companies refused to participate. Their concern was that injecting water into the oilfield might open them up to litigation from other operators who could claim that injection damaged their oil production. Another issue was the fact that some marginal wells might need to be taken out of production for use as injection wells.[25]

But in the event, cooperation was forthcoming. With the attack on Pearl Harbor, the nation was roused from a false sense of security. The war did not suspend the laws of economics, but it did provide planners with some additional leverage in encouraging compliance. Speaking to East Texas producers after the attack, DeGolyer warned, "Unless the operators themselves take steps to conserve the field's oil reservoir, the Federal Government will."[26] Whether motivated by patriotism or fear, they took this message to heart. Closing ranks, producers formed the disposal company and DeGolyer used the resources of the OPC to secure the necessary permits and equipment authorization for the project to go forward.[27]

But even more important than the measures that maintained East Texas production was meeting the challenge of transportation. It was not enough to produce oil abundantly, as Texas oilfields were already doing effectively. It was also necessary to transport that oil to refineries where crude could be converted into lubricants, fuel oil, gasoline, and aviation fuel. And here petroleum planners faced a major problem in Texas.

Transportation resources were inadequate to bring optimum amounts of crude oil to the nation's refineries. Railroad-borne tank cars could meet only a fraction of the need, and existing pipelines were inadequate. Texas and other Gulf Coast refineries could be served by local fields but much of the nation's refining capacity was located in the Northeast. These East Coast refineries had been relying in part on tanker shipments for crude oil, but after the war began, those transport lines were vulnerable to submarine strikes. Before hostilities, about 95 percent of the oil delivered to East Coast refineries from the Gulf Coast in Texas and Louisiana arrived by oil tankers. Only 2 percent arrived by pipeline. The transportation problem during the war was addressed by a number of pipeline projects, the most important being the "Big Inch" and "Little Inch" lines. The construction of the Big Inch and Little Inch lines were critical to the Texas oil industry's wartime contribution. By linking the oilfields with northeastern refiners, and linking Texas refineries with northeastern markets, these pipelines made possible a massive contribution to the war effort on the part of Texas producers and refiners. Big Inch, the largest oil pipeline in the world during its operation, was a 24-inch crude oil pipeline with a transport capacity of 300,000 barrels of oil per day. The line would ultimately link Longview, Texas, with Philadelphia and New York refiners. Little Inch was a 20-inch products line, moving refined crude oil products from Beaumont, Texas, to Linden, New Jersey, at a capacity of 235,000 barrels per day.[28]

Planning for these massive lines had begun even before the outbreak of hostilities. First proposed by a group of East Coast oil executives, the idea was taken up by Secretary Ickes, who faced significant opposition from the federal Supply Priorities and Allocation Board. In view of the Board, the scarcity of steel would not allow for construction on such a large scale. It took sustained pressure on the part of Ickes, as well as the army, navy, and congressional committees to win approval for the project, which did not take place until June 1942. Construction of the lines was rapid, with Big Inch in operation by August 1943 and Little Inch delivering refined petroleum to New York by March 1944.[29]

The scale of the contribution of the Texas oil industry to the Allied war effort was staggering. Even before the completion of the Big Inch and Little Inch lines, the state was producing in excess of one million barrels of oil per day. And at that point, Texas oilfields represented about 57 percent of known oil reserves in the United States. "Downstream," the petroleum industry also expanded and contributed to the war effort, with the Houston area representing more than one-third of national refining capacity. Texans played leading roles in the coordination of the industry, and Texas oil operators large and small were responsible for approximately 40 percent of national oil production. As the Allied bombers flew and the tanks rolled toward victory, an enormous share of them was fueled by petroleum pumped from the prolific oilfields of the Lone Star State. And although the efforts of planners and producers alike have been largely forgotten, the strategic advantages that this oil gave to the Allies should be recalled as a crucial contribution by Texas to the war effort.[30]

Notes

1. Houston Faust Mount II is an Associate Professor of History at East Central University. He is the author of *Oilfield Revolutionary: The Career of Everette Lee DeGolyer* (College Station: Texas A&M University Press, 2014), from which parts of this chapter are excerpted.

2. For a general examination of the oil industry in the first half of the twentieth century in the United States, see Harold Williamson, *The American Petroleum Revolution, 1899–1959* (Evanston, IL: Northwestern University Press, 1964). Works examining the twentieth-century military's reliance upon mechanized warfare include Simon Dunstan, *Mechanized Warfare* (New York: Chartwell Books, 2005); George F. Hofmann and Donn A. Starry, eds., *Camp Colt to Desert Storm: The History of US Armored Forces* (Lexington: University Press of Kentucky, 1999); George Hofmann, *Through Mobility We Conquer: The Mechanization of US Cavalry* (Lexington: University Press of Kentucky, 2006); and Mathew Darlington Morton, *Men on Iron Ponies: The Death and Rebirth of the Modern US Cavalry* (DeKalb, IL: Northern Illinois University Press, 2009). The rise of the railroad to warfare is detailed in Martin Van Creveld, *Supplying War* (Cambridge, UK: Cambridge University Press, 1984); and Christian Wolman, *Engines of War: How Wars Were Won and Lost on the Railways* (New York: Public Affairs, 2011). The development of air power can be seen in John Andreas Olsen, *A History of Air Warfare* (Lincoln,

NE: Potomac Books, 2011); and Vaclav Smil, *Creating the 20th Century: Technical Innovations of 1867 to 1914 and Their Lasting Impact* (Oxford, UK: Oxford University Press, 2005).

3. Daniel Yergin, *The Prize: The Epic Quest for Oil, Money, and Power* (New York: Simon and Schuster, 1992), 328–50. For a more detailed examination of the importance of oil to industrial and mechanized powers and the global role of oil in the events of the Second World War, see Jay Stout, *Fortress Ploesti: The Campaign to Destroy Hitler's Oil Supply* (Havertown, PA: Casemate, 2003); Henrietta M. Larson, et al., *New Horizons: History of Standard Oil Company (New Jersey), 1927–1950* (New York: Harper and Row, 1971); Emanuel Horowitz, "Were There Strategic Oil Targets in Japan in 1945?," *Air Power History* 51 (Spring 2004); Worrall Reed Carter, *Beans, Bullets, and Black Oil: The Story of Fleet Logistics Afloat in the Pacific during World War II* (Washington, DC: US Government Printing Office, 1953); Thomas J. Petty, "Fueling the Front Lines: Army Pipeline Units—Part I," *Engineer Magazine* 32 (October–December 2007); *United States Strategic Bombing Survey (USSBS): The 5th Air Force in the War Against Japan* (Washington, DC: US Government Printing Office, 1947); Anthony A. Stranges, "Synthetic Fuel Production in Prewar and World War II Japan: A Case Study in Technological Failure," *Annals of Science* 50 (1993); Chapay Sultanov, *Would the Allies Have Won without Baku Oil?* (Baku, Azerbaijan: Nurlar, 2008); Dietrich Eichholtz, *War for Oil: The Nazi Quest for an Oil Empire* (Washington, DC: Potomac Books, 2012); Wilhelm Tieke, *The Caucasus and the Oil: The German-Soviet War in the Caucasus, 1942–1943* (Winnipeg, CN: J. J. Fedorowicz, 1995); Robert Goralski and Russell W. Freeburg, *Oil and War: How the Deadly Struggle for Fuel in WWII Meant Victory or Defeat* (New York: William Morrow and Company, 1987); Robert Forczyk, *The Caucasus 1942–1943: Kleist's Race for Oil* (Oxford: Osprey Publishing, 2015); Richard A. Stewart, *Sunrise at Abadan: The British and Soviet Invasion of Iran, 1941* (New York: Praeger, 1988); Guy H. Woodward and Grace Steele Woodward, *The Secret of Sherwood Forest: Oil Production in England during World War II* (Norman, OK: University of Oklahoma Press, 1973); T. H. Vail Motter, *United States Army in World War II: The Middle East Theater: The Persian Corridor and Aid to Russia* (Washington, DC: US Government Printing Office, 1952); Süleyman Erkan, "The Invasion of Iran by the Allies during World War II," *Cordrul Cosminului* 16 (2010); Kenneth Pollack, *The Persian Puzzle: The Conflict between Iran and America* (New York: Random House, 2005); Mohammad Gholi Majd, *Iran under Allied Occupation in World War II: The Bridge to Victory and the Land of Famine* (Lanham, MD: University Press of America, 2016); James Gadea, "'*Ulei Român*' During World War II and Beyond: Development of the Romanian Oil Industry," *Yale Review of International Studies* 6 (October 2014); Irvine H. Anderson, *Aramco, the United States, and Saudi Arabia: The Study of Dynamics of Foreign Oil Policy, 1933–1950* (Princeton, NJ: Princeton University Press, 1981); Maurice Pearton, *Oil and the Roumanian State, 1895–1948* (Oxford: Clarendon Press, 1971); Hanson Baldwin, "Oil Strategy in World War II," *American Petroleum Institute Quarterly—Centennial*

Issue (Washington, DC: American Petroleum, 1959); and Stephen Howarth and Joost Jonker, *A History of Royal Dutch Shell: Powering the Hydrocarbon Revolution, 1939–1973* (Oxford: Oxford University Press, 2007).

4. Yergin, *The Prize*, 305–27. For more specific examinations of the United States' use of oil to alter Japanese policy, see Roland H. Worth Jr., *No Choice but War: The United States Embargo against Japan and the Eruption of War in the Pacific* (Jefferson, NC: McFarland and Company, 1995); Herbert Feis, *Petroleum and American Foreign Policy* (Stanford University: Food Research Institute, 1944); and Walter J. Levy, *Oil Strategy and Politics, 1941–1981* (Boulder, CO: Westview Press, 1982). A good examination of US interdiction of Japanese oil supplies during the war is Stephen L. Wolborsky, "Choke Hold: The Attack on Japanese Oil in World War II" (master's thesis: School of Advanced Airpower Studies Air University, 1994).

5. Works examining the effect of Allied bombing on German oil production and Germany's alternative (synthetic) fuels are Earl R. Beck, *Under the Bombs: The German Home Front, 1942–1945* (Lexington: University of Kentucky Press, 1986); Peter W. Becker, "The Role of Synthetic Fuel in World War II Germany," *Air University Review* (July–August 1981); Conrad Crane, *Bombs, Cities, Civilians, and Oil: American Airpower Strength in World War II* (Lawrence: University of Kansas Press, 1993); and *Anthony N. Stranges,* "Friedrich Bergius and the Rise of the German Synthetic Fuel Industry," *Isis* 75 (December 1984). The Allied effort to deprive Germany of oil imports from neutral countries can be seen in Leonard Caruana and Hugh Rockoff, "An Elephant in the Garden: The Allies, Spain, and Oil in World War II," *European Review of Economic History* 11 (2007).

6. American Petroleum Institute, *Petroleum Facts and Figures*, 7th ed. (New York: American Petroleum Institute, 1941), 16. For works (besides the ones already listed above and below) chronicling the development and operations of the Texas oil industry and its greater importance to the United States, see C. A. Warner, *Texas Oil and Gas Since 1543* (Houston: Gulf Publishing Company, 1939); Mody C. Boatright and William A. Owens, *Tales from the Derrick Floor: A People's History of the Oil Industry* (Lincoln: University of Nebraska, 1982); Christopher J. Castaneda and Joseph A. Pratt, *From Texas to the East: A Strategic History of Texas Eastern Corporation* (College Station: Texas A&M University Press, 1993); Joseph A. Pratt, *The Growth of a Refining Region* (Greenwich, CT: JAI, 1980); Edgar Wesley Owen, *The Trek of the Oil Finders: A History of Exploration for Petroleum* (Tulsa, OK: American Association of Petroleum Geologists, 1975); James Presley, *A Saga of Wealth: The Rise of the Texas Oil Men* (New York: Putnam, 1978); Carl Coke Rister, *Oil! Titan of the Southwest* (Norman: University of Oklahoma Press, 2013); and John S. Spratt, *The Road to Spindletop: Economic Change in Texas, 1875–1901* (Austin: University of Texas Press, 1955). For a detailed examination of the emergence of Houston as a petroleum industry center, see Paul Alejandro Levengood, "For the Duration and Beyond: World War II and the Creation of Modern Houston, Texas," (PhD diss., Rice University, 1999). To see oil and the war effort's

influence on a smaller city and rural region, see Irene Paulette, "Odessa during the War Years, 1941–1945: A Microcosm of the Nation," *Permian Historical Annual* 22 (1992); and James R. Pfluger, "Fuel for Victory: Texas Panhandle Petroleum, 1941–1945," *Panhandle-Plains Historical Review* 62 (1989).

7. Emilio Zamora, "The Failed Promise of Wartime Opportunity," in *Texas Labor History*, eds. Bruce Glasrud and James C. Maroney (College Station: Texas A&M University Press, 2013). The number of new major oil-field discoveries in Texas during the war came from "Oil and Texas: A Cultural History" from the Texas State Historical Association's, *Texas Almanac*, accessed June 13, 2021, https://texasalmanac.com/topics/business/oil-and-texas-cultural-history. The twelve refineries were located in Houston (3), Port Neches (2), Texas City (3), Port Arthur (2), Baytown (1), and Beaumont (1).

8. Diana Davids Olien and Roger M. Olien, *Oil in Texas: The Gusher Age, 1895–1945* (Austin: University of Texas Press, 2002), 220–21.

9. Earl Oliver, "Changes Needed in Oil Ownership Law," *Oil and Gas Journal*, 23 (July 1931); Yergin, *The Prize*, 244–47; *Twentieth Century Petroleum Statistics, 1946* (Dallas: DeGolyer and MaNaughton, 1946), 21; Olien and Olien, *Oil in Texas*, 183; Roger M. Olien and Diana Davids Olien, *Oil and Ideology: The Cultural Creation of the American Petroleum Industry* (Chapel Hill: University of North Carolina Press, 2000), 185–86; Houston Faust Mount, II, *Oilfield Revolutionary: The Career of Everette Lee DeGolyer* (College Station: Texas A&M University Press, 2014), 181.

10. Olien and Olien, *Oil and Ideology*, 195–98; Mount, *Oilfield Revolutionary*, 183. Other works chronicling the development of government regulation of the oil industry are Norman E. Nordhauser, *The Quest for Stability: Domestic Oil Regulation, 1917–1935* (New York: Garland Publishing, 1979); Steve Isser, *The Economics and Politics of the United States Oil Industry, 1920–1990: Profits, Populism, and Petroleum* (New York: Routledge, 1996); Jeanne Nienaber Clarke, *Roosevelt's Warrior: Harold L. Ickes and the New Deal* (Baltimore, MD: Johns Hopkins University Press, 1996); M. Elizabeth Sanders, *The Regulation of Natural Gas: Policy and Politics, 1938–1978* (Philadelphia: Temple University Press, 1981); and Peter H. Irons, *The New Deal Lawyers* (Princeton, NJ: Princeton University Press, 1993).

11. David M. Kennedy, *Freedom from Fear: The American People in Depression and War, 1929–1945* (New York: Oxford University Press, 1999), 182–88, 328; Hugh D. Mallon, "Petroleum Code and P.A.B. Knocked out by Supreme Court," *Oil and Gas Journal*, 30 (May 1935); Olien and Olien, *Oil and Ideology*, 197–98; Mount, *Oilfield Revolutionary*, 86, 183.

12. Kenny A. Franks, *The Oklahoma Petroleum Industry* (Norman: University of Oklahoma Press, 1980), 139–50; Olien and Olien, *Oil in Texas*, 182–83; Olien and Olien, *Oil and Ideology*, 189, 205; Mount, *Oilfield Revolutionary*, 181–82. The standard work on the Texas Railroad Commission and the Texas oil industry is David E. Prindle, *Petroleum Politics and the Texas Railroad Commission* (Austin: University of Texas Press, 1984).

13. James A. Clark, *Three Stars for the Colonel: The Biography of Ernest O.*

Thompson (New York: Random House, 1954), 16–17, 30, 38–39, 40–43, 47–68; William R. Childs, *The Texas Railroad Commission: Understanding Regulation in America to the Mid-Twentieth Century* (College Station: Texas A&M University Press, 2005), 209–24; Olien and Olien, *Oil and Ideology*, 199–200; Mount, *Oilfield Revolutionary*, 186.

14. Olien and Olien, *Oil and Ideology*, 228; Gerald D. Nash, *United States Oil Policy, 1890–1964* (Pittsburgh: University of Pittsburgh Press, 1968), 159–60; Mount, *Oilfield Revolutionary*, 193.

15. Nash, *United States Oil Policy*, 165–67; Mount, *Oilfield Revolutionary*, 203. The standard work on the Petroleum Administration for War is Petroleum Administration for War, *History of the Petroleum Administration for War, 1941–1945* (Washington, DC: US Government Printing Office, 1946).

16. For more on Everette Lee DeGolyer beyond those works cited in the footnotes of this work, see Carl C. Branson, "E. L. DeGolyer, 1886–1956," *Oklahoma Geology Notes* 17 (January 1957); and Lon Tinkle, *Mr. De: A Biography of Everette Lee DeGolyer* (Boston: Little, Brown, 1970).

17. "Texas, OPC Row Nears Settlement," *Dallas Morning News*, June 19, 1942; "Dove of Peace About to Light on Rail Board," *Dallas Morning News*, June 20, 1942; Mount, *Oilfield Revolutionary*, 200–3.

18. Olien and Olien, *Oil in Texas*, 222; Nash, *United States Oil Policy*, 167–68; John W. Frey and H. Chandler Ide, eds., *A History of the Petroleum Administration for War, 1941–1945* (Washington, DC: US Government Printing Office, 1946), 178–79.

19. Olien and Olien, *Oil in Texas*, 224–25. For an examination of unions and the oil industry, see Ray Davidson, *Challenging the Giants: A History of the Oil, Chemical and Atomic Workers International Union* (Denver: Oil, Chemical and Atomic Workers International Union, 1988); John Wooding, Charles Levenstein, Beth Rosenberg, "The Oil, Chemical and Atomic Workers International Union: Refining Strategies for Labor," *International Journal of Health Services* 27 (1997); and Harvey O'Connor, *History of the Oil Workers International Union (CIO)* (Denver, CO: Oil Workers International Union, 1950). See also In the Matter of Hughes Tool Company and Independent Metal Workers Union Locals Nos. 1 and 2, 36 N.L.R.B. 904 (1941). On history of IMW locals at Hughes, see Michael R. Botson Jr., *Labor, Civil Rights, and the Hughes Tool Company* (College Station: Texas A&M University Press, 2005). See also Clyde Johnson, "CIO Oil Workers' Organizing Campaign in Texas, 1942–1943," in *Essays in Southern Labor History Conference, 1976*, eds. Gary M. Fink and Merl E. Reed (Westport, CT: Greenwood Press, 1976). For racial dynamics of unions in the Texas petroleum industry, see F. Ray Marshall, "Some Factors Influencing the Upgrading of Negroes in the Southern Petroleum Refining Industry," *Social Forces* 42 (December 1963); and Zachary A. Montz, "Negro Laborers to the Crossroads: Organized Labor and the Traditions Black Unionism in Houston, Texas, 1935–1964" (PhD diss., University of Texas, 2013). Works chronicling the operations of the Fair Employment Practices Committee are Herbert Garfinkel, *When Negroes March: The March on Washington*

Movement in the Organizational Policies for FEPC (Glencoe, IL: Free Press, 1959); Andrew E. Kersten, *Race, Jobs, and the War: The FEPC in the Midwest, 1941–1946* (Urbana: University of Illinois Press, 2007); Louis C. Kesselman, *The Social Politics of FEPC: A Study in Reform Pressure Movements* (Chapel Hill: University of North Carolina Press, 1948); and Louis Ruchames, *Race, Jobs, and Politics: The Story of FEPC* (Westport, CT: Negro Universities Press, 1953).

20. Everette Lee DeGolyer, "Memorandum for Mr. Davies," February 27, 1943, box 51, folder 3423, Everette Lee DeGolyer Collection, Southern Methodist University; Olien and Olien, *Oil and Ideology*, 245; "Texas Pleads for Increase in Oil Prices," *Dallas Morning News*, April 16, 1943; Mount, *Oilfield Revolutionary*, 196. Additional works on the Office of Price Administration and its charge during the war are Andrew Bartels, "The Office of Price Administration and the Legacy of the New Deal, 1939–1946," *Public Historian* 5 (Summer 1983); and Julius Hirsch, *Price Control in the War Economy* (New York: Harper and Brothers, 1943). For other works chronicling price controls on corporations during the Second World War, see Hugh Rockoff, "Price and Wage Controls in Four Wartime Periods," *Journal of Economic History* 41 (June 1981); Meg Jacobs, "'How About Some Meat?' The Office of Price Administration, Consumption Politics, and State Building from the Bottom Up, 1941–1946," *Journal of American History* 84 (December 1997); Paul Evans, "The Effects of General Price Controls in the United States during World War II," *Journal of Political Economy* 90 (October 1982); Hugh Rockoff and Geofrey T. Mills, "Business Attitudes towards Wage and Price Controls in World War II," *Business and Economic History* 12 (1983); and Hugh Rockoff, "The Response of the Giant Corporations to Wage and Prime Control in World War II," *Journal of Economic History* 41 (March 1981).

21. DeGolyer, "Memorandum for Mr. Ralph K. Davies," August 20, 1941, box 56, folder 3538, Everette Lee DeGolyer Collection, Southern Methodist University; Mount, *Oilfield Revolutionary*, 197.

22. DeGolyer, "Memorandum for Mr. Ralph K. Davies"; Mount, *Oilfield Revolutionary*, 197; Harry F. Simons, "East Texas' Future Directly Related to Return of Water to Woodbine Sand," *Oil and Gas Journal* 28 (January 1943): 177. Ralph A. Wooster's "East Texas in World War II," *East Texas Historical Journal* 45 (2007) and Bill O'Neal's, *East Texas World War II* (Charleston, SC: Arcadia Publishing, 1970) are good overviews of the region during the war.

23. DeGolyer, "Memorandum for Mr. Ralph K. Davies"; Mount, *Oilfield Revolutionary*, 197; Simons, "East Texas' Future Directly Related to Return of Water to Woodbine Sand," 176; Mount, *Oilfield Revolutionary*, 197–98.

24. DeGolyer, "Memorandum for Mr. Ralph K. Davies"; Mount, *Oilfield Revolutionary*, 198.

25. DeGolyer, "memorandum for Mr. Ralph K. Davies"; Mount, *Oilfield Revolutionary*, 198. Ibid.

26. "Plans Mapped here for Etex Salt Disposal," *Dallas Morning News*, December 11, 1941.

27. "Plans Mapped here for Etex Sal Disposal"; Frey and Ide, eds., *A History*

of the Petroleum Administration for War, 1941–1945, 189; Mount, *Oilfield Revolutionary*, 198–99.

28. Frey and Ide, eds., *A History of the Petroleum Administration for War, 1941–1945*, 3, 104; Olien and Olien, *Oil in Texas*, 226; Castaneda and Pratt, *From Texas to the East*, 16–17. Standard works on the Little Inch and Big Inch pipelines are Texas Eastern Transportation Corporation, *The Big Inch and Little Big Inch Pipelines: The Most Amazing Government-Industry Cooperation Ever Achieved* (Houston: Texas Eastern Transportation Corporation, 2000); *Christopher James Castaneda, Regulated Enterprise: Natural Gas Pipelines and Northeastern Markets, 1938–1954* (Columbus: Ohio State University Press, 1993); Christopher J. Castaneda, "The Texas-Northeast Connection: The Rise of the Post-World War II Gas Pipeline Industry," *Houston Review* 12 (1990); and Maury Klein, *A Call to Arms: Mobilizing America for World War II* (New York: Bloomsbury Press, 2013).

29. Frey and Ide, eds., *A History of the Petroleum Administration for War, 1941–1945*, 104–05.

30. *Twentieth Century Petroleum Statistics, 1946* (Dallas: DeGolyer and MacNaughton, 1947), 8, 28; Olien and Olien, *Oil in Texas*, 236; Clark, *Three Stars for the Colonel*, 183.

7

The Better Half

Women, the Home Front, and World War II Texas

Christopher B. Bean

The Second World War was a total affair. Not only did governments go to war, but also its people. Equally decisive as any theater to victory, the home front necessitated constituents previously excluded from conflict. Most numerous, and important, were women, who represented approximately half the population. From time immemorial, women's dominant role regarding combat generally was as the "passive sweetheart," anxiously awaiting the return of her conquering hero in all his masculine glory. Women were not much beyond invaluable objects to be protected or desired, whose memory steeled their men's resolve against an enemy bent on degrading her honor. Modern warfare, with its nationalism and total objective, however, redefined women's role in the fight. She still anxiously awaited the return of her "conquering hero." But she was now no longer passively doing so. Mobilization required economies of scale previously inconceivable. Peasants, once relatively excepted from the conflict, were now citizens, invested and endowed with certain expectations to the nation and fully aware of the consequences of victory and defeat. The line between combatant and noncombatant had been blurred. All, young and old, man and woman, were now stakeholders in the affair, fully invested whether their country won or lost. Victory could come only by the combined effort of manpower as well as womanpower.[1]

Following Pearl Harbor in 1941, Texans immediately rallied to the defense of the country. Millions of men worked in the factories and plants constructing the tools of war or tilled the fields, reaping the food for victory. Alongside them were hundreds of thousands of women, including 310,000 new entries into the workforce during the war. Seven hundred and fifty thousand people from the Lone Star State entered military service, including 12,000 women, a demographic that could not immediately serve (outside the army and Navy Nurse Corps) since no military branch yet accepted them as enlistees. Within a year, due to wartime necessity and intense lobbying by prominent female governmental officials, including First Lady Eleanor Roosevelt, every branch would accept women, although, initially, only in an auxiliary status. Where and what a woman in uniform did during the war was soon defined by an acronym. By war's end, 350,000 US women were WACs (Women's Army Corps), WAVES (Women Accepted for Volunteer Emergency Service), WASP (Women Airforce Service Pilots), and "Bams," among other things, effectively doing nearly everything short of combat for the armed forces. This represented approximately a quarter of all Allied female military personnel during the war.[2]

Less profile yet more numerous and, in certain ways, more indispensable to the country's war effort were the millions of women whose uniform was not military issued. The vast majority of women in the country at the time either did not qualify for military service or had no intention of joining. They followed different paths, contributing in other ways. Instead of cockpits and khakis, they punched timeclocks, hammered rivets, tilled the fields, husbanded livestock, or typed inventory receipts. Some even invested their time to volunteering, organizing letter-writing campaigns, bond drives, or a myriad of different means to assist the war effort. There were even some who "contributed" through illegal and immoral ways. These women "did their part" by literally "doing their part." Most women, however, never really entered the workforce (or entered in a sporadic, part-time nature when economic needs arose). These women remained at home, contributed in quiet, yet vital ways. They were mothers, regardless of a war, who still had children to raise. They anxiously went through their daily lives not wanting to think too in-depth about what the son serving overseas was going through. Or perhaps they were wives, spending days on end alone from a husband who was cities away in war work or a continent away fighting the enemy. Many wives, both those who worked and those who did not, spent lonely days without their husband's comfort due to a war that needed to be won.

Society at the time was most comfortable when women remained in traditional gendered roles. Outside the home, perhaps the only occupation that everyone accepted women doing was the nurse. Traditionally a female occupation (both in peacetime and war) without causing any undue anxiety, nursing was "ideal" for women's nurturing nature. Of all the ways women served, this one, although romanticized, was one fraught with danger, both physical and psychological. Nurses generally were the first women in theater, sometimes literally going ashore with the attack forces. Not shielded from the war, they encountered all its sights, sounds, and smells. Consider the case of Lucy Wilson. A native of Big Sandy (East Texas), Wilson worked for the Red Cross in Tyler when she responded to an invite to enlist with the Army Nurse Corps. Wanting to get as far away from home as possible, she chose service in El Paso, before accepting overseas duty in the Philippines. Literally on the day her enlistment was up, the Japanese bombed Pearl Harbor. The Japanese immediately followed up with an attack on the Philippines. Wilson and her fellow nurses, prior to the American retreat, were evacuated to the Bataan Peninsula to prepare for the wounded. Prior to the surrender of Bataan, she was further evacuated to the island of Corregidor. She and twenty fellow nurses tended the wounded until ordered to depart on one of the last ships out to Australia. "Walking out in the middle of an operation with hundreds lined up under the trees waiting for surgery was devastating to me," she confessed. "This I have to live with for the rest of my life." Wilson's ordeal on the islands and subsequent evacuation was dramatized in a wartime movie starring Claudette Colbert, Paulette Goddard, and Veronica Lake, *So Proudly We Hail.*[3]

The clear majority of Texas women mobilized for the war effort did not wear a military uniform. Instead they donned denim sailor pants, nudeedudee overalls, or ration-induced simple rayon dresses. They worked in the private businesses prevalent during peacetime that continued during the war; they worked in offices, both for the government and private industries; they worked in the fields and pastures; or they worked in war and industrial manufacturing. Of those working, approximately a third worked in clerical and sales. Often forgotten about the US armed forces, it is a bureaucracy. A large majority of its personnel, in fact, do not actually fight or experience combat. This is as true today as it was in World War II. Of the sixteen million uniformed personnel, approximately 800,000 witnessed combat (5 percent). The rest made it possible for the combatants to fight. Many had to type and file each soldier's paperwork; many had to fulfill war industrial contracts; and many had to coordinate the war-material logistics. War is not fought simply with guns and bombs, but also pencils, paperwork, and typewriters (or for those who cannot remember the Cold War, spreadsheets, computers, global positioning systems [GPS], and smartphones). As the number of military personnel increased, inversely, so too did the size of the civilian white-collar workforce. During the war, its size increased four-fold, from one million in 1940 to four million in 1945. A benefactor of this increase was black women.[4]

Women also increased their numbers in the fields. The manpower shortage greatly affected agriculture as the draft and more promising war work siphoned off millions. The government, naturally, turned to women to fill the void. In total, 1.4 million women worked the fields during the war, increasing their percentage in agriculture from 8 percent in 1940 to more than 22 percent by war's end. Formally created in spring 1943, the Women's Land Army (WLA) was formed in the image of its Great War predecessor. Although hindered at times by the gender sensibilities and worries of the time and fears about "a socialized labor force," the WLA was administered at the state and local level. While some women labored year-round, living on-site at the respective farms, others engaged in seasonal work, receiving only cursory "on the job training." At its height, almost 76,000 women worked in the program in Texas in 1943. Despite a precipitous decline in 1944 and 1945, WLA workers in Texas still remained above 51,000 each year. The majority of Texas women (most Hispanic and African American) who worked the fields, however, did so in the same capacity before the war. This was not necessarily "an outing" or opportunity to "play farmer" for a time. It was their livelihood, as it was for their parents and grandparents before. For many, if not for the war, it was to be their future as well. Hermaninia Guerrero Cadena remembered how she and her family made a game out of their fieldwork by pretending the weeds in the field were enemy soldiers in need of plucking. Herlinda Mendoza Buitron Estrada from Bastrop worked the cotton fields as a teenager. Her family relied not only on her labor but also on her proficiency in recordkeeping. This ensured that she and her family received the maximum fruits of their labor. As her fiancé served in the Pacific, Victoria Partida Guerrero worked the fields, often alongside German prisoners of war. She admitted that this situation created unease. She worried they would escape.[5]

Women also assisted with livestock. Unlike other work for which women replaced departed men, ranching was one that they had always assisted. Ranching required "all hands on deck," and that included women's hands. Although long since the days of the frontier existed, the same spirit of rugged individualism, liberty, and egalitarianism still pervaded in the ranching life. Just as with men, women were expected to work. She also did not feel the same societal pressures as women working in manufacturing or the military. Her work during the war, for the most part, was her work before it and would be her work after it. Ranching communities "did not ridicule a woman for swinging a rope if she knew how to use it." "Rosie the Rancher," war or not, declared Wanda Harper Bush, was "nothing out of the ordinary." Not out of the ordinary was the work these women had to do, for it was exactly the work men did. "We worked hard," Celia Ann Smith Hill, a high school student from Alpine (West Texas) remembered. "Didn't make a difference how cool it was. It didn't matter if we would freeze to death, we'd get there and they'd have a horse saddled for us." Camella Menotti, also a teenaged girl, remembered working her father's farm in Galveston County. She recalled assisting him in many ways, including feeding the animals, vaccinating the animals, and dipping the animals against parasites. Menotti, a self-proclaimed "city girl," further added that she was taught the proper way to skin cattle.[6]

War mobilization perhaps had its most profound effect on the economics for women. Jobs traditionally exclusive to men now opened to women, including labor-intensive occupations such as lumberjacks, crane operators, welders, to name a few. In fact, approximately two million women labored in heavy industries by war's end. Such influx contributed to women increasing their share of the workforce from approximately a quarter in 1940 to more than a third by 1945. Perhaps understated, the actual number of women who worked during the war was higher, since many moved in and out of the economy depending on circumstances at home. In hindsight traditional gender roles were not revolutionized, in part because of sensitivities about "proper roles" for men and women and in part because women did not necessarily want them revolutionized. But to say there was not a profound benefit would miss the point. Millions of women found greater opportunities to move from the home to the factory or, more prevalent, from one job, possibly with limited opportunities and pay, to another with greater opportunities and higher wages. The war presented mobility to an otherwise static population. For a brief time, female agency, especially economic, was the strongest it had been since the beginning of the industrial revolution in the United States. In World War I, the percentage of women in the workforce at the beginning of the war changed little by war's end. Women moved laterally—those working prior to the conflict simply transitioned to other jobs. There was not a massive influx of new female employment. During the Second World War, however, there was both lateral and vertical transition. Women were not just moving into occupations previously deemed "man's work," but millions, many of which either worked part-time or not at all, moved into the workforce economy. The number of employed women during the war increased from eleven million to nearly twenty million, with perhaps a quarter of those new to the workforce. By 1945, with the depletion of men from the labor market, with sixteen million serving in the armed forces, and a large influx of women into the economy to fill that void, women accounted for approximately 50 percent of the nation's workforce.[7]

This, of course, included 310,000 Texas women who entered the workforce during the war. The Lone Star State not only welcomed numerous military facilities, but also proved instrumental in war-related industries. Women moved to industrial hot spots such as Houston, Dallas, Fort Worth, and Amarillo, refining, assembling, welding, lathing, and pressing the necessary material and machines for war. The country's necessity temporarily disrupted prewar gender segregation in the private sector. The iconic image of female empowerment and contribution during the war had to be "Rosie the Riveter." Empowered and capable, yet still feminine, desirable, and aware of her temporariness, this icon was in contrast to the gender-bending "Amazon" who threatened both men and women by her perceived "manliness" or "unnatural lesbianism." Rosie (as well as her female contemporary serving in the armed forces) could still contribute to victory, yet would not disrupt traditional gender roles necessary for a return to postwar normality nor undermine what mainstream society defined what it meant to be a woman in the United States. Although defined as an aircraft worker, the image expanded to include women in war production, from the aircraft production floor to the shipyards, to the ordnance factory to the steel plant, each had their version of Rosie. This icon spawned in part to include and acknowledge the contribution of women to the effort, and their numbers in these industries exploded. In Fort Worth, a hub for aircraft construction in Texas, Consolidated Aircraft set up eight schools for female workers within five months of the attack on Pearl Harbor. Within two years, women comprised 38 percent of the company's workforce and were employed in almost all its departments. Female workers at Hughes Tool Company in Houston comprised only 1.4 percent of the company's workforce in May 1942; by September of the following year, that number had increased to 26.6. The Lufkin Foundry (Deep East Texas) had women operating all the heavy machinery necessary to construct tank gears, transmissions, Howitzers, and machine guns. By 1944, there were 1.7 million women working in heavy industries, nearly an 800 percent increase from 1940—a situation made possible only through state legislatures amending labor laws to allow women to do heavy work and work more than eight hours in a day.[8]

One would think that women's entry into the workforce would be applauded by organized labor. On the surface, both women and unions could benefit from the relationship: unions with increased membership and women with increased security and agency. Women's experience with labor unions, however, is mixed. It is even less for African American women, who had two strikes against them: sex and race. Unions outwardly welcomed women into their ranks, even advocating for benefits such as equal work for equal pay—although female workers rarely received the same pay as their male counterparts. Gender inequality was a persistent aspect of war work. Even when they performed the same tasks as men, women generally received "women's work" pay or basic labor pay. Yet much of the activism on the part of unions came with a caveat. Unions were male-dominated entities whose first loyalty often was not with women, or even female members, but with its male constituents. Women could be a benefit to the union during the war, but few unions saw them as anything other than temporary. Moreover, they were routinely segregated from male counterparts who often harassed them with crude jeers and taunts. Union men routinely let it be known their presence was not wanted. For unions, they were a necessary measure for the war emergency, and once that emergency passed, so too would women. At times, unions colluded with management against female workers. Management, with support from organized labor, would segregate workers according to sex. In addition, although the federal government created new regulatory bodies to safeguard against discriminatory practices—such as the War Manpower Commission and the Fair Employment Practices Committee—the ability (and willingness) for Uncle Sam to effect change was circumscribed by a strong federalist attitude and constraints built in at their conception.[9]

Those who entered fields previously gender exclusive discovered much more than discrimination. Although by no means universal, since many women attest to being treated well when occupying "these men's spheres," women did experience sexual harassment. This behavior ranged from sexual propositions to crude jokes, from gawking stares to expressive whistles. For some, it was enlightening to enter these male-dominated spheres and witness the interactions that only exist between men. "We were like on parade when we went in [the construction yard]," remembered Aileen Noguess who worked at Consolidated Steel in Orange, Texas. "[F]rom the shop where I worked we had almost a mile to walk, and men up in the gantries whistled down at the women going by and things like that." Julia Wingate, a twenty-year-old, was also hired at Consolidated Steel. She was, in fact, the first female employee to "work out in the yard." She logged all the material coming in for construction and equipping the ships. Wingate was hesitant, until she discovered a male cousin working in the yard who she believed would watch out for her. That cousin warned her the men in the yard often teased and played jokes on one another, and now that she was the only female, she most definitely was now a target for such ribbing. She should be on guard for orders for "left-handed monkey wrenches" or the like. Wingate continued:

> So sometime later we got a report turned in on a bunch of steam strainers. Well, I knew you didn't strain steam, so I just sent it back. I didn't pay any attention to it, and about three days later everybody was looking for steam strainers. They came and asked me for them, and I said, "Oh, you can't fool me. You don't strain steam." The top guy over the warehouse division said, "You take her out there and show her some steam strainers." I came in and typed 'em up and sent the report through.[10]

Wingate admitted that, at times, the ribbing crossed from good-natured fun to something more serious, if not darker. Along with the dirty jokes so often told by men that she "resented being told, because I felt they had no respect for me," Wingate acknowledged the animosity toward her and other women by male colleagues who exhibited hostility to a female presence. "Now the men resented the women being out in the yard," she remembered. "They resented it. They had all kinds of jokes. They were very condescending, and when a woman could do the job as well as they could they didn't like it. They were threatened. Their superiority was threatened."[11]

María Isabella Solis (Thomas), who dreamed of being a teacher, found herself traveling a different course due to the war. Relocating from the border town of Brownsville, Texas, to the center of aircraft production in Richmond, California, Solis wanted to be Rosie the Riveter. Her diminutive stature benefited her, as she recalled the recruiter wanted small, short, and thin women. Such stature was a benefit in the cramped confines of aircraft production. "I was proud because . . . I did it just exactly the way they wanted [me] to," she recalled. "And here I come out, and they said, 'Hi, shorty. You did pretty good.'" Wilhelmina and Delfina Cooremans, Mexican nationals whose family relocated to San Antonio, were inseparable sisters. They joined the war mobilization effort together. They initially took jobs at Kelly Field in San Antonio, balancing aircraft propellers. In 1945, Boeing recruited the sisters to their Seattle aircraft plant. This move was promising, as the pay was higher and this enabled the two young women, "cloistered" their whole life, to strike out on an "adventure." Delfina acknowledged that her and her sister's experience during the war was for the better. "When we got back," Delfina stated, "we didn't expect anything from our parents. We helped our parents, not expected them to help us."[12]

California had a particular draw on black Texans. It was generally believed by African Americans in Texas that the promise of racial equality lay west. Although exactitude is difficult, it is generally estimated that about 10 percent of the Southern black population migrated out of the South during the war. In addition, a further 10 percent migrated within the South, generally from rural regions to urban. Seeking work in the aircraft-production industry, Fanny Christina Hill migrated to Los Angeles, California. She found work with North American Aviation, a company known for its willingness to hire minorities. Although she liked her wages, and the noticeable African American workforce was promising, she quickly noticed how the workforce was racially segregated. "I could see where they made a different [approach] in placing you in certain jobs," she remembered. "They had fifteen or twenty departments, but all the Negroes went to Department 17 because there was nothing but shooting and bucking rivets . . . I just didn't like it." Dona Irwin, whose husband had previously gone to Oakland, California, to find work in the shipyards, summoned her to follow. With two small children in tow, Dona relocated to what she hoped would be a better future. The ideal, however, did not match the reality. Although the Irwins relished the better job and pay as well as the relaxed segregation, since they could sit in the same establishments and shop in the same stores as whites, the situation was not the dreamed-of Shangri-la. Housing was a nightmare and the influx of so many African Americans into the Bay Area exacerbated racial tensions. To make matters worse, her eldest child died from a routine tonsillectomy. "I seriously considered returning to Houston," she admitted, perhaps with a tinge of doubt whether the relocation was the right move.[13]

For all the acclaim Rosie the Riveter received as the female icon of the war, she represented a fraction of women during the war. Most women did not enter the workforce as full-time employees, either unable or unwilling. In fact, of the twenty-eight million wives, approximately three-quarters were homemakers throughout the war. They were "Rosie the Homemaker" or "Rosie the Servicemen's Wife." The war only disrupted daily life; it did not replace it, and, it was always assumed, "Rosie" was simply a seat warmer for a "more deserving" returning male worker. Women, especially those who were married, who experienced economic agency during the war and may have dreamed of continuing it afterward soon discovered a hostile postwar environment. Established society derisively dismissed her as a "selfish, exploitative neurotic who callously neglected her home. . . ." As one student of the home front during war noted, "the years of war are remembered by older women today less as a time of gender revolution than as a crisis of logistics and work . . ." Nor did the war fundamentally alter prewar gender work patterns—something, despite the war necessity, society and most women did not desire. Children still had to be raised and elderly parents cared for. Houses still needed to be cleaned, dishes and clothes washed and dried. These wives, mothers, and, at times, oldest daughter remained at home, perhaps taking part-time work, but primarily focusing their attention on the family and contributing in volunteer ways such as buying war bonds, collecting necessary war material, or adhering to the government's insistence that housewives be ever vigilante in combating evasion and inflation. In many ways, the dutiful housewife was the nonthreatening feminized counterpart to the gender-bending female manufacturer, possibly "coarsened by having to get out in the business world."[14]

Often overlooked in this ideal, these women did this with the inescapable fear from death. These women knew today could be the day they would be notified of their husband's or their son's death. Consider the case of Mary Lacy's mother. "What really has always been ingrained in my memory," recalled Lacy, "is when my mom got the telegram. She was next door visiting the neighbor lady." When she opened it, "she gave out this blood curdling scream. . . ." Mary admitted after all these years, "I can tell you, it was awful because I still remember it to this day." Despite her unimaginable grief and then uncertainty about raising four little children (she was expecting her fourth) on her own, Mary, with pride in her voice, admired how her mother "didn't fall apart." In addition, these wives went without the physical and emotional assistance of the male head of household laboring in a vital war production plant states away or serving overseas in the armed forces.

Many housewives, including one from Amarillo (in the Panhandle) who admitted as much, struggled with the workload and loneliness, devoid of adult relationships and someone to confide in. At times, this fell to the eldest daughter, who either was thrust into the motherly role by war work or the unfortunate death of a mother. Housewives, although not in the high-profile positions of female factory workers whose contribution would not be in question, contributed in other ways to the war effort. No longer should the housewife struggle with the "kitchen-sink complex"; she was as profound and important to the country's mission as those constructing the tools of war. Her battlefield was the kitchen. The Office of Price Administration (OPA), the chief governmental agency charged with administering wage and price controls as well as wartime rationing, focused much attention on organizing the assistance of housewives in their cause to combat the adverse effects of such interventionist measures. Women were encouraged to "make do and mend." By doing, so contributing to the war effort. The OPA—with much self-interested assistance from the umbrella organization of unskilled labor unions, Congress of Industrial Organizations (CIO)—hoped to organize the private sphere, introducing the "Home Front Pledge Campaign." Homemakers were challenged to take the pledge to combat inflation through their consumer practices. "Planning meals is the way *I* can fight," became her war cry.[15]

Many Texas women had similar thoughts. There were many ways to assist the war effort beyond serving in uniform or assembling the tools of war. These ways, in fact, allowed all from the young to the old to feel part of the war effort. Children collected metal or other necessary material for war, often in conjunction with a community group or church. Female college students at North Texas State University (today University of North Texas) in Denton were trained by the Women's Defense Corps. In turn, these ladies could then organize and instruct their hometowns in defense. Young girls joined the 4-H in assisting in a plethora of ways. A popular way to bolster morale for servicemen was letter writing. Many women and young girls wrote letters to men overseas, simply letting them know they were not forgotten. One young girl from San Marcos created a club called the "Blue Horizon" in which its members exchanged names of soldiers to correspond with.

Teenage girls often babysat the children of working mothers of service personnel. Nita Boyd Brooks-Lewallen, while attending Hardin Simmons, a Baptist school in Abilene, Texas, that was part of the school's Six White Horses troop, taught horseback riding at Camp Mystic at Kerrville, Kerr County. A few employed their talent to the effort. Teresa Herrera Cásarez from Austin had a talent for singing and dancing. As her brothers served overseas, the sixteen-year-old Cásarez joined a dance troupe that entertained at United Service Organizations (USO) clubs and at Camp Swift in Bastrop, not far from Austin. "We did the typical dances, the *jarabe taptio*, the *zandunga* . . . ," she recalled, "just about any dance that was typical at the time." Such mingling by Latin women and Anglo servicemen in Texas was not such a third rail for Texas society. Never as entrenched or effective against Tejanos as against black Texans, in part because of outward appearances and in part because of the law recognizing Hispanics as white, segregation against the Anglo Texans called "Mexicans" was often sporadic. Where one establishment practiced it with zeal, another did not. Thus, there was not a uniform policy. Consider the example of the USO club in Del Rio, a town along the United States–Mexico border. It resisted such fraternization between Hispanic women and Anglo soldiers, turning away any such serviceman arriving with a Latin woman draped on his arm. When a Hispanic civil rights organization registered a complaint with the national USO, it was rebuffed with a terse reply this was a local matter.[16]

For all the newfound economic agency and influx of women into the workforce during the war, the leading occupation for women remained domestic servant. In fact, it would not be until the following decade that more women worked outside the home than in it. Although both black and white women worked as domestics in large numbers, it was not comparable. African American women were far more represented than white. A black woman was twice as likely as her white counterpart to be a domestic servant. This notwithstanding, the war greatly altered the possibilities for female minorities. Greater opportunities dropped the percentage of black women working as domestics from 60 percent in 1940 to 45 percent by the war's end. To be sure, black domestics as a whole of the African American working population dropped almost 10 percent through the war years, from almost a third to a fifth. This exodus raised concerns. "American home life needs an efficient servant class," a leading sociologist at the time declared about the war's disruptions to the possibility of returning to prewar norms, "and this element in the population must have positions in domestic service if any program for their peacetime employment is to be realized." White women as well as black women felt the pull of war work with its better pay and sense of pride and dignity.

The path out of domestic work, of course, was easier for white women, who were not limited by racial constraints. Black women, although their options circumscribed, were not powerless. At the time of the war, the popular image of female empowerment, whether in the factories constructing aircraft, in the fields tilling the land, in uniform assisting the fighting man, or at home as the dutiful wife, was a white woman. The black domestic woman, primarily, was to assist the white woman as a dutiful servant. She was to contribute to "a behind-the scenes cadre of support workers for gainfully employed white wives." Her service to the nation literally came through her contented, and generally believed natural, service to the white mistress. This image, however, had a major flaw—black women's agency contradicted their contentedness. Some domestics learned to "leverage" their positions. As Anna Mae Dickson, an African American domestic, later admitted, "You learn to be two persons." This strategy enabled many to still maintain a living yet not at the price of their dignity and "independent inner self." Those who could left their white employers without help, something well-to-do white women redefined publicly as proof of their sacrifice to the war effort as they did their own household duties. Some estimates have nearly half the whites used to having household help actually losing it. Those African Americans who remained experienced increased agency, less demeaning treatment and derogatory epithets (at least within earshot), and better pay, since those whites fortunate enough to retain their help did not necessarily want to lose her. Consider the experience of Annie Mae Hunt. A domestic in Dallas, she remembered how the domestic shortage benefited her. "That's when housework begin to go up," she noticed as her pay increased nearly five-fold to 7 dollars a day.[17]

The promise of the war was in part offset by its disruption. The displacement of large numbers of peoples, both voluntarily and through governmental compulsion, strained the sinews of familial relationships. Husbands were separated from wives, mothers separated from children, and children separated from parents. Increased mobility was a war by-product. Such dislocation, naturally, had profound consequences, both beneficial and adverse, for society. The war produced the circumstances that both resulted in marriages (the marriage rate actually increased by 25 percent, peaking in 1942) and destroyed them. "In every war," declared the National Conference on Family Relations, "the family is the first and greatest casualty." Most marriages survived the war, remaining intact for subsequent decades or in perpetuity. The war, nevertheless, rippled the idea that matrimonial bliss was permanent. With long periods apart, increased infidelity, and increased opportunities of agency, including economic, divorce rates noticeably increased. Exacerbating this increase were impulsive "wartime marriages." Often happening within days, and sometimes hours, these relationships lacked foundation, since the couples hardly knew each other before their nuptials. Sixteen percent of marriages ended in divorce in 1940, and five years later it jumped to 27 percent. The trend peaked in 1946 with a divorce rate not surpassed until 1980, which witnessed the highest divorce rate in American history. In the war, more than three million US marriages ended in divorce, and by 1950 there were one million veterans who were divorced.[18]

Americans did not just worry about the profound and certain changings to familial relations and traditional gender roles precipitated by the war. Morality and societal norms, for many, appeared loosened if not dismissed by the emergency situation. Women's sexuality was highlighted in advertisement and commodified as a way to benefit the war effort, but it was also threatening. At the same time the war emergency was unleashing benefits such as ingenuity, innovation, and selflessness, it was also loosening female morality—rarely was male immorality addressed as vigorously. Societal guardians understood the war was temporary, and once the country achieved victory, it was a return to "normality." It was imperative that the society that entered the war come out of it as relatively unchanged as possible. If not, the change had to be for the better and not adversely transformative. Sexual failings, deviancy, and immorality were of pressing concern. Fears of mothers "repudiating their children in their newly found freedom" further increased societal angst. With "absent" mothers working outside the home, it was worried their children would become delinquents and their teenagers self-indulgent hedonists. The massive upsurge in female employment occurred in demographics that either had no children or were young adults. Nonetheless, popular fears and societal "boogeymen" scoff at facts. Of particular concern was the morality of young women. Interdiction was necessary before they became Hester Prynnes. Like all concerns, there was a kernel of legitimacy. The war and its social disorganization and dislocation "accelerated the rate of departure from conventional sex behavior." There existed teenage girls and young women who made themselves sexually available for servicemen. These girls went by names such as "Victory Girls," "Patriotutes," and "Liberty Belles" and sometimes competed with one another in promiscuity. A few even discriminated by only sleeping with soldiers or only sailors. Those raising the concern were not necessarily parental worry warts or irrational social Puritans wishing to eradicate the natural sexual impulses. Promiscuity noticeably increased during the war. Moreover, according to one survey, in 1942 only 25 percent of single men and 40 percent of single women abstained from premarital sex. From 1939 to 1945, illegitimate births increased by 42 percent. It is estimated that 650,000 illegitimate children were born during the war years.[19]

Ironically, teenagers did not experience the highest increase in illegitimate pregnancies during the war. It was women between the ages of 20 and 30 who almost doubled their rate of illegitimate pregnancy. By 1940s standards, society considered these women mature, with many already married. This perhaps questions the actual rate of illegitimacy, considering the state did not consider children born in wedlock illegitimate. Due to the social stigma, the woman, if possible, would not disclose otherwise. Women in their twenties were also the ideal demographic for prostitution. With large congregations of men with disposable income, with many people working and living in communities where anonymity ruled, and the economic and societal constraints creating only so many economic possibilities for women, naturally some turned to the world's oldest profession. In Texas during the 1930s, prostitution was something to be managed or even regulated. City and state officials moved only when the practice became too overt or moved beyond generally acceptable red-light districts, so-called Zones of Tolerance. There had not been a crusading campaign of elimination since the days of World War I. With entry into World War II, an initial attitude change occurred. What was once tolerated now became a threat to the war effort. Military officials initiated a nationwide campaign against prostitution. This came at a time when the profession, due to the war's increase in economic opportunities for women, was declining. From its inception, however, there lacked any uniformity in the military's approach. Officials also primarily focused on the women and not their male solicitors. Furthermore, some zealously focused on eliminating prostitution, primarily in and around military facilities, while others directed their efforts toward what they saw as the most threatening aspect of prostitution: venereal disease (VD).[20]

Many believed VD more threatening to the war effort than the actual profession of prostitution and focused instead on public health. Thus arose the "classic debate concerning the regulation versus the suppression of prostitution." Further complicating matters were those military bases near the Mexican border, where the prostitutes and brothels were beyond US control. This left either diplomatically problematic solutions such as periodic closing of the international border or prohibiting military personnel access into Mexico, or the perception of accepting (some might say encouraging) immorality by having federal officials at the border passing prophylactics to all servicemen crossing into Mexico. To assist military officials, a newly created federal agency headed by Eliot Ness (yes, that Ness) called the Division of Social Protection was charged with enforcing a recent congressional statute that made prostitution near military bases a federal offense. Ness considered "diseased women" the "Military Saboteur Number 1" and effected through this agency his personal campaign against syphilis. The war necessitated a renewed effort to regulate female promiscuity and sexuality. Fearing that military officials would declare their cities and thus their business establishments off-limits to their personnel, city and state officials in Texas also intensified their efforts in combatting elicit sexual activity. In conjunction with federal efforts, state and local attitudes initially focused on elimination not regulation of the profession. The state's largest cities, including Austin, Beaumont, Corpus Christi, El Paso, Galveston, and San Antonio, moved to close the "hotel system." Officials in many urban areas in the state, realizing their limited resources and perhaps desire to combat something in which, on its surface, both parties were willing participants, instead focused on regulating the profession, aiming their efforts on the more problematic problem of venereal disease. Such "oversight" even occurred in small towns and rural communities. In Gainesville, Texas, north of Dallas, the police tolerated prostitution as long as trouble did not ensue, instead focusing on abatement of venereal disease. East of Dallas, officials in Greenville, in Hunt County, cooperated their efforts with military health officials at Majors Field to combat VD, resulting in the city being declared "not a bad 'source of infection.'" Prostitution in Galveston seemed to become more prevalent, and city officials in Amarillo convinced the military to accept its existence so long as city officials regulated the women against disease. Ultimately in El Paso, public officials and law enforcement, although at times reverting to a punitive approach of incarceration, mainly focused their attention on VD reduction and compassionate intervention rather than trying to eliminate "the world's oldest profession."[21]

Despite the efforts against elicit sexual activity, the actions of the vast majority of women in Texas during the war were honorable. Their contribution to victory in the Second World War is undeniable. Without their assistance, the United States would have at least struggled to fight a two-front war, with the country effectively fighting on one front exclusively. This monumental effort necessitated their contribution. They were needed in the homes, in the fields, in the factories, and in uniform. Their effort further caused society to reevaluate the capabilities of women. Although returned to the home as wife and mother after victory, these women put to lie the popular beliefs about female capabilities. For a moment, those who flew planes; repaired vehicles; trained soldiers, sailors, pilots, and marines; constructed ships and aircraft; and all the other millions of women who performed a task that otherwise was closed off or beyond their reach but for the war glimpsed a different path that millions of women could only dream. Horizons and aspirations were broadened. The genie saw a crack and, over the next generation, would wiggle from her confines. Their pride, so expressed in letters home and subsequent oral interviews, from flying planes, constructing ships, and contributing to the war effort in a myriad of other ways would be paid forward to subsequent generations of girls and women. "I felt like I's [sic] doing something to help the war," one shipbuilding woman expressed. "I loved it." One WASP exclaimed, "OOOOOOO, Mom. I'm so happy I could die. So you see, your baby chile [sic] is enjoying life to the fullest. I have *everything* I want . . . I'm doing what I love better than anything in the world." The fact that women were pilots, mechanics, manufacturers, technicians, among many other occupations, further precluded society from honestly denying the capabilities of women. Women displayed they were physically, psychologically, and mentally capable of much more than society granted. Preclusion now would be based on what men (and many women, to be sure) *wanted* women to be and their fast-diminishing ideas and definitions of "the proper place for women."[22]

War tends to compress time and space. Movements and experiences that otherwise would have occurred decades later are accelerated. The Second World War, with its scope and intensity, not only expanded changes already begun before the war, but also initiated ripples that would become transformative swells in the postwar decades. Most profound were those that affected women. Millions of women experienced for the first time economic empowerment. For the first time, they earned and spent their own money, earned through their own labor. Many of these women, whose identity was often enmeshed with their husbands, found themselves. They discovered internal aspects they never knew existed. They discovered a life beyond just wife and mother.

Notes

1. D'Ann Campbell, "Women in Combat: The World War II Experience in the United States, Great Britain, and the Soviet Union," *Journal of Military History* 57 (April 1993), 302.

2. Campbell, "Women in Combat," 302; Julia Brock et al., eds., *Beyond Rosie: A Documentary History of Women and World War II* (Fayetteville: University of Arkansas Press, 2015), 89.

3. Judith N. McArthur and Harold L. Smith, *Texas through Women's Eyes: The Twentieth-Century Experience* (Austin: University of Texas Press, 2010), 131–34

(quotation on p. 134). For a detailed chronicle of Wilson's story during the war, see Lucy Wilson Jopling, *Warrior in White* (San Antonio: Watercress Press, 1990). For additional stories of nurses during the war, see Kathryn J. Atwood, *Women Heroes of World War II: The Pacific Theater: 15 Stories of Resistance, Rescue, Sabotage, & Survival* (Chicago: Chicago Review Press Incorporated, 2017); Charissa J. Threat, *Nursing Civil Rights: Gender and Race in the Army Nurse Corps* (Urbana: University of Illinois Press, 2015); June Wandrey, *Bedpan Commando: The Story of a Combat Nurse during World War II* (Elmore, OH: Elmore Publishing Company, 1989); and Theresa Archard, *G.I. Nightingale: The Story of an American Army Nurse* (New York: W. W. Norton & Company, 1945).

4. John W. Jeffries, *Wartime America: The World War II Home Front* (Chicago: Ivan R. Dee, 1996), 72; D'Ann Campbell, *Women at War with America: Private Lives in a Patriotic Era* (Cambridge, MA: Harvard University Press, 1984), 104. For more on black women in the wartime economy, see Joshua Freeman et al., *Who Built America? Working People and the Nation's Economy, Politics, Culture, and Society,* 2 vols. (New York: Pantheon Books, 1992), especially volume II; Maureen Honey, ed., *Bitter Fruit: African American Women in World War II* (Columbia: University of Missouri Press, 1999); and Harold G. Vatter, *The US Economy in World War II* (New York: Columbia University Press, 1985).

5. Maggie Rivas-Rodriguez et al., *A Legacy Greater than Words: Stories of US Latinos and Latinas of the WWII Generation* (Austin: University of Texas Press, 2006), 227, 233–34. The 1.3 million number came from Richard R. Lingeman, *Don't You Know There's a War On? The American Home Front 1941–1945* (New York: G. P. Putnam's Sons, 1970). The other information for this and the preceding paragraphs come from Judy Barrett Litoff and David C. Smith, "'To the Rescue of the Crops': The Women's Land Army during World War II," *Prologue: The Journal of the National Archives* 25 (Winter 1993), n.p., https://www.archives.gov/publications/prologue/1993/winter/landarmy.html; Judy Barrett Litoff and David C. Smith, *American Women in a World at War: Contemporary Accounts from World War II* (Wilmington, DE: SR Books, 1997), 167; Herminia Guerrero Cadena Interview, June 25, 2002, The University of Texas at Austin Voices Oral History Center, accessed June 13, 2021, https://voces.lib.utexas.edu/collections/stories/herminia-guerrero-cadena; Stephanie Ann Carpenter, "Regular Farm Girl: The Women's Land Army in World War II," *Agricultural History* 71 (Spring 1997); Carpenter, *On the Farm Front*; Roger Meyer, "Cultivating Victory: The Women's Land Army," *Michigan History Magazine* 98 (September/October 2014); Cecilia Gowdy-Wygant, *Cultivating Victory: The Women's Land Army and the Victory Garden Movement* (Pittsburgh: University of Pittsburgh, 2013); and D Wayne D. Rasmussen, *A History of the Emergency Farm Labor Supply Program, 1943–1947* (Washington, DC: United States Department of Agriculture, 1951). For additional works on the Women's Land Army, see Dorit Geva, *Conscription, Family, and the Modern State: A Comparative Study of France and the United States* (New York: Cambridge University Press, 2013); Sandra K. Schackel, ed., *Western Women's Lives: Continuity*

and Change in the Twentieth Century (Albuquerque: University of New Mexico Press, 2003); Mary Cunningham Baur, "The Farm Homemaker Faces War," *Journal of Home Economics* (October 1942); Bryon Fairchild and Johnathan Grossman, *The Army and Industrial Manpower* (Washington, DC: US Government Printing Office, 1988); and W. E. Shewell-Cooper, *Land Girl: A Handbook for the Women's Land Army* (Gloucestershire, UK: Amberley Publishing, 2011). For the Women's Land Army's predecessor in the Great War, see Elaine F. Weiss, *Fruits of Victory: The Women's Land Army in the Great War* (Washington, DC: Potomac Books, 2008); Mart A. Stewart, "*'What Nature Suffers to Groe': Life, Labor, and Landscape on the Georgia Coast, 1680–1920* (Athens: University of Georgia Press, 1996); Rebecca Sharpless, *Fertile Ground, Narrow Choices: Women on Texas Cotton Farms, 1900–1940* (Chapel Hill: University of North Carolina Press, 1999); and Elaine F. Weiss, "Before Rosie the Riveter, Farmerettes Went to Work," *Smithsonianmag.com*, May 28, 2009. Studies of the British and Australian versions of the Women's Land Army in both world wars are Margaret Hilary Bullock, "The Women's Land Army 1939–1950: A Study of Policy and Practice with Particular Preference to the Craven District" (PhD diss., University of Leeds, 2002); Carol Twinch, *Women on the Land: Their Story during Two World Wars* (Cambridge, UK: Lutterworth Press, 1990); Bob Powell and Nigel Westacott, *The Women's Land Army* (Gloucestershire, UK: The History Press, 2009); Bonnie White, *The Women's Land Army in First World War Britain* (New York: Palgrave Macmillan, 2014); Sue Hardisty, *Thanks Girls and Goodbye! The Story of the Australian Women's Land Army 1942–1945* (Chicago: Spinifex Press, 1990); and Shirley Threlfo, *The Australian Women's Land Army, 1942–1945: The Experiences of Mabs Keppie* (Paterson, NSW: Paterson Historical Society, 1997). For a few instances of the need for labor in the fields in Texas are, *Dallas Morning News*, October 5 and 6, 1944.

6. Tanya Krause Randall, "Texas Ranch Women Remember World War II," *Sound Historian: Journal of the Texas Oral History Association* 13 (2011), 47–48, 53. For more on women ranching during the war, see Joyce Gibson Roach, *The Cowgirls* (Denton: University of North Texas Press, 1990); and Barney Nelson, *The Last Campfire: The Life Story of Ted Gray, A West Texas Rancher* (College Station: Texas A&M University Press, 1984).

7. Freeman et al., *Who Built America?*, II: 455–58; Jeffries, *Wartime America*, 72; Neil A. Wynn, *The Afro-American and the Second World War* (New York: Holmes & Meier Publishers, 1976), 17; Eugenia Kaledin, *Daily Life in the United States, 1940–1959* (Westport, CT: Greenwood Press, 2000), 19.

8. Maureen Honey, *Creating Rosie the Riveter: Class, Gender, and Propaganda during World War II* (Amherst: University of Massachusetts Press, 1984), 102–03, 116–17; McArthur and Smith, *Texas through Women's Eyes*, 92–93; Maureen Honey, "Remembering Rosie: Advertising Images of Women in World War II," in *The Home-Front War: World War II and American Society*, eds. Kenneth Paul O'Brien and Lynn Hudson Parsons (Westport, CT: Greenwood Press, 1995), 94; Jeffries, *Wartime America*, 72–73; Freeman et al., *Who Built America?*, II: 458–59; Kaledin,

Daily Life in the United States, 19. For more on women in industrial defense in Texas, see Donna Bonin, "Baytown's Rosie the Riveter," in *From Humble Beginnings: Exxon Baytown Seventy-fifth Anniversary, 1920–1995* (Baytown, TX: Exxon Baytown Public Relations Office, 1995); Mary Potchernick Cook, "Angelina's Rosies: Women at War in World War II East Texas" (master's thesis, Stephen F. Austin University, 1998). A detailed examination of the iconic Rosie is Sherna B. Gluck, *Rosie the Riveter Revisited: Women, the War, and Social Change* (Boston: Twayne Publishers, 1987).

9. Lingeman, *Don't You Know There's a War On?*, 163–94; Richard Polenberg, *War and Society: The United States, 1941–1945* (New York: J. B. Lippincott Company, 1972), 146; Nancy Gabin, "The Hand That Rocks the Cradle Can Build Tractors, Too," *Michigan History Magazine* 76 (March/April 1992), 14; McArthur and Smith, *Texas through Women's Eyes*, 93; William Henry Chafe, *The American Woman: Her Changing Social, Economic, and Political Roles, 1920–1970* (Oxford, UK: Oxford University Press, 1972), 151–73. For more on the experience of women, both white and black, and unions during the war, see Melinda Chateauvert, *Marching Together: Women of the Brotherhood of Sleeping Car Porters* (Urbana, IL: University of Illinois Press, 1998); Nancy F. Gabin, *Feminism in the Labor Movement: Women and the United Auto Workers, 1935–1975* (Ithaca, NY: Cornell University Press, 1990). A good study of the attitude of women blurring the gender lines in the workforce in another state, see Kelly Duda, "It's a Man's World: Women's Entrance into Male Spaces during World War II in Florida" (master's thesis, Florida State University, 2013). For more on the relationship between unions and women, primarily white, see Ruth Milkman, *Gender at Work: The Dynamics of Job Segregation by Sex during World War II* (Urbana: University of Illinois Press, 1987); Gary J. Rabalais, "Humble Women at War: The Case of Humble's Baytown Refinery, 1942–1945," *Houston Review of History and Culture* 2 (Spring 2005); and Charlotte A. Holliman, "Beaumont Women during World War II," *Texas Gulf and Historical Record* XXXI (November 1995). For the dynamic between unions and black women, see George N. Green, "Texas State Industrial Union Council" *Handbook of Texas Online*, https://tshaonline.org/handbook/online/articles/octbg; and Joseph Abel, "African Americans, Labor Unions, and the Struggle for Fair Employment in the Aircraft Manufacturing Industry of Texas, 1941–1945," *Journal of Southern History* 77 (August 2011); Philip S. Foner, *Women and the American Labor Movement* (New York: Free Press, 1979); Emily Yellin, *Our Mothers' War: American Women at Home and at the Front during World War II* (New York: Free Press, 2004); Katherine Turk, "'A Fair Chance to Do My Part of Work': Black Women, War Work, and Rights Claims at the Kingsbury Ordnance Plant," *Indiana Magazine of History* 108 (2012); Jacqueline Jones, *Labor of Love, Labor of Sorrow: Black Women, Work, and the Family from Slavery to the Present* (New York: Basic Books, 2010); and Jacqueline Jones, *American Work: Four Centuries of Black and White Labor* (New York: W. W. Norton and Company, 1998). Those interested in the limits of federal involvement and inability to effect change through the War

Manpower Commission and Fair Employment Practices Commission can read Deborah Fink, "What Kind of Woman Would Work in Meatpacking, Anyway? World War II and the Road to Fair Employment," *Great Plains Research* 5 (Fall 1995); and William J. Breen, "Women and Work: The Limit of War Manpower Commission Policy in World War II," *Australasian Journal of American Studies* 20 (December 2001).

10. Louis Fairchild, *They Called It the War Effort: Oral Histories from WWII Orange, Texas*, 2nd ed. (Denton: Texas State Historical Association, 2012), 166; McArthur and Smith, *Texas through Women's Eyes*, 130–31. For more on the experience of women in shipyards, see Katherine Archibald, *Wartime Shipyard: A Study in Social Disunity* (Berkeley: University of California Press, 1947).

11. McArthur and Smith, *Texas through Women's Eyes*, 131.

12. Rivas-Rodriguez et al., *A Legacy Greater than Words*, 213.

13. Honey, ed., *Bitter Fruit*, 9; James N. Gregory, "The Second Great Migration: A Historical Overview," in *African American Urban History: The Dynamics of Race, Class and Gender since World War II*, in eds. Joe W. Trotter and Kenneth L. Kusmer (Chicago: University of Chicago Press, 2009), 20–21, 25, 27; Cheryl Mullenbach, *Double Victory: How African American Women Broke Race and Gender Barriers to Help Win World War II* (Chicago: Chicago Review Press, 2013), 20–21. The estimates on Southern black migration out of and within the South came from Freeman et al., *Who Built America?*, II: 458–59.

14. Catherine Lutz, *Homefront: A Military City and the American Twentieth Century* (Boston, MA: Beacon Press, 2001), 84; Honey, *Creating Rosie the Riveter*, 70, 99, 102–3; William L. O'Neill, *A Democracy at War: America's Fight at Home & Abroad in World War II* (Cambridge, MA: Harvard University Press, 1993), 242–43. A few wives, instead of remaining at home waiting for their husband's return, decided to follow him to each assignment, including overseas. For worries about femininity being coarsened, see Karen Anderson, *Wartime Women: Sex Roles, Family Relations, and the Status of Women during World War II* (Westport, CT: Greenwood Press, 1981), especially Chapter 2. For their story during the war, see Doris Weatherford, *American Women and World War II* (Edison, NJ: Castle Books, 2008); and Duncan Barrett and Nuala Calvi, *GI Brides: The Wartime Girls Who Crossed the Atlantic for Love* (New York: HarperCollins, 2013). For the experience of wives who remained at home absent from their husbands serving overseas, see Judy Barrett Litoff et al., *Miss You: The World War II Letters of Barbara Wooddall Taylor and Charles E. Taylor* (Athens: University of Georgia Press, 2013); Judy Barrett Litoff and David C. Smith, eds., *Since You Went Away: World War II Letters from American Women on the Home Front* (Lawrence: University Press of Kansas, 1991). Works that show how this image of the homemaker was reinforced and the ideal highlighted include Hartmann, *The Home Front and Beyond*; Linda Gordon, *Heroes of Their Own Lives: The Politics and History of Family Violence, Boston, 1880–1960* (New York: Viking, 1988); and Linda Gordon, *Woman's Body, Woman's Right: Birth Control in America*, rev. ed. (New York: Penguin Books, 1990).

15. Rebecca Craver, "Homefront with a Border Twist: El Paso Juárez during World War II," *Sound Historian: Journal of the Texas Oral History Association* 5 (1999), 3; Campbell, *Women at War with America*, 72, 81, 83, 113, 191; Amy Bentley, *Eating for Victory: Food Rationing and the Politics of Domesticity* (Urbana: University of Illinois Press, 1998), 31, 33; Brock et al., eds., *Beyond Rosie*, xxvii, 123–29; Emily E. LB. Twarog, *Politics of the Pantry: Housewives, Food, and Consumer Protest in Twentieth-Century America* (New York: Oxford University Press, 2017), 30–31. For the exhaustion and loneliness experienced by housewives, see Evelyn Millis Duvall, "Loneliness and the Servicemen's Wives," *Marriage and Family Living* 7 (November 1945). A sort of road map for housewives to traverse the demands of war work and war marriage, see Gulielma Fell Alsop and Mary F. McBride, *Arms and the Girl: Guide to Personal Adjustment in War Work and War Marriage* (New York: Vanguard Press, 1943). Three examples of a teenager girl forced into the "motherly" role of younger siblings are the experiences of Gloria Araguz Alaníz, whose mother passed when Gloria was fifteen; Elvira Orta Pardo López whose mother died in 1940 when Elvira was fifteen and who prayed her brother Pablo would return from serving overseas unharmed; and Davie Elizardo whose younger brother returned from the war scarred. "His mind was different when he came back," she lamented. She was now forced to care for her siblings and the household (see Rivas-Rodriguez et al., *A Legacy Greater than Words*, 222, 225, 235). The government magnified the image of the housewife as vital to the war effort. These women were to be applauded and deemed necessary to victory. For a reframing of household duties, although never at the expense of "women's proper role in society," see Leila J. Rupp, *Mobilizing Women for War: German and American Propaganda, 1939–1945* (Princeton, NJ: Princeton University Press, 1978).

16. Rivas-Rodriguez et al., *A Legacy Greater than Words*, 222–23, 229, 239, 242; "Growing Up Green: 1941–2015: The WWII Years (1941–1949), University Libraries Exhibit, accessed June 13, 2021, https://exhibits.library.unt.edu/growingupgreen/wwii-years/); Elizabeth R. Escobedo, *From Coveralls to Zoot Suits: The Lives of Mexican American Women on the World War II Home Front* (Chapel Hill: University of North Carolina Press, 2013), 115; Francis E. Merrill, *Social Problems on the Home Front: A Study of War-time Influences* (New York: Harper & Brothers Publishers, 1948), 92–95; Randall, "Texas Ranch Women Remember World War II," 51. For the role of the 4-H in the war, see Gabriel N. Rosenberg, *The 4-H Harvest: Sexuality and the State in Rural America* (Philadelphia: University of Pennsylvania Press, 2016). A detailed examination of children during the war are Stephen Mintz, *Huck's Raft: A History of American Childhood* (Cambridge, MA: Belknap Press of Harvard University Press, 2004); Calvin L. Christman, *Lost in the Victory: Reflections of American War Orphans of World War II* (Denton: University of North Texas Press, 1998). A work that examines one woman's letter-writing campaign to servicemen serving overseas to boost morale, see Mrs. Keith Frazier Somerville, *Dear Boys: World War II Letters from a Woman Back Home*, eds. Judy Barrett Litoff and David C. Smith (Jackson: University Press of Mississippi, 2009). Also see essay on agriculture by Christopher B. Bean and Henry C. Dethloff.

17. Bentley, *Eating for Victory*, 76–78; Jones, *Labor of Love, Labor of Sorrow*, 235, 237; McArthur and Smith, *Texas through Women's Eyes*, 119; Winegarten, *Black Texas Women*, 234; Wynn, *Afro-American and the Second World War*, 16; Phyllis Palmer, "Black Domestics during the Depression: Workers, Organizers, Social Commentators," *Prologue: The Journal of the National Archives* 29 (Summer 1997), 127; Campbell, *Women at War with America*, 173–74; Alwyn Barr, *Black Texans: A History of Negroes in Texas 1528–1971* (Austin: Jenkins Publishing Company, 1971), 198; Vatter, *The US Economy in World War II*, 130; Judith Rollins, *Between Women: Domestics and Their Employers* (Philadelphia: Temple University Press, 1985), 56; Phyllis Palmer, *Domesticity and Dirt: Housewives and Domestic Servants in the United States, 1920–1945* (Philadelphia: Temple University Press, 1989), 12. The experience of Annie Mae Hunt during the war is in Ruthe Winegarten and Annie Mae Hunt, *I Am Annie Mae: An Extraordinary Woman in Her Own Words: The Personal Story of a Black Texas Woman* (Austin: University of Texas Press, 1983). For more on domestic servants during the war and their changing image and empowerment, see David M. Katzman, *Seven Days a Week: Women and Domestic Service in Industrializing America* (New York: Oxford University Press, 1981); Bonnie Thornton Dill, "Across the Barriers of Race and Class: An Exploration of the Relationship between Work and Family among Black Female Domestic Servants" (PhD diss., New York University, 1979); K. Sue Jewell, *From Mammy to Miss America and Beyond: Cultural Images and the Shaping of US Social Policy* (London, UK: Routledge, 1993); Patricia Morton, *Disfigured Images: The Historical Assault on Afro-American Women* (Westport, CT: Greenwood Press, 1991); John Langston Gwaltney, *Drylongso: A Self-Portrait of Black America* (New York: Random House, 1980); Margaret Allen, "The Domestic Ideal and the Mobilization of Womanpower in World War II," *Women's Studies International Forum* 6 (1983); and Daniel E. Sutherland, *Americans and Their Servants: Domestic Service in the United States from 1880–1920* (Baton Rouge: Louisiana State University Press, 1981).

18. John Costello, *Virtue under Fire: How World War II Changed Our Social and Sexual Attitudes* (Boston: Little, Brown and Company, 1985), 205; Adams, *The Best War Ever*, 123; Jessica Weiss, *To Have and to Hold: Marriage, the Baby Boom, and Social Change* (Chicago: University of Chicago Press, 2000), 179; Merrill, *Social Problems on the Home Front*, 33–43; Jeffries, *Wartime America*, 67–68. More on the reasons and consternation of changing familial dynamics, see Stephen Mintz and Susan Kellogg, *Domestic Revolutions: A Social History of American Family Life* (New York: Free Press, 1988); Eliza K. Pavalko and Glen H. Elder Jr., "World War II and Divorce: A Life-Course Perspective," *American Journal of Sociology* 95 (March 1990); and William L. Anderson and Derek W. Little, "All's Fair: War and Other Causes of Divorce from a Beckerian Perspective," *American Journal of Economics and Sociology* 58 (October 1999).

19. Merrill, *Social Problems on the Home Front*, 102; Polenberg, *War and Society*, 147; Adams, *Best War Ever*, 123; Cari Romm, "During World War II, Sex Was a National-Security Threat," the *Atlantic*, October 8, 2015, https://www.theatlantic.

com/health/archive/2015/10/during-world-war-ii-sexually-active-women-were-a-national-security-threat/409555/; Leslie J. Reagan, *When Abortion Was a Crime: Women, Medicine, and Law in the United States, 1867–1973* (Berkeley: University of California Press, 1997), 163–64; Melissa A. McEuen, *Making War, Making Women: Femininity and Duty on the American Home Front, 1941–1945* (Athens: University of Georgia Press, 2011), 17; Costello, *Virtue under Fire*, 203. One of the best works on regulation of female sexuality during the war is Marilyn E. Hegarty, *Victory Girls, Khaki-Wackies, and Patriotutes: The Regulation of Female Sexuality during World War II* (New York: New York University Press, 2008). Another, although entirely focused on female sexuality, is Marilynn S. Johnson, *The Second Gold Rush: Oakland and the East Bay in World War II* (Berkeley: University of California Press, 1993).

20. Allan M. Brandt, *No Magic Bullet: A Social History of Venereal Disease in the United States Since 1880* (New York: Oxford University Press, 1985), 166; Fred H. Allison, "Patriotic Prosperity and Social Change in World War II: The Impact of Majors Field on Greenville, Texas," *Sound Historian: Journal of the Texas Oral History Association* 5 (1999), 44–45; Costello, *Virtue under Fire*, 203; David C. Humphrey, "Prostitution in Texas: From the 1830s to the 1960s," *East Texas Historical Quarterly* 33 (1995), 34–35.

21. Brandt, *No Magic Bullet*, 166; Costello, *Virtue under Fire*, 203; Merrill, *Social Problems on the Home Front*, 122; Craver, "Homefront with a Border Twist," 11; John Parascandola, *Sex, Sin, and Science: A History of Syphilis in America* (Westport, CT: Praeger, 2008), 101–8; Christopher B. Bean, "Boom Town: The Effect of Camp Howze on Cooke County and Gainesville, Texas," *Red River Valley Historical Journal* 4 (Winter 2006), 64–65, 74–75; H. Gordon Frost, *The Gentlemen's Club: The Story of Prostitution in El Paso* (El Paso, TX: Mangan Books, 1983), 236–60. For Ness's administration and campaign against perceived and actual sexual immorality, see Eliot Ness, *What About Girls?* (New York: Public Affairs Committee [YMCA], 1943). To see how the neighboring city of New Orleans dealt with prostitution during the war, see Allison Baffoni, "'It is the Promiscuous Woman Who Is Giving Us the Most Trouble': The Internal War on Prostitution in New Orleans during World War II" (master's thesis, American University, 2007). The military also took the regulating approach in Hawaii, focusing on venereal disease and not necessarily the act of prostitution. For this, see Beth Bailey and David Farber, "Prostitutes on Strike: The Women of Hotel Street during World War II," *Radical History Review* 52 (Winter 1992).

22. Fairchild, *They Called It the War Effort*, 177; Litoff and Smith, *We're in This War, Too*, 116.

8

Oral History and World War II, 1941–45

From the Front Line to the Lone Star State

Stephen M. Sloan[1]

What you are doing is better than an epitaph on a tombstone for me.
—*World War II Veteran on His Oral History Interview*[2]

In the United States, no subject has received more attention from oral historians than World War II. For more than seventy years now, interviewers have worked with a wide range of individuals affected by the war. From elementary-aged students to seasoned scholars, from institutionally based efforts to community initiatives, the mass of interviewers interested in recording these stories has been as diverse as the stories themselves. The bulk of this large effort has been directed at the servicemen and servicewomen of World War II, but the project also addresses the home front and a wide range of features of the conflict's long reach. Oral history, with its long form, deep listening, and co-creation, has proved itself as a valuable tool to record the human experience of the war. Throughout the nation, hundreds of thousands of interviews have been conducted over the years, an effort that began long before the guns of war fell silent.[3]

The origins of the World War II oral history project lie in the war itself. The lack of a depth and breadth of information on military actions in the Great War led the US Army to create the position of combat historian to help guarantee a fuller record of the second global conflict. Initially, the combat historian worked in the field to document actions and gather historical resources for the archives. They soon discovered, however, such material insufficient. For combat historians, oral history became a powerful tool to actively create a historical record, rather than receiving or filing away print materials they were able to acquire. The vanguard of combat historians using interview research was Lieutenant Colonel Samuel Lyman Atwood Marshall,[4] who drew on the long tradition of "critiques" (post-maneuver assembling of primary officers) and "briefings" (the discussions that take place before actions) to create a new conversation that he called the "interview after combat." The technique included reassembling participants from an action and guiding them back through the battle, step by step, asking questions to draw out detail and the personal experiences of soldiers in the engagement. It was much more detailed and complete than any other type of action review used in the past.[5]

The first instance of employing this technique was after a night battle in the Pacific—Makin Island, November 1943. Marshall published a book based on his approach titled *Island Victory*. It was a landmark publication written "from the very words of the men who fought—from the words of *all* men who fought . . . not merely those of the commanders or a few other leaders." The significance of this was that "no book like it has ever appeared before. And it is most probable that no days of battle in this or any previous war have ever been described as accurately as *Island Victory* describes the combat on Kwajalein." In 1944, Marshall would bring the technique to the other theater of the war, where it became a widely adopted device used by combat historians to understand maneuvers throughout Europe. For army historian Forrest C. Pogue,[6] interviews he conducted with dozens of men who went in on the morning of June 6, 1944, formed his understanding of the D-Day invasion. Pogue, like Marshall, began gathering interviews immediately: "Some I talked to shortly after they were wounded, others I interviewed as they rested near the front lines."[7]

The drive to do interviews, however, was not just about gathering more information. As combat historian Hugh M. Cole later maintained, the after-action reports and journals of the sixty-one American divisions fighting in Europe alone weighed some thirty-seven tons. The challenge for the historian was "not that of finding information, but of cutting down and compressing the materials at hand." It was not just about amassing more data, but also capturing additional perspectives and experiences. For Cole, the corpus of combat interviews became one of the most valuable sources of information available to the historian. The interviews "fleshed out the framework of events chronicled in the unit journals and provided additional testimony to help resolve disputed questions of fact. As army historian Stephen E. Everett has noted, the informal processes through which planning and execution of military activities often happen "has resulted in less information committed to paper or into permanent electronic databases, again emphasizing the importance of supplementing the written record."[8]

Pogue noted that through the course of collecting their interviews, the methods and approaches the historians used evolved. He reflected later that "all of us learned a great deal about army organization and tactics that we hadn't known before. We picked up each new item casually, tried it out cautiously on the next interviewees, and if it worked, we then demanded information about that particular point from the next officer we met." The frenzied fieldwork of combat historians continued up until VE (Victory in Europe) Day. When the dust settled, more than 2,000 interviews had been gathered and collected in the European theater alone during the war years. For oral history as an approach, as historian Stephen J. Lofgren argues, the army effort established the "relative institutional acceptance of oral history as a necessary requirement for capturing experiences of war and organizational history." This would be the beginning of a long army tradition.[9]

What began during World War II as a specialized internal strategy has since become a varied and ongoing effort to gather oral histories. Whereas the aims of the work of combat historians were quite focused, the broader project, as it has continued and evolved, has been driven by a wide range of impulses—to document, to memorialize, to celebrate, to provide tribute, to understand, to instruct, to remember, to thank, to not forget, and a host of other motivations and desires. Despite the varied impetuses for conducting interviews, those who took on the mantle of recording World War II oral histories built upon the strengths of the approach that combat historians had already discovered. Oral history offered an approach to actively capture more detailed and more complete information to add to the historical record. It was a tool that brought texture to the understanding of events, assembling multiple perspectives to inform a richer composite. The framework of events became more fleshed out, building not just a broader knowledge of *what happened*, but the myriad of perspectives on *how* and *why* events occurred. Oral history brought candor, honesty, and simple statements to topics that seemed increasingly complex and distant. Like combat historians, the succeeding generations of oral historians continued to experiment and develop their approach and often worked with a sense of urgency, aware that the passage of time threatened the loss of voices and often brought the tangled considerations of working with memory.

The next wave of World War II oral historians worked to gather not just a history of the battlefield, but also the variety of ways in which individuals experienced the conflict. For many, it was the defining event of their generation. The World War II oral history project would be an effort that would grow with the expansion of recording technology and only increase in its pace as the country moved toward the new millennium. The growth of World War II oral history work, like the rise of the postwar oral history movement in general, was closely tied to the evolution, availability, and affordability of recording technology. Buoyed by the introduction of analog reel-to-reel recorders that replaced wire recording in the electronics boom of the late 1940s and 1950s, several US oral history efforts emerged in the generation following the war. This technology would be replaced by a second wave of lower-fidelity, yet much less expensive, cassette recorders. Invented by the Philips company in 1963, the portable cassette recorder opened new possibilities. The price point for recording oral history dropped considerably with its introduction and adoption, and it would be central in many projects from the late 1960s to the turn of the century. The ease of recording and playback that this device offered multiplied the initiatives to capture stories, popularizing an effort that had been fairly centralized up to that point. The turn from analog to digital came slowly, and the transition to a standard format was by no means seamless, but digital became the norm by the new millennium. Digital recording offered increased fidelity for amateur efforts and created new possibilities for sharing recordings. Overall, the majority of oral history interviews have been audio only, but sound and image have grown in popularity since the 1970s. Like audio, the growth of quality audiovisual work hinged on issues of access, affordability, and preservation.[10]

The rise of professional oral history can be seen through several surveys and publications from the mid-1960s to the early 1980s. These surveys reveal a landscape where the number of nationwide oral history projects grew from less than 100 to a list of approximately 500 oral history programs by 1982. Each of these programs, wide-ranging in size and scope, could contain several diverse individual and ongoing projects. Of the 89 projects included in a 1965 survey, only 5 initiatives addressed topics related to World War II.[11] None of these was particularly interested in the broad American experience of the war; instead, they focused on individuals such as political leaders and generals, thus reflecting the early US oral history movement's emphasis on elites. By 1971, a follow-up survey found more than a 250 percent increase in projects nationwide. Oral History Association president Louis M. Starr reported, oral history is "developing so rapidly that no guide can keep abreast of it." The variety of the emerging projects was impressive, including nine new major projects concerning World War II oral history. Notable among this group was the listing of the US Navy, Air Force, and Marines, each following the early lead of the US Army in hosting ongoing oral history projects. Overall, however, it is not until the broader study ten years later that the popular movement to capture oral histories had truly gained great momentum.[12]

The much more ambitious survey of oral history programs in the early 1980s identified 500 total programs, wide ranging in focus with an ongoing effort in every state in the union. The number of projects concerned with World War II grew to forty-three with wide ranges of emphases. From oral histories with Tuskegee Airmen in Alabama to workers in Oregon World War II shipyards, from interned Japanese Americans in California to Holocaust survivors in Connecticut, a broader examination of the experience of World War II was emerging. These efforts, however, were just suggestive of the dramatic increase in oral history work in subsequent decades. Although the ongoing work by institutional and academic oral history programs continued to impress, the flexibility and accessibility of the approach made it a favored methodology for diverse practitioners. Whether it be individual researchers, family members, small-town institutions, or regional associations, the World War II oral history project had entered its age of popularization.[13]

In examining the broad scope of World War II oral history work, it becomes clear that the motivations to collect and the approaches for sharing World War II oral histories are as diverse as the stories themselves. These stories hold popular appeal, and in a country shaken by events of the 1960s and 1970s, the struggle and victory of the 1940s took on renewed meaning. One popular work that typified this sentiment was Studs Terkel's *"The Good War": An Oral History of World War II*. Terkel noted in his foreword that he chose that name because the "Good War" was a phrase often voiced by men of an earlier generation "to distinguish that war from other wars, declared and undeclared." In the post–Vietnam War era, looking back past the social and economic tensions of recent memory was an exercise wholeheartedly endorsed by the public. The tests that Americans met, both at home and abroad, created a yearning to hear stories of those who had not only faced clear and dire challenges in the past, but had also met them decisively. Journalist Tom Brokaw collected stories of the men and women who lived through the Second World War. In *The Greatest Generation*, Brokaw paid "tribute to those men and women who have given us the lives we have today," those who faced the Great Depression and the challenge of World War II and were still here to speak of it. The book was a tribute that resonated, selling more than two million copies in its first two years in print.[14]

Along with popular publications that came from oral history, the approach also became the backbone of academic research and publications on the war years. Some of these titles used personal narratives to inform biography, while others relied upon large collections of interviews to examine everything in between the attack on Pearl Harbor in 1941 to the settlement at Potsdam in 1945. Called "true stories," "memoirs," "personal accounts," "recollections," "remembrances," "accounts," and "experiences," these titles that number in the hundreds use interview research of first-person experiences with events to add depth and authenticity to our understanding of a wide range of issues and events on the home front and battlefield alike. The early 1990s witnessed a dramatic increase in the drive to record and present World War II stories. The fiftieth anniversary of World War II (1991–95) provided a springboard for the work, with institutions and communities of all sizes contributing to the effort. For example, "Cincinnati Goes to War: A Community Responds to World War II," an exhibit produced by the Cincinnati Historical Society, positioned oral histories in a primary role in their conception and design. As one exhibit reviewer noted, these interviews had a focus "fully on Cincinnati but in a way . . . [r]eal people and their ordinary experiences are kept at center stage throughout."[15]

The rise in the popularity of historian Stephen E. Ambrose's work matched the spate of interest around the conflict's fiftieth anniversary. Ambrose relied extensively on oral history for his research. His work also reached beyond print media and guided the production of the popular HBO miniseries *Band of Brothers* and the film *Saving Private Ryan*. His career also represents a bridge to other public programming from oral histories as well. His work with D-Day veterans inspired him to found the National World War II Museum in New Orleans, a noted museum of the conflict and repository of thousands of World War II oral histories.[16]

In 2000, the federal government established a new historic site to interpret the American home-front experience in World War II, the Rosie the Riveter/World War II Home Front National Historical Park in Richmond, California. A central part of this new site was a partnership with the Regional History Office at University of California, Berkeley, to conduct oral history interviews. To date, more than 250 interviews have been gathered. This project is indicative of the growing desire in the 1980s and 1990s to document stories of the home front in World War II. Although these efforts have not been nearly as extensive as those that concentrate on veterans, they represent much needed examinations of the ways in which World War II affected the country beyond the battlefield.[17]

For veterans of World War II, the fullest expression of the drive to conduct oral histories has been the Veterans History Project (VHP) in the American Folklife Center of the Library of Congress. In October 2000, Congress passed the Veterans' Oral History Project Act, which authorized the creation of the VHP. With an initial authorization of $250,000, the VHP was charged to "collect video and audio recordings of personal histories and testimonials of veterans of the Armed Forces who served during a period of war." The language of the act highlighted the importance of gathering oral histories of the approximately six million living veterans of World War II, noting that "almost 1,500 die each day." In laying out the rationale for creating the project, the enabling legislation stated the following:

> It is in the Nation's best interest to collect and catalog oral histories of American war veterans so that future generations will have original sources of information regarding the lives and times of

> those who served in war and the conditions under which they endured, so that Americans will always remember those who served in war and may learn first-hand of the heroics, tediousness, horrors, and triumphs of war.[18]

The VHP offered forms, training opportunities, and a prominent archive in which to store and access the collection, but collecting the oral histories relied on the willingness of veterans to contribute and the work of volunteer interviewers. Within a relatively short time, the initiative created the largest oral history collection on the planet. The Library of Congress currently holds approximately 75,000 audio and video recordings in the VHP, with approximately two-thirds regarding the Second World War.[19]

In 2016, new legislation passed to expand the Veterans History Project to include oral histories with members of Gold Star Families. With this, the project invites interviews of immediate relatives of those lost fighting for their country. This extension of the VHP's mission promises to have a significant effect on the ongoing contributions of World War II interviews by calling for oral histories with spouses and descendants of veterans lost in this conflict. This change in mission, however, also promises to make the record that the Library of Congress holds a much more honest compilation of World War II. These will be stories of immediate loss and death, often stopped at a painful moment in time some seventy-plus years ago. This shift also presents opportunities by capturing more civilian experiences, including bringing significantly more voices of women to the archive. As the bill's sponsor, Representative Chris Smith from New Jersey stated this "will honor the men and women who gave 'the last full measure of devotion' in the service of our nation by allowing their families to tell their stories—so that all Americans can hear, appreciate, remember and honor these patriots."[20]

Recording World War II Oral Histories in Texas

For Texans, the oral histories of the state and its citizens' involvement in World War II are critical records to gather and preserve, and to share in a variety of ways. It was a war, of course, that not only realigned global alliances and set the stage for the modern international order, but also had a dramatic transforming effect on the state and on several generations of its people. As the broader effort to record World War II oral histories picked up around the nation, that effort was especially active in Texas. More than 750,000 Texans[21] served during the war, and each person's service intimately touched a much broader circle of family and friends. The enormity of the war effort meant those who lived through the conflict have stories to tell. For institutional oral history programs in the state, North Texas State University, now University of North Texas, created an early focus on recording veterans of World War II. When Ronald E. Marcello[22] came to the program in 1967, he expanded the focus of the oral history program from Texas politics to the Great Depression and veterans of World War II. Assisted by veterans' organizations, he completed projects on prisoners of war, the attack on Pearl Harbor, and World War II aviation. To date, more than 1,000 interviews from World War II veterans have been collected by the program.[23]

In 1999, Maggie Rivas-Rodriguez led the creation of the US Latino & Latina World War II Oral History Project at the University of Texas at Austin.[24] The initiative's objective was to recognize the many contributions that Hispanics made to the war effort, since "the general histories of the period have not included the experiences of this generation of Latinos." The project has interviewed over 700 men and women on World War II since that time and has published eight issues of a newspaper dedicated to the interviews. Rivas-Rodriguez has also produced several academic publications that draw on the work of the project.[25] Although the project's scope is much broader than Texas, the majority of World War II interviewees come from the Lone Star State. The effort has truly broadened the narrative of the World War II experience.

With its launch in 2000, the Veterans History Project energized efforts by community groups throughout Texas to partner with World War II veterans to record their histories. Texas has been one of the largest contributors to the VHP collection with approximately 3,600 interviews on World War II to date. The list of organizations and affiliations of the partners whose interviewers have accomplished this work in Texas is remarkably diverse—American Red Cross, American Association of Retired Persons (AARP), Boy Scouts of America, Daughters of the American Revolution, Texas Court Reporters Association, universities, archives, museums, public libraries, senior living centers, Veterans Affairs offices and hospitals, high schools, rotary clubs, Veterans of Foreign Wars (VFW) posts, and the American Legion. The commitment to World War II oral histories peaks on annual occasions when we recognize our veterans (Veterans Day, Memorial Day, or Independence Day) or on anniversaries of significant dates in the war. This has been true in Texas as well. In 2005, spurred on by the recognition of the sixtieth anniversary of the war's official end, the Texas Historical Commission initiated an effort to document the places and stories of Texans connected to the global conflict. *Texas in World War II* sought to document the physical footprint of the war, recognizing that Texas was home to a host of major and minor military installations, nearly seventy bases and branch prisoner-of-war camps, and four internment camps. Along with designating these places, some with a special series of historical markers, the initiative placed high importance on gathering the experiences of Texans more generally involved in the conflict. Community partners were organized to stage fifty-five local and regional oral history workshops titled *Here and There: Recollections of Texas in World War II*. Trainers encouraged participating interviewers collecting oral histories to make sure these recordings were deposited with the nationwide Veterans History Project.[26]

Interpreting the Experiences of Texas and Texans in World War II

Emerging from the collections of rich oral history research gathered are publications on various aspects of World War II in Texas. Louis Fairchild's *They Called It the War Effort: Oral Histories from WWII Orange, TX* is representative of scholarship in the state produced from oral history interviews. This study of Orange, which grew from a population of 7,500 prior to the war to a city of approximately 60,000 by war's end, emphasizes oral histories in understanding the life of the coastal community and the impact shipbuilding had during the conflict. These home-front stories highlight the shifting social constraints and the high cost of "increased opportunities, profits, and a more cosmopolitan lifestyle." Fairchild's work is representative of several studies relying extensively on oral history to understand World War II's effect on Texas communities, including El Paso, Greenville, Fort Worth, Abilene, and Sweetwater. World War II was a watershed for such places large and small. Juxtaposed between the Great Depression and the boom of the 1950s, these Texas communities would never be the same. For oral historians, the best way to understand these fundamental changes has been to interview those who experienced it firsthand.[27]

A central energy in the shifting social structures, modernization, and enlarged capital that transformed the state in World War II was the many ways in which the federal government expanded in Texas. Most notably were the many military facilities throughout the state created to support the war effort. Oral history has proven to be a useful tool in understanding these as well: from studies of individual camps and airfields, like Camp Kenedy, Pyote Air Force Base, and Hondo Army Airfield, to treatments of the overall impact of the army air force or POW installations on the surrounding communities. Jan Jarboe Russell's 2015 publication on the family internment camp at Crystal City is a great example of how narrative can reveal the full range of human experience. Her interviewees provided what other sources could not, including, as one review puts it, the "child's-eye descriptions of what the long, strange journey to their unknown new home was like." These are stories of sorrow, betrayal, and destruction, but also narratives of an enduring community overcoming great odds.[28]

The largest body of World War II literature informed by oral history, however, examines less the war's impact on the Texas communities it touched; instead, it focused on experiences of Texans in combat. Notable publications have woven these stories together, adding texture to our understanding of the experiences of service personnel. In this category, narratives of the women who joined the war effort hold a significant place. Special attention has been paid to the experiences of the Women Airforce Service Pilots (WASP). Trained in Houston and at Avenger Field in Sweetwater, the WASP contributed to the war effort by freeing up men for overseas service through ferrying aircraft, towing gunnery targets, transporting equipment and personnel, and flight-testing aircraft. They also broke new barriers for women with their service. Oral history has proven especially effective in capturing and sharing the stories of these women. Of special note is the work of historian Katherine Sharp Landdeck at Texas Woman's University who was nominated for an Emmy Award for her work on the film

Silver Wings, Flying Dreams: The Complete Story of the Women Airforce Service Pilots. Her expertise on the experiences of WASP has informed several public history projects and presentations.[29]

The desire to record and share the stories of veterans has led to several collections of works informed by oral history. Though primarily focused on the individual experiences of veterans, these works further bring together a chorus of experiences to impart a richer understanding. Reflective of the maturation of the World War II oral history project in the state, these works, William Adams's work on veterans of the Lower Rio Grande Valley notwithstanding, were published in the new millennium. Kelley Crager's *Hell under the Rising Sun: Texan POWs and the Building of the Burma-Thailand Death Railway* shows the power of oral history to capture and impart the varied experiences of veterans. In this case, he attempts to understand those men who endured forced labor and privation in their three and a half years of imprisonment by the Japanese. It is a story other sources fail to provide. "Even those official sources that are available," declares Crager, "do not adequately reflect the former prisoners' thoughts and feelings regarding their experiences."[30]

As oral historians work in an interview to capture and detail an individual story, it has provided a rich vehicle for works of individuals affected by World War II. These treatments range from broad academic studies to self-published memoirs. The multitude are too numerous to include. One example, however, that reveals the ways in which oral history works to both broaden the understanding of a life and tell us much more than the story of an individual is Michael S. Sweeney's *Sound Historian* piece on Henry T. Waskow, the subject of a much-heralded story dispatched by correspondent Ernie Pyle during the war. Waskow, a lieutenant in the 36th Infantry Division who was killed in Italy, was memorialized by Pyle in a column that was widely circulated in the national and international press. Despite the popularity of the piece titled "Who Was Henry T. Waskow of Belton, Texas?," the answer posed would be not answered adequately until Sweeney's research and oral history interviews with Waskow's comrades, friends, and family members. As oral historian Ronald E. Marcello noted, "Sweeney has taken Pyle's personalized story of Waskow and made it even more personalized, as well as more detailed." Oral history has offered authors a path to bring texture and complexity to the understanding of a life lived, and this has been especially true in its application in works on World War II.[31]

The Texas World War II Oral History Project

Several archives within Texas have prioritized recording World War II experiences through oral history. The collections with significant holdings are outlined below. For the researcher interested in using oral history to explore a multitude of perspectives on the war, these collections are indispensable. The oral histories below, and scores of others held by smaller organizations, have informed exhibits, programs, theatrical productions, curriculum projects, and publications. As we witness the final act of World War II oral history efforts in the state, it is important to note the impressive work that has been accomplished to date.

Baylor University Institute for Oral History—Waco, Texas

- Collection: 378 interviews (primarily audio, some video)
- Special Topics: Sweethearts of the 36th Infantry Division, Utilization of World War II Prisoners of War in Texas, Liberators of World War II Concentration Camps, Wage-Earning Women of World War II
- Availability: Transcripts and audio/video available at www.baylor.edu/oralhistory

Commemorative Air Force—Dallas, Texas

- Collection: Approximately 4,500 interviews (primarily audio, some video)
- Special Topics: US Aviation in World War II in the Pacific and Europe, German and Japanese Pilots, WWII Home Front
- Availability: Collection currently not available to the public. Plans for creating public archive.

General Land Office Voices of Veterans Oral History Program—Austin, Texas

- Collection: Approximately 90 interviews
- Special Topics: Veterans, WASP, and WAVES
- Availability: Interviews are searchable, with summaries, audio files of the interviews, and selected downloadable transcripts at voicesofveterans.org

Lamar University—Beaumont, Texas

- Collection: Approximately 20 interviews (primarily audio, some video)
- Special Topics: Home-Front Experiences, War Experiences, Prisoners of War
- Availability: Located in the Mary and John Gray Library for public access to the audio files. Interviews inventoried at https://www.lamar.edu/library/services/university-archive/index.html

National Museum of the Pacific War—Fredericksburg, Texas

- Collection: Over 4,100 veteran interviews (audio format, few video)
- Special Topics: War against Japan, Admiral Chester Nimitz, Prisoners of War
- Availability: Transcripts and selected audio are available and downloadable at https://digitalarchive.pacificwarmuseum.org/digital/collection/p16769coll1/search?_ga=2.144171698.626239612.1623547120-157734893.1623547120

South Texas Archives and Special Collections at Texas A&M University, Kingsville—Kingsville, Texas

- Collection: More than 200 interviews (Spanish and English)
- Special Topics: World War II Veterans
- Availability: All interviews are available to researchers on location and records are available at http://libguides.tamuk.edu/content.php?pid=585404&sid=4824652

Stephen F. Austin State University—Nacogdoches, Texas

- Collection: Approximately 50 interviews (audio)
- Special Topics: East Texans in World War II
- Availability: Interview transcripts and audio accessible at the Ralph W. Steen Library. Selected transcripts at http://digital.sfasu.edu/cdm/landingpage/collection/OH

Texas A&M University—College Station, Texas

- Collection: 16 interviews (audio)
- Special Topics: Veterans, War's Impact on Texas A&M
- Availability: Transcripts available at Cushing Memorial Library on the Texas A&M University campus.

East Texas War and Memory Project, Texas A&M University, Commerce—Commerce, Texas

- Collection: 182 interviews (video)
- Special Topics: Home Front, Spouses of Veterans, Army Specialized Training Program, Texans Who Lived in Europe during World War II
- Availability: Full video of interviews is available in the library's digital collections at http://dmc.tamuc.edu

Texas City Library Local History Department—Texas City, Texas

- Collection: 21 interviews (most audio, few video)
- Special Topics: General Histories of World War II from Residents of Texas City
- Availability: Transcripts and audio available at www.texascity-library.org

Texas Military Forces Museum—Austin, Texas

- Collection: 12 interviews (audio)
- Special Topics: 36th Infantry Division, 442nd Regimental Combat Team
- Availability: Audio available at museum.

Texas Women's Oral History—Denton, Texas

- Collection: Over 700 interviews (audio and video)
- Special Topics: Training and Experience of Women Air Force Service Pilots
- Availability: Interviews available at www.twu.edu/library/wc-oral-history-project-page.asp

University of North Texas Oral History Program—Denton, Texas

- Collection: Over 1,000 interviews (audio)
- Special Topics: Pearl Harbor Survivors, Prisoners of War from the European and Eastern Theaters, Lost Battalion, Air Force Personnel from European theater
- Availability: Transcripts held in the UNT Special Collections in Willis Library. Select transcripts available online with UNT access code or from an on-campus computer.

Institute of Oral History at University of Texas at El Paso—El Paso, TX

- Collection: Approximately 180 interviews (primarily audio)
- Special Topics: El Paso during the War, Bracero Project, Mexico in World War II
- Availability: Interview transcripts and audio are available on the UTEP Digital Commons at https://scholarworks.utep.edu/oral_history/

The University of Texas Institute of Texas Cultures at San Antonio—San Antonio, Texas

- Collection: Approximately 12 interviews (audio)
- Special Topics: Aviation, Women in Military in World War II
- Availability: Some transcripts available, audio available online through UTSA Libraries Special Collections—www.lib.utexas.edu/taro/utsa/00317/utsa-00317.html

VOCES Oral History Project University of Texas—Austin, Texas

- Collection: Approximately 700 interviews (most video, only 10 audio)
- Special Topics: Army, Army Bands, Bataan Death March, Battle of the Bulge, Citizenship, Civil Rights, Civil Service, Education, Ending the War, European Theater, GI Bill, Health Issues, Home Front, Killed in Action, Latinas in the Military, Medics, Normandy, Nurses, Postwar Service, Poverty, Prisoner of War, Pro-Veteran Activist, Racism/Discrimination, Great Depression, Voting Rights Act, WWII, Wounded in Action
- Availability: Interviews are accessible at the Benson Latin American Collection at the University of Texas. Some transcripts are available at http://www.lib.utexas.edu/voces/browse-index.html

37th Training Wing Office of History and Research, Texas—San Antonio, Texas

- Collection: About 30 interviews (audio)
- Special Topics: General Histories of World War II Servicemen
- Availability: Public must contact them for information about the collection.

The repositories above, along with the Veterans History Project, are excellent recipients for World War II oral history interviews as this mammoth and important project enters its final stage. Interviewing work still needs to be done on the experience of veterans. In a 2016 study by the US Department of Veterans Affairs, Texas was fifth in terms of population, with approximately 35,000 World War II veterans living in the state. Along with new interviews to be conducted, it remains especially important to guarantee the preservation of existing recordings currently held only in private collections.[32]

Conclusion

Taken together, the effort to collect an oral history of the American experience in World War II has produced some impressive results on both the state and national scale. Oral history, which developed as a practice since 1945, has grown and evolved as a methodology while documenting the Second World War. Oral historians, both professional and amateurs, have worked as intensively on World War II, and consequently, the overall historical record of this event is marked by a wealth of personal remembrances.

Unlike what the combat historians were looking for, however, the bulk of World War II oral histories are not merely a play-by-play recounting of events, but expansive perspectives on *how* and *why* events happened the way they did. Perhaps more meaningful than this is the capacity these interviews possess to express the *significance* of the war—not as a static construct, but as it has shifted and changed over time, expressed by those who experienced it most closely. Several years ago, I interviewed nineteen US servicemen who participated in the liberation of concentration camps near the end of World War II.[33] Some seventy years after events, these individuals related their experience emancipating those interned at camps such as Buchenwald, Dachau, and Nordhausen. Their stories were vivid memories of the sights, smells, sounds, and stories from, what was for some, encounters with sites that lasted only a few hours. Embodied in these interviews is the tangible and vivid reality of the camps. What the interviews also achieve for these liberators is to relate the significance of those singular experiences over time, revealing layers of meaning. When interviewed in October 2011, William Dippo, a liberator of Mauthausen, had lived a long life since the spring of 1945. As he testified to witnessing Mauthausen, he did so in fluid terms, even connecting it to events in the new millennia. In 2005, his experience in World War II gained further meaning when Tibor Rubin, a Hungarian-born Jewish survivor of Mauthausen and later a private in the US Army, was awarded the Medal of Honor by President George W. Bush for actions during the Korean War.[34] As Mr. Dippo stated in his interview, "I'm puffed up about a lot of things I know of people and the things they have done and their accomplishments, but I'm puffed up on myself that I was able to do something."[35]

While educating how to conduct oral history, I have been asked this question about the work to record World War II interviews: "When do we know when we have enough?" It is an interesting question, and I confess that World War II is the only subject on which I have been asked that question. A fundamental flaw in the question posed, however, is a misunderstanding about the nature of oral history. Oral history is not about the drive to accomplish one narrative, to fill in gaps until they are gone and a seamless record is complete. It is not a puzzle for which we seek the final piece. A more useful metaphor is oral history as chorus. Adding voices enriches the refrain, maybe underscoring the melody, perhaps bringing in useful dissonance. Additional voices bring more texture, color, depth, and range to the piece. Oftentimes, we think of this subject as "the war," but oral history reveals and reminds us that there were many Second World Wars, millions of them, each grounded in a unique individual experience.

Notes

1. Stephen M. Sloan is Associate Professor of History at Baylor University. Former head of the Oral History Association, he currently is Director of the Institute for Oral History at Baylor. He has authored and edited several works on oral history as research and on Texas oral history.

2. A comment to interviewer Ronald E. Marcello upon reflecting on the meaning of their work together. Dr. Marcello directed the Oral History Program at the University of North Texas for thirty-five years, conducting more than 1,500 interviews on World War II and authoring several books on the topic.

3. Oral histories represent an interviewer and interviewee working together to create a sound or video recording of historical information that preserves and shares a person's life history or eyewitness account of past experience. For general works on oral history, see Donald A. Ritchie, *Doing Oral History: Using Interviews to Uncover the Past and Preserve It for the Future* (New York: Oxford University Press, 2003); James Hoopes, *Oral History: An Introduction for Students* (Chapel Hill: University of North Carolina Press, 1979); Robert Perks and Alistair Thomson, eds., *The Oral History Reader* (New York: Routledge, 2006); and Valerie Raleigh Yow, *Recording Oral History: A Guide for the Humanities and Social Sciences*, 2nd ed. (Lanham, MD: Altamira Press, 2005).

4. S.L.A. Marshall would rise to the rank of brigadier general over a long career in the US Army, serving in World War I, World War II, and the Korean War. He also authored over thirty books on warfare, including the pioneering and controversial *Men Against Fire: The Problem of Battle Command* (New York: William Morrow & Company, 1947), and, with assistance from Captain John G. Westover

and Lieutenant A. Joseph Webber, *Bastogne: The Story of the First Eight Days: In Which the 101st Airborne Division Was Closed within the Ring of German Forces*, rev. ed. (Washington, DC: Zenger Publishing Company, 1979).

5. S.L.A. Marshall, *Island Victory: The Battle for Kwajalein*, rev. ed. (Washington, DC: Zenger Publishing Company, 1982), vii.

6. Master Sergeant Forrest C. Pogue later became a biographer of General George C. Marshall and the longtime director of both the George C. Marshall Foundation and Marshall Library at Virginia Military Institute. Pogue would also serve, in 1971, as one of the first presidents of the Oral History Association in the United States.

7. Stephen E. Everett, *Oral History Techniques and Procedures* (Washington, DC: Center of Military History, 1992), vii, 5; Forrest C. Pogue, *Pogue's War: Diaries of a WWII Combat Historian* (Lexington: University Press of Kentucky, 2001), 51.

8. Hugh M. Cole, *The Lorraine Campaign, US Army in World War II* (Washington, DC: Historical Division, Department of the Army, 1950), 616–17; Everett, *Oral History*, iii.

9. Pogue, *Pogue's War*, 99; Stephen J. Lofgren, "The Status of Oral History in the Army: Expanding a Tradition," *Oral History Review* 30 (Summer–Autumn 2003): 82. As part of the Office of the Administrative Assistant to the Secretary of the Army, the United States Army Center of Military History continues to record the history of the US Army in both times of war and peace.

10. Rebecca Sharpless, "The History of Oral History" in *History of Oral History: Foundations and Methodology*, eds. Thomas L. Charlton, Lois E. Myers, and Rebecca Sharpless (Lanham, MD: Altamirà Press, 2007), 13. These included Betamax digital audio and LaserDiscs in the 1970s; compact discs, digital audiotape, and digital compact cassettes in the 1980s; and MiniDiscs and DVDs in the 1990s. Although the media on which recordings are stored still varies greatly, oral historians have agreed on WAV as the best format for digital audio in the new millennium. The standards for digital video formats are still less established than audio.

11. Columbia University, Oral History Research Office, *Oral History in the United States: A Report from the Oral History Research Office of Columbia University* (New York: Columbia University Press, 1966); Gary L. Shumway, *Oral History in the United States: A Directory* (New York: The Oral History Association, 1971); Patsy A. Cook, ed., *Directory of Oral History Programs in the United States* (New York: Microfilming Corporation of America, 1982). The five that dealt with the Second World War are Claremont Graduate School, Claremont, California (California aircraft industry); Hoover Institute on War, Revolution and Peace, Stanford University, California (leaders of World War II); Harry S. Truman Library, Independence, Missouri (affairs of Truman administration); University of Oklahoma, Norman, Oklahoma (career of General Pat Hurley); and the George C. Marshall Research Foundation, Arlington, Virginia (career of General George C. Marshall).

12. Shumway, *Oral History in the United States*, 6. Included in the variety of new oral history programs are the American Society for Microbiology in Bloomington, Indiana; the Hogan Archive of New Orleans Music and New Orleans

Jazz in New Orleans, Louisiana; the Social Security Administration in Baltimore, Maryland; and the International Business Machines Corporation (IBM) in New York. The nine are American Aviation Historical Society, University of Southern California, US Air Force Academy, US Marine Corps, Dwight D. Eisenhower Presidential Library, US Naval Institute, North Texas State University, Southwest Texas State University, and World Tapes for Education.

13. Patsy A. Cook, ed., *Directory of Oral History Programs in the United States* (New York: Microfilming Corporation of America, 1982). In addition to the oral histories of white male combatants, the new social history in the 1960s and 1970s began focusing attention on racial minorities and noncombatants. Black soldiers, Holocaust survivors, Japanese internees, and female defense plant workers became the subject of detail. Whether audio or visual testimonies, their stories further enlighten us to the varied experiences of the Second World War. For such published works, see John Tateishi, *And Justice for All: An Oral History of the Japanese American Detention Camps* (New York: Random House, 1984); Tony Kushner, "Oral History at the Extremes of Human Experience: Holocaust Testimony in a Museum Setting," *Oral History* 29 (Autumn 2001); Mary Penick Motley, *The Invisible Soldier: The Experience of the Black Soldier, World War II* (Detroit: Wayne State University Press, 1975); Roger Horowitz, "Oral History and the Story of America and World War II," *Journal of American History* 82 (September 1995); Noah Shenker, *Reframing Holocaust Testimony* (Bloomington: Indiana University Press, 2015); and Sherna Berger Gluck, *Rosie the Riveter Revisited: Women, the War, and Social Change* (New York: New American Library, 1988). Noteworthy depositories of audio/visual testimonies of Holocaust survivors include the Fortunoff Video Archive at Yale University Library and the University of South California Shoah Foundation Institute for Visual History and Education. The latter collection now also contains testimonies of the 1994 Rwandan Genocide, the 1937 Nanjing Massacre, the Armenian Genocide, and the Guatemalan Genocide. More information on their work is available at https://sfi.usc.edu/about.

14. Studs Terkel, *"The Good War": An Oral History of World War II* (New York: Pantheon Books, 1984), vi; Tom Brokaw, *The Greatest Generation* (New York: Random House, 1998), xxxviii; Larry King Live Transcript, "Tom Brokaw Discusses 'The Greatest Generation,'" aired March 6, 2000, accessed June 13, 2021, http://transcripts.cnn.com/TRANSCRIPTS/lkl.html.

15. James H. Madison, review of "Cincinnati Goes to War: A Community Responds to World War II," by Cincinnati Historical Society, Cincinnati History Museum, Cincinnati, Ohio, *Journal of American History* "Discovering America: A Special Issue" 79 (December 1992), 1106.

16. Stephen E. Ambrose, a student of Forrest C. Pogue, published several titles on General Dwight D. Eisenhower, as well as *Band of Brothers, E Company, 506th Regiment, 101st Airborne: From Normandy to Hitler's Eagle's Nest* (New York: Simon & Schuster, 1992); *D-Day, June 6, 1944: The Climactic Battle of World War II* (New York: Simon & Schuster, 1994); *Citizen Soldiers: The US Army from the Normandy Beaches to the Bulge to the Surrender of Germany, June 7, 1944–May*

7, 1945 (New York: Simon & Schuster, 1997); *The Victors: Eisenhower and His Boys—The Men of World War II* (New York: Simon & Schuster, 1998); *Comrades: Brothers, Fathers, Heroes, Sons, Pals* (New York: Simon & Schuster, 1999); and *The Wild Blue: The Men and Boys Who Flew the B-24s over Germany* (New York: Simon & Schuster, 2001). The museum was founded as the National D-Day Museum in 2000. On September 25, 2003, Congress awarded the museum the designation of "America's National World War II Museum."

17. Public Law 106–35 designated the area centered on the old Kaiser shipyards, "In order to preserve for the benefit and inspiration of the people of the United States as a national park certain sites, structures, and areas located in Richmond, California that are associated with the industrial, governmental, and citizens efforts that led to victory in World War II." In 2014, the Regional History Office became the Oral History Center of the Bancroft Library at the University of California at Berkeley.

18. Public Law 106–380, October 27, 2000, [H.R. 5212] Congressional Record, vol. 146 (2000).

19. Public Law 106–380. VHP oral histories are searchable through an online database by biological information, name of veteran/civilian, name of interviewer/donor, war, branch of service, unit of service, and service location, http://memory.loc.gov/diglib/vhp/html/search/search.html. Approximately 10 percent of the oral histories have been digitized and are available online. If interviews are searched in the database and not found online, you can schedule an appointment ten days in advance of your visit. Reviewing the collection takes place in the American Folklife Center at the Library of Congress.

20. Elise Viebeck, "House Approves Gold Star Families Bill after Trump's Feud with Khans," *Washington Post*, September 6, 2016, https://www.washingtonpost.com/news/powerpost/wp/2016/09/06/house-approves-gold-star-families-bill-after-trumps-feud-with-khans/. A term that has evolved in reference to the service flag used since World War I. This flag displayed a blue star for every family member in the service, with a gold star replacing the blue star upon loss of that serviceman or servicewoman. According to the US Army, "The nation recognizes the sacrifice that all Gold Star Family members make when a father, mother, brother, sister, son, daughter, or other loved one dies in service to the nation." For additional information, see https://www.army.mil/goldstar/. Approximately 6.5 percent of the interviews currently in the Veterans History Project, World War II oral history collection are with female narrators.

21. This number includes approximately 20,000 women. Texas had the only all-female military training base in the United States during the war—Avenger Field in Sweetwater, home of the Women Airforce Service Pilots.

22. Marcello was also a leader in the Oral History Association—president in 1989 and secretary/treasurer from 1976 to 1986—and helped found the Texas Oral History Association.

23. Michelle M. Mears, "Ron Marcello: His Life and Career in Oral History,"

Sound Historian: Journal of the Texas Oral History Association 13 (2011): 5; Partial catalog in University of North Texas, Christopher N. Koontz, Ronald E. Marcello, and Kelly E. Crager, *Heroes: Oral History Interviews with World War II Veterans* (Denton: Oral History Program, University of North Texas Press, 2002).

24. In 2009, the project changed its name and expanded its mission. The Voces Oral History Center at the University of Texas at Austin now interviews, preserves, and shares the stories of men and women from the Korean and Vietnam War eras.

25. Maggie Rivas-Rodriguez, *Texas Mexican Americans and Postwar Civil Rights* (Austin: University of Texas Press, 2015); Maggie Rivas-Rodriguez and B.V. Olguin, eds., *Latina/os and World War II: Mobility, Agency, and Ideology* (Austin: University of Texas Press, 2014); Maggie Rivas-Rodriguez and Emilio Zamora, eds., *Beyond the Latino WWII Hero: Social and Political Legacies of the Latino WWII Generation* (Austin: University of Texas Press, 2009); Maggie Rivas-Rodriguez, Juliana Torres, Melissa DiPiero-D'Sa, Lindsay Fitzpatrick, eds., *A Legacy More than Words: Stories of US Latinos & Latinas of the WWII Generation* (Austin: US Latino & Latina WWII Oral History Project, University of Texas Press, 2006); and Maggie Rivas-Rodriguez, ed., *Mexican Americans and World War II* (Austin: University of Texas Press, 2005).

26. Texas Historical Commission, *Texas in World War II: Fundamentals of Military Oral History*, 2009. With material adapted from Baylor University's *Introduction to Oral History Manual*, 2; Texas Historical Commission, "Texas in World War II," accessed April 19, 2017, http://www.thc.texas.gov/preserve/projects-and-programs/military-sites/texas-world-war-ii.

27. JoAnn Stiles, review of *They Called It the War Effort: Oral Histories from WWII Orange, Texas*, by Louis Fairchild, *Sound Historian: Journal of the Texas Oral History Association* 3 (1995–1996): 73; Louis Fairchild, *They Called It the War Effort: Oral Histories from WWII Orange, TX*. This work was published in 1993 by Eakin Press with a second edition published in 2012 with the Texas State Historical Association. The second edition expands the number of interviews with nonwhite residents of Orange, including Japanese American and African American perspectives on this period of rapid change. Those works referenced above are Rebecca Craver, "Homefront with a Border Twist: El Paso during World War II," *Sound Historian: Journal of the Texas Oral History Association* 5 (1999); Fred H. Allison, "Patriotic Prosperity and Social Change in World War II: The Impact of Majors Field on Greenville, Texas," *Sound Historian: Journal of the Texas Oral History Association* 5 (1999); J'Neil L. Pate, *Arsenal of Defense: Fort Worth's Military Legacy* (Denton: Texas State Historical Association, 2011); Tracy M. Shilcutt, "'Soldiers Were Everywhere': Camp Barkley and Abilene, Texas, 1940–1945," *Sound Historian: Journal of the Texas Oral History Association* 12 (2009); and Dawn Letson, "Girl Pilots of Avenger Field: Sweetwater's Romance with the WASP of World War II," *Sound Historian: Journal of the Texas Oral History Association* 13 (2011).

28. Janet Maslin, "Purgatory at Home in Wartime," review of Jan Jarboe Russell, *The Train to Crystal City: FDR's Secret Prisoner Exchange Program and America's*

Only Family Internment Camp during World War II, in *New York Times* (January 18, 2015), accessed December 14, 2016, http://www.nytimes.com/2015/01/19/books/the-train-to-crystal-city-by-jan-jarboe-russell.html; Jan Jarboe Russell, *The Train to Crystal City: FDR's Secret Prisoner Exchange Program and America's Only Family Internment Camp during World War II* (New York: Scribner, 2015). For those oral history works concerning military facilities referenced, see Robert H. Thonhoff, *Camp Kenedy, Texas: World War I: Training Camp, Depression-Era: CCC Camp, World War II: Alien Detention Camp, German POW Camp, Japanese POW Camp* (Austin: Eakin Press, 2003); Robert D. Thompson, *We'll Find the Way: The History of Hondo Army Air Field during World War II* (Austin: Eakin Press, 1992); Thomas E. Alexander, *Rattlesnake Bomber Base: Peyote Army Airfield in World War II* (Abilene, TX: State House Press, 2005); Thomas E. Alexander, *The Wings of Change: The Army Air Force Experience in Texas during World War II* (Abilene, TX: McWhiney Foundation Press, 2003); Thomas E. Alexander, *The Stars Were Big and Bright: The United States Army Air Forces and Texas during World War II* (Austin: Eakin Press, 2000); Richard Paul Walker, *Prisoners of War in Texas during World War II* (Denton: North Texas State University Press, 1980); Michael R. Waters, *Lone Star Stalag: German Prisoners of War at Camp Hearne* (College Station: Texas A&M University Press, 2004).

29. The National WASP WWII Museum is located at Avenger Field in Sweetwater, Texas. For more information see http://waspmuseum.org/. Works focusing on the WASP include Jean Hascall Cole, *Women Pilots of World War II* (Salt Lake City: University of Utah Press, 1992); Harry Franklin Snapp, *Pioneer Women in West Texas Skies: Women Airforce Service Pilots of World War II* (Abilene, TX: Rupert N. Richardson Press, Hardin-Simmons University, 1994); Cindy J. Weigand, *Texas Women in World War II* (Lanham, MD: Republic of Texas Press, 2003); and Sarah Byrn Rickman, *Nancy Love and the WASP Ferry Pilots of World War II* (Denton: University of North Texas Press, 2008). *Silver Wings/Flying Dreams: The Complete Story of the Women Airforce Service Pilots*, directed by Bill Suchy (Orlando, FL: Bill Suchy Productions, 2015).

30. Kelly E. Crager, *Hell under the Rising Sun: Texan POWs and the Building of the Burma-Thailand Death Railway* (College Station: Texas A&M University Press, 2008), xii. Those works included in the project's maturation are William L. Adams, *Valley Vets: An Oral History of World War II Veterans of the Lower Rio Grande Valley* (Austin: Eakin Press, 1999); Larue Harper Barnes, *They Were There: Texas Veterans Remember World War II* (Hillsboro, TX: Hill College Press, 2006); Brenda J. Cooper, *World War II 50th Anniversary Veteran Interviews* (Baytown, TX: Lee College Press, 2002); Stephen Neal Manning, *The Courage of Common Men: Texans Remember World War II* (Plano: Republic of Texas Press, 2001); Stephen Neal Manning, *Texans Touched by World War II* (Plano: Republic of Texas Press, 2003); Ronald E. Marcello, "Lone Star POWs: Texas National Guardsmen and the Building of the Burma-Thailand Railroad, 1942–1944," *Southwestern Historical*

Quarterly 95 (January 1992); Patrick B. Simpson, "Survival: American Prisoners of War of the Japanese, 1941–1945," *Sound Historian: Journal of the Texas Oral History Association* 5 (1999); Stephen M. Sloan, Lois E. Myers, and Michelle Holland, eds., *Tattooed on My Soul: Texas Veterans Remember World War II* (College Station: Texas A&M University Press, 2015); and Ralph A. Wooster, *Texas and Texans in World War II* (Austin: Eakin Press, 2005).

31. Ronald E. Marcello, "Introduction," *Sound Historian: Journal of the Texas Oral History Association* 2 (1995–96): iv; Michael S. Sweeney, "War Correspondent Ernie Pyle's 'Beloved Captain': The Life and Death of Henry T. Waskow of Belton, Texas, and the Column that Touched America," *Sound Historian: Journal of the Texas Oral History Association* 2 (1995–96).

32. For those interested in learning more about oral history or identifying additional resources to assist in conducting an interview, the Texas Oral History Association (www.baylor.edu/toha) is the network and professional association for oral historians in the state. You may also access *The Introduction to Oral History Manual* by the Institute for Oral History at Baylor University at www.baylor.edu/oralhistory. The VA reported approximately 620,000 World War II veterans were living in 2016, less than 4 percent of the sixteen million who served in the war. The review also estimated that approximately 372 veterans were lost each day. See http://www.nationalww2museum.org/honor/wwii-veterans-statistics.html. For additional guidelines for interviewing veterans, see Barbara W. Sommer, *Doing Veterans Oral History* (Oral History Association and the Veterans History Project, 2015).

33. The Texas Liberators of World War II Concentration Camps Oral History Project was funded by a grant from the Texas Holocaust and Genocide Commission. The initiative ran from August 2011 to August 2013 and collected nineteen video oral histories on the liberation of camps, including Bergen-Belsen, Buchenwald, Dachau, Landsberg, Mauthausen, and Nordhausen. More information about the project is available at www.thgc.texas.gov and www.baylor.edu/oralhistory/liberators.

34. Teddy "Tibor" Rubin, liberated from Mauthausen, immigrated to the United States following the war. Wounded in action during the Korean War, Rubin spent thirty months in a POW camp, where his bravery and sacrifice saved many lives. For a recent biography on Tibor Rubin, see Daniel M. Cohen, *Single Handed: The Inspiring True Story of Tibor "Teddy" Rubin, Holocaust Survivor, Korean War Hero, and Medal of Honor Recipient* (New York: Berkley Caliber, 2015).

35. William Dippo, *Oral Memoirs of William Dippo*, Texas Liberators of World War II Concentration Camps Oral History Project, Texas Holocaust and Genocide Commission, interviewed by Stephen M. Sloan on October 21, 2011, in San Antonio, Texas (Waco, TX: Baylor University Institute for Oral History, 2012), 63.

9

Texas Agriculture and World War II

Christopher B. Bean and Henry C. Dethloff[1]

The attack by the Japanese Empire on Pearl Harbor on December 7, 1941, and the entrance of the United States into a war already involving Great Britain and Europe had profound effects upon Texas agriculture in all dimensions—feed, food, and fiber production; the processing, storage, and distribution of grain; cotton, cattle, poultry, beef, and pork production; and veterinary medicine. Transitioning from its nineteenth-century image of a provincial, backwater state from the South, Texas was on the cusp of becoming the economic powerhouse it is today, attractive to millions of people and industries from around the country and the world due to its innovation and opportunities. Although today known for its oil, banking, culture, and industrial population centers, Texas has always had a prominent and vibrant agricultural sector. As a result, Texas agriculture was going to profoundly affect the American and allied war effort during World War II, and conversely the war significantly affected Texas and American agriculture. In the words of Napoleon, armies march on their stomachs, and this still remained true in the mechanized forces of the mid-twentieth century. American farm productivity thus accelerated under the urgent stimulus of providing food and fiber for Allied military forces. Land-grant colleges, such as Texas A&M University, and associated agencies such as the agricultural extension service, agricultural experiment stations, and even 4-H clubs became significant contributors to the war effort. More than 20,000 Texas Aggies served in World War II, including more than 14,000 officers, 29 of whom were at the rank of general officer, and many of them agricultural and engineering students at Texas A&M.[2]

Texans and Americans of every age and locale became engaged in World War II. Farming was a vital war industry, and many laborers remained on the farm, critical to the American war effort. In the words of Secretary of Agriculture Claude R. Wickard, "Our farm resources must be used toward but one end—Victory." At home, war bonds, scrap-metal drives, home canning, and victory gardens became a way to help win the war. Victory gardens flourished in the Lone Star State, with their number increasing each year. In 1943 alone, Texans tended 1.4 million gardens, a 14 percent increase from 1942. Texas agricultural extension 4-H clubs began the "Feed a Fighter" program. With older children lured away to paying defense work, most 4-Hers challenged to meet governmental goals were prepubescent kids. Despite their age, this "4-H Army" took to heart the call "to be a loyal, effective, and courageous soldier on the home front." Their contributions were quite astonishing. Nationally, these young people were directly responsible for more than 77,000 head of dairy cattle, 250,000 swine, and 210,000 head of livestock. This group further contributed 40,000 tons of forage crops and 109,000 bushels of root crops. The average soldier ate approximately 1 ton of food in a year. With sixteen million men and women in uniform, the food necessary to feed the United States (and overall Allied forces) was astronomical. In Texas in 1942, it is estimated that the 4-H produced enough "to keep 17,000 fighting men in food and fiber for a year." By raising enough food to feed at least one soldier for an entire year, boys and girls gained membership into the Feed a Fighter Club, and in Texas they were rewarded with a trip to Randolph Air Force Field (San Antonio) and the neighboring army camps. Home "victory gardens" were promoted to encourage households to grow and consume their own produce and reduce dependence on commercial or imported food products—which could in turn be directed to military uses.[3]

Agricultural experiment station staff taught courses in army mess management in the military science program, and in special short courses. One important development, perfected by Professor Robert E. Karper at Texas A&M University, related to the production of starch from grain sorghum. Starch was in short supply during the war because the sources of supply of cassava roots imported from the East Indies was lost. More broadly, Texas agricultural experiment stations engaged in research to stimulate and increase crop production with studies indicating improved plowing, fertilizing, seed selection, irrigation, and harvest techniques. Paradoxically, from 1940 to 1945, farm population in Texas declined sharply, from 2,160,000 to 1,520,000 (see Table 9.1). Many of those who remained on the farm received deferments from military service in that their services to the country as farmers was more critical than their service in the military. Notably, the number of operating farms declined from 418,000 to 385,000. These numbers would suggest that farming and farm productivity declined markedly. Quite the opposite was true. While the number of farms and farmers declined, farm production expanded significantly. From 1940 to 1950, the acreage in Texas farms rose from 137,683,000 million to 145,389,000 acres, and by 1959, acreage had stabilized in the 140-million-plus range. Per capita farm production increased from $288 per person in 1940 to $2,452 in 1960. From 1940 to 1945, Texas farm population declined by 640,000! In 1945, there were 33,000 fewer farms in operation than there had been in 1940![4]

Table 9.1.

Texas Agriculture, 1935–50

	1935	1940	1945	1950
Farm Population	2,369,000	2,160,000	1,520,000	1,292,000
Number of Farms	501,000	418,000	385,000	332,000
Total Acreage in Farms	137,597,000	137,683,000	141,338,000	145,389,000
Average Acreage per Farm	275	329	367	439
Value of Farm Products Sold	(na)	439 million	1 billion	1.53 billion

Source: Historical Statistics of the United States: Colonial Times to 1970 (Washington, DC: US Department of Commerce: Bureau of the Census, Part 1, Series K 1–81, 1975), 457–64.

The cotton industry, in particular, was affected by the war. Farmers looked forward to increased production and, of course, profits. But due to low prices and a labor shortage in the field, cotton production in early 1942 in Texas slumped, declining to 82 percent of the year's projection. But promise was in the air. By year's end, those same farmers were now anticipating the state's largest cotton crop. In fact, in Lamb County (northwest of Lubbock), farmers harvested the biggest crop in the county's history. Ideal conditions allowed the cotton to establish a deep root system, thus shielding the plant from heavy rains. Throughout the summer of 1942, cotton blooms "appeared if by magic, and in the fall, heavy . . . [l]oaded stalks bent nearly to the ground." The boom disguised the fact that there existed a pressing need for labor. Whether they offered higher wages or aggressively recruited workers, farmers each year experienced a tightening labor pool. Growers looked to the government for assistance, hoping the War Production Board would intervene and obtain rationed materials for the manufacture of cotton strippers in Dallas and Wichita Falls. If so, cotton production would skyrocket. On average, one field-worker picked 150 to 250 pounds of cotton a day. A stripper, by contrast, could collect ten bales of cotton, or two and a half tons in the same period! Strippers would also save cotton farmers 90 percent on their labor costs. And it was in part increased mechanization and trends begun in the 1930s that contributed to the shift in the state from cotton to other agricultural and livestock endeavors.[5]

Further affecting Texas agriculture was the alteration to its structure. The war benefited those wanting to farm their own land. Farm tenancy in Texas decreased from 60 percent in 1930 to 37.6 percent by 1945. Governmental loans and easy credit contributed to this trend. So too did mechanization. The need for mechanization proved all the more important as the war effort drained labor from the fields. In the cotton industry, for instance, mechanical cotton harvesters filled the gap. The use of spindle-type pickers and roll or finger strippers reduced the time to gather an acre of cotton from 150 to 6.5 man-hours. After a few technical hiccups, the cotton industry in Texas would be fully mechanized by the 1970s. Mechanization also permeated the entire agricultural industry in the state. By war's end, draft animals had been replaced by tractors, and "a trend toward greater horsepower permitted farmers to utilize heavier and more sophisticated equipment." Plows continued to increase in size as the one- and two-row implements were replaced by the six-, eight-, and ultimately twelve- and sixteen-row plows. Furthermore, machines with the ability to gather a "multiplicity of crops enhanced the grain-harvesting ability."[6]

Drought and the shift toward profit-driven agribusiness in the 1930s moved Texas farmers to a willingness to embrace scientific innovations in the 1940s. Resistance to fertilizers waned as the application of ammonia-based fertilizers became commonplace. Similar changes occurred with the use of herbicides. Practices such as preplanting (to maintain proper soil moisture for planting) and preemergence (inhibiting germination of weeds before "ugly little heads show") and postemergence (killing the weeds after "ugly little heads show") herbicides all proved effective in controlling weeds. A secondary benefit was to drive down labor costs, since farmers no longer needed costly "hand labor" to control weeds prior to seeding. Farmers on the Texas plains relied less and less on the uncertainty of weather and turned to irrigation. Although the war created a shortage in irrigation equipment, drastically reducing the number of new wells drilled in the first year of the war, the demand never dissipated. In fact, during the wars, the number of irrigation wells drilled nearly doubled: 2,560 in 1941 to 4,300 in 1945. Well demand occurred at a time when rainfall was more than sufficient to produce "dry-land crops." Irrigation, however, permitted "a greater flexibility in crop selection" and increased production, rather than a fail-safe against drought. Texas farmers tapped the Ogallala Aquifer—one of the world's largest that encompasses 174,000 square miles in eight states under the Great Plains. Future hydrological and environmental concerns of depleting this vital aquifer would not be a concern for several generations. Even had the war's generation known of the ecological trade-off it probably would have mattered little, since watered acreage throughout the 1940s increased drastically and made it possible for crop selection previously prohibited on the dryer South Plains. With a reliable source of water, Texas farmers could for the first time produce Irish potatoes, cabbages, cantaloupes, carrots, cucumbers, onions, and peppers. Grapes, soybeans, alfalfa, and corn soon followed. These commodities were only possible in Texas because of the availability of water.[7]

Even as the number of farms decreased and the reliance on mechanization increased, the need for labor never completely disappeared. As the war effort pulled more and more men into vital (and better-paying) defense industries and the armed forces, fewer and fewer were available for farmwork: between April 1940 and July 1942, two million men and six million people total vacated the fields. In fact, in Texas alone, there were 200,000 fewer agricultural workers in 1943 than in 1939. To fill this need, the government tapped other pools of labor, including importing Mexican migrant workers, prisoners of war, and women. Of the three, women accounted for the largest group. Approximately three million women (27 percent of the agricultural workforce) responded to the nation's call to arms. In fact, the percentage of women working on farms rose from 8 percent in 1940 to 22.4 percent by 1945. The US Department of Agriculture estimated that nearly one and a half million nonfarm women were placed in agriculture jobs, while an equal number were directly recruited by farmers or found farmwork on their own. "Whether the forces consisted of farm wives driving tractors," notes students of the women's roles on farms during the war, "college women milking cows, housewives picking apples, or secretaries spending summer vacations harvesting, these workers responded with energy and ingenuity and ingenuity to the wartime need for farm labor." Most surely, these women came "to the rescue of the crops."

Officially titled the Women's Land Army (WLA), this organization was formally created in April 1943 in the image of its predecessor during the First World War. Although a federally funded program and hindered, at times, by reluctance at the federal and state level to employ women outside the traditional gender roles and some farmers critical of what they deemed "a socialized labor force" and not free labor, the WLA was administered at the state and local level. It operated in all but seven states, with some states such as Iowa and Minnesota prohibiting female farmworkers. The WLA organized women into three laboring groups. While some labored year-round, living on-site at the respective farms, others engaged in seasonal work. Still others were assigned to emergency labor. This included short-term assignments such as crop harvesting for a day or weekend. Since many women retained a primary job, they often commuted from home to a nearby farm to work in designated shifts. Those who traveled long distances would be housed in camps or farms. By war's end, most states offered formal training courses on various aspects of farming, such as livestock husbandry or machinery operation. The overwhelming majority of women, however, received cursory "on the job training." Women were paid "regular unskilled labor wages," ranging from 25 to 50 cents an hour, although more technical and skilled jobs that required training could pay more. Most workers in the WLA labored seasonally and consisted of middle-class urbanites and students, soldiers' wives, office clerks, school teachers, and secretaries, and it was not uncommon to have mother-daughter teams working together. At its height, almost 76,000 women worked in the program in Texas in 1943. Despite a precipitous decline in 1944 and 1945, WLA workers in Texas still remained above 51,000 each year.[8]

In order to achieve victory, the entire nation had to be mobilized. No longer was warfare simply a "man's affair." Women, civilians, and those beyond military age now had to contribute for victory. This even included children and marginalized groups such as African Americans. A seasonal occurrence in the South throughout the first half of the twentieth century, school cancellation became a regular occurrence in the farming communities throughout the country. In Lamb County, Texas, the district closed all schools for most of November to allow students to assist with the harvest. The students welcomed anything to get out of school and get paid in the process, but soon many had regret, for the district had to make up the lost days canceled over the Thanksgiving and Christmas holidays. Those in 4-H also contributed. In Texas, more than 26,000 performed emergency farm labor. Much more limited in the ways to assist the country in victory due to racial policies and sensibilities at the time, black Americans were marginalized to effectively manual labor. This held in both the military and on home front. Thus, within the African American community ran a strain of indifference if not resistance and resentment to assist Uncle Sam's crusade to liberate and democratize peoples abroad, while simultaneously denying it to many of its own citizens at home. Black community leaders at the national, state, and local levels battled this small yet persistent attitudes. African American civic leaders and pastors continuously reminded their constituents and parishioners of the stakes in the war. In the Texas Panhandle, black pastors encouraged their congregations that a white victory or loss would be their victory or loss.[9]

Another way to address the labor shortage was to import it. The Farm Labor Transportation Program, more commonly referred to as the "Bracero program," legalized and defined the standards for recruitment and employment of Mexican laborers. The genesis of this program actually predates the country's entry into the war. The passage of the Selective Training and Service Act of 1940 greatly drained military-age men from the fields. The following summer, a group calling itself the Dirt Farmers' Congress, formed in San Antonio, began lobbying federal officials for labor assistance by importing Mexican field hands. Despite intense lobbying, no redress was forthcoming until America's entry into war surpassed sticky racial or nationality issues. In August 1942, the United States and Mexico negotiated the Mexican Farm Labor Program. Under this agreement, those hiring imported Mexican workers agreed to pay a minimum wage and promised humane treatment, such as adequate shelter and food. The program was overseen by multiple federal agencies. Approximately 200,000 braceros were contracted to farmers in the United States. But none of these went to Texas. Texas farmers did not participate in the program, citing its "restrictive" obligations. They lobbied to have its requirements either weakened or simply done away with. In addition, Mexican officials, despite the state's Caucasian Race Resolution, which prohibited discrimination against Hispanics in Texas (legally, Hispanics were considered white), and the Good Neighbor Commission, which was to investigate and propose solutions to remedy discrimination, dismissed what they considered a hollow gesture that the state had no intention of enforcing. Thus they "embargoed" Mexican national workers from going to the Lone Star State. This prohibition would be lifted in 1947, but in the meantime Texas farmers secreted Mexican workers across the border and into their fields. Derisively called "wetbacks," these unofficial workers filled the fields, benefiting their employers by keeping wages down. The exact number of illegal workers during the war years in Texas may never be known, but most certainly it numbered in the tens, perhaps hundreds, of thousands. Off the books and illegal, these workers had little recourse for injustices. They often experienced unlivable wages, grinding poverty, and violent discrimination.[10]

With the armed forces and industry drawing more and more individuals from the fields, the War Department authorized a program that assisted labor-strapped farmers. Instead of Axis soldiers fighting for Allied defeat, the government had them working toward Allied victory. Texas held 78,982 prisoners in 14 military installations and 7 smaller installations constructed specifically for housing captives. The number of prisoner camps in the Lone Star State was twice that of any other state in the Union. There also existed branch camps. These camps contained only dozens of prisoners and provided labor to the remote regions of the state not in the immediate vicinity of the main camps. Due to their ephemerality, these camps were often housed in schools or makeshift tent cities on the town's fairgrounds. One labor camp in Navasota was housed in circus tents. For this labor, farmers paid the government $1.50. The government, in turn, gave each laborer 80 cents in canteen coupons. The remaining amount offset the cost of the program. By war's end, POWs worked the fields picking, harvesting, baling, threshing, chopping, and gathering everything from peaches to rice, from wood to hay, and from pecans to cotton. In Liberty County, northeast of Houston, the prisoners dazzled the locals by catching and killing by hand the numerous water moccasins and copperheads in the rice fields. One famous photograph has a prisoner posing with a dead snake draped around his neck in all his sartorial and masculine glory. By all accounts, Texas farmers were quite satisfied with the labor of the prisoners, even continuing relationships with them after the war.[11]

What else was going on besides mechanization, fertilization, irrigation, and labor procurement? In a few words, electrification, crop diversification, drainage programs, wind erosion and insect control, crop rotation, and biological seed and plant improvement, as well as war, were creating a new world, not just in agriculture but also in the total life experience of Texans and Americans. Poultry, hog, and beef production became more organized and efficient. Raising crops was the fundamental base of agriculture. Processing, storage, and shipment of food and grain products became a critical component of the American war effort. In 1940, at the beginning of World War II, the Texas Grain & Feed Association, the Panhandle Grain & Feed Association, and the Texas Feed Manufacturers' Association handled virtually all Texas feed and grain storage and transport. Those associations collaborated closely during the war and soon merged to become one as the Texas Grain & Feed Association. War changed the character of the Texas grain and feed industry and the environment in which that business was conducted—and indeed all agricultural industries became more nationally oriented under federal oversight. The War Production

Board regulated manufacturing and the allocation of raw materials. The War Shipping Administration directed ocean shipping. The Office of Defense Transportation controlled railroad freight uses and rates, and the Interstate Commerce Commission allocated domestic and international shipping. The Office of Price Administration (OPA) set wage and price controls. The character of the Texas and national agricultural and agribusiness industries, including the Texas Grain & Feed Association, changed dramatically. A great part of that change had to do with growth and expansion.[12]

The Texas livestock and feedlot industry as well as the feed and grain industry, while being introduced in the 1920s and 1930s, experienced their real birth during World War II as the demand for beef spiraled. Correspondingly, meat packing and storage operations and facilities expanded and became more structured, while the open-range cattle industry, already in decline, also became more constrained and structured. While the number of Texas farmers and cattle raisers declined sharply from 1940 to 1950, from 2.1 million to 1.5 million, total acreage in production during that same period rose from 137.5 million acres to 141.3 million, and value of farm products soared from $439 million to $1.7 billion. More surprising was the shift in the cattle industry in the state from the open fields in the western part of the state to the more forested east. By the end of 1945, there was in fact more cattle in East Texas than in West Texas. It was during the war that grain sorghum emerged as a commercial commodity in Texas. The Texas Panhandle became the most productive sorghum-growing region in the country. Irrigation (and later the development of a drought-resistant hybrid) increased production throughout the war. Used as a feed grain, sorghum helped pioneer the practice of fattening cattle in pens, thus reducing the need for open-range grazing. By 1970, Texas was the leading cattle-feeding state in the United States, marketing three million fattened animals annually (Texas also led the nation in horses, sheep, goats, and turkeys). The storage, processing, and transport of Texas grain and feed products became a war industry managed largely by the Texas Grain & Feed Association. Sorghum was part of a greater agricultural diversification in the state during the war. By war's end, 135 different crops were being grown in the state, with cotton, feed grains, rice, wheat, and citrus fruits being the most important. Such diversification and various and conducive climates resulted in Texas leading the nation in production of cotton, grain sorghums, tomatoes, onions, spinach, pecans, and, one of the most purchased items by soldiers on leave, roses.[13]

Despite the war's benefit to the cattle business, the industry's tolerance of government intrusion only went so far. US servicemen had meals high in calories (4,300 calories on average) and much of that came from meat. Compared to his civilian counterpart, in fact, the American soldier during the war received two and a half times more red meat a day, or about a pound a day. One advertisement boldly declared the American fighting man "the greatest meat eater in the world." Government regulators and bureaucrats who threatened future profits and the industry's reliance on the free market often drew the ire of cattlemen. For example, the Texas and Southwestern Cattle Raisers Association opposed ceiling prices on live cattle. Such ceilings, they argued, were unenforceable and damaging to livestock production. Ceiling prices "would create insurmountable administrative problems and encourage the spread of black markets." At a time when production was paramount, cattlemen warned such restrictions would "damage morale" and limit profits and thus production. The industry's vigilance seemed warranted when Fred Vinson, the director of the Office of Economic Stabilization, moved to set price levels for bulls and cattle. Cattlemen responded to this move by "flooding the markets with cattle to receive the highest possible price before fixed prices became effective." Consequently, a shortage soon appeared, with less high-quality beef and fewer pounds of beef flowing into the market.[14]

The war created further problems to an already problem-plagued livestock industry. The 1930s negatively affected demand. Exacerbating this decline in customer demand was the biting drought. The war only brought a new challenge to the industry. The war's demand denuded the workforce on cattle farms (as well as any other farm). Men were either siphoned off by the promise of war work or drafted into service. Nessye Mae Proffitt Roach, from Reagan County (West Texas), remembers working alongside her father as a ranch hand. "It was so hard to get quality help," she recalled, "because nearly all of the men who were in good health and the right age were in the service." This shortage, however, was not as difficult for the industry to meet as in other economic endeavors also plagued by a labor shortage. While some ranchers unwisely employed any able-bodied individual off the streets, forgetting the demands of the job and the importance of knowledge about everything from the weather to the instincts of animals, many looked to hands already on the ranch. Some ranchers employed cooperation. Known as "neighboring," those in close proximity combined their efforts to work each other's ranches. This usually occurred with those who shared some portion of the fence lines. Due to the nature of the pastures, this cooperation even occurred across state borders. Pansy Evans Espy recalled how her husband and father, who had farms in different states (one in New Mexico, the other Texas), helped "no matter what you had planned to do—you stopped it because your neighbor came and helped you, and no matter what comes up, you say, 'No, I've got to neighbor today.'" Long before the war, ranching had been a rather equal endeavor, with women routinely filling in or performing ranch duties "as one of the boys." "Texas ranch women filled the void in manpower so well," one student of the industry admitted, "that few outside the ranching industry even knew of the shortage." Mary Nan West, who was raised by her mother to do ranch work, admitted the obvious. "It's not about what you are allowed to do on the ranch as a woman; it's what you are expected to do." And do they did . . . no matter the conditions or year. "We worked hard," remembered Alpine, Texas, native Celia Ann Smith Hill, who went to high school during the week but worked on the ranch on weekends. "Didn't make a difference how cool it was. It didn't matter if we would freeze to death, we'd get there and they'd have a horse saddled for us."[15]

Despite the uniqueness of their occupation, cattle ranchers still experienced many of the same war-related issues as everyone else. That included fear. The country was gripped by the possibility of an Axis attack or invasion immediately following the country's entry into the war. With its coastline, industries, and shared border with Mexico, many in the state considered Texas, as well as citizens in other states with similar features, a prime target. Communities along the Rio Grande readied their citizenry by staging blackouts. The anger and uncertainty following what most believed to be an impossibility, an attack launched from across the Pacific, shattered Americans' sense of security as well as superiority and created an atmosphere of anxiety in late 1941 and early 1942. Americans saw "boogeymen" everywhere and mobilized the country not just for war production, but also for war defense. Civil organizations, both federal, state, and private, sprouted to meet what many considered certain invasion. In South Texas, farmers organized a local militia (perhaps a vigilante group) they dubbed "the Guerrillas." These farmers saw themselves as the first line of defense in the case of a Japanese airborne assault across the Rio Grande. Membership required only that prospects possess "a high-powered rifle, five hundred rounds of ammunition, and a car with a full tank of gas." Shortages caused by the war soon became as prevalent as "war scares." Where food rationing did not present the same problem for ranchers as for urbanites, rationing of war material, such as metals and equipment proved especially problematic. "You just didn't fix it until the war was over," recalled Betty Baker about the situation her father faced. Ranchers improvised where possible or simply did without. In fact, of all the items rationed during the war, the one they had most difficulty doing without was ammunition. For a brief time, trapping troublesome predators came back in vogue. Cattle theft also returned as a problem. Meat rationing resulted in some people bypassing the middleman and obtaining meat in a rather nineteenth-century fashion. This possibly further added to the workload of ranchers as "putting down tracks" (range riding) returned in force.[16]

Although nothing on the farm more personified Texas than beef, the war had a more profound effect on poultry. The US Department of Agriculture set national goals for the war effort that routinely listed the goal for eggs for the following year: "Poultry & Eggs: lots more." Prior to the Second World War, chicken was primarily eaten on Sunday or only on special occasions. The value in the chicken lay in its eggs not its meat. In 1935, the average American consumed only fifteen pounds of chicken compared to forty-nine pounds of pork and fifty-three pounds of beef. By 1943, chicken consumption had nearly doubled to twenty-eight pounds per person. The expansive nature of the war, however, gave opportunity for those Southerners who envisioned the South as a major source of poultry. Furthermore, the government did not ration poultry. The epicenter of poultry began its shift from New England to the South. Its mild climate, cheap and abundant labor, and limitless market possibilities favored prospective chicken farmers. Also, those Texas farmers who lacked the farm size and finances for cattle could more easily shift from raising crops to poultry. Poultry's profitability only continued to brighten throughout the 1940s and beyond. Farmers, with the assistance of scientists, greatly increased their efficiency with breeding faster-growing birds with superior meat quality and increased egg-laying production. Mechanization of feeding, watering, and egg-gathering further reduced labor costs. Integral to the industry was "vertical integration." With integration, all components of the production process, including the breeding, hatching, and feeding, were owned by the feed company or "integrator." To contracted farmers, the company provided the chicks and feed. The farmers raised them in a company-owned facility, where the chickens would also be processed. The farmer was then paid for raising the birds. This streamlined poultry raising shifted financial liability from the farmer to the "integrator." The result was a noticeable inverse trend of the amount of feed to produce a pound of chicken. For example, in 1940, it took 4.2 pounds of feed to produce a pound of live weight. By 1950, that had declined to 3.3 pounds. In the succeeding decades, the relationship only continued in the favor of the farmers. Thus, by 1950, Texas was one of the leading poultry producers in the country, with 9,669 poultry farms.[17]

In addition to chicken, government officials also needed increased production of eggs. The need was 1,500 additional carloads for 1942. Prior to the United States' entry into the war, Texas egg producers were pivotal in providing eggs for Great Britain in the lend-lease program, which authorized the president to lend, lease, or sell material to any country he deemed vital to American interests. In order for the eggs to be sent overseas, the federal government first purchased them from the farmers. The eggs were then broken and put through a fast-drying process and shipped to their destination. In doing their part, egg producers did not just profit but so too did their hens. "We stayed home all day," noted Texas farmer William G. DeLoach. "Save rubber and gas. Help defense. The hens helped out today to the tune of 80 eggs. Maybe so we will be getting 100 eggs per day soon." Similar increased need and production occurred with Irish potatoes, sweet potatoes, tomatoes, carrots, and onions. In the war years, Texas farmers increased the production of these crops by 30 percent.[18]

"The Peanut promises to play an important role in the war economy," boldly declared one governmental publication. The Japanese expansion throughout Asia and the Pacific (China and East Indies, specifically) placed under their control approximately half of the world's supply of vegetable fats and oils. This critical shortage for the Allies forced improvisation. Prior to the war, peanuts were consumed as a food and was a "minor domestic product," but the war necessitated their use for oils, especially in replacing the now unavailable coconut oil in the manufacturing of glycerin, a vital component to "make things blow up." Throughout the country, from Virginia in the East to Oklahoma and Texas in the Southwest, to Georgia and Alabama in the Southeast, peanut acreage nearly doubled in the years from 1935 to 1944. Within the first year of the war, peanut production increased 75 percent. In its "Peanut for Oil" campaign, the federal government challenged Texas farmers to contribute their share in this expansion to plant an additional one million acres of peanuts. Texas met that challenge, producing on average 645,200 harvested acres and 283,952,000 pounds of peanuts from 1938 to 1948. The peak for the Oklahoma–Texas region came in 1943, when the area produced 3.8 times more than prewar levels of peanut acreage. This program was run through the Agricultural Adjustment Administration, and many planters signed up for additional rows to be planted. In fact, in 1942, farmers in Lamb County (northwest of Lubbock) set a county high in profits from peanuts at $150,000. This shifted Texas peanut production to a point that Texas today is the country's second largest producer (often trading with Alabama) of peanuts behind only Georgia. Contrary to popular wisdom, the government's effort to increase production of vegetables, peanuts, fruits, and eggs for the war effort was not going to happen through large agricultural producers, but rather through small farmers. Small farms were somewhat insulated by the war's adverse effects (labor and equipment shortages) in ways large farms were not. In 1942, the production of large farms actually decreased compared to the previous year. Small farms, on the other hand, rarely experienced labor shortages, but instead lacked capital for investment. It was easier for Uncle Sam to loan money to small farmers than to reallocate an already diminishing labor supply.[19]

A necessary yet, at times, criticized governmental measure during the war was rationing. As demand outpaced supply, rationing promised a remedy to spiraling inflation, undermining black markets, and inequitable distributions. This aspect of the wartime mobilization was a "substantial restructuring of US society." In short order, the Office of Price Administration froze prices on some things and rationed many others. This included food, which Uncle Sam reminded its citizens almost daily was now a weapon. For rural Texans, although every bit as patriotic as their urban counterparts, the constriction of rationing was not as biting. This was due in part to many inhabitants already being poor, so they did not notice any appreciable decline in their standard of living. But mostly it was because they had the means and space to supplement in ways that those in urban areas could not. Their victory gardens were much more than simple, small plots crammed into a vacant lot or rooftop. In fact, they continued to produce much of their own food. Those who raised cattle, hogs, or chicken always had a ready supply of meat. Those Texans who grew corn worried little about the government rationing cornmeal, a staple of the South's diet. A quick trip to a grist mill with a bag of corn solved the problem. Excess would be preserved for personal culinary use or giving, bartering, or selling it to neighbors, friends, or town folk. This practice also included anything else on the farm, such as excess eggs and surplus milk or butter. Buck Young, a resident of Baytown along the Gulf Coast, recalled "even with rationing our family did all right. We had plenty of butter from our cow, eggs from our chickens, and fresh vegetables from our garden, or from the Mason jars of my mother's canning efforts." Another man from Lovelady, Houston County, Texas (East Texas) often shared his excess milk, butter, and eggs with less fortunate neighbors. This practice continued, however, until governmental officials intervened, forcing him to accept ration coupons for the goods or destroy the surplus.[20]

With rationing of steel making it increasingly difficult to obtain cans, and the hold on consumer goods such as refrigerators, people had to improvise. Often one of the busiest places in the county, especially rural regions, was the cannery. Excess from a bumper crop or produce from a victory garden often found its way here. A percentage went to the cannery, usually 15 percent. Those wanting more food could often work at the cannery for a percentage of the canned goods. In rural Texas communities, where governmental and philanthropic measures for the most indigent were either nonexistent or stretched to capacity, this system of canning ensured a distribution of food processed for the community and the war effort. The cannery received some, workers and volunteers received some, and producers retained some. During the war, Texas A&M University pioneered this effort for food preservation. This industry had become critical to the war effort and to the sustainment of family health and welfare. Then US representative Lyndon B. Johnson (later president of the United States) worked with Texas A&M horticulturist Guy W. Adriance to establish a food-canning facility on the A&M campus, and Professor F. R. Brison was the first professor to teach commercial food preservation at Texas A&M. The canning, storage, preservation, and transport of foodstuff was one of the most critical and progressive wartime farm and food industries.[21]

The mobilization of all manner of manufacturing plants for war production impacted agricultural equipment manufacturers. Food and fiber production was as important to the war effort as weapons. Agribusiness—mixing agriculture, engineering, science, and technology—and free enterprise became an increasingly prominent part of the war effort and accelerated the transformation of postwar American agriculture. As Texas A&M's Edwin Jackson Kyle, dean of the A&M College of Agriculture, explained in 1944, "In the opportunity to render a real service, there is hardly any other profession that will equal agriculture. The entire nation is deeply interested today in the successful solution of many pressing problems connected with agriculture. The study of agriculture in a standard agricultural college prepares a young man to assist in the solution to these vital problems." And, in 1944, Texas A&M's president Gibb Gilchrist announced a "New Vision at Texas A&M," which included a focus on engineering and agricultural research and instruction, in conjunction with the basic sciences and the establishment of a "technical training center" throughout Texas for instruction in agriculture and engineering in short-term training programs. Part of wartime mobilization had to do with creating a civilian workforce of men and women trained to provide feed, food, and fiber to the nation and its military forces at home and abroad.[22]

Military forces have been historically decimated, not only by combat casualties, but also by illnesses such as dysentery, gastrointestinal maladies, toxins, and other epidemiological disasters arising from unsanitary conditions and poorly and hastily prepared, and sometimes spoiled, foods. Contaminated foods could produce bacterial infections such as salmonella, *Clostridium botulism*, typhoid fever, septic sore throat, Weil's disease, dysentery, scarlet fever, or diphtheria. The list is formidable. Veterinarians served in the Quartermaster Corps and with medical and transportation units engaged in moving food products from farms to the battlefields. During the year 1944, US military forces required on a daily basis 19,000 head of cattle, 27,000 hogs, 600 calves, and 5,000 sheep to meet meal requirements. Each unit of meat or meat products had to be cleared for consumption by a veterinary medical inspection. Veterinarians methodically examined transport facilities, stored food, or food products in transit. That is an aspect of war that is largely unknown to most people. Military personnel's health related directly to the procurement, processing, and serving of foodstuffs. More than 90 percent of veterinarians in military service during World War II were involved in food inspection and environmental hygiene. Many veterans returning from the war were often aided in their pursuit of studies in veterinary medicine by the GI Bill, and the profession became more widely recognized as an integral component of society, urban and rural. Public health became an increasingly critical component of veterinary medicine. Texas towns and cities began to adopt animal control, sanitation, and public health codes. Disease prevention and control became an integral part of veterinary medicine and public health—particularly in diseases such as rabies that are easily and often transmitted from animals to humans. Vaccination of animals was critical to human health. And concurrently, as human populations expanded, animal populations, and the human-animal bond among cats, dogs, and horses, seemed to have magnified.[23]

Moreover, as trade and commerce expanded and became increasingly global, veterinary medicine became an increasingly urban and global profession. The same applied to agriculture. By 1945, the United States was supplying 75 percent of the world's soybeans, 50 percent of the feed grains, and 40 percent of the wheat entering international markets. Another export that the United States was increasing its share of was rice. Rice production in the United States centered in South Carolina, Louisiana, and Texas, and rose sharply during World War II. In 1940, rice farmers produced 24,495,000 pounds of rice, which sold at an average of $1.80 per hundred. In 1946, farmers were producing 32,497,000 pounds of rice, which sold at $5.00 per hundred. From

1942 to 1946, the Department of Agriculture established production goals linked to price guarantees. Goals were raised for each farmer by 5 percent a year. Farms that did not meet the goals lost 10 percent of the maximum rice payment for each 1 percent underplanted. Farmers could also borrow up to 85 percent of the estimated value of the crop before planting or harvest. During the war, the OPA set rice prices under a directive first entitled MPR 150, "a document which was revised and amended 31 times in the 5 years which it remained in effect." By the close of the war, rice millers were required to reserve 60 percent of the total rice milled for sale to the government. The postwar conversion of the economy from essentially military to civilian consumption created considerable marketing chaos in the rice industry and in other agricultural crops. During the war, the OPA held the lid on price increases, and with the release of those controls, prices increased an average of 33 percent between 1945 and 1947. Part of the conversion from the war to a peacetime economy also involved the absorption of some five million men and women from the military into the civilian economy. It was a time of celebration, but also of tribulation and restoration of the peacetime economy.[24]

With the close of the war, Texas farmers and ranchers could not fully realize how much their industries had changed. Although there were noticeably fewer of them in the state, the future for those who managed to remain on the farm looked promising. The war brought changes that augured a limitless future . . . at least for those who could remain on the farm or ranch. The livestock industry's reliance on vaccines and antibiotics as well as selective breeding resulted in not only more animals to slaughter (or for wool or for milking or for eggs) but also larger and healthier animals. Diversification of crops, the adoption of science and pre- and post-planting techniques, and the availability of mechanization all promised achieving more with less. This inverted relationship further meant increased profits. The hardships and uncertainty that accompanied all agricultural endeavors, quite prematurely of course, appeared to be something of the past. All this was made possible by the necessities of war. A war had to be won, and Texas agricultural provided the means. The nation needed fibers for uniforms and grains for food. High-calorie meats were needed to fuel the taxing work of fighting and manufacturing. Texas agriculture and ranching following war was transformed. Little did anyone really understand exactly how.

Notes

1. Henry C. Dethloff authored more than a dozen books about Texas history. He was Professor Emeritus of History at Texas A&M University at College Station. He unfortunately passed away during the process of creating this manuscript.

2. Henry C. Dethloff, *A Centennial History of Texas A&M University, 1876–1976*, 2 vols. (College Station: Texas A&M University Press, 1975), II: 451–71. For the agricultural experiment stations, see volume II of Dethloff's history of Texas A&M University.

3. For the first quotation, see Gabriel N. Rosenberg, *The 4-H Harvest: Sexuality and the State in Rural America* (Philadelphia: University of Pennsylvania Press, 2016), 166; Amy Bentley, *Eating for Victory: Food Rationing and the Politics of Domesticity* (Urbana: University of Illinois Press, 1998), 118. For the second quotation and the amount of food the average soldier eats in a year, see US Department of Agriculture, *Food for Freedom: Information Handbook, 1943* (Washington, DC: US Government Printing Office, 1943). For the number of dairy cattle, swine, and livestock and tons of forage and root crops and the quotation regarding the number of troops kept in food and fiber, see National 4-H History Preservation Program, "Wartime 4-H Support—World War II," https://4-hhistorypreservation.com/History/WW-II_Support/#TOC-07. For the "Feed a Fighter" program in Texas, see Henry C. Dethloff and A. Shurgin, *The Land-Grant Legacy in the Lone Star State* (College Station: Texas A&M Agrilife, Texas A&M University Press, 2013). Works detailing the history (including during the war) of the 4-H Club are William L. Carpenter and Dean W. Colvard, *Knowledge Is Power* (Raleigh: North Carolina State University, 1987); Joanne Rouche and Debra Jones, "Covering Our Bases: A Military 4-H Youth Development Program," *Journal of Youth Development* 3 (Fall 2008); James W. Clark, *Clover All Over: North Carolina 4-H in Action* (Raleigh: North Carolina State, 1984); Jerry H. Rayburn, *4-H in Pennsylvania* (University Park, PA: Penn State University Press, 1980); and Franklin M. Reck, *The 4-H Story: A History of 4-H Club Work* (Ames: Iowa State College Press, 1951). Important works on victory gardens in World War II (and their predecessors in the Great War) and their importance to the war effort are E. Hallock, "Bringing Victory Gardens to the Classroom," *Instructor* 53 (1943); P. R. Young, "Victory Gardens for School and Home," *Journal of National Educational Association* 31 (1942); Stephanie A. Carpenter, *On the Farm Front: The Women's Land Army in World War II* (DeKalb: Northern Illinois University Press, 2003); Judy Barrett and David C. Smith, "'To the Rescue of the Crops': The Women's Land Army during World War II," *Prologue: The Journal of the National Archives* 25 (Winter 1993); Paul D. Casdorph, *"Let the good Times Roll": Life at Home in American during World War II* (New York: Paragon House, 1989); William J. Furdell, "The Great Falls Home Front during World War II," *Montana: The Magazine of Western History* 48 (Winter 1998); Rose Hayden-Smith, *Sowing the Seeds of Victory: American Gardening Programs of World War I* (Jefferson, NC: McFarland & Company, 2014); Clifford M. Kuhn, "'It Was a Long Way from Perfect, but It Was Working': The Canning and Home Production Initiatives in Greene County, Georgia,

1940–1942," *Agricultural History* 86 (2012); Laura J. Lawson, *City Bountiful: A Century of Community Gardening in America* (Berkeley: University of California Press, 2005); Kenneth Helphand, *Defiant Gardens: Making Gardens in Wartime* (San Antonio: Trinity University Press, 2006); Pennsylvania State Council of Defense, *Handbook of the Victory Garden Committee War Services, 1944* (University Park: Pennsylvania State University Press, 1944); Richard Goldstein, *Helluva Town: The Story of New York City during World War II* (New York: Free Press, 2013); and Christopher Michael Head, "The Armor of Democracy: Volunteers on the Home Front in World War II California" (master's thesis, California Polytechnic State University–San Luis Obispo, 2009). Thought-provoking works about food's primacy to the combatants of World War II is Lizzie Collingham, *The Taste of War: World War II and the Battle for Food* (New York: Penguin Books, 2013); and Michael J. Grant, "'Food Will Win the War and Win the Peace': The Federal Government and Kansas Farmers during World War II," *Kansas History* 20 (Winter 1997–1998). For the improvisation because wartime limitations and government rationing of foodstuffs, see Richard R. Lingeman, *Don't You Know There's a War On? The American Home Front, 1941–1945* (New York: Nation Books, 2003); Mark H. Leff, "The Politics of Sacrifice on the American Home Front in World War II," *Journal of American History* 77 (March 1991); Irene Paulette, "Odessa during the War Years 1941–1945: A Microcosm of the Nation," *Permian Historical Annual* 22 (1982); Michael C. C. Adams, *The Best War Ever: America and World War II* (Baltimore, MD: Johns Hopkins University Press, 1994); R. Douglas Hurt, *The Great Plains during World War II* (Lincoln: University of Nebraska Press, 2008); Susan M. Hartmann, *The Home Front and Beyond: American Women in the 1940s* (New York: MacMillan Publishing Company, 1983); Maureen Honey, ed., *Bitter Fruit: African American Women in World War II* (Columbia: University of Missouri Press, 1999); D'Ann Campbell, *Women at War with America: Private Lives in a Patriotic Era* (Cambridge, MA: Harvard University Press, 1984); John W. Jeffries, *Wartime America: The World War II Home Front* (New York: Ivan R. Dee, 1998); Stephen J. Leonard, "Denver at War: The Home Front in World War II," *Colorado Heritage* (1987); Robert F. Karolevitz, "Life on the Home Front: South Dakota in World War II," *South Dakota History* 19 (Fall 1989); Emily Yellin, *Our Mother's War: American Women at Home and at the Front during World War II* (New York: Free Press, 2005); Alistair Cooke, *The American Home Front, 1941–1942* (New York: Atlantic Monthly Press, 2006); and Ronald H. Bailey, *The Home Front: USA* (New York: Time-Life Books, 1978).

4. Dethloff, *The Centennial History of Texas A&M University*, II: 460–61. Background on the Cooperative Extension Services can be found in L. Kelsey and C. Hearne, eds., *Cooperative Extension Work*, 3rd ed. (Ithaca, NY: Cornell University Press, 1963). The effect of governmental regulation on productivity can be found in Sally H. Clarke, *Regulation and the Revolution in the United States Farm Productivity* (New York: Cambridge University Press, 1994); and Alan S. Milward, *War, Economy, and Society, 1939–1945* (Berkeley: University of California, 1977).

5. Janet M. Neugebauer, ed., *Plains Farmer: The Diary of William G. De Loach, 1914–1964* (College Station: Texas A&M University Press, 1991), 219; Hurt, *Great Plains during World War II*, 160, 168, 212; Texas Agricultural Statistics Service, comp., *Texas Historical Crop Statistics, 1866–1989* (n.c.: n.p., 1991), 11–13; Ralph Wooster, "East Texas in World War II," *East Texas Historical Journal* 45 (2007), 46. In fact, as farmers moved away from cotton, many turned to livestock, particularly hogs. Throughout the war, the Texas hog industry expanded greatly. By 1946, the state ranked ninth, with a total of 1,857,000 hogs. As many a Texas farmer knows, "when cotton declines, hogs prosper." This information can be found in Neugebauer, ed., *Plains Farmer*, 256.

6. Garry L. Nall, "Farming on the High Plains: Innovation and Adaptation on Arid Lands in Texas," *Journal of the West* 29 (October 1990): 26; Cecil Harper Jr. and E. Dale Odom, "Farm Tenancy," *New Handbook of Texas*, https://tshaonline.org/handbook/online/articles/aefmu. The history and developments in the cotton industry in Texas (including the war) can be found in Karen G. Britton, *Bale o' Cotton* (College Station: Texas A&M University Press, 1992); Neil Foley, *White Scourge: Mexicans, Blacks, and Poor Whites in Texas Cotton Culture* (Berkeley: University of California Press, 1997); Gilbert C. Fite, *Cotton Fields No More: Southern Agriculture, 1865–1980* (Lexington: University of Kentucky Press, 2009); and Robert L. Haney, *Milestones: Marking Ten Decades of Research* (College Station: Texas A&M University Press, 1989). Similar developments in other crops and the way they are farmed in Texas can be found in Irvin Milburn Atkins, *A History of Small Grain Crops in Texas: Wheat, Oats, Barley, Rice, 1582–1976* (College Station: Texas A&M University Press, 1980); Paul Mangelsdorf, *Corn: Its Origin, Evolution, and Development* (Cambridge, MA: Belknap Press, 1964); Henry C. Dethloff and Stephen W. Searcy, *Engineering Agriculture at Texas A&M: The First Hundred Years* (College Station: Texas A&M University Press, 2015); and Paul H. Carlson, *Texas Woolybacks: The Range Sheep and Goat Industry* (College Station: Texas A&M University Press, 1982).

7. Nall, "Farming on the High Plains," 27–28; Donald E. Green, *Land of the Underground Rain: Irrigation on the Texas High Plains, 1910–1970* (Austin: University of Texas Press, 1973), 146–47; V. L. McGuire, "Changes in Water Levels and Storage in the High Plains Aquifer, Predevelopment to 2005," *USGS Fact Sheet 2007–3029*, https://pubs.usgs.gov/fs/2007/3029/. For the effect (for better and worse) of technology and innovation, much of which came about due to the Second World War, on American farmers in the twentieth century, see R. Douglas Hurt, *Problems of Plenty: The American Farmer in the Twentieth Century* (New York: Ivan R. Dee, 2003); John L. Shover, *First Majority–Last Minority: The Transforming of Rural Life in America* (De Kalb: Northern Illinois University Press, 1976); Robert Paarlberg and Don Paarlberg, "Agricultural Policy in the Twentieth Century," *Agricultural History* 74 (Spring 2000); Murray R. Benedict, *Farm Policies of the United States, 1790–1950* (New York: Octagon Books, 1966); Donald C. Blaisdell, *Government and Agriculture: The Growth of Federal Farm Aid* (New York: Farrar and Rinehart,

1940); Donald Worster, *Dust Bowl: The Southern Plains in the 1930s* (New York: Oxford University Press, 1979); John T. Schlebecker, *Whereby We Thrive: A History of American Farming, 1607–1972* (Ames: Iowa State University Press, 1975); Nancy A. Blanpied, ed., *Farm Policy: The Politics of Soil, Surpluses, and Subsidies* (Washington, DC: Congressional Quarterly, 1984); Walter Wilcox, *The Farmer in the Second World War* (Ames: Iowa State College Press, 1947); Gilbert C. Fite, *American Farmers: The New Minority* (Bloomington: Indiana University Press, 1981); Bruce L. Gardner, *American Agriculture in the Twentieth Century: How It Flourished and What It Cost* (Cambridge, MA: Harvard University Press, 2002); Anne Hallam, ed., *Size, Structure, and the Changing Face of American Agriculture* (Boulder, CO: Westview Press, 1993); and Paul K. Conkin, *A Revolution Down on the Farm: The Transformation of American Agriculture Since 1929* (Lexington: University of Kentucky Press, 2009).

8. The information for this and the preceding paragraphs come from Judy Barrett Litoff and David C. Smith, "'To the Rescue of the Crops': The Women's Land Army during World War II," *Prologue* 25 (Winter 1993), n.p., https://www.archives.gov/publications/prologue/1993/winter/landarmy.html; Judy Barrett Litoff and David C. Smith, *American Women in a World at War: Contemporary Accounts from World War II* (Wilmington, DE: SR Books, 1997), 167; Stephanie Ann Carpenter, "Regular Farm Girl: The Women's Land Army in World War II," *Agricultural History* 71 (Spring 1997); Carpenter, *On the Farm Front*; Roger Meyer, "Cultivating Victory: The Women's Land Army," *Michigan History Magazine* 98 (September/October 2014); Cecilia Gowdy-Wygant, *Cultivating Victory: The Women's Land Army and the Victory Garden Movement* (Pittsburgh: University of Pittsburgh, 2013); and D Wayne D. Rasmussen, *A History of the Emergency Farm Labor Supply Program, 1943–1947* (Washington, DC: United States Department of Agriculture, 1951). The significant difference in field labor in Texas from 1939 to 1943 is in Neugebauer, ed., *Plains Farmer*, 229. For additional works on the Women's Land Army, see Judy Barrett Litoff and David C. Smith, *Since You Went Away: World War II Letters from American Women on the Home Front* (Lawrence: University Press of Kansas, 1991); Dorit Geva, *Conscription, Family, and the Modern State: A Comparative Study of France and the United States* (New York: Cambridge University Press, 2013); Sandra K. Schackel, ed., *Western Women's Lives: Continuity and Change in the Twentieth Century* (Albuquerque: University of New Mexico Press, 2003); Mary Cunningham Baur, "The Farm Homemaker Faces War," *Journal of Home Economics* (October 1942); Bryon Fairchild and Johnathan Grossman, *The Army and Industrial Manpower* (Washington, DC: US Government Printing Office, 1988); and W. E. Shewell-Cooper, *Land Girl: A Handbook for the Women's Land Army* (Gloucestershire, UK: Amberley Publishing, 2011). For the Women's Land Army's predecessor in the Great War, see Elaine F. Weiss, *Fruits of Victory: The Women's Land Army in the Great War* (Washington, DC: Potomac Books, 2008); Mart A. Stewart, "'*What Nature Suffers to Groe*': *Life, Labor, and Landscape on the Georgia Coast, 1680–1920* (Athens: University of Georgia Press, 1996);

Rebecca Sharpless, *Fertile Ground, Narrow Choices: Women on Texas Cotton Farms, 1900–1940* (Chapel Hill: University of North Carolina Press, 1999); and Elaine F. Weiss, "Before Rosie the Riveter, Farmerettes Went to Work," *Smithsonianmag.com*, May 28, 2009. Studies of the British and Australian versions of the Women's Land Army in both World Wars are Margaret Hilary Bullock, "The Women's Land Army 1939–1950: A Study of Policy and Practice with Particular Preference to the Craven District" (PhD diss., University of Leeds, 2002); Carol Twinch, *Women on the Land: Their Story during Two World Wars* (Cambridge, UK: Lutterworth Press, 1990); Bob Powell and Nigel Westacott, *The Women's Land Army* (Gloucestershire, UK: The History Press, 2009); Bonnie White, *The Women's Land Army in First World War Britain* (New York: Palgrave Macmillan, 2014); Sue Hardisty, *Thanks Girls and Goodbye! The Story of the Australian Women's Land Army 1942–1945* (Chicago: Spinifex Press, 1990); and Shirley Threlfo, *The Australian Women's Land Army, 1942–1945: The Experiences of Mabs Keppie* (Paterson, NSW: Paterson Historical Society, 1997). For a few instances of the need for labor in the fields in Texas are *Dallas Morning News*, October 5 and 6, 1944.

9. Neugebauer, ed., *Plains Farmer*, 220, 224; *Progressive Farmer*, February and November 1943; National 4-H History Preservation Program, "Wartime 4-H Support—World War II," https://4-hhistorypreservation.com/History/WW-II_Support/#TOC-07; *County Wide News*, November 1942. For a comparison of the contribution of children to victory in England, see R. J. Morre-Colyer, "Kids in the Corn: School Harvest Camps and Farm Labor Supply in England, 1940–1950," *Agricultural History Review* 52 (2004). For additional accounts outside of Texas, see *Salina* (Kansas) *Journal*, September 23, 1942, and August 24, 1943; and *Roswell Daily Record*, October 16, 1942. You can also find the biography of a young African American boy who worked the fields during the Second World War and grew up to lead the Nation of Islam. For Elijah Muhammad's wartime experience, see June Skinner Sawyers, *Chicago Portraits* (Evanston, IL: Northwestern University Press, 2012); Karl Evanzz, *The Messenger: The Rise and Fall of Elijah Muhammad* (New York: Pantheon Books, 1999); and Herbert Berg, *Elijah Muhammad* (London, UK: Oneworld Publications, 2013).

10. Hurt, *Great Plains during World War II*, 216–18; Thomas A. Guglielmo, "Fighting for Caucasian Rights: Mexicans, Mexican Americans, and the Transnational Struggle for Civil Rights in World War II Texas," *Journal of American History* 92 (March 2006), 1223–27. For the number of braceros during the war, see, Armando Navarro, *Mexican Political Experience in Occupied Aztlán: Struggles and Change* (Walnut Creek, CA: AltaMira Press, 2005). For more on the Caucasian Race Resolution, see Matt S. Meier and Feliciano Ribera, *Mexican Americans, American Mexicans: From Conquistadors to Chicanos* (New York: Hill and Wang, 1993). Some insight into the Bracero program can be found in Ana Elizabeth Rosas, "Breaking the Silence: Mexican Children and Women's Confrontation of *Bracero* Family Separation, 1942–1964," *Gender and History* 23 (August 2011); John Weber, *From South Texas to the Nation: The Exploitation of Mexican Labor*

in the *Twentieth Century* (Chapel Hill: University of North Carolina Press, 2015); J. Justin Castro, "Mexican Braceros and Arkansas Cotton: Agricultural Labor and Civil Rights in the Post-World War II South," *Arkansas Historical Quarterly* 75 (Spring 2016); Ronald Takaki, *Double Victory: A Multicultural History of America in World War II* (New York: Back Bay Books, 2000); Rocio Gomez, "Braceros in the Arkansas Delta, 1943–1964," *Ozark Historical Review* 39 (Spring 2010); Marietta Ann Lucas, "Bracero Labor in Northeast Arkansas," *Craighead County Historical Quarterly* 6 (Summer 1968); Barbara Driscoll De Alvarado, *The Tracks North: The Railroad Bracero Program of World War II* (Austin: Center for Mexican American Studies and the University of Texas Press, 1999); Don Mitchell, *They Saved the Crops: Labor, Landscape, and the Struggle Over Industrial Farming in Bracero-Era California* (Athens: University of Georgia Press, 2012); Julie M. Weise, *Corazón de Dixie: Mexicanos in the US South Since 1910* (Chapel Hill: University of North Carolina Press, 2015); Erasmo Gamboa and Kevin Leonard, *Mexican Labor and World War II: Braceros in the Pacific Northwest, 1942–1947* (Seattle: University of Washington Press, 2000); Michael Snodgrass, "The Bracero Program, 1942–1964," in *Beyond the Border: The History of Mexican-US Migration*, ed. Mark Overmyer-Velásquez (New York: Oxford University Press, 2011); Otey M. Scruggs, "Texas and the Bracero Program, 1942–1947," *Pacific Historical Review* 32 (1963); Richard B. Craig, *The Bracero Program: Interest Groups and Foreign Policy* (Austin: University of Texas Press, 1971); HannaLore Hein, "The Mexican Invasion . . . By Invitation Only: A Critical Look at the Legacy and Consequences of the Bracero Program, 1942–1964," (undergraduate honors thesis, University of Colorado, 2011); and Ana Elizabeth Rosas, *Abrazando el Espíritu: Bracero Families Confront the US-Mexico Border* (Oakland: University of California Press, 2014). For additional work on the cooperation between the United States and Latin American countries during the war years, see John Granato II, "Dennis Chavez and the Inter-American Ideal, 1936–1962" (master's thesis, University of New Mexico, 2012); and Roy Lujan, "Dennis Chavez and the National Agenda: 1933–1946," *New Mexico Historical Review* 74 (January 1999).

11. Arnold P. Krammer, *Nazi Prisoners of War in America* (New York: Stein and Day, 1979); Arnold P. Krammer, "When the Afrika Korps Came to Texas," *Southwestern Historical Quarterly* 80 (January 1977); Robert Tissing, "Stalag Texas, 1943–1945," *Military History of Texas and the Southwest* 13 (Fall 1976); Richard Paul Walker, "Prisoners of War in Texas during World War II" (PhD diss., North Texas State University, 1980); Richard Paul Walker, "The Swastika and the Lone Star: Nazi Activity in Texas POW Camps," *Military History of the Southwest* 19 (Spring 1989); *The Vindicator* (Liberty County), October 13, 2010; and *Weekly and Semi-Monthly Reports on Prisoners of War, June 1942–30 June 1946*, Office of the Provost Marshall General (US National Archives, Washington). In addition to the works concerning Axis prisoners of war cited above, further works chronicling the Axis prisoner of war experience in Texas and the United States at large, particularly in agricultural work, see Thomas Jaehn, "Unlikely Harvesters: German

Prisoners of War as Agricultural Workers in the Northwest," *Montana: The Magazine of Western Heritage* 50 (Autumn 2000); James E. Fickle and Donald W. Ellis, "POWs in the Piney Woods: German Prisoners of War in the Southern Lumber Industry, 1943–1945," *Journal of Southern History* 56 (November 1990); William L. Shea and Merrill R. Pritchett, "The Wehrmacht in Louisiana," *Louisiana History* 23 (Winter 1982); Lowell A. May, *Camp Concordia: German POWs in the Midwest* (Manhattan, KS: Sunflower University Press, 1995); William L. Shea and Merrill R. Pritchett, "The Afrika Korps in Arkansas, 1943–1946," *Arkansas Historical Quarterly* 37 (Spring 1978); Jake W. Spidle, "Axis Invasion of the American West: POWs in New Mexico, 1942–1946," *New Mexico Historical Review* 19 (April 1974); Joseph T. Butler Jr., "Prisoner of War Labor in the Sugar Cane Fields of Lafourche Parish, Louisiana, 1943–1944," *Louisiana History* 14 (Summer 1973); Penny Clark, "Farm Work and Friendship: The German Prisoner of War Camp at Lake Wabaunsee," *Emporia State Research Studies* 36 (Winter 1988); Lowell Bangerter, "German Prisoners of War in Wyoming," *Journal of German-American Studies* 14 (1979); Barbara Wyatt, ed., *Japanese Americans in World War II: A National Historic Landmarks Theme Study* (Washington, DC: National Historic Landmarks Program National Park Service, 2012); Robert D. Billinger Jr., "With Wehrmacht in Florida: German POW Facility at Camp Blanding, 1942–1946," *Florida Historical Quarterly* 58 (October 1979); Matthias Reiss, "Bronzed Bodies behind Barbed Wire: Masculinity and the Treatment of German Prisoners of War in the United States during World War II," *Journal of Military History* 69 (April 2005); Michael Walzer, "Prisoners of War: Does the Fight Continue After the Battle?," *American Political Science Review* 63 (September 1969); Robert D. Billinger Jr., "Behind the Wire: German Prisoners of War at Camp Sutton, 1944–1946," *North Carolina Historical Review* 61 (October 1984); Robert D. Billinger Jr., *Hitler's Soldiers in the Sunshine State: German POW's in Florida* (Gainesville: University Press of Florida, 2009); Allen V. Koop, *Stark Decency: German Prisoners of War in an New England Village* (Hanover, NH: University Press of New England, 1988); Richard E. Holl, "Swastikas in the Bluegrass State: Axis Prisoners of War in Kentucky, 1942–1946," *Register of the Kentucky Historical Society* 100 (Spring 2002); Richard E. Holl, "German Prisoners of War Visit Henry County, Kentucky, September-October 1944," *Quarterly Review* 22 (September 1999); Daniel Hutchinson, "'We . . . Are the Most Fortunate of Prisoners': The Axis POW Experience at Camp Opelika during World War II," *Alabama Review* 64 (October 2011); Daniel A. Jepson, "Camp Carson, Colorado: European Prisoners of War in the American West during World War II," *Midwest Review* 13 (1991); William P. Corbett, "'They Hired Every Farmer in the Country': Establishing the Prisoner of War Camp at Tonkawa," *Chronicles of Oklahoma* 69 (Winter 1992); Harold Zimmerman, "Harvesting Peaches with German Prisoners of War," *Journal of the Western Slope* 2 (Winter 1987); Ralph Spencer, "Prisoners of War in Cheyenne Country, 1943–1946," *Nebraska State Historical Society* 63 (Fall 1982); Jason Ward Morgan, "'Nazis Hoe Cotton': Planters, POWs, and the Future of Farm Labor in the Deep South," *Agricultural History* 81 (Fall 2007); Melissa Amateis

Marsh, *Nebraska POW Camps: A History of World War II Prisoners in the Heartland* (Charleston, SC: The History Press, 2014); David W. Fiedler, *The Enemy Among Us: POWs in Missouri during World War II* (St. Louis: Missouri Historical Society Press, 2003); and Richard S. Warner, "Barbed Wire and Nazilagers: PW Camps in Oklahoma," *Chronicles of Oklahoma* 64 (Spring 1986).

12. The information for this paragraph came from Henry C. Dethloff, *From Field to Fork: A History of Texas Grain and Feed Association, 1898–1998* (Fort Worth: Texas Grain and Feed Association, 1998). The War Production Board formed the foundation of the government's role in the "arsenal of democracy." Arthur Herman's, *Freedom Forge: How American Business Produced Victory in World War II* (New York: Random House Trade Paperbacks, 2013) is the standard work on the War Production Board. Bruce Catton's, *The War Lords of Washington* (New York: Harcourt Brace, 1948) remains helpful. A detailed exposition of the War Shipping Administration can be found in Frederic C. Lane's, *Ships to Victory: A History of Shipbuilding under the US Maritime Commission in World War II* (Baltimore, MD: Johns Hopkins University Press, 2001). The Office of Price Administration played a pivotal (and often criticized) role in the government's oversight of food production and consumption. At times, however, the organization that enforced rationing operated "irrationally." In the early days of the war, Representative Lyndon B. Johnson denounced the "overs-staff, over-stuffed" OPA in a message to his Texas constituents that the organization "has gone irrational, [with] administrators who spent too much time laying down the law to us and not enough time in reading upon on the law?" The Johnson quotation can be found in William K. Klingaman, *The Darkest Year: The American Home Front 1941–1942* (New York: St. Martin's Press, 2019), 296. For additional information on rationing and the above paragraph, see M. Jacobs, "'How About Some Meat?': The Office of Price Administration, Consumption Politics, and State Building from the Bottom Up," *Journal of American History* 84 (December 1997); Harvey C. Mansfield, *A Short History of OPA* (Washington, DC: US Government Printing Office, 1947); Andrew H. Bartels, "The Office of Price Administration and the Legacy of the New Deal, 1939–1946," *Public Historian* 5 (1983); and Julius Hirsch, *Price Control in the War Economy* (New York: Harper and Brothers, 1943).

13. For information on the Feed Associations, see Dethloff, *From Field to Fork*. For more cattle in East Texas than West, see Wooster, "East Texas in World War II," 46. For information on the production level of products such as cotton, spinach, onions, and so on, see Seth S. McKay and Odie B. Faulk, *Texas After Spindletop: The Saga of Texas, 1901–1965* (Austin: Steck-Vaughn Company, 1965). Further discussion on the cattle industry in Texas and the nation during World War II can be found in J'Nell Pate, *Livestock Legacy: The Fort Worth Stockyards, 1887–1987* (College Station: Texas A&M University Press, 2000); Roger Horowitz, *Putting Meat on the American Table: Taste, Technology, Transformation* (Baltimore, MD: Johns Hopkins University Press, 2006); John T. Schlebecker, *Cattle Raising on the Plains, 1900–1950* (Lincoln: University of Nebraska Press, 1963); Garry L. Nall, "The Cattle-Feeding Industry on the Texas High Plains," in *Southwestern*

Agriculture: Pre-Colombian to Modern, eds. Henry C. Dethloff and Irvin May Jr. (College Station: Texas A&M University Press, 1982); Marion Clawson, *The Western Range Livestock Industry* (New York: McGraw-Hill, 1950); Kenneth Charles Dragel, "Ranchers' Adjustments in a Marginal Environment" (PhD diss., University of Nebraska, 1994); and Jimmy M. Skaggs, *Prime Cut: Livestock Raising and Meat-packing in the United States, 1607–1983* (College Station: Texas A&M University Press, 1986). Sorghum is discussed in Neugebauer, ed., *Plains Farmer*, 241; J. Roy Quinby, "Hybrid Sorghum: A Triumph of Research," in *Southwestern Agriculture: Pre-Colombian to Modern*, eds. Henry C. Dethloff and Irvin May Jr. (College Station: Texas A&M University Press, 1982); J. Roy Quinby et al., *Grain Sorghum Production in Texas* (College Station: Texas A&M University Press, 1958); Hurt, *Great Plains during World War II*; and William F. Bennett, Billy B. Tucker, and A. Bruce Maunder, *Modern Grain Sorghum Production* (Ames: Iowa State University Press, 1990). The role of women in that industry, including during the war, can be found in Elizabeth Maret, *Women of the Range: Women's Roles in the Texas Beef Cattle Industry* (College Station: Texas A&M University Press, 2017).

14. Bentley, *Eating for Victory*, 94; Hurt, *Great Plains during World War II*, 183.

15. Tanya Kraus Randall, "Texas Ranch Women Remember World War II," *Sound Historian: Journal of the Texas Oral History Association* 13 (2011), 41, 43–44, 47. For more studies about ranch women, see "The Young Ranch Girls Help Too!" *Sheep and Goat Raiser*, August 1944; Joyce Gibson Roach, *The Cowgirls* (Denton: University of North Texas Press, 1990); Barney Nelson, *The Last Campfire: The Life Story of Ted Gray, A West Texas Rancher* (College Station: Texas A&M University Press, 1984).

16. Klingaman, *The Darkest Year*, 56, 76; Randall, "Texas Ranch Women Remember World War II," 44–45. For more on the fears experienced in other states, see *Antiaircraft Journal* 92 (May–June 1949); *Seattle Times*, December 7, 2016; Lorraine Boissoneault, "The Great Los Angeles Air Raid Terrified Citizens—Even Though No Bombs Were Dropped," *Smithsonian.com*, January 19, 2018, https://www.smithsonianmag.com/history/great-los-angeles-air-raid-terrified-citizen-seven-though-no-bombs-were-dropped-180967890/; *New York Times*, December 18, 1941; Lorraine B. Diehl, *Over Here! New York City during World War II* (New York: HarperCollins, 2010); Gary Glynn, *Montana's Home Front during World War II* (Missoula, MT: Pictorial Histories Publishing, 1994); and John Caughey and LaRee Caughey, *Los Angeles: A Biography of a City* (Oakland: University of California Press, 1976).

17. US Department of Agriculture, *Food for Freedom*, 4; Fite, *Cotton Fields No More*, 200–03; *Progressive Farmer*, December 1943. For more on the evolution of the industry in the 1940s, see D. F. King and S. L. Chestnutt, *Poultry Production in the South* (Danville, IL: Interstate Printers and Publishers, 1948).

18. Neugebauer, ed., *Plains Farmer*, 214; Wooster, "East Texas in World War II," 46; *Lamb County Leader*, January 29 and February 5, 1942; Bentley, *Eating for Victory*, 100.

19. *Monthly Review* of the Federal Reserve Bank of Atlanta, July 31, 1942;

Neugebauer, ed., *Plains Farmer*, 215–16, 218; C. Wayne Smith, *Crop Production: Evolution, History, and Technology* (New York: John Wiley & Sons, 1995), 413; Andrew F. Smith, *Peanuts: The Illustrious History of the Goober Pea* (Urbana: University of Illinois Press, 2002), 101–3; Tom Oder, "How Peanuts Changed the World," *Mother Nature Network*, September 24, 2015, https://www.mnn.com/your-home/organic-farming-gardening/stories/how-peanuts-changed-world; B. C. Langley, "Peanut Culture," in *The New Handbook of Texas*, 6 vols, eds. Ron Tyler et al. (Austin: Texas State Historical Association, 1996), V: 108; Sherman Ellsworth Johnson, *Changes in American Farming* (Washington, DC: US Department of Agriculture, Miscellaneous Publication No. 707, 1949), 28. The quote "make things blow up" is in Adee Bruan, "Turning Bacon into Bombs: The American Fat Salvage Committee," *Atlantic*, accessed June 14, 2021, https://www.theatlantic.com/health/archive/2014/04/reluctantly-turning-bacon-into-bombs-during-world-war-ii/360298/ . The *Monthly Review* further highlighted how Japanese expansion hurt US and Western needs: "In addition to increased demands placed upon ordinary domestic production, the problem is accentuated by the cutting off of 68 percent of our supplies of imported oils, or 10 percent of our total normal consumption requirements. The quantity lost, however, is overshadowed in importance by the strategic nature of many of the oils that were imported from the East Indies. Coconut oil for soap making, of which an important by-product is glycerine, which in turn is used in the manufacture of nitroglycerine, formerly came from the Philippines. Supplies of palm oil and palm kernel oil, which were likewise used by the soap industry, are also cut off. If domestic oils are substituted in the production of glycerine, larger quantities will be necessary than if the imported oils were used, since domestic oils yield only from 10 to 11 percent glycerine, while the imported oil yielded 14 percent. Other important oils, such as castor oil, tung oil, linseed oil, and olive oil, were supplied almost entirely by imports." There are four types of peanuts: runner, Spanish, Virginia, and Valencia. Texas has the necessary soil and climate and farmer interest to be a leading producer of all four types. (See "Texas Peanut Production Guide," Texas Cooperative Extension, Texas A&M University System, http://peanut.tamu.edu.)

20. Lauren Shaubhut, "World War II Sacrifices on the Home Front Houston County, Texas," *East Texas Historical Journal* 45 (2007), 581; Rebecca Craver, "Homefront Border Twist: El Paso-Juárez during World War II," *Sound Historian: Journal of the Texas Oral History Association* 5 (1999), 10; Bentley, *Eating for Victory*, 15, 23, 61–62. Additional works on rationing and its effects are Barbara McLean Ward, ed., *Produce & Conserve, Share & Play Square: The Grocer and the Consumer on the Home-Front Battlefield during World War II* (Hanover, NH: University Press of New England, 1994); Jill Norman, *Eating for Victory: Healthy Home Front Cooking on War Rations* (London, UK: Michael O'Mara Books Limited, 2007); Joanne Lamb Hayes, *Grandma's Wartime Kitchen, World War II and the Way We Cooked* (New York: St. Martin's Press, 2000); Lingeman, *Don't You*

Know There's a War On? David M. Kennedy, Freedom from Fear: The American People in Depression and War, 1929–1945 (New York: Oxford University Press, 1999); Emily E. LB. Twarog, *Politics of the Pantry: Housewives, Food, and Consumer Protest in Twentieth-Century America* (New York: Oxford University Press, 2017); Paul D. Casdorph, *Let the Good Times Roll: Life at Home in America during WWII* (New York: Paragon House Publishers, 1989); John Morton Blum, *V Was for Victory: Politics and American Culture during World War II* (New York: Harcourt Brace & Company, 1976); Richard Polenberg, *War and Society: The United States, 1941–1945* (Westport, CT: J. B. Lippincott Company, 1972); Emmanuel B. Halper, "Evolution and Maturity of the American Supermarket during World War II," *Real Property, Probate, and Trust Journal* 41 (Summer 2006); James Ward Lee et al., eds., *1941: Texas Goes to War* (Denton: University of North Texas Press, 2000).

21. Dethloff and Shurgin, *Land-Grant Legacy*, 44–52; *Lamb County Leader*, July 25, 1940; *County Wide News*, August 6, 1942; Bentley, *Eating for Victory*, 136–37; Neugebauer, ed., *Plains Farmer*, 228. For more also consult Dethloff and Searcy, *Engineering Agriculture at Texas A&M.*

22. "What Shall a Young Man Study?" Radio Talk, May 1, 1931; Dethloff and Shurgin, *Land-Grant Legacy*, 48. For more on Kyle's time at Texas A&M University, see Dethloff, *A Centennial History of Texas A&M University*, volume II.

23. See Dethloff, *From Field to Fork: A History of Texas Grain and Feed Association, 1898–1998.*

24. The rice industry is covered in greater detail in Henry C. Dethloff, *A History of the American Rice Industry, 1685–1985* (College Station: Texas A&M University Press, 1988); John Norman Efferson, *The Production and Marketing of Rice* (New Orleans: Simmons Press, 1952); and Edward Hake Philips, "The Gulf Coast Rice Industry," *Journal of Agricultural History* 25 (April 1954). The engineering aspect in Texas is covered in Dethloff and Searcy, *Engineering Agriculture at Texas A&M.* For the operations of the Office of Defense Transportation, see Joseph B. Eastman, "The Office of Defense Transportation," *Annals of the American Academy of Political and Social Science* 230 (November 1943).

10

Serving the Nation in Time of War

Training Camps, Prison Camps, and Major Texas Units in the Second World War

Kelly E. Crager[1]

The Second World War transformed the state of Texas in numerous ways. The New Deal programs of President Franklin D. Roosevelt began to draw Texans' attention toward Washington, DC. In the 1930s, they began to embrace a more national-focused identity. The Japanese attack on Pearl Harbor seared this nationalism into the minds of most Texans, and they showed their support for the war effort immediately and with great vigor. Seven hundred and fifty thousand Texans entered the US armed services during the war, while millions of others supported the war effort in their homes, farms, factories, churches, and businesses. Federal spending for the war, as it did elsewhere, alleviated the economic and financial pressures of the Great Depression in Texas, and this infusion of dollars would propel Texas into the postwar giant it would become. The federal government in Texas during the war brought about deep and fundamental changes to the state and helped usher in a new era in postwar Texas.[2]

It was not simply the government's domestic spending, however, that spurred growth in the Lone Star State. American entry into the war necessitated a massive military buildup in men and materiel, and much of this occurred in Texas. Geography and climate influenced the state's role during the war as much as federal spending. Texas, in fact, became a major training ground for American forces, with the state boasting dozens of military facilities. The relative geographic isolation of many Texas towns also appealed to authorities who suddenly found the pressing need to administer to and care for hundreds of thousands of Axis prisoners of war, helping to build a mutually beneficial relationship with Texas farmers, federal authorities, and even the prisoners themselves. Texas also hosted internment camps during the war, administering to the thousands of alien enemy civilians who found themselves caught in the legal murkiness of their home countries' war.

Within Texas there existed 175 military installations during the war, boasting numerous training facilities as well as defense installations along the Gulf Coast. By war's end, 1.5 million men passed through Texas training facilities. Many of the camps that existed before the war were greatly expanded in size and in purpose as lessons learned on the battlefields of Europe and in the Pacific necessitated increased specialized training with new weapons and tactics. El Paso's Fort Bliss, a home for horse cavalry prior to and during the early war years, underwent a vast expansion once it was deemed the mounted cavalry would have a role in the Second World War. As the efficacy of traditional cavalry units disappeared and horse units were phased out, the open spaces of far West Texas proved an ideal environment for artillery training and later for antiaircraft artillery training during World War II. Fort Bliss, unlike smaller cavalry posts in the state that did not survive the war, was in a prime position to transition into the Cold War world after 1945. Similarly, Fort Sam Houston at San Antonio served as the training home of hundreds of thousands of American soldiers during the war, undergoing a profound facilities expansion to house and train Lieutenant General Walter Krueger's Third Army. Throughout the war, the fort would also be the headquarters for the Sixth, Ninth, Tenth, and Fifteenth Armies.[3]

The army, heeding the call for further preparedness prior to the Pearl Harbor attack, expanded the number of training facilities in Texas, opening camps across the state and insuring lasting benefits for the local economies near these newer facilities. Camp Bowie near Brownwood (Central Texas) serves as a good example of this expansion. The federal mobilization of the Texas National Guard in November 1940 demanded the rapid completion of training facilities at Bowie. The camp was still not completed by the time troops arrived in November and December 1940, but the additional manpower of the newly federalized Texans and trainees from other parts of the country quickly brought the new camp online. During the preparedness years, leaders in Taylor County successfully lobbied for the creation of Camp

Barkeley near Abilene, a sprawling facility that, like Bowie, was unfinished when the troops of the US 45th Infantry Division arrived in late 1940 but served as a major training facility for thousands of men prior to the war's end. Killeen's Camp Hood (later designated the permanent status Fort Hood by 1950), opened in January 1942, initially served as the home to tank destroyer units but eventually grew to a sprawling infantry training facility that would survive the war and become a bastion of US military preparedness during the Cold War era. Indeed, Texas abounded with major and minor installations serving and preparing ground forces for the European and Pacific theaters.[4]

The wide-open skies of Texas proved invaluable to US military aviation during the war, and the state hosted dozens of pilot training facilities. Although the San Antonio area was a hub of flying activity with facilities at Kelly, Brooks, Lackland, and Randolph Fields, the US Army established bases throughout the state, from Dalhart in the northwestern Panhandle to Brownsville in far South Texas, from Biggs Army Airfield near El Paso to Galveston Army Airfield on the Gulf Coast. In fact, pilots learned to fly nearly every aircraft in the nation's arsenal at the many airfields in the state. East of Dallas, in Greenville, Hunt County, there existed a complex of one major airfield—Majors Field—and its three satellite facilities. These initially housed a basic flight training school but eventually hosted fighter pilot training not only for American air forces but also for the most recent partner in the allied cause against the Axis, the 201st Fighter Squadron of the Mexican Expeditionary Air Force. Raytheon Corporation, a company that specializes in defense-related aviation, further set up a division at the field and continues to be a major employer in the region to this day. Naval aviation training also called Texas home during the war as the newly completed Naval Air Station Corpus Christi opened in the summer of 1941. In fact, from January 1942 through May 1944, more than 200,000 men trained in Texas. That included 45,000 pilots, 12,000 bombardiers, 12,000 navigators, and many aerial gunners, photographers, and mechanics. Navy pilots earned their wings and trained at Corpus Christi and its six auxiliary stations, earning it the moniker "University of the Air."[5]

Unbeknownst to many, the Lone Star State not only trained pilots for the US Army Air Forces but also for the Royal Air Force. In the early days of the war, with Britain standing alone against Nazi Germany, the United States and Great Britain negotiated a series of programs to assist the island nation in its "time of need." Out of this came the British Flying Training Schools (BFTS). Utilizing already existing flight schools that trained Army Air Corps pilots, these schools trained British pilots from "primary through advanced" in a program lasting twenty weeks at six locations in four states, including Terrell, Texas (east of Dallas). This all-in-one scheme offered "faster training and greater efficiency." In total, more than 13,000 British pilots trained in the United States, with almost half of those in one of the six BFTS schools. At Terrell, around 2,200 trained, with 19 pilots dying in accidents and 1 from natural causes. These men are still interred in the local cemetery.[6]

Thousands of fighter and bomber pilots alike trained in Texas, but perhaps the most intriguing story of World War II Texas aviation belongs to female pilots. It was readily apparent early in the war that the country lacked enough trained male pilots to serve in combat overseas while performing vital support roles in the United States. To alleviate this strain and to free male pilots for combat duty, the US Army Air Forces, under the command of General Henry "Hap" Arnold, created what eventually became the Women Airforce Service Pilots (WASP), which ultimately trained at Avenger Field in Sweetwater (West Texas). Chosen as its director was famed aerial racer and the first woman to break the sound barrier (in 1953), Jacqueline Cochran, who had been doggedly determined and relentless in lobbying for the creation of this female unit. The necessity of war and assistance of First Lady Eleanor Roosevelt certainly did not hurt her cause. The graduates of this all-volunteer program of female pilots received approximately 500 hours of training; that included both flying time and ground-school training. Following their seven-month training period, these women performed numerous flying tasks in the continental United States, ferrying planes on cross-country trips, towing targets for aerial gunnery training, and fulfilling a variety of other responsibilities. In fact, by the time of their deactivation in late December 1944, the WASP had flown approximately 60 million miles, delivered more than 12,000 aircraft, and flew every aircraft in the army's arsenal, including the B-17. More than 1,000 women served (this included two Chinese American women, two Mexican American women, and one Native American woman; black women were excluded) with the WASP during the war, and their contribution to the war effort was timely and essential. Thirty-eight female pilots lost their lives. In spite of these women's military-style training and obvious role they played in supporting the Army Air Forces, the army refused to militarize the WASP program and its members went without military recognition and veterans' status and benefits until 1977. In 2009, the WASP were awarded a Congressional Gold Medal, and after years of lobbying and bureaucratic reversals and delays, Congress finally passed legislation allowing these female pilots to be interred in Arlington National Cemetery. Following this final reversal, in late 2016, WASP pilot Elaine Harmon was buried.[7]

It is worth noting that both the existing and new military facilities brought with them a huge injection of federal dollars for the Texas economy, in addition to the massive numbers of men and women who arrived to serve in the armed forces. The construction of new and expansion of existing facilities meant the creation of thousands of new jobs for Texas workers and the accompanying influx of non-Texan workers in the labor force. Local businesses saw a marked increase in profits resulting from government contracts and provided the material, food, and services necessary to supply the war effort, the military presence in the state, and the growing state population. Texas industry (especially the petroleum and chemical industries, as well as aircraft production) thrived during the war years. Texas agriculture also witnessed a significant shift toward specialization as farmers and ranchers provided the wheat, cotton, and cattle to feed an all-consuming military. Both industry and agriculture in the Lone Star State were able to rebound from the Depression-era collapse in prices and profits and entered the postwar years poised for future growth. Consider the example of Texas City. Already benefiting from the state's petroleum-centered economy, Texas City housed industrial and transportation networks that the government could expand and that had a straight channel port that operated twenty-four hours a day with no need for tugs or pilots. The military's infusion of federal dollars greatly expedited the coastal city's economic and industrial growth and thus married Uncle Sam and private industry in the common goal of victory. Through the Defense Plant Corporation (DPC)—a subsidiary of the Reconstruction Finance Corporation, which was a Depression-era government organization that provided federal assistance to state and local governments through massive loans to large corporations—the government granted several defense contracts to Texas City's oil refineries. The DPC also initiated the construction of two new strategic industries in the city: One was a tin-processing corporation and the other a chemical corporation that produced styrene used in synthetic rubber and explosives. Texas City also produced aviation fuel and asphalt in huge quantities, productions that would continue in the postwar era. Such investments contributed to the city's population tripling in the 1940s and, consequently, massive new development of public works, schools, businesses, and new residences. The army coming to town also precipitated many undesirable changes, such as overcrowding, stressing of existing infrastructure, rising prices, increasing vice, and fraying of local tensions and sensibilities.[8]

Similar in size to Texas City, Odessa also experienced profound change when it answered the bell for mobilization. This West Texas town built the Midland Army Flying School (school for bombardiers) about ten miles outside of town. In fact, it was approved and constructed even before the United States entered World War II. After America's entry into the conflict, however, the city became a true military boomtown, for better or worse. Adding to the city's importance was its prewar oil industry. Production increased astronomically, with the volume of business in 1938 measured at seven million dollars and seven years later, at eighty-two million dollars. The local government accepted construction by the DPC of the Carbon Black Plant, which processed carbon black. This was an essential ingredient in truck and car tires and proved to be a bit of an environmental concern for Odessa. Food and housing shortages, increased school enrollment and decreased number of teachers, massive influx of females into the workforce, and outsiders into town all characterized the changes that Odessa experienced throughout the war and that irrevocably changed the city afterward. With the military came a cost. A cost that every community hoped to avoid but ultimately paid: vice, immorality as defined by contemporary standards, and crime. In Abilene, for example, a city that lobbied hard for an army installation, local officials and moral leaders struggled to accommodate the need for entertainment for the troops yet still preserve the West Texas town's moral attitude. Any problems arising, however, were quickly mitigated because the soldiers "had money to spend and did so by eating great quantities of steak, buying clothes, toilet articles, and carting 'armloads' of purchases back to the camp." A proprietor exclaimed that "Abilene's economic revival looked secure." San Antonio's concern focused more on "regulat[ing] sexual activity considered deviant and immoral," such as dens of prostitution and "homosexuality havens," deeming them off-limits and out-of-bounds to enlisted personnel. Just east of Dallas, Greenville, in Hunt Texas, worried about the immorality, especially alcohol, that Majors Field might bring to their "church town."[9]

While many migrated to Texas during the war to better their lives and contribute to the war effort, other populations arrived against their will. The United States housed 435,788 Axis prisoners of war by war's end: 378,898 Germans, 51,455 Italians, and 5,435 Japanese. Texas, in fact, held 78,982 prisoners in fourteen military installations and seven smaller installations constructed specifically for housing captives. The number of prisoner camps in the Lone Star State was twice that of any other state in the Union. Authorities believed the state's size and, ironically, "similar" climate to North Africa warranted its use. American and Allied victories in North Africa in early 1943 resulted in the capture of tens of thousands of German prisoners and necessitated a reasonable and effective policy and program to care for new POWs. A signatory to the Geneva Convention of 1929, the United States found itself bound to the agreement's regulations pertaining to the capture and treatment of enemy soldiers in its care. Since the Convention specified that enemy soldiers must be detained in a climate similar to the one in which they were captured, the German soldiers of the Afrika Korps found themselves bound for the warm and dry climate of Texas.[10]

To a large degree, the POW system in the United States resembled what one might expect: shipment of German prisoners across the Atlantic, processing at various facilities on the East Coast, then traveling by rail to predetermined camps located throughout the country, and internment until the war's end. Officials insisted that POW camps not be located in or near major cities and remain a considerable distance from important war industries. This was typically the case for those who came to Texas, but the sheer volume of German POWs and the peculiar situation in the Lone Star State made this impractical. Many prisoners found themselves in military base camps at established military bases in Texas, such as Fort Bliss, Fort Sam Houston, Camp Hood, Camp Bowie, and Camp Maxey. The US Army, through the Provost Marshal General's Office (PMGO), established six permanent base camps in Texas located near Hereford and McLean in the Panhandle, Brady in the Hill Country, and Hearne, Mexia, and Huntsville in East Texas. For the most part, each of these camps had been fully constructed and ready to accept prisoners by early 1943. Initially, officials tried to keep the public uninformed about the construction of the base camps, and concerned local residents would resent the presence of the enemy prisoners in their midst. Potential threats to prisoners' safety were also a concern. Secrecy was difficult in these small towns, and local curiosity eventually overwhelmed the desire for secrecy. Authorities employed locals in the construction of these large camps. This cooperation and the camps' presence would soon act as a minor boon to the local economies and assuaged any security concerns from the local populace. The "cat was certainly out of the bag" when prisoners from famed Field Marshal Erwin Rommel's Afrika Korps began arriving by the trainloads in early 1943, and the curious locals met the trains at the depots to get a look at their communities' newest arrivals: haggard, defeated German prisoners, still in dirty and oftentimes bloodied uniforms, marching to their new home in the base camps.[11]

The PMGO saw to it that each camp was constructed according to its overall design, with each of the base camps having a capacity of 3,000 to 4,000 prisoners. Officer prisoners remained segregated from enlisted prisoners, with sections of each camp assigned to each group. Open floors, bunk beds, and coal stoves characterized the barracks, and each camp was surrounded by numerous barbed-wire fences, interspersed with high guard towers and floodlights. All contained a hospital and mess facilities, as well as a post exchange, chapel, laundry, and library. Many prisoners took advantage of opportunities to further their education while in captivity, organizing courses on numerous topics they believed would benefit them in their careers following the war. Camps offered traditional liberal arts courses such as the languages (English, French, and Latin), math, chemistry, geography, and history, as well as vocational offerings, including fruit culture, agriculture, and shorthand. Courses ranged from quite informal affairs, while others were more in line with college or university classes and taught by qualified civilians or POW instructors. Seeking to prevent the unrest that often accompanies boredom and confinement, camp officials offered dozens of recreational activities to the prisoners. POWs participated in sports, organized teams and tournaments (soccer being the most popular), and handicraft activities such as woodworking, leatherworking, metalworking, pottery, and other leisurely pursuits.[12]

As is often the case during war, American captors immediately found use of the large numbers of prisoners as a labor force. The war hit Texas agriculture particularly hard, losing thousands of farm workers to the military, and it was not long before the German-enlisted prisoners worked fields and forests throughout the state. Local farmers and timbermen contracted with camps for prisoner labor, paying 80 cents per prisoner per day for their efforts. Prisoners chopped cotton, baled hay, farmed rice, and felled trees. In addition to countless other farm-related jobs, prisoners worked local businesses, provided that none of the work directly involved prosecuting the war. In the congressional district of Speaker of the House Sam T. Rayburn, along the Red River, German POWs cleared trees for the Denison Dam–Lake Texoma project. To be sure, such labor arrangements suited both the farmers and the prisoners, as each received benefits from such labor.[13]

The success of the POW labor system, along with the pressing need for labor in Texas, resulted in the creation of dozens of smaller camps throughout the state. These branch camps were clustered mostly in the eastern half of Texas and located in closer proximity to areas in need of agricultural workers. Typically housing a few hundred prisoners, these camps existed to provide labor to local farmers who would file requests for a certain number of prisoners to work each day, transporting them to work sites, overseeing their labor, feeding them, and then returning them to the camp at day's end. Although it was understood that POW labor could not compete with paid labor in terms of efficiency or production, Texas farmers were pleased to have access to the new and growing labor pool. For their part, the prisoners seemed to enjoy the arrangement. Though certainly not all prisoners volunteered to work under the program, the thousands who did took advantage of the opportunities to leave the confines of the camp, to see more of the state, and to be engaged in productive activity under what must have seemed like pleasant circumstances, given their overall predicament. Many learned English as a result of the labor program, as well as trades, and they found themselves exposed to American culture. They built relationships with the Texans they encountered, many of which continued into the postwar years as they exchanged letters, and hundreds of the German prisoners returned to the United States following the war.[14]

Although the rules for and legality of detaining prisoners of war were relatively clear, as laid forth in the internationally approved Geneva Convention, the circumstances relating to noncombatant foreign nationals was open to interpretation. Shortly after the outbreak of hostilities, the US Department of Justice established a program intended to identify and detain alien nationals from Axis nations residing in the United States. Deeming these "alien enemies" potential espionage and sabotage security threats, the Department of Justice empowered the Immigration and Naturalization Service (INS) to assemble and detain foreign nationals living in the United States for the duration of the war. In the name of hemispheric security, the US Department of State also encouraged many Latin American governments to transfer to the United States any alien enemies living within their borders.[15]

Despite the dubious legality of the program (incarcerating individuals without due process, for starters), tens of thousands of citizens from the Axis nations were processed through the INS program during the war. Although some were repatriated to their home countries, usually as part of an exchange with American nationals who were caught in Axis nations when the war commenced, and others were freed after proceedings concluded that they posed no threat to national security, the vast majority of the Axis nationals spent the war's duration in geographically isolated camps around the United States. At one time or another, there existed eight such camps in the Lone Star State. Three temporary camps would be administered by the state and were located in Houston, San Antonio, and Laredo. The army ran two "temporary detention stations" at Fort Sam Houston and Fort Bliss.

There existed three INS camps, and each offered an interesting glimpse into the context and prevailing attitudes of wartime America. One of the camps was the Kenedy Alien Detention Camp, located just outside of Kenedy, Texas, some sixty miles southeast of San Antonio. Opened in April 1942 on the site of a former Civilian Conservation Corps camp, the facility underwent a speedy renovation to help accommodate hundreds of mostly German civilians. In all, 3,500 enemy alien single men (the vast majority being German) passed through its gates, with repatriation of internees frequent. It remained a detention center until the US Army assumed operations in October 1944 and repurposed it as a POW camp. Another INS camp existed in

Seagoville, Texas, twenty miles southeast of Dallas. Again making use of available facilities, INS took possession of a newly constructed, minimum-security women's prison in Seagoville in April 1942, renaming it the Seagoville Enemy Alien Detention Station. Of all the INS camps in Texas, this camp was perhaps the most unique and comfortable, with its colonial-style, redbrick buildings, resembling more of a college campus than a detention center. Growing to 600 internees, the camp at Seagoville served as a clearinghouse of sorts, holding single women, some families without children, and fifty Japanese language teachers from California until they were repatriated or moved to a larger camp near Crystal City, Texas, near the border between Texas and Mexico. The number of Japanese in Texas was quite small, due mainly to the hostile attitude by the legislature "scaring off" potential migrants with legislation limiting their franchise, land ownership, and business licensing. Both of these camps closely followed regulations regarding care and treatment of internees, including plentiful access to health care, education, food from their native countries, and physical activity. By early summer 1945, the Seagoville camp was closed and the facility returned to the Federal Bureau of Prisons after VE Day.[16]

The facility at Crystal City was the largest and most impressive of the INS camps in Texas. Upon acquiring the former Farm Security Administration facility near Crystal City (115 miles southwest of San Antonio), the INS commenced a major reconstruction effort to transform and greatly increase the camp's facilities: 500 buildings on 290 acres. At its height, it held more than 3,000 internees. The Crystal City Alien Enemy Detention Facility was designed to hold both Japanese and German internee families, most of whom arrived from Latin America, and served as a model camp for the INS program. Although not officially segregated from each other, the Japanese and German internees rarely interacted. This camp boasted modern housing facilities, camp stores for both Japanese and German internees, and access to education through the Japanese- and German-language schools, as well as through accredited American schools. Personnel and facilities for worship were also provided. Officials permitted limited access beyond the camp's perimeter for picnics and dozens of softball teams competed in leagues and tournaments. US officials further catered to the unique Japanese cuisine, providing them with rice, soy sauce, tofu, and dried seaweed. Despite making the camp as hospitable as possible, censorship and surveillance of the detainees were pervasive and a constant reminder of the facilities' true nature. Security was vital with daily head counts; consequently, the camp experienced no successful escape attempts. Being a foreign national taken from one's home and being detained in a strange land, surrounded by barbed-wire fences with searchlights and guard towers hardly represents the ideal family environment; and there is plenty to question the legality, wisdom, and racial implications of the INS program. In spite of the common complaints by internees about typical everyday issues, the stories of most of those detained at Crystal City were quite positive, given the very difficult circumstances.[17]

In total, 750,000 Texans served[18] during the Second World War: Texas, in fact, represented only 5 percent of the national population but 7 percent of the military's personnel. They experienced the beginning of the country's involvement at Pearl Harbor and witnessed the surrender and occupation of the Axis powers. Twelve admirals and 155 generals were native to the state. That was a greater percentage of its population into the armed forces than any other state (approximately 12 percent). From Houston County, Texas, machinist Leon Bennett was serving on the *Neosho* when it arrived at Pearl Harbor on December 6. Shortly after unloading its cargo of aviation fuel, the Japanese planes attacked. Bennett recalled how he initially believed the planes to be friendly planes dropping sandbags. Lance Cleo Wade from East Texas had twenty-five confirmed victories while flying for the Royal Air Force until his death in 1944, making him the "top scoring ace" from Texas. Thomas W. Fowler, a tank-platoon leader, closed a breach that the Germans had opened in the operations around Anzio in 1944. Reorganizing scattered tanks caught in a mine field, Fowler, a Wichita Falls native, cleared a path through the field, at one time leaving his tank and physically pulling mines from the ground. All the while, despite the focus of enemy fire, he emerged unscathed. His luck ran out ten days later when he was killed in action. For his action at Anzio, Fowler received the Medal of Honor. Lloyd D. Hughes left Texas A&M University and volunteered for the Army Air Corps. With the Ninth Air Force in North Africa, Hughes commanded a B-24 Liberator. While on a bombing mission against the Ploesti oil fields in Romania, his plane received two direct hits. His plane heavily damaged and in flames, Hughes attempted to crash-land. He was killed on impact, but his actions saved most of his crew. He was posthumously awarded the Medal of Honor. Born near Austin, General Ira Clarence Eaker served as commander of the Eighth Air Force in England until 1943. He contributed to the development of strategic bombing against Germany. Major General Charles R. Bond served in the famed "Flying Tigers" in China. Native of San Antonio, Walter L. McCreary was a Tuskegee Airman. A Houstonian perhaps doing the simplest of acts expedited the end of the war. Kermit Beahan, a bombardier on the B-29 Bockscar, pushed the button that released the atomic bomb "Fat Man" that detonated over Nagasaki on August 9, 1945.[19]

Although most served valiantly with little acclaim and fanfare, a few Texans went on to legendary status. In the aftermath of Pearl Harbor, Admiral Chester W. Nimitz was chosen as commander in chief of the US Pacific Fleet during the war. The Fredericksburg native also commanded the Pacific Ocean theaters, overseeing the famed island-hopping campaigns toward Japan. Although never officially retiring from the navy, Nimitz continued to serve after the war, eventually accepting various political and academic positions. He died at age eighty in 1966. Although he considered his home Kansas, Dwight D. Eisenhower was Texan by birth. Born in Denison, Eisenhower was graduated from West Point and, prior to World War II, served largely in staff positions, including as General Douglas MacArthur's chief of staff in the Philippines. At war's beginning, he was serving under chief of staff of the US Army, General George C. Marshall. "Ike's" organizational, diplomatic, and political skills led to his command of Allied forces invading North Africa and Sicily in 1942 and 1943, and by 1944, he was appointed supreme allied commander in Europe for the invasion of France. Brief stints as army chief of staff, president of Columbia University, and supreme commander of North Atlantic Treaty Organization (NATO) forces marked his time from the end of the war to his ascension to the White House in 1953. Eisenhower served two terms as president of the United States and retired to Gettysburg before dying in 1969 at age seventy-eight.[20]

One noted Texan joined the fight even before his country. Claire Lee Chennault, born in Commerce, Texas (east of Dallas), served in World War I as a flight instructor before retiring from the army in

1937 due to health issues and disagreements with superiors. Related to Sam Houston on his father's side and Robert E. Lee on his mother's, Chennault became an advisor to Chiang Kai-shek, the nominal ruler of China at the time, fighting a civil war against communist insurgents. In early 1941, Chennault organized the American Volunteer Group. Including Chennault, seven Texans served in the unit. This organization comprised American pilots volunteering to serve the Chinese effort against the invading Japanese. It was better known by their unique painted nose on their airplanes, which had the iconic shark face and thus were named "the Flying Tigers." Although his unit's actions resulted in international fame, Chennault's time in China was characterized by an acerbic relationship with the theater commander—Joseph Stilwell—once the United States entered the war. Following the war and his forced retirement, Chennault continued to author books about aerial tactics and organized and chaired the Civil Air Transport. In 1958, he died of cancer.[21]

Perhaps the most famous combat soldier in World War II was born in Kingston, Texas (northeast of Dallas). Audie L. Murphy fought in campaigns in North Africa, Sicily, Italy, and France. For his valor, he was awarded thirty-three medals, decorations, and citations, including the Medal of Honor. He, in fact, won every medal the US military bestows. A sort of postwar Renaissance man, Murphy wrote songs, acted in movies, dated movie stars, and authored a best-selling autobiography. Murphy died in an airplane crash in 1971 just shy of his forty-seventh birthday. He was buried with full military honors in Arlington National Cemetery. James Earl Rudder led one of the most daring exploits during the Normandy campaign. Born in Eden, Texas, Rudder commanded the 2nd Ranger Battalion ("Rudder's Rangers") in its mission storming Pointe du Hoc, a hundred-foot cliff located at the westernmost edge of Omaha Beach, where Allied planners believed there were German guns that could imperil the invasion. In attacking and holding the Pointe, Rudder's men suffered more than 50 percent casualties. Rudder himself suffered two wounds. By war's end, he was a full colonel and commanding the 109th Infantry Regiment, 28th Infantry Division, which saw action during the Battle of the Bulge. He was one of the most decorated American soldiers in the war, receiving the Distinguished Service Cross and Silver Star, as well as several honors from the French government. After serving as mayor of

Brady, Texas, and Texas Land Commissioner, Rudder became president of Texas A&M University. He died in 1970. A native of Willow Grove (near Waco), Doris (Dorie) Miller, an African American messman, was awarded the Navy Cross for his actions manning a machine gun against the Japanese sneak attack on Pearl Harbor. He was lost at sea when the ship he served on was torpedoed during the Gilbert Islands Campaign in late 1943. Dallas-born Samuel D. Dealey became forever known as the "Destroyer Killer" before the Japanese ultimately stopped his deadly ways in late 1944. During his command of the submarine USS *Harder*, Dealey sank sixteen enemy vessels, receiving the Navy Cross with three gold stars and the Purple Heart. General MacArthur was so appreciative of this navy man's exploits he awarded him the army's Distinguished Service Cross. Congress posthumously awarded Dealey the Medal of Honor, making him one of thirty-three Texans to earn the country's highest military honor. Both Miller and Dealey were two of twenty-three thousand Texans who paid the ultimate price defending the country during the Second World War.[22]

These men, although as varied in background as the population in Texas, generally shared a common experience during war: It returned with them. As with those returning from the Vietnam War, shell shock, war neurosis, battle exhaustion, battle fatigue—or its modern name, post-traumatic stress disorder (PTSD)—haunted millions of returning servicemen. Although statistics for World War II remain speculative compared to succeeding conflicts, it is generally believed that out of the 16 million in uniform, 800,000 experienced combat. Of those, almost 40 percent displayed "severe symptoms of combat stress" resulting in their permanent discharge. In the US Army alone, nearly 2 million men were either removed permanently or temporarily due to combat stress–related ailments. Their time in theater, which was much longer than later wars; the nature of the combat; and, of course, the wartime horrors witnessed by liberation of areas once occupied by the enemy all contributed to stamp the war on the minds of America's finest. Their combat experiences "produce[d] emotions stronger than civilians can know, emotions of terror, panic, anger, sorrow, bewilderment, helplessness, uselessness, and each of these feelings drained energy and mental stability." For some, it came immediately; for others not until decades later. This struggle, however, was one only recently dealt with.

The mentally scarred GI plagued by nightmares in a constant state of agitation, anxiety, and fear who lashes out in violent verbal or physical outbursts. Sailors physically back home yet psychologically tense from Japanese kamikazes, torpedoes, or depth charges. The marine detached from society and his family characterized by his itinerancy, alcoholism, or suicidal thoughts. For the greatest generation, these were caricatures and did not fit the sanitized narrative of the American man fighting a noble cause against the very epitome of evil. War's psychological by-products, easily undiagnosed and difficult to comprehend, were simply ignored or dismissed as an individual's weakness.[23]

The number of Texans who struggled with the psychological effects of the war may never be known, but certainly it's in the thousands. These men struggled with everything from common nightmares to the more debilitating suicidal thoughts. Hernan Cortez, still only seventeen when he returned home, lost his right hand when "a grenade hit the foxhole where he was tending to an injured man." Instinctively, he grabbed it to throw it out, and the grenade exploded in his hand. So young to be a "cripple," Hernan struggled with thoughts of suicide. While in Temple (Central Texas) during his rehabilitation, he steeled himself to relearn basic utilities with his left hand, including writing and tying his shoes. He even learned to play the organ. He became a police officer in the Laredo Police Department and later a private detective. Willie Garcia served in North Africa and Italy in the army transporting ammunition. He returned "100 percent disabled" from shell shock. His wife recalled how "the stress was so bad he couldn't eat, he couldn't walk." He remained prostrate in a hospital for nearly a year after the war. His wife, Elizabeth, was warned by doctors upon his discharge about possible violent tendencies. Until his death, she noted, he never laid a hand on her. Army Air Corps waist gunner Enrique Rodriguez Falcón initially struggled upon returning home. In contrast to the excitement of war, peace was difficult for him to adjust to. "When I came home," he admitted, "I couldn't find myself. It was hard."[24]

A number of Texas military units, and units with very strong ties to the state, played important roles in both the Pacific and European theaters of the war. The Texas National Guard, mobilized into federal service in November 1940, became the US 36th Infantry Division. Between the two world wars and especially during the Great Depression, the

Texas Guard swelled with volunteers looking for adventure and, to be blunt, a paying job. "Times was pretty rough," admitted Pete Evans from Hamby, a small town just northeast of Abilene. "I quit school [to join the National Guard]. . . . Well, we drew maybe a dollar-and-a-half a drill, I believe it was, and, of course, back in those days, a dollar-and-a-half was as big as a wagon wheel . . . It would supplement our sort of meager existence. You know, there's a lot of difference between 'poor' and '*poor*,' but we were *poor*."[25]

Arriving at Brownwood's unfinished Camp Bowie (the first major defense construction project in the state in World War II) in the winter of 1940, the 36th Infantry Division prepared for war like many other Guard units around the country. Hamstrung by the dearth of prewar preparation and military spending, the 36th embarked on a program to bring about rapid growth and training. When war came in December 1941, the division under Major General Fred Walker prepared for combat in the European theater. These "T-Patchers" (so called due to their distinctive arrowhead-shaped shoulder patch with a large block *T*) were witness to some of the most brutal fighting of the Italian campaign. The 36th participated in the controversial crossing of the Rapido River in January 1944, suffering 50 percent casualties in the tragic effort. US 5th Army commander Lieutenant General Mark Clark intended for the river crossing near Monte Cassino to serve as a diversion for the upcoming landing at Anzio, an operation deemed essential for liberating Rome. In spite of Walker's strenuous objection to the operation and plagued by shortages of vital supplies, poor geographical circumstances, and heavy German defenses on the opposite side of the river, the T-Patchers made two valiant, yet disastrous, efforts before Clark abandoned the operation. Controversy about the Rapido operation following the war manifested in a congressional investigation that exonerated both Clark and Walker, but scholars continue to debate the wisdom and necessity of this operation. After regrouping from the Rapido debacle, the division eventually participated in the breakout at Anzio later that spring before marching into Rome in June 1944 to liberate the city. The 36th also saw extensive action in Northern Europe, and participated in liberating those held in Nazi concentration camps near the war's end.[26]

The 2nd Battalion of the 131st Field Artillery Regiment, pared from the 36th Infantry Division following the Louisiana Maneuvers in the summer of 1941, saw brief action in the Pacific theater. It endured a different kind of tragedy during the war. The battalion consisted mostly of young Texans who hailed from North and West Texas. Sent to help bolster American defenses in the Pacific, the unit was captured in battle against the Japanese on the Dutch island of Java (today part of Indonesia). Along with the survivors of the sunken heavy cruiser USS *Houston* (many of whom were also Texans), which had been destroyed during the Battle of Sunda Strait on February 28 through March 1, 1942, the artillerymen spent the remainder of the war in a Japanese POW camp. More than 600 of these POWs labored on the infamous Thai–Burma "Death Railway" under appalling conditions, suffering from rampant disease, starvation, extreme overwork, and the brutality of their captors. The men of the 2nd Battalion's E Battery did not labor on the railway, but instead spent the remainder of the war working in war industries on the Japanese home islands. They also labored under brutal conditions in just another example of the Japanese contravening the requirements of the Geneva Convention.[27]

Other units with a strong Texas lineage saw action in Europe and the Pacific. Interestingly, the 112th and 124th Regiments (formerly of the Texas National Guard) were cavalry units, the last to serve on horseback in the Second World War. The 112th gave up its mounts early in the conflict but served in numerous battles in the Pacific, including at the Driniumor River on Papua New Guinea where the regiment suffered 50 percent casualties. In 1944, the regiment assisted the commander of the Southwest Pacific, General Douglas MacArthur, to fulfill his wartime promise to liberate the Philippines. The 124th, also giving up its horses, deployed to India before moving on to Burma to fight alongside guerillas to keep open the vital Burma Road. The 90th Infantry Division, originally made up of mostly Texans and Oklahomans and known by the moniker T-O Division, or "Tough 'Ombres" and also "Texas' Own," arrived in Europe in 1944. Elements of the 90th came ashore on D-Day, and the division suffered enormous casualties fighting its way through the bocage country in northern France in the breakout from Normandy. The division eventually fought its way into Germany, participating in the Rhineland and Ardennes campaigns, including the largest and bloodiest battle in Western Europe during the Second World War, the Battle of the Bulge. As the end of the war neared, the Tough 'Ombres (largely consisting of replacement troops from around the United States) were in southern Germany where they participated in the liberation of the Flossenbürg concentration camp in southern Bavaria. The division was in the Sudetenland (Czechoslovakia) when word arrived on May 7, 1945, that the war had ended.[28]

With the war's conclusion, it was time to move forward. American veterans returned home, hopeful and optimistic following their wartime experiences; those Axis prisoners who found themselves in Texas camps were repatriated with the same aspirations in mind. Many of the prisoners were encouraged by the freedom and opportunities available in the United States and voluntarily returned to America to seek a better life. The Lone Star State's last INS camps were shuttered by 1948 as the United States and its former enemies completed the repatriation processes. Some of the camps that provided training to American fighting men during the war were similarly closed, having outlived their usefulness, while others such as Camp Hood, Fort Bliss, and the numerous camps in and around San Antonio not only survived the war but also thrived in the new global order brought about in the aftermath of World War II. Peace and the Cold War economy (among many other factors) allowed Texas and Texans to enjoy the hard-won fruits of victory.

Notes

1. Kelly E. Crager has authored many works on Texas POWs during the Second World War. He currently heads the Oral History Project at the Vietnam Center and Archive at Texas Tech University.

2. For further examination of the war's mobilization on local, state, and national economies, see Robert Hough Connery, *The Navy and the Industrial Mobilization in World War II* (Princeton, NJ: Princeton University Press, 1951); James Ward Lee et al., eds., *1941: Texas Goes to War* (Denton: University of North Texas Press, 2000); Mark Harrison, ed., *The Economies of World War II: Six Great Powers in Industrial Comparison* (New York: Cambridge University Press, 1998); Harold G. Vatter, *The US Economy in World War II* (New York: Columbia University Press, 1985); A. J. Baime, *The Arsenal of Democracy: FDR, Detroit, and an Epic Quest to Arm an America at War* (New York: Houghton Mifflin Harcourt, 2014); Alan S. Milward, *War, Economy, and Society, 1939–1945* (Berkeley: University of California Press, 1977); Paul Kennedy, *Engineers of Victory: The Problem Solvers Who Turned the Tide in the Second World War* (New York: Random House Trade Paperbacks, 2013); Norman Beasley, *Knudsen: A Biography* (New York: McGraw-Hill Book Company, 1947); Donald M. Nelson, *Arsenal of Democracy: The Story of*

American War Production (New York: Harcourt, Brace, and Company, 1946); Paul A. C. Koistinen, *Arsenal of World War II: The Political Economy of American Warfare, 1940–1945* (Lawrence: University Press of Kansas, 2004); Gerald D. Nash, *The American West Transformed: The Impact of the Second World War* (Lincoln: University of Nebraska Press, 1990); and Robert Higgs, "Wartime Prosperity? A Reassessment of the US Economy in the 1940s," *Journal of Economic History* 52 (March 1992).

3. The number of Texans who trained in Texas military facilities can be found at Texas Historical Commission's website, www.thc.texas.gov/preserve/projects-and-programs/military-sites/texas-world-war-ii, which proves to be one of the better and more reliable educational sites. Other facilities, such as Rio Grande City's Fort Ringgold, were used during the war but the size and transportation advantages of larger posts like Fort Bliss supported consolidation and spelled the end for many smaller facilities. For a good history of Fort Bliss, including during the Second World War, see Leon Metz, *Desert Army: Fort Bliss on the Texas Border* (El Paso, TX: Mangan Books, 1995). More details on the role that Fort Sam Houston had during the Second World War are Eldon Cagle Jr., *Fort Sam: The Story of Fort Sam Houston, Texas* (San Antonio: Maverick Publishing Company, 2003); Fort Sam Houston Museum, *Commodious Homes for the Troops: A Centennial History of the Cavalry and Light Artillery Addition, Fort Sam Houston, Texas 1905–2005* (San Antonio: Fort Sam Houston, 2006); and Fort Sam Houston Museum, *The Quadrangle: Hub of Military Activity in Texas: An Outline History* (San Antonio: Fort Sam Houston, 2009); and Ron Tyler, ed., *The New Handbook of Texas*, 6 vols. (Austin: Texas State Historical Association, 1996), II: 1117.

4. Useful works covering the development of these camps are Sylvia Ann Edwards, "Land Acquisition in Coryell County, Texas, for the Formation of Camp Hood, 1942–1945: A Civilian Perspective" (master's thesis, Baylor University, 1988); John J. Hatcher, "Camp Barkeley: Abilene, Texas," *Texas Military History* 3 (Winter 1963); William McWhorter, "Together They Won: Sam T. Rayburn and the Fourth Congressional District during World War II," *East Texas Historical Journal* 49 (Fall 2011); Duncan Gra'Delle, *Killeen: Tale of Two Cities, 1882–1982* (Austin: Eakin Press, 1984); and James M. Myers's "World War II as an Instrument of Social Modernization: The Social and Economic Influence of Camp Barkeley on Abilene, Texas" (master's thesis, Hardin Simmons University, 1981).

5. For a more detailed description and list of the many Texas army airfields during the war, little of which remains today to signify there ever existed a military training facility or airfield, see Lou Thole's four-volume set *Forgotten Fields of America: World War II Bases and Training, Then and Now* (Missoula, MT: Pictorial Histories Publishing Company, 1999). For the number of pilots, bombardiers, and navigators, see Seth S. McKay and Odie B. Faulk, *Texas After Spindletop: The Saga of Texas, 1901–1965* (Austin: Steck-Vaughn Company, 1965). For Raytheon Corporation in Greenville, see Fred H. Allison "Patriotic Prosperity and Social Change in World War II: The Impact of Majors Field on Greenville, Texas," *Sound Historian:*

Journal of the Texas Oral History Association 5 (1999); and W. Walworth Harrison, *History of Greenville & Hunt County, Texas* (Waco, TX: Texian Press, 1977). For works on individual airfields in the state during the war, see San Antonio Air Logistics Center Office of History, Kelly AFB, Texas, *A Brief History of Kelly Air Force Base* (San Antonio: Air Force Logistics Command, 1993); Mel Brown, *Wings Over San Antonio* (Charleston, SC: Arcadia Publishing, 2001); Thomas E. Alexander, "'*The Stars Were Big and Bright*': *The United States Army Air Forces and Texas during World War II* (Denton: University of North Texas Press, 2000); Thomas E. Alexander, *Rattlesnake Bomber Base*: *Pyote Army Airfield in World War II* (Abilene, TX: State House Press, 2005); W. A. Caplinger and Jim Conrad, *A History of Majors Air Field, Greenville, Texas* (Hunt, TX: Hunt County Historical Commission, n.d.); Thomas E. Alexander and Dan K. Utley, *Faded Glory*: *A Century of Forgotten Texas Military Sites, Then and Now* (College Station: Texas A&M University Press, 2012); Bennet B. Monde, "A History of Avenger Field, Texas" (master's thesis, Hardin-Simmons University, 1980); Aaron D. Horton, "The Long Road Home: Alfred Andersch Hans Werner Richter, and the German Search for Meaning in Catastrophe" (PhD diss., Louisiana State University, 2011); Anne Krueger Hussey, *A Heritage of Service*: *Seventy-Five Years of Military Aviation at Kelly Air Force Base, 1916–1991* (San Antonio: Air Force Logistics Command, 1992); Scott Huddleston, "A Simple Aviation Camp Helped S.A. Land the Role of 'Military City,'" *mysantonio.com*, July 11, 2011; Robert Mueller, *Air Force Bases: Active Air Force Bases within the United States of America on 17 September 1982* (Washington, DC: Office of Air Force History United States Air Force, 1982); Mark L. Morgan, "Air Force Bases: 1946–1987," *AAHS Journal* 32 (Winter 1987); Harriett Sue Pohl, "Webb Air Force Base," *Junior Historian* 29 (January 1969); William Head, *Every Inch a Soldier*: *Augustine Warner Robins and the Building of US Airpower* (College Station: Texas A&M University Press, 1995); Thomas A. Manning, *History of Air Education and Training Command, 1942–2002* (Randolph Air Force Base, TX: Office of History and Research Headquarters Air Education and Training Command, 2005); Cecilia Thompson, *History of Marfa and Presidio County, 1535–1946*, 2 vols. (Austin: Nortex, 1985); Galveston *Daily News*, November 15, 1945; Norman C. Delaney, "Corpus Christi's 'University of the Air,'" *Naval History Magazine* 27 (June 2013); *Wingspan*, March 10, 2016; and Frederick J. Shaw, ed., *Locating Air Force Base Sites History's Legacy* (Washington, DC: Air Force History and Museums Program United States Air Force, 2004, updated version 2014).

6. Tom Killebrew, *The Royal Air Force in Texas*: *Training British Pilots in Terrell during World War II* (Denton: University of North Texas Press, 2003), 10; Jan Adamson, "United Skies Over Terrell: Many Lessons Awaited RAF Cadets Stationed at No. 1 British Flying Training School," *Texas Coop Power*, August 2014, www.texascooppwer.com. For additional works chronicling the cooperation between the British and the United States regarding pilot training, see M. W. Palmer, "British Flying Training Schools in America," *Transatlantic* (April 1945); Robert F. Schirmer, "AAC & AAF Primary Flying Schools 1939–1945, Part VII, Dallas Primary,"

Journal of American Aviation Historical Society 37 (Fall 1992); and Gilbert S. Guin, "British Aircrew Training in the United States 1941–1945," *Air Power History* 42 (Summer 1995).

7. A more detailed examination of the WASP as well as female Texans' contribution to the war effort is in Katherine Sharp Landdeck's essay. But for those wanting works on the WASP, see Molly Merriman *Clipped Wings: The Rise and Fall of the Women Airforce Service Pilots (WASPs) of World War II* (New York: New York University Press, 1998); Sarah Byrn Rickman's *WASP of the Ferry Command: Women Pilots, Uncommon Deeds* (Denton: University of North Texas Press, 2016); Marianne Verges, *On Silver Wings: The Women Airforce Service Pilots of World War II, 1942–1944* (New York: Ballentine Books, 1991); James W. Ure, *Seized by the Sun: The Life and Disappearance of World War II Pilot Gertrude Tompkins* (Chicago: Chicago Review Press, 2017); Sarah Byrn Rickman, *The Originals: The Women's Auxiliary Ferrying Squadron of World War II* (Sarasota, FL: Disc Books, 2001); Sally Van Wagenen Keil, *These Wonderful Women in Their Flying Machines: The Unknown Heroines of World War II* (Rhinebeck, NY: Four Directions Press, 1979); Anne Noggle, *For God, Country and the Thrill of It: Women Airforce Service Pilots during WWII* (College Station: Texas A&M University Press, 1990); Amy Strebe, *Flying for Her Country: The American and Soviet Women Military Pilots of World War II* (Westport, CT: Greenwood Publishing Group, 2007); Harry F. Snapp, "Pioneering Women in West Texas Skies: Women Airforce Service Pilots of World War II," *West Texas Historical Association Year Book* 70 (1994); Jean Hascall Cole, *Women Pilots of World War II* (Salt Lake City: University of Utah Press, 1992); Ann B. Carl, *A WASP Among Eagles: A Woman Military Test Pilot in World War II* (Washington, DC: Smithsonian Books, 2010); William M. Miller, *To Live and Die a WASP: 38 Women Pilots Who Died in WWII* (n.c.: CreateSpace Independent Publishing Platform, 2016); Amy Nathan, *Yankee Doodle Gals: Women Pilots of World War II* (Washington, DC: National Geographic Society, 2001); Byrd Howell Granger, *On Final Approach: The Women Airforce Service Pilots of World War II* (Scottsdale, AZ: Falconer Publishing, 1991); Marie Mountain Clark, *Dear Mother and Daddy: World War II Letters Home from a WASP* (Livonia, MI: First Page Publications, 2005); Leslie Haynsworth and David Toomey, *Amelia Earhart's Daughters* (New York: William Morrow and Company, 1998); Vera S. Williams, *WASPs: Women Airforce Service Pilots of World War II* (St. Paul, MN: Motorbooks International, 1994); Helena Schrader, *Sisters in Arms: British and American Women Pilots during World War II* (Barnsley, South Yorkshire, UK: Pen and Sword Books, 2006); Marion Stegeman Hodgson, *Winning My Wings: A Woman Airforce Service Pilot in World War II* (Annapolis, MD: Naval Institute Press, 1996); Nancy Robison, "'*We Love to Fly*': *Women Airforce Service Pilots* (n.c.: CreateSpace Independent Publishing Platform, 2013); David A. Stallman, *Women in the Wild Blue: Target Towing WASP at Camp Davis* (Sugar Creek, OH: Carlisle Printing, 2011); Jaqueline Cochran, *Jackie Cochran: An Autobiography of the Greatest Woman Pilot in Aviation History* (New York: Bantam Books, 1987); Jacqueline Cochran, *The*

Stars at Noon (Boston: Little, Brown 1954); and Sarah Byrn Rickman, *Nancy Batson Crews: Alabama's First Lady of Flight* (Tuscaloosa: University of Alabama Press, 2009). The first WASP pilot was buried in Arlington National Cemetery with full military honors as early as 2002. The Secretary of the Army, however, who believed these women should not have been buried in the cemetery, reversed the policy, citing the superintendent of the cemetery lacked the authority to grant burial to the female pilots. Thus, until Congress intervened, further burials were barred. Full details of the struggle to be buried in Arlington National Cemetery can be found in Katherine Sharp Landdeck, "A Woman Pilot Receives the Military Funeral the Army Denied Her," *Atlantic*, September 8, 2016; Leo Shane, III, "Female WWII Pilots Now Allowed Burial at Arlington," *Military Times*, May 20, 2016; and *Washington Post*, September 7, 2016. The premier work on Texas women who served in all branches during the war is Cindy Weigand, *Texas Women in World War II* (Lanham, MD: Republic of Texas Press, 2003).

8. For a more detailed examination of Texas City during the war, see Priscilla Myers-Benham, "Texas City: Port of Industrial Opportunity" (PhD diss., University of Houston, 1987); and Priscilla Myers-Benham, "Texas City Port of Opportunity," *Houston Review* 10 (1988). The role the Reconstruction Finance Corporation had in prewar Texas is briefly discussed in Joseph "Chip" Dawson's essay as well as in Jesse H. Jones (with Edward Angly), *Fifty Billion Dollars: My Thirteen Years with the RFC (1932–1945)* (New York: Macmillan, 1951). Assessments of the growth of the government-business relationship are Paul A. C. Koistinen, *The Military-Industrial Complex: A Historical Perspective* (New York: Praeger Publishers, 1980); James Titus, ed., *The Home Front War in the 20th Century: The American Experience in Comparative Perspective* (Washington, DC: Government Printing Office, 1984); Richard E. Holl, *Committed to Victory: The Kentucky Home Front during World War II* (Lexington: University Press of Kentucky, 2015); Allen Cronenberg, *Forth to the Mighty Conflict: Alabama and World War II* (Tuscaloosa: University of Alabama Press, 1995); Gregory Hooks, *Forging the Military-Industrial Complex: World War II's Battle of the Potomac* (Urbana: University of Illinois Press, 1991); and Joe R. Feagin and Kelly Riddell, "The State, Capitalism, and World War II: The US Case," *Armed Forces and Society* 17 (Fall 1990).

9. Irene Paulette, "Odessa during the War Years, 1941–1945: A Microcosm of the Nation," *Permian Historical Annual* 22 (December 1982); Tracy M. Shilcutt, "'Soldiers Were Everywhere': Camp Barkeley and Abilene, Texas 1940–1945," *Sound Historian: Journal of the Texas Oral History Association* 12 (2009), 34–35. The best work on Abilene's experience with the "army coming to town" is James Myer, "The Army Comes to Abilene," *West Texas Historical Association Year Book* 65 (1985). The concerns of citizens in Greenville about the army coming to town is in Allison, "Patriotic Prosperity and Social Change in World War II," 41–44. The story concerning San Antonio and the homosexual community can be found in Melissa Gohlke, "Off-Limits and Out-of Bounds, World War II and San Antonio's Queer Community," *The Top Shelf: A Blog About Special Collections at the UTSA Libraries*, February 25, 2013; and Allan Berube, *Coming Out Under Fire: The History*

of Gay Men and Women in World War II (New York: The Free Press, 1990). For further works examining the effects of "the military coming to town" in Texas, see J'Nell L. Pate, *Arsenal of Defense: Fort Worth's Military Legacy* (Denton: Texas State Historical Association, 2011); James L. Colwell, "'Hell from Heaven': Midland Army Air Field in World War II," *Permian Historical Annual* Pt. 1, 25 (1985); Pt. 2, 26 (1986); and Pt. 3, 27 (1987); James L. Colwell, "Wings over West Texas: Pecos Army Air Field in World War II," *West Texas Historical Association Yearbook* 63 (1987); Elizabeth Wheaton, *Texas City, Texas: Is Beginning Its Destruction Its Revitalization* (Texas City: Texas City Chamber of Commerce, 1959); Bill O'Neal, *East Texas in World War II* (Mt. Pleasant, SC: Arcadia Publishing, 2010); Paul Alejandro Levengood, "For the Duration and Beyond: World War II and the Creation of Modern Houston, Texas" (PhD diss., Rice University, 1999); Christopher B. Bean, "'When the Army Comes to Town': The Effects of Camp Howze on Gainesville and Cooke Country," *Red River Valley Historical Journal* 4 (Winter 2006); and Melanie Wiggins, *Torpedoes in the Gulf: Galveston and the U-boats, 1942–1943* (College Station: Texas A&M University Press, 1995). The effects concerning cities in the nation as a whole can be found in Stephen Herman Dew, *The Queen City at War: Charlotte, North Carolina, during World War II, 1939–1945* (Lanham, MD: University Press of America, 2011); Roger W. Lotchin, "California Cities and the Hurricane of Change: World War II in the San Francisco, Los Angeles, and San Diego Metropolitan Areas," *Pacific Historical Review* 63 (August 1994); Jacob Vander Meulen, "World War II Aircraft Industry in the West," *Journal of the West* 36 (July 1997); Catherine Lutz, *Homefront: A Military City and the American Twentieth Century* (Boston: Beacon Press, 2001); David Brinkley, *Washington Goes to War* (New York: Alfred A Knopf, 1988); Jacob Vander Meulen, "West Coast Labor and the Military Aircraft Industry, 1935–1941," *Pacific Northwest Quarterly* 88 (Spring 1997); Perry R. Duis and Scott LaFrance, *We've Got a Job to Do: Chicagoans and World War II* (Chicago: Chicago Historical Society, 1992); Jeffery M. Dorwart, *The Philadelphia Navy Yard: From the Birth of the US Navy to the Nuclear Age* (Philadelphia: University of Pennsylvania Press, 2001); Richard Goldstein, *Helluva Town: The Story of New York City during World War II* (New York: The Free Press, 2010); and Ruth Wallach et al., *Los Angeles in World War II* (Mt. Pleasant, SC: Arcadia Publishing, 2011).

10. Any study of prisoners of war in the United States, and especially in Texas, during World War II should begin with Arnold P. Krammer's extensive work on this topic, especially *Nazi Prisoners of War in America* (New York: Stein and Day, 1979); *Undue Process: The Untold Story of America's German Allie Internees* (New York: Rowman and Littlefield Publishers, 1997); and "When the 'Afrika Korps' Came to Texas," *Southwestern Historical Quarterly* 80 (January 1977). Other works that are especially useful are Richard P. Walker's *The Lone Star and the Swastika: Prisoners of War in Texas* (Austin: Eakin Press, 2001); Robert W. Tissing Jr., "Stalag Texas, 1943–1945," *Military History of Texas and the Southwest* 13 (Fall 1976); Mark Choate's *Nazis in the Pineywoods* (Lufkin: Best of East Texas Publishers, 1989); Jeffrey L. Littlejohn and Charles H. Ford, eds., *The Enemy within Never Did*

without: German and Japanese Prisoners of War at Camp Huntsville, 1942–1945 (Huntsville, TX: Texas Review Press, 2015); and Michael R. Waters, *Lone Star Stalag: German Prisoners of War at Camp Hearne* (College Station: Texas A&M University Press, 2004). A very interesting, though brief, examination of Italian prisoners of war held in Hereford, Texas, is Donald Mace Williams, *Interlude in Umbarger: Italian POWs and a Texas Church* (Lubbock: Texas Tech University Press, 1992).

11. Additional works that examine the internment of Axis POWs in Texas and other states are Danny Steelman, "German Prisoners of War in America: Oklahoma's Prisoner of War Operations during World War II," *Oklahoma State Historical Review* 4 (Spring 1983); George T. Mazuzan and Nancy Walker, "Restricted Areas: German Prisoner of War Camps in Western New York, 1944–1946," *New York History* 59 (January 1978); Anita Buck, *Behind Barbed Wire: German Prisoner of War Camps in Minnesota* (St. Cloud, MN: North Star Press, 1998); John Hammond Moore, "Hitler's Wehrmacht in Virginia, 1943–1946," *Virginia Magazine of History and Biography* 85 (1977); John Hammond Moore, "Italian POWs in America: War Is Not Always Hell," *Prologue: The Journal of the National Archives* 8 (Fall 1976); Edward Corbett, "Interned for the Duration: Axis Prisoners of War in Oklahoma, 1942–1946" (master's thesis, Oklahoma City University, 1967); John J. Culley, "A Troublesome Presence": World War II Internment of German Sailors in New Mexico," *Prologue: The Journal of the National Archives* 28 (Winter 1996); John Hammond Moore, "Nazi Troopers in South Carolina, 1944–1946," *South Carolina Historical Magazine* 81 (October 1980); Hazel Wages, "Memphis Armed Service Forces Depot Prisoner of War Camp: 1944–1946," *Tennessee Historical Quarterly* 52 (Spring 1993); John J. Culley, "World War II and a Western Town: The Internment of the Japanese Railroad Workers of Clovis, New Mexico," *Western Historical Quarterly* 13 (January 1982); Susan Badger Doyle, "German and Italian Prisoners of War in Albuquerque, 1943–1946," *New Mexico Historical Review* 66 (July 1991); Robert C. Doyle, *The Enemy in Our Hands: America's Treatment of Prisoners of War from the Revolution to the War on Terror* (Lexington: University of Kentucky Press, 2010); Terry Paul Wilson, "The Afrika Korps in Oklahoma: Fort Reno's Prisoner of War Compound," *Chronicles of Oklahoma* 52 (Fall 1974); Judith M. Gansberg, *Stalag USA: The Remarkable Story of German POWs in America* (New York: Thomas Y. Crowell, 1977); Antonio Thompson, "Winning the War behind the Lines: Colonel George Chescheir and the Axis POWs at Fort Benning, Georgia," *Register of the Kentucky Historical Society* 105 (2007); James Richard Keen, "The Captive Enemy? Italian Prisoners of War in Texas during World War II" (master's thesis, University of Texas at the Permian Basin, 1998); Arnold P. Krammer, "Japanese Prisoners of War in America," *Pacific Historical Review* 52 (February 1983); Richard Paul Walker, "Prisoners of War in Texas during World War II" (PhD diss., University of North Texas, 1980); Betty Cowley, *Stalag Wisconsin: Inside WWII Prisoner-of-War Camps* (Oregon, WI: Badger Books, 2002); Kate Faust, "Remembrances of the Prisoner of War Camp in West Helena, Arkansas," *Phillips County*

Historical Quarterly 16 (September 1978); Bert Page and Ken B. Harper, "Achtung! German WWII POWs in Pope County," *Pope County Historical Association Quarterly* 45 (July and December 2011); and Robert D. Billinger Jr., *Nazi POWs in the Tar Heel State* (Gainesville, FL: University Press of Florida, 2008). Memoirs and oral histories by German POWs in Texas and America are Lewis H. Carlson, *We Were Each Other's Prisoners: An Oral History of World War II American and German Prisoners of War* (New York: Basic Books, 1997); Heino R. Erichsen, *The Reluctant Warrior: Former German POW Finds Peace in Texas* (Austin: Eakin Press, 2001); Helmut Hörner, Translated and edited by Allan Kent Powell, *A German Odyssey: The Journal of a German Prisoner of War* (Golden, CO: Fulcrum, 1991); Berneda Koller, *An Ironic Point of Light: A Story of a German from Russia Who Survived an American World War II Prisoner of War Camp* (Freeman, SD: Pine Hill Press, 1994); Kathy Roe Coker, "World War II Prisoners of War in Georgia: German Memories of Camp Gordon, 1943–1945," *Georgia Historical Quarterly* 76 (Winter 1992): Walter Schmid, translated by Richard Rundell and edited by Wolfgang T. Schlauch, *A German POW in New Mexico* (Albuquerque: University of New Mexico Press, 2005); Fritz Ensslin, "A German Soldier Tells What It Is Like to Visit Ft. Leonard Wood in 1943 as a POW," *Essayons* (June 1991); and Jeffrey E. Geiger, *German Prisoners of War at Camp Cooke, California: Personal Accounts of 14 Soldiers, 1944–1946* (Jefferson, NC: McFarland and Company, 1996).

12. Along with the above cited works, details on such educational efforts (as well as re-educational efforts) in these facilities during the war can be found in Antonio Thompson, *Men in German Uniform: POWs in America during World War II* (Knoxville: University of Tennessee Press, 2010); Karen Riley, "Schools Behind Barbed Wire: A History of Schooling in the United States Department of Justice Internment Camp at Crystal City, Texas, during World War II, 1942–1946" (PhD diss., University of Texas, 1996); Ron Rabin, *The Barbed-Wire College: Reeducating German POWs in the United States during World War II* (Princeton, NJ: Princeton University Press, 1995); Curt Bondy, "Observation and Reeducation of German Prisoners of War," *Harvard Educational Review* 14 (January–December 1944); J. Barrie Williams, "Re-education of German Prisoners of War in the United States during World War II" (master's thesis, College of William and Mary, 1993); Wolfgang D. Schmidt, *The Education and Reeducation of POW 31G-23742357* (Bloomington, IN: Xlibris, 2001); and Chip Walker, "German Creative Activities in Camp Aliceville, 1943–1946" *Alabama Review* 38 (January 1985).

13. The information for German POWs working in Sam T. Rayburn's district is in McWhorter, "Together They Won." In addition to the works concerning Axis prisoners of war cited above, works chronicling the Axis prisoner of war experience in Texas and the United States at large, particularly in agricultural work, include Thomas Jaehn, "Unlikely Harvesters: German Prisoners of War as Agricultural Workers in the Northwest," *Montana: The Magazine of Western Heritage* 50 (Autumn 2000); James E. Fickle and Donald W. Ellis, "POWs in the Piney Woods: German Prisoners of War in the Southern Lumber Industry, 1943–1945,"

Journal of Southern History 56 (November 1990); William L. Shea and Merrill R. Pritchett, "The Wehrmacht in Louisiana," *Louisiana History* 23 (Winter 1982); Lowell A. May, *Camp Concordia: German POWs in the Midwest* (Manhattan, KS: Sunflower University Press, 1995); William L. Shea and Merrill R. Pritchett, "The Afrika Korps in Arkansas, 1943–1946," *Arkansas Historical Quarterly* 37 (Spring 1978); Jake W. Spidle, "Axis Invasion of the American West: POWs in New Mexico, 1942–1946," *New Mexico Historical Review* 19 (April 1974); Joseph T. Butler Jr., "Prisoner of War Labor in the Sugar Cane Fields of Lafourche Parish, Louisiana, 1943–1944," *Louisiana History* 14 (Summer 1973); Penny Clark, "Farm Work and Friendship: The German Prisoner of War Camp at Lake Wabaunsee," *Emporia State Research Studies* 36 (Winter 1988); Lowell Bangerter, "German Prisoners of War in Wyoming," *Journal of German-American Studies* 14 (June 1979); Barbara Wyatt, ed., *Japanese Americans in World War II: A National Historic Landmarks Theme Study* (Washington, DC: National Historic Landmarks Program National Park Service, 2012); Robert D. Billinger Jr., "With Wehrmacht in Florida: German POW Facility at Camp Blanding, 1942–1946," *Florida Historical Quarterly* 58 (October 1979); Matthias Reiss, "Bronzed Bodies behind Barbed Wire: Masculinity and the Treatment of German Prisoners of War in the United States during World War II," *Journal of Military History* 69 (April 2005); Michael Walzer, "Prisoners of War: Does the Fight Continue After the Battle?" *American Political Science Review* 63 (September 1969); Robert D. Billinger Jr., "Behind the Wire: German Prisoners of War at Camp Sutton, 1944–1946," *North Carolina Historical Review* 61 (October 1984); Robert D. Billinger Jr., *Hitler's Soldiers in the Sunshine State: German POW's in Florida* (Gainesville: University Press of Florida, 2009); Allen V. Koop, *Stark Decency: German Prisoners of War in an New England Village* (Hanover, NH: University Press of New England, 1988); Richard E. Holl, "Swastikas in the Bluegrass State: Axis Prisoners of War in Kentucky, 1942–1946," *Register of the Kentucky Historical Society* 100 (Spring 2002); Richard E. Holl, "German Prisoners of War Visit Henry County, Kentucky, September-October 1944," *Quarterly Review* 22 (September 1999); Daniel Hutchinson, "'We . . . Are the Most Fortunate of Prisoners': The Axis POW Experience at Camp Opelika during World War II," *Alabama Review* 64 (October 2011); Daniel A. Jepson, "Camp Carson, Colorado: European Prisoners of War in the American West during World War II," *Midwest Review* 13 (1991); William P. Corbett, "'They Hired Every Farmer in the Country': Establishing the Prisoner of War Camp at Tonkawa," *Chronicles of Oklahoma* 69 (Winter 1992); Harold Zimmerman, "Harvesting Peaches with German Prisoners of War," *Journal of the Western Slope* 2 (Winter 1987); Ralph Spencer, "Prisoners of War in Cheyenne Country, 1943–1946," *Nebraska State Historical Society* 63 (Fall 1982); Jason Ward Morgan, "'Nazis Hoe Cotton': Planters, POWs, and the Future of Farm Labor in the Deep South," *Agricultural History* 81 (Fall 2007); Melissa Amateis Marsh, *Nebraska POW Camps: A History of World War II Prisoners in the Heartland* (Charleston, SC: The History Press, 2014); David W. Fiedler, *The Enemy among Us: POWs in Missouri during World War II* (St. Louis: Missouri Historical Society

Press, 2003); and Richard S. Warner, "Barbed Wire and Nazilagers: PW Camps in Oklahoma," *Chronicles of Oklahoma* 64 (Spring 1986).

14. A more extensive examination of the use of POW labor in the United States, beyond those works cited above is George G. Lewis and John Mewha, *History of Prisoner of War Utilization by the United States Army, 1776–1945* (Washington, DC: Department of the Army, 1955). To see the relationships that could be formed between POW and members of the local population, see Ruth Beaumont Cook, *Guests Behind Barbed Wire: German POWS in America: A True Story of Hope and Friendship* (Birmingham, AL: Crane Hill Publishers, 2007); Howard S. Levie, "The Employment of Prisoners of War," *American Journal of International Law* 57 (April 1963); Barbara Schmitter Heisler, *From German Prisoner of War to American Citizen: A Social History with 35 Interviews* (Jefferson, NC: McFarland and Company, 2013); and Bean, "'When the Army Comes to Town.'"

15. The best work detailing the rules and regulations regarding prisoners of war throughout the years is Doyle, *The Enemy in Our* Hands. Important compilations of individual accounts of those held in INS camps are Daniels et al., *Japanese Americans*; Thomas Connell, *America's Japanese Hostages: The World War II Plan for a Japanese Free Latin America* (New York: Praeger, 2002); and C. Harvey Gardiner, *Pawns in a Triangle of Hate: The Peruvian Japanese and the United States* (Seattle: University of Washington Press, 1981). Works examining the internment of Japanese, German, and Italian civilians throughout the United States are Lawson Fusao Inada, ed., *"'Only What We Could Carry': The Japanese American Internment Experiment* (Berkeley, CA: Heyday Books, 2000); Roger Daniels et al., eds., *Japanese Americans: From Relocation to Redress* (Salt Lake City: University of Utah Press, 1986); Richard Reeves, *Infamy: The Shocking Story of the Japanese American Internment in World War II* (New York: Henry Holt and Company, 2015); Roger Daniels, *Prisoners without Trial: Japanese Americans in World War II* (New York: Hill and Wang, 2004); Eric L. Muller, *American Inquisition: The Hunt for Japanese American Disloyalty in World War II* (Chapel Hill: University of North Carolina Press, 2997); Roger Daniels, *Concentration Camps North America: Japanese in the United States and Canada during World War II* (Malabar, FL: Krieger Publishing Company, 1993); Dorothy Swaine Thomas and Richard S. Nishimito, *The Spoilage* (Berkeley: University of California Press, 1946); Heidi Donald, *We Were Not the Enemy: Remembering the United States Latin American Civilian Internment Program of World War II* (Lincoln, NE: iUniverse, 2008); Stephen Fox, ed., *The Unknown Internment: An Oral History of the Relocation of Italian-Americans during World War II* (Boston: Twayne Publishers, 1990); Rose D. Scherini, "Executive Order 9066 and Italian Americans: The San Francisco Story," *California History* 70 (Winter 1991); Mary Elizabeth Basile Chopas, "Law, Security, and Ethnic Profiling: Italians in the United States during World War II" (PhD diss., University of North Carolina, 2013); Paula Branca-Santos, "Injustice Ignored: The Internment of Italian Americans during World War II," *Pace International Law Review* 13 (Spring 2001); Stephen Seng-hau Mak, "America's Other Internment: World War II and

the Making of Modern Human Rights" (PhD diss., Northwestern University, 2009); Allan W. Austin, *From Concentration Camps to Campus: Japanese American Students and World War II* (Urbana, IL: University of Illinois Press, 2004); Jeffrey F. Burton, *Confinement and Ethnicity: An Overview of World War II Japanese American Relocation Sites* (Tuscon: Western Archeological and Conservation Center, 1999); Alan R. Bosworth, *America's Concentration Camps* (New York: W. W. Norton Company, 1967); US Commission on Wartime Relocation and Internment of Civilians, *Personal Justice Denied* (Washington, DC: Government Printing Office, 1983); John Christgau, *Enemies: World War II Alien Internment* (Lincoln, NE: Authors Choice Press, 2001); and Russell L. Estlack, *Shattered Lives Shattered Dreams: The Disrupted Lives of Families in America's Internment Camps* (Springville, UT: Bonneville Books, 2011). Specific administrative information concerning the INS program and various camps can be found in Record Group 85, National Archives and Records Administration, Washington, DC, and College Park, Maryland. A poignant study of individuals' experiences is Jan Jarboe Russell, *The Train to Crystal City: FDR's Secret Prisoner Exchange Program and America's Only Family Internment Camp during World War II* (New York: Scribner, 2015).

16. Because the Geneva Convention forbade housing prisoners of war and detained civilians in prison facilities, the INS took possession of the Seagoville facility from the Federal Bureau of Prisons earlier in 1942. For the number of alien enemy facilities in Texas, see the Texas Historical Commissions previously cited online. For the hostile attitude by the Texas Legislature, see Richard Polenberg, *War and Society: The United States, 1941–1945* (New York: J. B. Lippincott Company, 1972).

17. See the above-mentioned specified works in footnotes 6,7, 9, and 10 concerning Crystal City and its operations.

18. Very good sources to a few of the many Texans who served during the Second World War are Stephen M. Sloan et al., eds., *Tattooed on My Soul: Texas Veterans Remember World War II* (College Station: Texas A&M University Press, 2015); Rupert N. Richardson et al., *Texas: The Lone Star State*, 10th ed. (New York: Routledge, 2010), 339; and the website www.texasescapes.com.

19. The population of Texas in 1940 was approximately 6.4 million. Information about the number of Texans serving and the percentage of the population, the number of Texans awarded the Medal of Honor, and the number of Texans who died in this footnote and the next can be found at the Texas Historical Commission website. The information concerning the number of generals from the state came from Seth S. McKay and Odie B. Faulk, *Texas after Spindletop: The Saga of Texas, 1901–1965* (Austin: Steck-Vaughn Company, 1965). For brief biographies of Bennett, Wade, Fowler, Hughes, Eaker, Bond, and McCreary, see Ralph Wooster, "East Texas in World War II," *East Texas Historical Journal* 45 (2007); Barbara Anne Ganson, *Texas Takes Wing: A Century of Flight in the Lone Star State* (Austin: University of Texas Press, 2014); Lee et al., *1941: Texas Goes to War*, 217; "Bombings of Hiroshima and Nagasaki—1945," Atomic Heritage Foundation, June 5,

2014, https://www.atomicheritage.org/history/bombings-hiroshima-and-nagasaki-1945; and Henry C. Dethloff, *A Centennial History of Texas A&M University, 1876–1976*, 2 vols. (College Station: Texas A&M University Press), II: 463–64.

20. Works on Chester W. Nimitz include Frank A. Driskill, *Chester W. Nimitz: Admiral of the Hills* (Austin: Eakin Press, 1983); Edwin Hoyt, *How They Won the War in the Pacific: Nimitz and His Admirals* (New York: Weybright and Talley, 1970); Walter R. Borneman, *The Admirals: Nimitz, Halsey, Leahy and King—The Five-Star Admirals Who Won the War at Sea* (New York: Little, Brown and Company, 2012); E. B. Potter, *Nimitz* (Annapolis, MD: Naval Institute Press, 1976); and Brayton Harris, *Admiral Nimitz: The Commander of the Pacific Ocean Theater* (New York: St. Martin's Press, 2012). For a more detailed examination of Dwight D. Eisenhower, see Forrest C. Pogue, *The Supreme Command* (Washington, DC: Government Printing Office, 1954); Stephen E. Ambrose, *The Supreme Commander: The War Years of Dwight D. Eisenhower* (New York: Anchor Books, 1970); Stephen E. Ambrose, *Eisenhower: Soldier, General of the Army, President-Elect, 1893–1952* (New York: Simon & Schuster, 1983); Stephen E. Ambrose, *Eisenhower: The President* (New York: Simon & Schuster, 1984); Jean Edward Smith, *Eisenhower in War and Peace* (New York: Random House, 2012); Robert R. Bowie and Richard H. Immerman, *Waging Peace: How Eisenhower Shaped an Enduring Cold War Strategy* (New York: Oxford University Press, 1998); Dwight D. Eisenhower, *Crusade in Europe* (Garden City, NY: Doubleday & Company, 1948); and Chester J. Pach and Elmo Richardson, *The Presidency of Dwight D. Eisenhower* (Lawrence: University Press of Kansas, 1991).

21. James W. Pohl, "Claire Lee Chennault," *Handbook of Texas Online*, https://tshaonline.org/handbook/online/articles/fch20. For more on Claire Chennault and the Flying Tigers, see Keith Ayling, *Old Leatherface of the Flying Tigers: The Story of General Chennault* (Indianapolis, IN: Bobbs-Merrill, 1945); Sam Kleiner, *The Flying Tigers: The Untold Story of the American Pilots Who Waged a Secret War against Japan* (New York: Penguin Random House, 2018); Martha Byrd, *Chennault: Giving Wings to the Tiger* (Tuscaloosa: University of Alabama Press, 1987); Duane Schultz, *The Maverick War: Chennault and the Flying Tigers* (New York: St. Martin's Press, 1987); and Anna Chennault, *Chennault and His Flying Tigers* (New York: P. S Eriksson, 1963). The seven Texans who served in the unit were Claire Lee Chennault, Charles Rankin Bond Jr., David Lee "Tex" Hill, Paul J. Green, Mathew W. Kuykendall, Neil Martin, and Robert W. Prescott.

22. The best works on Audie L. Murphy's life are Don Graham, *No Name on the Bullet: A Biography of Audie Murphy* (New York: Viking Penguin, 1989); David A. Smith, *The Price of Valor: The Life of Audie Murphy, America's Most Decorated Hero of World War II* (Washington, DC: Regnery History, 2015); Harold B. Simpson, *Audie Murphy, American Soldier* (Hillsboro, TX: Hill Junior College Press, 1975); and Audie L. Murphy, *To Hell and Back* (New York: Henry Holt and Company, 1977). For works on James Earl Rudder, see Ronald L. Lane, *Rudder's Rangers: The True Story of the 2nd United States Ranger Battalion's D-Day Combat Action*

(Longwood, FL: Ranger Associates, 2008); Garry Mauro, *The Land Commissioners of Texas: 150 Years of the General Land Office* (Austin: Texas General Land Office, 1986); Christopher B. Bean, "James Earl Rudder: A Lesson in Leadership" (master's thesis, University of North Texas, 2003); and Thomas M. Hatfield, *Rudder: From Leader to Legend* (College Station: Texas A&M University Press, 2011). Those interested in Doris Miller can read Thomas W. Cutrer and T. Michael Parrish, *Doris Miller, Pearl Harbor, and the Birth of the Civil Rights Movement* (College Station: Texas A&M University Press, 2017); and Neil Sapper, "Aboard the Wrong Ship in the Right Books: Doris Miller and Historical Accuracy," *East Texas Historical Journal* 18 (January 1980). More on Samuel D. Dealey is contained in Charles A. Lockwood and Hans Christian Adamson, *Through Hell and Deep Water: The Stirring Story of the Navy's Deadly Submarine, the USS Harder, under the Command of Sam Dealey, "Destroyer Killer!* (New York: Greenburg, 1956); and Clay Blair Jr., *Silent Victory: The US Submarine War against Japan* (Philadelphia: J. B. Lippincott Company, 1975). To explore the stories of other Texans who served, see Henry C. Dethloff, *Texas Aggies Go to War: In Service of the Country* (College Station: Texas A&M University Press, 2006); John A. Adams Jr., *The Fightin' Texas Aggie Defenders of Bataan and Corregidor* (College Station: Texas A&M University Press, 2015); Jerry C. Cooper, John A. Adams, and Henry C. Dethloff, *To Bataan and Back: The World War II Diary of Major Thomas Dooley* (College Station: Texas A&M University Press, 2016); and James R. Woodall, *Twelve Texas Aggie War Heroes: From World War I to Vietnam* (College Station: Texas A&M University Press, 2015). For the adjustment of Texas veterans to peace time, see Michael D. Gambone, *Long Journeys Home: American Veterans of World War II, Korea, and Vietnam* (College Station: Texas A&M University Press, 288).

23. Stephen A. Ambrose, *Band of Brothers: E Company, 506th Regiment, 101st Airborne: From Normandy to Hitler's Eagle's Nest* (New York: Simon and Schuster, 2001), 203; and Joshua A. Jones, "From Nostalgia to Post-Traumatic Stress Disorder: A Mass Society Theory of Psychological Reactions to Combat," *Inquiries Journal* 5 (2013), 3. The numbers of World War II veterans suffering psychological ailments come from Steve Bentley, "A Short History of PTSD: From Thermopylae to Hue, Soldiers Have Always Had a Disturbing Reaction to War," *The VVA Veteran* (March/April 2005). The mental effects of combat have existed since the dawn of warfare. The condition has been chronicled by Herotodus, mentioned in the *Book of Job*, described by William Shakespeare in *Henry IV*, experienced by E. B. Sledge in *With the Old Breed*, and popularized (both negatively and sympathetically) on the big screen by movies such as *Taxi Driver*, *First Blood*, and *American Sniper*. Throughout the years, what today is diagnosed as post-traumatic stress disorder (PTSD) has gone by more than eighty names. First coined in 1980, PTSD was officially added to the *Diagnostic and Statistical Manual of Mental Disorders*, 3rd edition (*DSM-III*), published by the American Psychiatric Association. Although fraught with quackery and, at times, remedies that did more harm than help, the medical establishment has studied war's psychological casualties for well over a century. Historians, however, have only recently begun studying the cost to

combatants and society. Some of the best works are Gerald F. Linderman, *The World within War: America's Combat Experience in World War II* (Cambridge, MA: Harvard University Press, 1997); Richard A. Gabriel, *No More Heroes: Madness & Psychiatry in War* (New York: Hill & Wang, 1987); P. Watson, *War on the Mind: The Military Uses and Abuses of Psychology* (New York: Basic Books, 1978); Charlie Jane Anders, "From 'Irritable Heart' to 'Shellshock': How Post-Traumatic Stress Became a Disease," *Gizmodo.com*, April 4, 2012, accessed June 14, 2021, https://gizmodo.com/from-irritable-heart-to-shellshock-how-post-trauma-5898560; Joe Stein, "Examining Post-Traumatic Stress Disorder and the Plight of Vietnam Veterans," *Iowa Historical Review* 5 (2015); N. C. Andreasen, "Acute and Delayed Posttraumatic Stress Disorders: A History and Some Issues," *American Journal of Psychology* 161 (2004); Pamela Engel, "US Veterans Affairs Lobotomized WWII Vets Suffering from PTSD," *Business Insider*, December 11, 2013, accessed 2021, http://www.businessinsider.com/us-veterans-affairs-lobotomized-soldiers-after-world-war-ii-2013–12; Chris R. Brewin, *Posttraumatic Stress Disorder: Malady or Myth?* (New Haven, CT: Yale University Press, 2007); Johnathan Shay, *Achilles in Vietnam: Combat Trauma and the Undoing of Character* (New York: Scribner, 1994); Aphrodite Matsakis, *Vietnam Wives: Facing the Challenge of Life with Veterans Suffering Post-Traumatic Stress*, 2nd ed. (Brooklandville, MD: Sidran Press, 1996); Eric T. Dean Jr., *Shook Over Hell: Post-Traumatic Stress, Vietnam, and the Civil War* (Cambridge, MA: Harvard University Press, 1997); Dave Grossman, *On Killing: The Psychological Cost of Learning to Kill in War and Society*, rev. ed. (New York: Back Bay Books, 2009); and Charles R. Figley, eds., *Trauma and Its Wake: The Study and Treatment of Post-Traumatic Stress Disorder* (New York: Brunner/Mazel, 1985). The pioneers in what became PTSD were the Europeans, especially the British. Works on Europe's "war lunatics" are Peter Barham, *Forgotten Lunatics of the Great War* (New Haven, CT: Yale University Press, 2004); Paul Lerner, *Hysterical Men, War, Psychiatry, and the Politics of Trauma in Germany, 1890–1930* (Ithaca, NY: Cornell University Press, 2003); Fiona Reid and Christine Van Everbroeck, "Shell Shock and the Kloppe: War Neuroses amongst British and Belgian Troops during and After the First World War," *Medicine, Conflict, and Survival* 30 (September 2014); Tracy Loughran, *Shell-Shock and Medical Culture in First World War Britain* (Cambridge, UK: Cambridge University Press, 2016); and A. D. Macleod, "Shell Shock, Gordon Holmes and the Great War," *Journal of the Royal Society of Medicine* 97 (February 2007).

24. Maggie Rivas-Rodriguez et al., *A Legacy Greater than Words: Stories of US Latinos & Latinas of the WWII Generation* (Austin: University of Texas Press, 2006), 30, 230, 234.

25. Pete Evans to Ronald E. Marcello, February 15, 1984, interview transcript (OH 624), 2–4. This important collection of oral history interviews with World War II veterans is housed at the University of North Texas Archives, Denton, Texas.

26. See Major General Fred Walker's memoir of this period, *From Texas to Rome: A General's Journey* (Dallas: Taylor Publishing Company, 1969); Duane

Schultz, *Crossing the Rapido: A Tragedy of World War II* (Yardley, PA: Westholme Publishing, 2011); Mark W. Clark, *Calculated Risk* (New York: Harpers and Brothers, 1950); Rick Atkinson, *The Day of Battle: The War in Sicily and Italy, 1943–1944* (New York: Henry Holt and Company, 2007); Jon Mikolashek, *General Mark Clark: Commander of US Fifth Army and Liberator of Rome* (Philadelphia: Casemate, 2013); Robert L. Wagner, "The Rapido River Controversy: A Review," *East Texas Historical Journal* 28 (1990); Robert L. Wagner, *The Texas Army: A History of the 36th Division in the Italian Campaign* (Austin: State House Press, 1991); Martin Blumenson, *Mark Clark: The Last of the Great World War II Commanders* (New York: St. Martin's Press, 1984); Martin Blumenson, *Bloody River: The Real Tragedy of the Rapido* (Boston: Houghton Mifflin, 1970); and Bruce L. Brager, *The Texas 36th Division: A History* (Austin: Eakin Press, 2000).

27. See Ronald E. Marcello, "Lone Star POWs: Texas National Guardsmen and the Building of the Burma-Thailand Railroad, 1942–1944," *Southwestern Historical Quarterly* 95 (January 1992); Alexander Mendoza and Charles David Grear, *Texans and War: New Interpretations of the State's Military History* (College Station: Texas A&M University Press, 2012); Kelly E. Crager, *Hell under the Rising Sun: Texan POWs and the Building of the Burma-Thailand Death Railway* (College Station: Texas A&M University Press, 2008); and Kelly E. Crager, "'God Knows What's Going to Happen to Us': The Lost Battery of Texas's 'Lost Battalion' during World War II," *Southwestern Historical Quarterly* 112 (July 2008).

28. See Glenn Johnston's compilation of oral history interviews with members of the 112th Cavalry in "We Ain't No Heroes: The 112th Cavalry in World War II" (Denton: University of North Texas Oral History Program, 2005). Another interesting account is Robert Peyton Wiggins, *Jungle Combat with the 112th Cavalry: Three Texans in the Pacific in World War II* (Jefferson, NC: McFarland and Company, 2011). Accounts of the New Guinea campaign are Edward J. Drea, *Defending the Driniumor: Covering Force Operations in the New Guinea, 1944* (Fort Leavenworth, KS: US Army Command and General Staff College, 1984); James P. Duffy, *War at the End of the World: Douglas MacArthur and the Forgotten Fight for New Guinea, 1942–1948* (New York: New American Library, 2016); Stephen R. Taafe, *MacArthur's Jungle War: The 1944 New Guinea* (Lawrence: University of Kansas Press, 2006); John Vader, *New Guineas: The Tide Is Stemmed* (New York: Ballantine Books, 1971); and Harry A. Gailey, *MacArthur's Victory: The War in New Guinea, 1943–1944* (New York: Random House, 2004). Famed author Norman Mailer served with the 112th Cavalry and used his experiences to write the incomparable novel *The Naked and the Dead*. For operations of the 90th Division, see Joe Abrams, *A History of the 90th Division in World War II: 6 June 1944 to 9 May 1945* (Nashville, TN: Battery Press, 1999); and Benjamin L. Bradley, *Searching for Competence: The Initial Combat Experience of Untested US Army Divisions in World War II* (n.c.: Lucknow Books, 2015). To see how a cavalry post adjusted to mechanization during World War II, see Caleb Pirtle, III, and Michael F. Cusack, *The Lonely Sentinel, Fort Clarke: On Texas' Western Frontier* (Austin: Eakin Pres, 2000).

11

A New Texas Emerges

The Long-Term Impact of World War II, 1945–60

Keith J. Volanto[1]

Momentous transformations were beginning to occur in Texas during World War II, and the pace of social, cultural, and economic change only accelerated in the decades after the conflict's conclusion. While some of the postwar developments were inevitable, others were only unleashed because of the war. In either case, daily life for countless Texans would be far different by the early 1960s than previous generations. Many have observed that Texans did not return to the farm after the Second World War. In fact, this immense movement had already begun during the war as rural inhabitants either left the land to serve in the military or were lured to the cities by high-paying industrial jobs. The result of this diaspora was a steep decline in the state's farm population, from a little more than 2 million residents in 1940 to 1.5 million just five years later. By 1950, for the first time in the state's history, more Texans lived in urban areas than in the countryside. This trend only continued with each passing year, as the farm population dropped to 800,000 by 1960 and continued to fall to 215,000 by 1980.[2]

Further exacerbating this shift from rural to urban centers was the severe drought that plagued Texas in the 1950s. What made the drought of the 1950s was not just its speed in engulfing the state, but also its length and intensity. The rapid expansion of agriculture on the Great Plains in Texas was not just because of the demands of the war effort. Above-average rainfall and few supply problems also contributed. Beginning in the lower valley in spring 1949, it soon extended to

West Texas by fall. By the summer of 1951, the drought covered nearly the entire state. By 1953, the situation in Texas had become dire. When farmers could no longer rely on rainfall, they turned to the water underground—a situation further exacerbated by the increasing reliance upon irrigation for agriculture following the war. Irrigation wells began littering the countryside. With a reliable source of water, farmers could now plant several different crops throughout the year. Farmers were now drawing from the water year-round. Thus, water tables were reduced to critical levels. Comal Springs, in fact, for the first and only time in recorded history, ceased flowing out of the Edwards Aquifer. This decline came as quite a shock, however, to farmers and experts alike, who believed the groundwater resources of the High Plains to be literally inexhaustible. The drought hit its peak between 1954 and 1956, when it abruptly ended with the return of the rains.[3]

The drought's impact went beyond water. The searing heat and dry conditions parched the state. One newspaper aptly described the situation as "the Great Dry Up." In South Texas, farmers went years between planting crops. For many, all they could do was laugh. "The Lord is a pretty good feller," went a popular joke at the time. "But he don't know a damn thing about farming." The dry soil brought back scenes from the infamous Dust Bowl of the 1930s as wind erosion wreaked havoc on the topsoil. "Our house wasn't sealed tight and dust would come in through the walls," remembered Herman Kellner Jr., a rancher from south of San Antonio. "You'd wipe your hand on the furniture and it was black." Others noted the barrenness of the land. New grass was unable to grow. This allowed cattle to overgraze the fields, thus damaging the land and permitting the intrusion of mesquite and cedar. Farmers had to feed their cattle prickly pear cactus, burning the needles off to make them edible. Reports of calves reduced in bodyweight by nearly 50 percent were common. By the end of the drought, 244 of the state's 254 counties had been declared disaster areas, and the farm population continued its precipitous decline as ranchers sold entire herds and headed for urban opportunities. In today's dollars, the drought cost Texans an average of 3.5 billion dollars each year from 1950 to 1957. Out of the hardships of the drought, however, came a silver lining. The dire situation further increased governmental action in the region on a scale that even surpassed the New Deal. It also moved the state to action in previously talked-about water planning and conservation measures, including doubling the number of reservoirs in the state.[4]

During the postwar years, industries initially spurred by the war coupled with the arrival of new companies continued to draw a sizeable number of migrants from the rural areas. In addition to the pull of opportunities away from the farm, many other factors conspired to drive Texans off the land. The resumption of the federal government's crop-reduction programs to balance supply with demand that were initiated during the Great Depression under the guidance of the Agricultural Adjustment Administration further reduced the demand for rural laborers. Even more significant to the rural exodus proved to be a host of technological developments, especially in the state's dominant cotton industry. Increased mechanization was profoundly transformative to Texas farm life. The widespread availability of the tractor, made possible by the economic benefits during the war, provided increased power and speed for a variety of tasks, contributing greatly to the reduced need for farm laborers and the virtual elimination of draft animals. The arrival of equipment for harvesting wheat, hay, peanuts, pecans, spinach, and other agricultural commodities further contributed to the reduction of farm labor, though none was more significant than the spindle-type mechanical cotton picker perfected by the Rust Brothers for the International Harvester near the end of the war.[5]

In order to take full advantage of mechanization in the postwar years, other scientific developments were needed, and soon provided, by research scientists and officials from the federal agricultural experiment stations, such as the Agricultural Extension Service at Texas A&M University. To maximize the efficiency of mechanical pickers, researchers developed new breeds of cotton in which the bolls opened higher and more fully on the stalks, while scientists reduced trash mixed with the fibers by developing herbicides and defoliants to combat weeds and remove leaves before harvesting. Gin equipment was also improved to properly clean machine-picked cotton. Ammonia- and nitrogen-based fertilizers became standard enhancers to improve production, while a host of commercial insecticides were increasingly deployed from tractor-mounted equipment or aircraft to reduce losses from the boll weevil and other pests.[6]

Only highly capitalized farmers working large tracts of land on open and flat terrain could compete successfully by taking full advantage of these developments. Tractors, mechanical pickers, and additional expenses for chemicals were cost-prohibitive for small growers operating twenty- and forty-acre plots, nor practical for most planters owning land on undulating ground. Huge tracts of former cotton lands would be gradually converted into cattle-raising and hay-growing operations as cotton raising in Texas shifted from its traditional home on family farms and sharecropper-worked plantations in eastern Texas to massive agribusinesses employing relatively small numbers of wage laborers commanding vast acreages in the Southern High Plains of Northwest Texas and the Lower Rio Grande Valley of South Texas—areas that also benefited from modern irrigation techniques. Overall, the number of farming units in Texas from 1930 to 1960 dropped 54.7 percent, from 501,017 to 227,071. Farm ownership during those years, however, shrunk only by 8 percent, from 193,829 to 177,907. The most precipitous decline occurred among white and black sharecropper families, whose numbers were reduced from 68,874 and 36,249, respectively, in 1930 to being virtually nonexistent thirty years later as Census Bureau officials in 1960 did not bother to record any remaining on the land.[7]

Moving forward, those operators involved in commercial farming were often heavily capitalized growers working large acreages and enjoying the benefits accruing from machinery, scientific advancements, and low-wage labor. Remaining farm owners tended to be white and living in comfortable homes with modern lighting and appliances, often powered by electricity provided by cooperatives established through the Rural Electrification Administration—a New Deal–era agency that made loans to groups of farmers and ranchers to provide electric power in rural areas. Rural isolation was further broken down; physically, through a network of "farm-to-market" county roads, state highways, and federal interstate highways, and culturally, via the growing number of radio and television stations broadcasting across most of the state.[8]

Many of those leaving the land, but by no means all, transitioned into the industries awakened by the war. Oil refiners and drillers continued to lead the state in both production value and industrial employment. Producers benefited greatly from the growing postwar demand for oil. The industry met this increased need. They achieved this in part by drilling new wells in the state's coastal waters, but also by making new discoveries inland in the Permian Basin of West Texas where men like George H. W. Bush began his career. Initially spurred by wartime needs for synthetic rubber and chemicals for explosives, increased postwar oil and natural gas production in Texas further stimulated the state's growing petrochemical industry. By the mid-1960s, more than 200 plants largely concentrated along the Gulf Coast created a majority of the chemical ingredients needed by the nation's plastic, rubber, and synthetic fiber companies. Meanwhile, petroleum-derived synthetic rubber produced at Gulf Coast facilities provided most of the nation's supply.[9]

Despite peacetime reductions, the aircraft industry established a permanent foothold in North Texas after World War II, spurred by the demands of the Cold War. In 1949, Chance Vought Aircraft took over Grand Prairie's North American plant to produce jet aircraft, specializing in US Navy fighters. The next year, the Bell Aircraft Corporation established the world's first helicopter-production facility on a site in Hurst and Euless, outside of Fort Worth. In 1954, General Dynamics Corporation purchased the massive Consolidated Vultee plant in Fort Worth whose 20,000 workers produced aircraft for the US military. By the 1960s, Texas aircraft companies employed 60,000 workers and the state ranked second in aircraft production behind only California. The aerospace industry, which had arrived in Texas during World War II when the US Army established an Air Defense Center at Fort Bliss near El Paso to test and develop military rockets, expanded greatly during the 1950s. The federal government provided millions of dollars in defense contracts to companies such as General Dynamics and Boeing to undertake ballistics research at many Texas facilities. In 1961, Texas became a major player in space exploration when the National Aeronautical and Space Administration (NASA) located the future Lyndon B. Johnson Space Center in Houston, making Texas's largest city home to NASA's command post for the effort to send men to the moon by the end of the decade. That challenge was answered on July 20, 1969, with the Apollo 11 mission landing on the moon. A significant step in the success of that mission occurred in 1965, when the first American to walk in space was a Texan, Edward H. White II. With the Apollo 12 mission, in November 1969, Alan Bean (no relation to the editor) became the first Texan to walk on the moon.[10]

Many Texas industries during the Cold War era benefited from both military and civilian clients. The construction business, which struggled during the Great Depression, recovered during and after World War II with the needed construction of military bases and transportation infrastructure projects. Such projects enriched Brown & Root Company and other builders while providing jobs for tens of thousands. Electronics companies witnessed tremendous growth during the 1950s. Small firms and large corporations developed a variety of consumer products, such as record players, radios, and televisions while also producing electronic navigation, guidance, radar, and communications equipment for the US military. Dallas-based Texas Instruments (TI) emerged as a leader in the postwar electronics industry. Previously known as Geophysical Service Incorporated (GSI), the company had made its first mark by applying electronic seismology techniques to aid in oil exploration. During the war, GSI modified this technology to produce submarine-detection equipment for the US Navy. The company changed its name to Texas Instruments in 1951 and became the first company to develop a means to mass-produce the recently invented transistor. While the company dominated transistor sales, one of its development teams in 1954 produced the first portable transistor radio. Four years later, TI engineer Jack Kilby would invent the world's first integrated circuit, a device that soon revolutionized the new computer industry. As a result, the net value of the state's industrial products went from 1.8 billion dollars in 1949 to approximately 5.01 billion in 1955. In a little more than half a decade, the net value increased by around 200 percent.[11]

By 1955, more than half a million Texans labored for manufacturing companies, ranking twelfth nationally in industrial employment. Postwar industrialization led to renewed recruitment efforts in Texas by national labor unions. By 1946, there were 350,000 Texans who were union members, with three-quarters of them affiliated with the American Federation of Labor (AFL) and the Congress of Industrial Organizations (CIO), which merged in 1955. Union membership increased over the next decade, largely the result of rapid economic expansion and population growth. Total union membership peaked in the 1950s at 400,000 workers, or only 17 percent of the state's nonagricultural workforce. The growth of labor unions was resisted by management and many Texas politicians alike, who decried them as politicized and criticized their supposedly corrupt and radical leaders. The majority of large industrial workplaces in Texas contained high union membership. More than 60 percent of manufacturing plants employing over 250 workers had organized laborers, compared to less than 10 percent of plants with fewer than 250 workers. Union membership tended to be higher in the newer industries such as oil refining and petrochemicals, automobile manufacturing, and communications.[12]

Table 11.1

Population of the Ten Largest Texas Cities, 1930–60[13]				
City	**1930**	**1940**	**1950**	**1960**
Houston	292,352	384,514	596, 163	938,219
Dallas	260,475	294,734	434,462	679,684
San Antonio	231,542	253,854	408,442	587,718
Fort Worth	163,447	177,662	278,778	356,268
El Paso	102,421	96,810	130,485	276,687
Austin	53,120	87,930	132,459	186,545
Corpus Christi	27,741	57,301	108,287	167,690
Amarillo	43,132	51,686	74,443	137,969
Lubbock	20,520	31,853	71,747	128,691
Beaumont	57,732	59,061	94,014	119,175

One consequence of this rural to urban movement was the growth of Texas cities (table 11.1). From 1940 to 1960, Houston's population increased from 384,514 in 1940, ranking as the country's twenty-first most populated city, to 938,219 in 1960, now the country's seventh most populated city and on the verge to pass Baltimore, Maryland.

Houston's population grew at approximately 250 percent in those decades. Dallas also saw significant growth, increasing from 294,734 in 1940 to 679,684 by 1960, a 230 percent increase. That moved "Big D" from the thirty-first most populated city to the fourteenth. Dallas's neighbor, Fort Worth, went from 177,662 people in 1940 to 356,268 in 1960. That doubling of the population brought the city from the forty-sixth to the thirty-fourth most populated. In all three of the cities, the largest population increase occurred in the ten years from 1940 to 1950, but each continued to grow at significant rates from 1950 to 1960.

These increases in population in Texas cities are even more profound when compared to other cities synonymous with World War II industry. For example, from 1940 to 1960, Los Angeles and San Francisco, California; Detroit, Michigan; Philadelphia, Pennsylvania; and New York, New York, all experienced population growth. But none came even close to the percentage of Houston, Dallas, or Forth Worth in the same years. Los Angeles saw the greatest growth with approximately 60 percent increase (1.5 million to 2.48). San Francisco saw the other double-digit growth with about 16.5 percent (634,536 to 740,316). Philadelphia, Detroit, and New York, however, saw minimal population increase as well as minimal percentage increase in the two decades from 1940 to 1960. The "City of Brotherly Love" increased in population by 70,000 people, an approximate 3.6 percent increase; the "Motor City" did not fare much better, with just under 47,000 new residents (an increase of just under 2.9 percent); and the "Big Apple" added slightly more than 300,000 residents, an increase of 4 percent. Where places like New York added hundreds of thousands, and Los Angeles added millions of new residents, and Detroit and Philadelphia added tens of thousands to their already impressive population totals, these cities had already experienced the infrastructural and civic service difficulties necessary to accommodate the citizenry in a major metropolis. Those cities had experienced for years the requirements of a national, and for a couple, international prominence. Houston, Dallas, and Fort Worth were still in the process of shedding their provinciality for national and international prominence. In the coming decades, their "coming of age" would be profound.[14]

By 1960, the ten largest Texas cities all contained more than 100,000 residents (see Table 11.1), with three-quarters of the state's population living in urban areas. As core industries came to be associated with many metropolises (e.g., oil refining in Houston, aircraft manufacturing in Dallas/Fort Worth, and cotton processing in Lubbock, which contributed to Texas leading the nation in the production of oil, petrochemicals, natural gas, carbon black, helium, and sulfur), other economic activities supportive of the growing consumer economy (food processing, wholesale and retail trade, and financial services) also grew extensively, employing collectively about a third of the state's total workforce.[15]

In addition to urban growth, suburbs surrounding major Texas metropolitan areas also expanded significantly during the 1950s. Though a few black suburban neighborhoods formed, such as Hamilton Park in Dallas, inexpensive land, availability of federal government loans, increased highway construction, and the strong desire by many whites to offset the effects of federal court rulings on school integration all contributed to middle- and upper-class "white flight" from the core population centers of Texas cities to white-dominated suburbs.[16]

Many Texans experienced the now-familiar images of 1950s suburban life. But this life did not end the way it began. The 1950s began under a pall of fear and uncertainty, with death lurking throughout society. By decade's end, however, a renewed sense of security and optimism returned. This transition had nothing to do with nuclear weapons, communist infiltrators, or the Cold War, but a disease. Paralytic poliomyelitis ("polio") had made the summer months a deadly venture as death lurked in every swimming pool or with every public gathering. The scourge of iron lungs, braces for disfigured and weakened legs, and the overall sadness of the vibrancy of youth stolen were ways of life for many Texas families. Within society, there existed a sort of morbid resignation with people coping with songs and nervous humor as all efforts to combat the disease proved ineffective. Not unlike the Europeans during the Black Death in the fourteenth century or, with qualifications, Americans decades later during the AIDS crisis, polio was a reminder of the fragility of life and randomness of death. That is until 1955 when Dr. Jonas Salk developed a successful vaccine. This renewed sense of optimism, in part from a growing economy, further increased demand for new consumer goods, and the desire to spend wartime savings and redeem war bonds led to the development of a mass postwar consumer culture. Purchases from this generation of Americans, deprived for so long by the economic uncertainty of the Great Depression and rationing during the war, fueled the postwar economy. Televisions began to be mass-purchased for the first time (by 1960, 81 percent of Texas households owned one), and merchants profited from sales of a variety of new devices such as TI's portable radios. Automobiles contributed to a postwar motor culture that included the popular drive-in theaters and restaurants and ever-lengthening commutes to work. The baby boom further expanded the state's economy. Texans, like the rest of the country, celebrated the return of stability by procreating at unprecedented levels, with 203,841 live births in 1950 and 249,142 in 1960. Though illegitimate births increased during the 1940s and 1950s than most realize, a majority of children joined families as products of the record number of marriages taking place during those years (the divorce rate in Texas, however, was also high at almost twice the national average). The baby boom stimulated the economy by creating a large demand for many consumer goods and services. The huge demand for houses, and accompanying mass-purchasing of items for those homes, aided builders, grocers, and furniture salesmen alike. The need for health care facilities provided jobs for doctors, nurses, and staff, while the higher birth rate led to increased opportunities in education for teachers, administrators, and custodians.[17]

Another such luxury of suburban life was the inauguration of major professional sports in Texas. From the early 1950s to the early 1960s, with the metropolitan populations to support it, Major League Baseball teams and American Football League (AFL) teams debuted in Houston and Dallas. Although known for its collegiate teams and stars, the state's entry into major professional sports came at a time when its collegiate impact began to wane. The first major professional team and the first professional football team in Texas was the short-lived Dallas Texans in 1952. Any optimism fans may have had was quickly dashed in the first game, when the Texans, although scoring first, were decisively defeated by the New York Giants, 24 to 6. By season's end, the Texans posted a 1–11 record, the only bright spot being an upset victory against the favored Chicago Bears. Plagued by low attendance, financial problems, and possibly a premature entry for professional sports into Texas, the team relocated to Baltimore at the end of the season, changing its name to the Colts. The team's fleeting existence in Texas disguised, however, a monumental precedent. In the midst of a still entrenched segregated society, the Texans fielded an integrated squad with two black players on the roster. It would be another eight years before professional football returned to the Lone Star State. In 1960, a reincarnated Dallas Texans, now a member of the AFL, a rival professional football league to the National Football League (NFL), began play in "Big D." For three seasons, the Dallas Texans competed for the city's heart with the rival NFL Dallas Cowboys, who began to play in 1960. After three years, the Texans conceded the hearts of Dallas to the Cowboys by relocating to Kansas City and renaming the team the Chiefs. The Chiefs left Dallas as the AFL Champions, however, defeating their intra-state rivals, the Houston Oilers. Most football fans in Dallas probably felt like they were being punished when the Texans relocated, because the Cowboys were an example in futility. Winless in 1960, the Cowboys would post losing seasons until 1965, when they broke even. Cowboys fans witnessed success but disappointment as well. "Always the bridesmaid never the bride" was the epithet its fans attached to the team as it lost two NFL championships to Vince Lombardi's Green Bay Packers in 1966 and 1967. Little did the fan base know that their patience would pay off in the next decade as the Cowboys truly became "America's Team."[18]

With the Texans' departure, only one AFL football remained in Texas. The most dominant team in the early days of the AFL, the Houston Oilers went to the first three AFL championship games, winning the first two in 1960 and 1961 and losing the 1962 game to the Dallas Texans in one of the all-time classic football championship games. Success returned to the Oilers in the late 1970s and early 1980s. For the next decade and a half, the team experienced a love-hate relationship with the fan base before relocating to Tennessee after the 1996 season. Sharing the professional spotlight in the "Bayou City" was the Major League Baseball team, the Houston Colt .45s. The Colt .45s debuted in 1962, and three years later, rechristened the Houston Astros, the team opened "the Eighth Wonder of the World," the Astrodome, the world's first completely enclosed sports stadium. The Astros also played home games on a new playing surface, dubbed AstroTurf, which contributed to the transition from unique, welcoming outdoor stadiums with grass playing surfaces to the sterile multipurpose indoor baseball and football stadiums. By the 1970s, these so-called cookie-cutter stadiums had little to differentiate themselves from one another. Throughout the 1960s, the Astros struggled, finishing with a losing record every year except 1969. The team would not experience success for nearly two decades into its existence.[19]

The decades following World War II profoundly affected politics in Texas. Not only were Texas statesmen national figures, but the state's political climate was also in flux. Following the Civil War, in the era known as Reconstruction, the Republican Party was politically dominant, controlling the state's levers of power until the 1870s. Since Reconstruction, however, the Republican Party considered Texas a political wasteland. In fact, from 1896 to 1950, the Republican Party elected no one to the US Senate and only three men to the House of Representatives. The deep-red state of today actually began its transition shortly after the Second World War. Forces unleashed by the war, such as the Cold War, fissures in the Democratic Party caused by the civil rights movement, and an increasing resistance to federal government involvement in state affairs greatly benefited the "Party of Lincoln" as an increasing number of Texans voted, yet still hesitated to register as, Republican. This dynamic was shown when Texas overwhelmingly voted for Republican Dwight D. Eisenhower both in 1952 and 1956. Ike did not just carry the state; he dominated it. In 1948, the Republican presidential candidate, Thomas Dewey, garnered 24.3 percent of the vote in Texas. Four years later, Eisenhower more than doubled that percentage with 53.2 percent. In subsequent decades, the state's support for the Republican presidential candidate remained strong. In the next five canvases, the Democrats won in 1960, 1964, and 1968, and only in 1964 was it decisive. In 1976, the Democrats saw their last presidential victory.[20]

Where their national outlook was bright, the Republican Party's prospects at the state and local level still remained gloomy in the years immediately following World War II. Although there were moments of promise, such as when the Republicans, for the first time since Reconstruction, actually determined a statewide race in 1957 as the

Democrats were divided. Thus, Republican cohesion led to the election of Republican John G. Tower to the Senate to fill the seat vacated by Lyndon B. Johnson. Throughout the 1950s, although defeated each time, Republican gubernatorial candidates improved their share of the vote. It increased from slightly more than 10 percent in 1954 to nearly 46 percent by 1962. Republicans finally won the governorship for the first time since Reconstruction in 1978, when William (Bill) Clements defeated John Luke Hill. Since then, Republicans have lost only two gubernatorial races in the state (1982 and 1990), and each of those the Republican ticket had flawed or scandalized candidates. Although Bruce Alger was elected to the House of Representatives in the 1950s, he remained the only Republican representative from Texas until 1966, when, for the first time in a century, the party elected two in the same year: George H. W. Bush of Houston and Robert D. Price of Pampa (Panhandle). Although the Democrats remained firmly in control of Texas in the 1950s, forces following the Second World War were trending for Texas to become a political wasteland for Democrats.[21]

The profound postwar changes in Texas occurred at a time when the United States was in the midst of beginning a new chapter in its history; one every bit as transformative and marked by fear and anxiety as the Second World War. For the next half century, Texas would lead in the country's struggle in the Cold War, the ideological struggle for global dominance between the forces of liberalism and totalitarianism. With the defeat of the Axis powers, the country breathed a sigh of relief. Little did Americans know a new, and more menacing, enemy was on the horizon, one that in the coming decades would move the world, on occasion, to the precipice of destruction. That enemy was the Soviet Union, and that ideology was communism. A threat that was even more magnified once the communist country developed its own superweapon, the atomic bomb, in 1949. Suddenly the world faced a prospective war that would dwarf the devastation and death of World War II.[22]

As they did against Adolf Hitler's Nazi Germany and Emperor Hirohito's Imperial Japan, Texans rallied to the challenge. That challenge harnessed both the best of Texas and, at times, highlighted its worst. An underlying insecurity in the soundness of its political and economic systems brought about anxiety that led to fear that transitioned into violations of liberty Americans only equated with fascism and communism. In an ironic twist, the most fervent defenders against communism actually engaged in communistic tactics to "cleanse the body politic" of subversive individuals and sentiments. Consider the case of George Ebey. Having served in the Army Air Corps during the war, George Ebey returned to his life as an educator. Active in progressive causes, Ebey led the liberal American Veterans Committee (AVC), an organization that championed many postwar causes identified with the left, such as cooperation between the United States and the Soviet Union, social welfare programs, and an end to discrimination against unions and racial minorities. His troubles began shortly after being hired as Houston's deputy superintendent of schools in 1952. Unbeknownst to Ebey, he walked into a situation already brewing with anti-communist fear. Virulently anti-communist organizations such as the Minute Women of the USA, whose Houston chapter looked to purge the city of anything ideologically threatening, crusaded against what they deemed "creeping socialism." This loosely translated to a more interventionist federal government aimed at social justice. Led by leading socialites in the city, the Houston chapter brought outside speakers and distributed propaganda. Its members also engaged in "McCarthyistic" tactics of heckling and silencing speakers, picketing businesses, and observing classroom curricula. "Houston . . . is," it was generally believed at the time due to the actions of the city's chapter of the Minute Women, "with the possible exception of Tulsa, Oklahoma, the most reactionary community in the United States." Denounced for his "subversive associations and activities . . . on behalf of racial harmony and progressive education," Ebey did not get his administrator contract renewed, despite a spirited defense and eventual exoneration of any specific affiliation. He was a victim of not only the fear of communist infiltration, but also the uncertainty about the progressive forces unleashed by the war that would drastically upend the segregated South in the coming decades.[23]

While reactionary forces attempted to cleanse society of "dangerous elements," local, state, and federal officials, in the name of national defense, prepared the country for the certain communist attack to be coming. In 1952, state and federal officials in Lampasas County, northwest of Austin, rehearsed the takeover of the town by communist forces. The invaders, this time the 82nd Airborne as the "Aggressor" stand-ins, arrested local officials and closed churches. They rewrote societal "dos and don'ts" for the occupied populace, imposing censorship, indoctrination, and surveillance. In the ensuing months, American forces from Fort Hood, with the assistance from town folk rallied by propaganda efforts to remember the Alamo and Goliad, retook the occupied city, but not before the exercise actually cost the lives of combat men due to accidents and greatly frayed the patience of many in the town when the "invading" forces trampled crops, killed livestock, and damaged property. Others lampooned the exercise as "cold war pageantry." Few in Lampasas shed tears when the next exercise was held in Louisiana. Despite such grumblings about inconvenience, the fear of communist invasion moved communities in the state to action. Although many in the state capital did not see the need for preparation, believing such activity for a nuclear conflict unnecessary and pointless. Austin, nonetheless, experienced "civil defense mania." The city distributed "Family and Home Survival Kits" filled with important contact numbers and instructional pamphlets concerning first aid, home food storage, and the national civil defense plan. Austin schools devised evacuation plans, while city officials cooperated with the Red Cross to devise an emergency plan. Houston-based oil companies sponsored international education in Asia and Africa in the decades following the war to stanch the movement of these newly independent former colonies toward radicalism. In the postwar years, the oil industry was in flux, and decolonization was a threat to the US oil industry's "economic hegemony." These oil companies, which monopolized oil field services, looked to sell itself instead of oil. As a result, Houston would become "global headquarters of oil expertise" and promote "a particular global political economy." The military also peppered defense forces and weapons throughout the state and placed millions in defense contracts with the various aircraft, shipping, and technology industries in the state. The US Air Force, for instance, housed the Atlas Intercontinental Ballistic Missiles at Dyess Air Force Base near Abilene.[24]

In addition to its economic developments, demographic shifts, political transitioning, and ideological struggles, the war also unleashed grass-roots civil rights movements by Tejanos and African

Americans. Their contributions to Allied victory drove the desire for equality. Rural Hispanics and black migration to urban areas, where discrimination on a daily basis in the form of segregated public facilities was more enhanced than in rural environments, further helped to galvanize civil rights efforts. Two highly publicized events involving Hispanic veterans fueled Tejano activism in these years. In September 1945, authorities in Richmond, Texas, arrested Congressional Medal of Honor recipient Macario Garcia for fighting with a restaurant owner who refused him service because of his ethnicity. Hispanics raised money for his defense and publicized Garcia's trial and subsequent acquittal. The second incident occurred when a funeral home director in Three Rivers, Texas (located halfway between San Antonio and Corpus Christi), refused burial services for the body of Felix Longoria, a Tejano veteran killed in action during the Philippines campaign. The American GI Forum, a new civil rights organization formed in 1948 by Hispanic war veterans to combat discrimination in benefits allocation from the Veterans Administration, represented the Longoria family. The negative publicity and lobbying effort by the Forum's leader, Dr. Héctor P. García, led to the intervention of Senator Lyndon B. Johnson to arrange for Longoria to be buried with full military honors at Arlington National Cemetery.[25]

Energized by returning war veterans, the League of United Latin American Citizens (LULAC), founded in 1929 by middle-class Latinos and by far the largest Mexican American civil rights organization in Texas, continued to press for acceptance during the postwar years. The group found success in a series of important court cases expanding civil rights for Hispanics in Texas, including a successful challenge of de facto school segregation. LULAC attorney Gus Garcia successfully argued in the 1948 case *Delgado v. Bastrop ISD* that Tejanos, being a "separate class of whites" than Anglos, should be freed from the customary practice of public school segregation in Texas, even though no such legislation specifically established the practice (as in the case of black Texans). In 1954, Garcia and fellow attorneys achieved a reversal of a Tejano farm laborer's murder conviction when the US Supreme Court unanimously ruled in *Hernandez v. State of Texas* that the defendant had been denied a fair trial since Hispanics had been expunged from jury pools for more than twenty-five years in Jackson County (near Victoria along the coast), where the trial had been held. The ruling meant that Mexican American citizens could not be excluded as jurors simply because of their ethnicity. By reestablishing protection against jury exclusion, the decision increased the probability of Tejanos being tried by a jury of their peers.[26]

During World War II, the National Association for the Advancement of Colored People (NAACP) continued to seek legal redress for discrimination against African Americans. With success in the 1944 *Smith v. Allwright* case that ended the all-white primary in Texas, the NAACP began to achieve a series of triumphs. This included a US Supreme Court ruling in *Sweatt v. Painter* (1950) that Heman Sweatt, an otherwise qualified applicant, had been unlawfully denied admission to the University of Texas Law School because of his race, since the state did not have a separate quality medical school for blacks. The decision opened the door for African Americans to attend the University of Texas Law School, its medical and dental schools, and all its postgraduate programs not existing at other black colleges in Texas.[27]

Though the *Sweatt v. Painter* decision was a major victory for school integration, the NAACP's victory before the Supreme Court in *Brown v. Board of Education of Topeka, Kansas* was transformative. In this 1954 case, the court ruled segregation at all levels of public education was inherently unequal and therefore unconstitutional under the Fourteenth Amendment's equal protection guarantee. True change, however, would take much time to be realized. First, the High Court clarified in a subsequent ruling that desegregation could take place gradually ("with all deliberate speed"). Second, many local school districts and public colleges in Texas, as elsewhere, slowed their implementation of the *Brown* decision. While desegregation tended to move relatively quickly in areas with few black students, the process faced resistance in Central and East Texas due to their large black populations. A contentious showdown over desegregation took place during the fall of 1956 in Mansfield (southeast of Fort Worth), where the NAACP won a desegregation order from a federal appeals court to integrate Mansfield High School. After angry protesters burned crosses in the African American section of town and hanged effigies on the campus and downtown area, a mob of several hundred whites denied entry to the black students. Governor Allan Shivers, a supporter of segregation, intervened by sending Texas Rangers to Mansfield to disperse the crowds and restore order, but gave specific orders to arrest any black students trying to attend the high school under the pretense of disturbing the peace and inciting a riot. The move succeeded, as President Dwight D. Eisenhower, then running for reelection, was unwilling to intervene. The governor's actions would encourage residents in Little Rock, Arkansas, the following year to replicate what had occurred in Mansfield, but with the presidential election out of the way, Eisenhower sent hundreds of federal troops to Little Rock to enforce the desegregation rulings of the federal courts.[28]

Despite Eisenhower's show of force, public school desegregation in Texas, as in many parts of the South, continued to move at a glacial pace. Or as one student of desegregation in Houston put it, they made haste slowly. By 1964, only 18,000 of Texas's 325,000 African American students attended integrated schools. Desegregation in higher education took place more smoothly. Though threatening crowds succeeded in turning away African American students at Texarkana College in 1955, and some education officials (such as those at North Texas State College in Denton, which today is University of North Texas) refused to integrate until ordered by a federal court, many colleges nevertheless began to desegregate during the mid-1950s. (A couple of Texas two-year institutions, Amarillo College and Del Mar College in Corpus Christi, had already desegregated voluntarily before the *Brown* decision.) In 1955, Texas Western (now University of Texas at El Paso) became the first four-year school in Texas to integrate, followed by the University of Texas and Southern Methodist University in 1956. By 1958, close to two-thirds of Texas colleges and universities had integrated their undergraduate classes, though such changes did not yet extend to immediate access to dormitories and cafeterias, equality in scholarship opportunities, or the hiring of black professors. By the end of the 1950s, black Texans had achieved much progress, yet more needed to be done to secure basic civil rights, as segregated public facilities and voting barriers continued to exist.[29]

Revolutionary changes in Texas were evident in the decades immediately following the Second World War. Though the Texas of today had not yet arrived, the Lone Star State stood on the threshold of modernization, with one foot in the past and the other stepping forward boldly into the future. Slowly dissipating was a Texas with a rural majority population engaged in agricultural pursuits with mostly small cities harboring a nascent industrial base while white supremacist ideology limited the civil rights of its minority citizens. Within a generation, changes fostered by the war began to usher in a new Texas, evolving into a predominantly urban-industrial state with a more egalitarian society, at least in terms of a rhetoric not always matched by reality.

Notes

1. Keith J. Volanto is Professor of History at Collin County Community College. Chair of the Department of History, Volanto has authored, co-authored, and edited many books and articles about Texas history.

2. Gilbert C. Fite, *Cotton Fields No More: Southern Agriculture, 1865–1980* (Lexington: University of Kentucky Press, 1984), 233. For additional effects the war had on Texas agriculture, see R. Douglas Hurt, *Problems of Plenty: The American Farmer in the Twentieth Century* (Chicago: Ivan R. Dee, 2001); Jess Gilbert, *Planning Democracy: Agrarian Intellectuals and the Intended New Deal* (New Haven, CT: Yale University Press, 2015); Murray R. Benedict, *Farm Policies of the United States, 1790–1950* (New York: Octagon Books, 1966); Glenn L. Johnson, *The Overproduction Trap in US Agriculture: A Study of Resource Allocation from World War I to the Late 1960s* (Baltimore: Johns Hopkins University Press, 1972); Nancy A. Blanpied, ed., *Farm Policy: The Politics of Soil, Surpluses, and Subsidies* (Washington, DC: Congressional Quarterly, 1984); Linda Loboa and Katherine Meyer, "The Great Agricultural Transition: Crisis, Change, and Social Consequences of Twentieth Century US Farming," *Annual Review of Sociology* 27 (2001); Robert Paarlberg and Don Paarlberg, "Agricultural Policy in the Twentieth Century," *Agricultural History* 74 (Spring, 2000); and Anne Hallam, ed., *Size, Structure, and the Changing Face of American Agriculture* (Boulder, CO: Westview Press, 1993).

3. R. L. Nace and E. J. Pluhowski, "Drought of the 1950s—With Special Reference to the Midcontinent," *Geological Survey Water-Supply Paper 1804* (Washington, DC: US Government Printing Office, 1965), 1, 84; Donald E. Green, *Land of the Underground Rain: Irrigation on the Texas High Plains, 1910–1970* (Austin: University of Texas Press, 1973), 147–48, 168–70; John D. Wiener et al., "Bite without bark: How the Socioeconomic Context of the 1950s US Drought Minimized Responses to a Multiyear Extreme Climate Even," *Weather and Climate Extremes* II (2016): 84–88. For comparison between the 1950s drought and one of the more recent Texas droughts, see Brian A. Smith and Brian B. Hunt, "A Comparison of the 1950s Drought of Record and the 2009 Drought, Barton Springs Segment of Edwards Aquifer, Central Texas," *Gulf Coast Association of Geological Societies Transactions* 60 (2010). For how a Texas Panhandle farmer experienced the drought and its effects on farming, see Janet M. Neugebauer, ed., *Plains Farmer: The Diary of William G. DeLoach, 1914–1964* (College Station: Texas A&M University Press, 1991). The best fictional, some say best account, of the 1950s drought is Elmer Kelton, *The Time It Never Rained* (New York: A Forge Book, 1973).

4. *San Antonio Express-News*, September 11, 2015; John Burnett, "When the Sky Ran Dry," *Texas Monthly*, July 2012; Kathy Wythe, "The Time It Never Rained: How Texas Water Management Has Changed Because of Recurring Droughts," *Texas H_2O: A Publication of the Texas Water Resources Institute* (Fall 2011), 12–14. For the Texas drought humor, see Rana K. Williamson, *When the Catfish Had Ticks: Texas Drought Humor* (Austin: Eakin Press, 1997). N. Richard Nash, a young playwright at the time, chronicled the experiences of farmers in drought-stricken Texas in the early 1950s with the folksy comedy play, and later movie starring Katherine Hepburn and Burt Lancaster, *The Rainmaker.* For this, see *New York Times*, December 19, 2000. For the lessons learned from the 1950s drought, see Jackson School of Geosciences, "Five Key Lessons (and Challenges) from the Great Texas Drought," *UTNews*, September 10, 2012, accessed June 14, 2021, https://news.utexas.edu/2012/09/10/five-key-lessons-and-challenges-from-the-great-texas-drought/.

5. Pete Daniel, *Breaking the Land: The Transformation of Cotton, Tobacco, and Rice Cultures since 1880* (Urbana: University of Illinois Press, 1985), 245–50; Fite, *Cotton Fields No More*, 184–87; Keith J. Volanto, *Texas, Cotton, and the New Deal* (College Station: Texas A&M University Press, 2005). By 1940, many growers on the Southern High Plains of Northwest Texas had already been utilizing cotton strippers, especially the "finger" types, which were basically wooden boxes containing an open front with iron rods projecting outward that pulled bolls (and leaves) off the stalks through the finger grooves. Though the accompanying trash resulted in a lower grade of cotton, use of the device significantly reduced labor costs. The effect and importance of the Agricultural Adjustment Administration (and other federal assistance) on agriculture before, during, and after the war can be found in Ann Folino White, *Plowed Under: Food Policy Protests and Performance in New Deal America* (Bloomington: University of Indiana Press, 2014); Donald Worster, *Dust Bowl: The Southern Plains in the 1930s* (New York: Oxford University Press, 1979); Van Perkins, *Crisis in Agriculture: The Agricultural Adjustment Administration and the New Deal, 1933* (Berkeley: University of California Press, 1969); Roger Biles, *The South and the New Deal* (Lexington: University of Kentucky Press, 2006); Paul K. Conkin, *A Revolution Down on the Farm: The Transformation of American Agriculture Since 1929* (Lexington: University of Kentucky Press, 2009); Donald C. Blaisdell, *Government and Agriculture: The Growth of Federal Farm Aid* (New York: Farrar and Rinehart, 1940); and Bruce L. Gardner, *American Agriculture in the Twentieth Century: How It Flourished and What It Cost* (Cambridge, MA: Harvard University Press, 2002).

6. Fite, *Cotton Fields No More*, 184–87; Karen Gerhardt Britton, *Bale o' Cotton: The Mechanical Art of Cotton Ginning* (College Station: Texas A&M University Press, 1992), 104–06; Henry C. Dethloff and Stephen W. Searcy, *Engineering Agriculture at Texas A&M: The First Hundred Years* (College Station: Texas A&M University Press, 2015); Henry C. Dethloff and Garry L. Nall, "Agriculture," *Handbook of Texas Online*, accessed June 1, 2017, http://www.tshaonline.org/

handbook/online/articles/ama01. Further reading on the importance of cotton to Texas, the United States, and the world at large can be found in Stephen Yafa, *Cotton: The Biography of a Revolutionary Fiber* (New York: Penguin Books, 2005); Sven Beckert, *Empire of Cotton: A Global History* (New York: Vintage Books, 2014); and Giorgio Riello, *Cotton: The Fabric That Made the Modern World* (New York: Cambridge University Press, 2013). An interesting study about the development of insecticides in the twentieth century is Edmund Russell, *War and Nature: Fighting Humans and Insects with Chemicals from World War I to Silent Spring* (New York: Cambridge University Press, 2001). For the adverse effects of insecticides, many of which were funded by the military following the Second World War, see Rachel Carson's *Silent Spring* (New York: Houghton Mifflin Harcourt, 2002).

7. D. Clayton Brown, *King Cotton in Modern America: A Cultural, Political, and Economic History since 1945* (Jackson: University Press of Mississippi, 2011), 233–50; Fite, *Cotton Fields No More*, 189, 208; Garry L. Nall, "Farming on the High Plains: Innovation and Adaptation on Arid Lands in Texas," *Journal of the West* 29 (October 1990), 22; Green, *Land of the Underground Rain*; J. Lee and Lillian J. Stambaugh, *The Lower Rio Grande Valley of Texas* (San Antonio, TX: Naylor, 1954); Volanto, *Texas, Cotton, and the New Deal*, 7.

8. Robert A. Calvert, Arnoldo De León, and Gregg Cantrell, *The History of Texas*, 3rd ed. (Wheeling, IL: Harlan Davidson, 2002), 358–59, 365; Deward Clayton Brown, *Electricity for America: The Fight for the REA* (Westport, CT: Greenwood Press, 1980); Paul Burka, "Texas Primer: The Farm-to-Market Road," *Texas Monthly* (April 1983), 134; Richard Schroeder, *Texas Signs On: The Early Days of Radio and Television* (College Station: Texas A&M University Press, 1998). In 1935, only 2 percent of Texas farms had electric power. Thirty years later, 2 percent of Texas farms did not have electricity. Works detailing the state's attempts at electrification and the Rural Electrification Administration are Henry Robert Hodges, "Rural Electrification Co-ops in Texas" (master's thesis, University of Texas Press, 1962); James E. Banks and John E. Babcock, *Corralling the Colorado: The First Fifty Years of the Lower Colorado River Authority* (Austin: Eakin Press, 1988); Comer Clay, "The Lower Colorado River Authority: A Study in Politics and Public Administration" (PhD diss., University of Texas Press, 1948); and John A. Adams Jr., *Damming the Colorado: The Rise of the Lower Colorado River Authority, 1933–1939* (College Station: Texas A&M University Press, 1940).

9. See Samuel D. Myres, *The Permian Basin: Petroleum Empire of the Southwest*, 2 vols. (El Paso, TX: Permian Press, 1977); Richard R. Moore, *West Texas after the Discovery of Oil: A Modern Frontier* (Austin: Jenkins Publishing, 1971); David F. Prindle, *Petroleum Politics and the Texas Railroad Commission* (Austin: University of Texas Press, 1981); Charles A. Warner, "The Oil Industry in Texas since Pearl Harbor," *Southwestern Historical Quarterly* LXI (January 1958): 327–40; Roger M. Olien, "Oil and Gas Industry," *Handbook of Texas Online*, accessed June 2, 2017, http://www.tshaonline.org/handbook/online/articles/doogz. George Herbert Walker Bush's life in the oil fields can be found in Tom Wicker, *George Herbert*

Walker Bush (New York: Viking, 2004); Bobby D. Weaver, *Oilfield Trash: Life and Labor in the Oil Patch* (College Station: Texas A&M University Press, 2013); Timothy Naftali, *George H. W. Bush* (New York: Times Books, 2007); and Kitty Kelley, *The Family: The Real Story of the Bush Dynasty* (New York: Doubleday, 2004). The stories of other oil wildcatters are in Bernard F. Clark Jr., *Oil Capital: The History of American Oil, Wildcatters, Independents, and Their Bankers* (Houston: Bernard F. Clark Jr., 2016); and Roger M. Olien and Diana David Hinton, *Wildcatters: Texas Independent Oilmen* (College Station: Texas A&M University Press, 2007).

10. See E.C. Barksdale, *The Genesis of the Aviation Industry in North Texas* (Austin: University of Texas Bureau of Business Research, 1958); Barbara Ganson, *Texas Takes Wing: A Century of Flight in the Lone Star State* (Austin: University of Texas Press, 2014); Roger Bilstein and Jay Miller, *Aviation in Texas* (Austin: Texas Monthly Press, 1985); Kenneth W. Howell et al., *Beyond Myths and Legends: A Narrative History of Texas*, 4th ed. (Wheaton, IL: Abigail Press, 2013); Henry C. Dethloff, *Suddenly Tomorrow Came: A History of the Johnson Space Center* (Washington, DC: NASA History Series SP-4307, 1993); Stephen B. Oates, "NASA's Manned Spacecraft Center at Houston, Texas," *Southwestern Historical Quarterly* 67 (January 1964); Charles C. Alexander and E. C. Barksdale, "Aeronautics and Aerospace Industry," *Handbook of Texas Online*, accessed June 4, 2017, http://www.tshaonline.org/handbook/online/articles/dnaul. For general treatments of General Dynamics, consult Roger Franklin, *The Defender: The Story of General Dynamics* (New York: Harper & Row Publishers, 1986); and Jacob Goodwin, *Brotherhood of Arms: General Dynamics and the Business of Defending America* (New York: Times Books, 1985). The importance of the Johnson Space Center is chronicled in Charles Murray and Catherine Bly Cox, *Apollo: The Race to the Moon* (Burkittsville, MD: South Mountain Books, 1989).

11. The information for this paragraph comes from Joseph A. Pratt and Christopher J. Castaneda, *Builders: Herman and George R. Brown* (College Station: Texas A&M University Press, 1999); Carroll Pursell, *Technology in Postwar America: A History* (New York: Columbia University Press, 2007); and Caleb Pirtle III, *Engineering the World: Stories from the First 75 Years of Texas Instruments* (Dallas: Southern Methodist University Press, 2005). The revolutionary development of the transistor to the electronic industry can be found in Michael Riordan and Lillian Hoddeson, *Crystal Fire: The Invention of the Transistor and the Birth of the Information Age* (New York: W. W. Norton and Company, 1997). The growth of the computer industry is examined in Christophe Lécuyer, *Making Silicon Valley: Innovation and the Growth of High Tech, 1930–1970* (Cambridge, MA: Massachusetts Institute of Technology Press, 2006). The net value can be found in Seth. S. McKay and Odie B. Faulk, *Texas After Spindletop: The Sage of Texas, 1901–1965* (Austin: Steck-Vaughn Company, 1965).

12. George N. Green and Michael R. Botson Jr., "Looking for Lefty: Liberal/Left Activism and Texas Labor, 1920s–1960s" in *The Texas Left: Radical Roots of Lone Star Liberalism*, eds. David O'Donald Cullen and Kyle G. Wilkison (College Station: Texas A&M University Press, 2010), 112–32; Ruth A. Allen, George N. Green,

and James V. Reese, "Labor Organizations," *Handbook of Texas Online*, accessed June 2, 2017, http://www.tshaonline.org/handbook/online/articles/om101; Robert A. Calvert et al., *The History of Texas*, 362–63. For unionization in the aviation industry, specifically Boeing, see Dana L. Cloud, *We Are the Union: Democratic Unionism and Dissent at Boeing* (Urbana, IL: University of Illinois Press, 2011). For a general treatment of the decline and evolution of private unions, see Jake Rosenfeld, *What Unions No Longer Do* (Cambridge, MA: Harvard University Press, 2014). To see the hostile environment faced by labor organization during the mid-twentieth century in one Texas city, see Patricia Evridge Hill, *Dallas: The Making of a Modern City* (Austin: University of Texas Press, 1996). For unionization in the oil industry, see Mount's and Montz's essays.

13. The source for these figures can be found in "Texas Almanac: City Population History from 1850–2000," available at http://texasalmanac.com/sites/default/files/images/CityPopHist%20web.pdf.

14. The information for the cities comes from Campbell Gibson, "Population of the 100 Largest Cities and Other Urban Places in the United States: 1790–1990," US Census Bureau, Population Division Working Paper No. 27, June 1998, accessed 2021, https://www.census.gov/library/working-papers/1998/demo/POP-twps0027.html. For a brief survey on the effects because of the increase population, see Randolph B. Campbell, *Gone to Texas: A History of the Lone Star State* (New York: Oxford University Press, 2003), 410–11.

15. This paragraph comes from the following works: David G. McComb, *The City in Texas: A History* (Austin: University of Texas Press, 2015); Robert B. Fairbanks, *For the City as a Whole: Planning, Politics, and the Public Interest in Dallas, 1900–1965* (Columbus: Ohio State University Press, 1998); Martin V. Melosi and Joseph A. Pratt, *Energy Metropolis: An Environmental History of Houston and the Gulf Coast* (Pittsburgh: University of Pittsburgh Press, 2007); Paul Alejandro Levengood, "For the Duration and Beyond: World War II and the Creation of Modern Houston, Texas" (PhD diss., Rice University, 1999); Walter L. Buenger and Joseph A. Pratt, *But Also Good Business: Texas Commerce Banks and the Financing of Houston and Texas* (College Station: Texas A&M University Press, 1986); Victoria Buenger and Walter L. Buenger, *Texas Merchant: Marvin Leonard and Fort Worth* (College Station: Texas A&M University Press, 2008); Robert L. Martin, *The City Moves West: Economic and Industrial Growth in Central West Texas* (Austin: University of Texas Press, 1969); and Kenneth B. Ragsdale, *Cleared for Takeoff: Aviators, Businessmen, and the Growth of an American City* (Austin: University of Texas Press, 2004).

16. See William H. Wilson, *Hamilton Park: A Planned Black Community in Dallas* (Baltimore, MD: Johns Hopkins University Press, 1998); Warren Leslie, *Dallas Public and Private: Aspects of an American City* (Dallas: Southern Methodist University Press, 1998); Darwin Payne, *Big D: Triumphs and Troubles of an American Supercity in the 20th Century* (Dallas: Three Forks Press, 2000); Michael Phillips, *White Metropolis: Race, Religion, and Ethnicity in Dallas, 1841–2001* (Austin: University of Texas Press, 2006); Jim Schutze, *The Accommodation: The Politics of*

Race in an American City (Dallas: Taylor Publishing Company, 1986); and Linda Scarbrough, *Road, River, and Good Ol' Boy Politics: A Texas County's Path from Farm to Supersuburb* (Austin: Texas State Historical Association, 2008). Works that document the effects of "white flight" in other American cities are Eric Avila, *Popular Culture in the Age of White Flight: Fear and Fantasy in Suburban Los Angeles* (Berkeley: University of California Press, 2006); Kevin M. Kruse, *White Flight: Atlanta and the Making of Modern Conservatism* (Princeton, NJ: Princeton University Press, 2005); Antero Petila, *Not in My Neighborhood: How Bigotry Shaped a Great American City* (New York: Ivan R. Dee, 2010); and Thomas J. Sugrue, *The Origins of the Urban Crisis: Race and Inequality in Postwar Detroit* (Princeton, NJ: Princeton University Press, 2014).

17. For the effect of polio on Texans and society, see Heather Green Wooten, *The Polio Years in Texas: Battling a Terrifying Unknown* (College Station: Texas A&M University Press, 2009). For the cultural changes in Texas that occurred following the Second World War , such as changes in marriage, divorce, the baby boom and its effects on consumerism, and increased employment in certain areas of the economy, see Kenneth T. Jackson, *Crabgrass Frontier: The Suburbanization of the United States* (New York: Oxford University Press, 1985); Jon C. Teaford, *The American Suburb: The Basics* (New York: Routledge, 2007); David G. McComb, *The City in Texas*; and Howell et al., *Beyond Myths and Legends*. For Texas birth statistics, see Robert D. Grove and Alice M. Hetzel, "Vital Statistics Rates in the United States, 1940–1960," *US Department of Health, Education, and Welfare, Public Health Service* (Washington, DC, 1960), 877–80. The divorce rates in Texas for 1950 and 1960 were 4.9 and 3.6 per 1,000 residents, respectively, compared to national rates of 2.6 and 2.2 for those same years. For this, see, "100 Years of Marriage and Divorce Statistics, United States, 1867–1967," *US Department of Health, Education, and Welfare Publication No. (HRA) 74–1902* (Rockville, MD: December 1973), 34–35. National examinations of the baby boom's importance are in Steve Gillon, *Boomer Nation: The Largest and Richest Generation Ever, and How It Changed America* (New York: Free Press, 2004); Jessica Weiss, *To Have and to Hold: Marriage, the Baby Boom, and Social Change* (Chicago: University of Chicago Press, 2000); and Diane J. Macunovich, *Birth Quake: The Baby Boom and Its Aftershocks* (Chicago: University of Chicago Press, 2002).

18. For more on the Dallas Texans (1952), see *Chicago Tribune*, January 21, 1952; *Dallas Morning News*, January 21 and 31, 1952, and January 18, 1953; Michael Olesker, *The Colts' Baltimore: A City and Its Love Affair in the 1950s* (Baltimore, MD: Johns Hopkins University Press, 2008); Pro Football Reference, Dallas Texans Franchise Encyclopedia, https://www.pro-football-reference.com/teams/dtx/; and Harold Rosenthal, ed., *American Football League Official History, 1960–1969* (St. Louis, MO: The Sporting News, 1970). For the AFL and Dallas Texans (1960), see Rosenthal, ed., *American Football League Official History, 1960–1969;* Bill Althaus, *The Good, the Bad, and the Ugly: Kansas City Chiefs: Heart-Pounding, Jaw-Dropping, and Gut-Wrenching Moments in Kansas City Chiefs History* (Chicago: Triumph Books, 2007); David Steidel, *Remember the AFL: The Ultimate Fan's*

Guide to the American Football League (Cincinnati: Cleristy Press, 2008); Ed Gruver, *The American Football League: A Year-by-Year History, 1960–1969* (Jefferson, NC: McFarland & Company Publishing, 1997); Jack Horrigan and Mike Rathet, *The Other League: The Fabulous Story of the American Football League* (Chicago: Follet Publishing Company, 1970); David A. F. Sweet, *Lamar Hunt: The Gentle Giant Who Revolutionized Professional Sports* (Chicago: Triumph Books, 2010); Jeff Miller, *Going Long: The Wild Ten Year Saga of the Renegade American Football League in the Words of Those Who Lived It* (New York: Contemporary Books, 2004); and Mark Stallard, *Kansas City Chiefs Encyclopedia*, 3rd ed. (New York: Sports Publishing, 2013); and Pro Football Reference, *Kansas City Chiefs Franchise Encyclopedia*, https://www.pro-football-reference.com/teams/kan/. For the Dallas Cowboys, see Pro Football Reference, *Dallas Cowboys Franchise Encyclopedia*, https://www.pro-football-reference.com/teams/dal/; Skip Bayless, *God's Coach: The Hymns, Hype and Hypocrisy of Tom Landry's Cowboys* (New York: Simon and Schuster, 1990); Sam Blair, *Dallas Cowboys, Pro or Con?* (Garden City, NY: Doubleday, 1970); Donald E. Chipman, Randolph Campbell, and Robert Calvert, *The Dallas Cowboys and the NFL* (Norman: University of Oklahoma Press, 1970); Tom Landry, *Tom Landry, An Autobiography* (Grand Rapids, MI: Zondervan Books, 1990); and Carlton Stowers, *Dallas Cowboys: The First Twenty-Five Years* (Dallas: Taylor Publishing, 1984).

19. For the Houston Oilers, Pro Football Reference, *Houston Oilers/Tennessee Oilers/Tennessee Titans Franchise Encyclopedia*, https://www.pro-football-reference.com/teams/oti/; Wade Philips, *Son of Bum: Lessons My Dad Taught Me about Football and Life* (New York: Diversion Books, 2017); O. A. "Bum" Philips and Ray Buck, *He Ain't No Bum* (Virginia Beach, VA: Jordan & Company Publishers, 1979); Kenny Hand, *Year of Pain: The 1989 Houston Oilers Season* (Austin: Eakin Press, 1990); Bum Philips and Gabe Semenza, *Bum Philips: Coach, Cowboy, Christian* (Brenham, TX: Lucid Books, 2010); Kevin Carroll, *Houston Oilers: The Early Years* (Austin: Eakin Press, 2001). For the Houston Astros, see Baseball Reference, *Houston Astros Team History & Encyclopedia*, https://www.baseball-reference.com/teams/HOU/; Mike Acosta, "Rain or Shine: How Houston Developed Space City Baseball," *Houston History* 6 (Summer 2009); James Gast, *The Astrodome: Building an American Spectacle* (Brookline, MA: The Aspinwall Press, 2014); Gregory H. Wolf et al., eds., *Dome Sweet Dome: History and Highlights from 35 Years of the Houston Astrodome* (Phoenix, AZ: Society for American Baseball Research, 2017); and Peter C. Bjarkman, ed., *Encyclopedia of Major League Baseball Team Histories: National League*, 2 vols. (Westport, CT: Mecklermedia, 1991).

20. For works on the influence and power of Texas statesmen at the national level, see D. B. Hardeman and Donald C. Bacon, *Rayburn: A Biography* (Austin: Texas Monthly Press, 1987); D. Clayton Brown, "Sam Rayburn and the Development of Public Power in the Southwest," *Southwestern Historical Quarterly* 78 (October 1974); McKay and Faulk, *Texas After Spindletop*; Anthony Champagne, *Congressman Sam Rayburn* (Brunswick, NJ: Rutgers University Press, 1984); Patrick L. Cox, *Ralph W. Yarborough, the People's Senator* (Austin: University of Texas

Press, 2010); Anthony Champagne, "Sam Rayburn: Achieving Party Leadership," *Southwestern Historical Quarterly* 90 (April 1987); Robert A. Caro, *The Years of Lyndon Johnson: Path to Power* (New York: Alfred K. Knopf, 1982); Robert A. Caro, *Master of the Senate: The Years of Lyndon Johnson* (New York: Alfred K. Knopf, 2002); and Robert A. Caro, *The Passage of Power: The Years of Lyndon Johnson* (New York: Vintage Books, 2012). For a history of the political environment, not just the Republican Party, in Texas following World War II, see George N. Green, *The Establishment in Texas Politics: The Primitive Years, 1938–1957* (Westport, CT: Greenwood Press, 1979); Paul D. Casdorph, *A History of the Republican Party in Texas, 1865–1965* (Austin: Pemberton Press, 1965); John R. Knaggs, *Two-Party Texas: The John Tower Era, 1961–1984* (Austin: Eakin Press, 1986); Roger M. Olien, *From Token to Triumph: The Texas Republicans since 1920* (Dallas: Southern Methodist University Press, 1982); Roger M. Olien, *From Token to Triumph: The Texas Republicans Since 1920* (Dallas: Southern Methodist University Press, 1982); and James R. Soukup et al., *Party and Factional Division in Texas* (Austin: University of Texas Press, 1964). A Republican insider's experience during this time is in Wayne Thorburn, *Red State: An Insider's Story of How the GOP Came to Dominate Texas Politics* (Austin: University of Texas Press, 2014). For the growing influence of the Republican Party prior to the Second World War, see Stacey Sprague, "James Evetts Haley and the New Deal: Laying the Foundations for the Modern Republican Party in Texas" (master's thesis, University of North Texas, 2004).

21. Green, *Establishment in Texas*, 197; Ron Tyler et al., *The New Handbook of Texas*, 6 vols. (Austin: Texas State Historical Association, 1996), V: 533–35; Campbell, *Gone to Texas*, 411–19.

22. A few books on the early days of the Cold War are John Lewis Gaddis, *The United States and the Origins of the Cold War, 1941–1947* (New York: Columbia University Press, 1973); John Lewis Gaddis, *We Now Know: Rethinking Cold War History* (New York: Oxford University Press, 1997); Melvyn P. Leffler, *A Preponderance of Power: National Security, the Truman Administration, and the Cold War* (Redwood City, CA: Stanford University Press, 1992); Melvyn P. Leffler, *The Specter of Communism: The United States and the Origins of the Cold War, 1917–1953* (New York: Hill and Wang, 1994); Daniel Yergin, *Shattered Peace: The Origins of the Cold War and the National Security State* (Boston: Houghton Mifflin, 1977); Nicolas Lewkowicz, *The German Question and the Origins of the Cold War* (Milan, IT: IPOC, 2008); and Wilson D. Miscamble, *From Roosevelt to Truman: Potsdam, Hiroshima, and the Cold War* (New York: Cambridge University Press, 2007).

23. For a more extensive discussion about the fear, anxiety, and paranoia about communism in Texas, see Green, *Establishment in Texas Politics*, 121–34. This paragraph comes from Don E. Carleton, "McCarthyism in Houston: The George Ebey Affair," *Southwestern Historical Quarterly* 80 (October 1976), with quotations on pages 167 and 173; Don E. Carleton, *Red Scare!" Right-Wing Hysteria, Fifties Fanaticism, and Their Legacy in Texas* (Austin: Texas Monthly Press, 1984). For more on McCarthyism, see Richard M. Fried, *Nightmare in Red: The McCarthy Era*

in Perspective (New York: Oxford University Press, 1991); Robert W. Griffith, *The Politics of Fear: Joseph R. McCarthy and the Senate*, 2nd ed. (Amherst: University of Massachusetts Press, 1987); Mark Jezer, *The Dark Ages: Life in the United States 1945–1960* (Boston: South End Press, 1982); McAuliffe Mary Sperling, *Crisis on the Left: Cold War Politics and American Liberals, 1947–1953* (Amherst: University of Massachusetts Press, 1978); John E. Haynes, *Red Scare or Red Menace? American Communism and Anticommunism in the Cold War Era* (Chicago: Ivan R. Dee, 1996); and Ellen Schrecker, *Many Are the Crimes: McCarthyism in America* (New York: Little, Brown and Company, 1998). The best works on the Cold War and civil rights are John David Skrentny, "The Effect of the Cold War on African-American Civil Rights: America and the World Audience, 1945–1968," *Theory and Society* 27 (April 1998); Mary L. Dudziak, *Cold War Civil Rights: Race and the Image of American Democracy* (Princeton, NJ: Princeton University Press, 2000); Thomas Borstelmann, *Apartheid's Reluctant Uncle: The United States and Southern Africa in the Early Cold War* (New York: Oxford University Press, 1993); Penny M. Von Eschen, *Race against Empire: Black Americans and Anticolonialism, 1937–1957* (Ithaca, NY: Cornell University Press, 1997); Brenda Gayle Plummer, *Rising Wind: Black Americans and US Foreign Affairs, 1935–1960* (Chapel Hill: University of North Carolina Press, 1996); Brenda Gayle Plummer, *In Search Power: African Americans in the Era of Colonization, 1956–1974* (New York: Cambridge University Press, 2013); and Thomas Borstelmann, *The Cold War and the Color Line: American Race Relations in the Global Arena* (Cambridge, MA: Harvard University Press, 2001).

24. James Marten, "Coping with the Cold War: Civil Defense in Austin, Texas, 1961–1962," *East Texas Historical Journal* 26 (1988): 4–6; *Lampasas Dispatch*, October 26, 2010; Betsy A. Beasley, "Service Learning: Oil, International Education, and Texas's Corporate Cold War," *Diplomatic History* 42 (2018): 178–79; *Houston Chronicle*, October 17, 2017; Michael Marks, "How One Texas Town Fell to Communist Rule in the 1950s," *Texas Standard*, April 12, 2017; Dan K. Utley and Cynthia J. Beeman, *History along the Way: Stories beyond the Texas Roadside Markers* (College Station: Texas A&M University Press, 2013), 145–47; "Texas in the Cold War," *Texas Historical Commission*, http://www.thc.texas.gov/texas-cold-war.

25. For this paragraph, see María-Cristina García, "Macario Garcia," *Handbook of Texas Online*, accessed June 3, 2017, http://www.tshaonline.org/handbook/online/articles/fga76; Patrick J. Carroll, *Felix Longoria's Wake: Bereavement, Racism, and the Rise of Mexican American Activism* (Austin: University of Texas Press, 2003); Carl Allsup, *The American G.I. Forum: Origins and Evolution* (University of Texas Center for Mexican American Studies Monograph 6, Austin, 1982); Ignacio M. García, *Hector P. García: In Relentless Pursuit of Justice* (Houston: Arte Publico Press, 2002); and Henry Ramos, *The American GI Forum: In Pursuit of the Dream, 1948–1983* (Houston: Arte Publico Press, 1998). Additional information on Mexican Americans, as well as Tejanos, in the war effort can be found in Manuel G. Gonzales, *Mexicanos: A History of Mexican-Americans in the United States*

(Bloomington: Indian University Press, 1999); Maggie Rivas-Rodriguez, *A Legacy Greater than Words: Stories of US Latinos & Latinas of the World War II Generation* (Austin: University of Texas Press, 2006); and Ian F. Hanner Lopez, *Racism on Trial: The Chicano Fight for Justice* (Cambridge, MA: Harvard University Press, 2003). An enlightening work on the complicated relationships between Lyndon B. Johnson and the Hispanic community in Texas and the United States as a whole is Julie Leininger Pycior, *LBJ and Mexican Americans: The Paradox of Power* (Austin: University of Texas Press, 1997). A more detailed examination can be found in De León's essay.

26. Works detailing the postwar struggle for equality for Mexican Americans are Guadalupe San Miguel Jr., *"Let All of Them Take Heed": Mexican Americans and the Campaign for Educational Equality in Texas* (Austin: University of Texas Press, 1987); Carlos Kevin Blanton, *George I.* Sánchez: *The Long Fight for Mexican American Integration* (New Haven, CT: Yale University Press, 2015); Mario T. Garcia, *Mexican Americans: Leadership, Ideology, and Identity, 1930–1960* (New Haven, CT: Yale University Press, 1989); Cynthia E. Orozco, *No Mexicans, Women, or Dogs Allowed: The Rise of the Mexican American Civil Rights Movement* (Austin: University of Texas Press, 2009); Benjamin Marquez, *LULAC: The Evolution of a Mexican American Political Organization* (Austin: University of Texas Press, 1993); Ian F. Haney-López, "Race, Ethnicity, Erasure: The Salience of Race to the LatCrit Theory," *California Law Review* 85 (October 1997); Michael A. Olivas, *Colored Men and Hombres Aquí: Hernandez v. Texas and the Emerging of Mexican-American Lawyering* (Houston: Arte Público Press, 2006); Carlos M. Alcala and Jorge C. Rangel, "Project Report: De Jure Segregation of Chicanos in Texas Schools," *Harvard Civil Rights-Civil Liberties Law Review* 7 (March 1972); and Craig A. Kaplowitz, *LULAC, Mexican Americans, and National Policy* (College Station: Texas A&M University Press, 2005).

27. Some good treatments of the legal battle and successes for black Americans against Jim Crow are Darlene Clark Hine, *Black Victory: The Rise and Fall of the White Primary in Texas*, 2nd ed. (Columbia, MO: University of Missouri Press, 2003); Charles L. Zelden, *The Battle for the Black Ballot: Smith v. Allwright and the Defeat of the All-White Primary* (Lawrence: University of Kansas Press, 2004); Alwyn Barr and Robert A. Calvert, eds., *Black Leaders: Texans for Their Times* (Austin: Texas State Historical Association, 1981); Gary M. Lavergne, *Before Brown: Heman Marion Sweatt, Thurgood Marshall, and the Long Road to Justice* (Austin: University of Texas Press, 2010); Amilcar Shabazz, *Advancing Democracy: African Americans and the Struggle for Access and Equity in Higher Education* (Chapel Hill: University of North Carolina Press, 2004); Dwonna Goldstone, *Integrating the 40 Acres: The Fifty-Year Struggle for Racial Equality at the University of Texas* (Athens: University of Georgia Press, 2006); Howard Beeth and Cary Wintz, eds., *Black Dixie: Afro-Texan History and Culture in Houston* (College Station: Texas A&M University Press, 1992); and Chandler Davidson, *Race and Class in Texas Politics* (Princeton, NJ: Princeton University Press, 1990).

28. This paragraph comes from Robyn Duff Ladino, *Desegregating Texas Schools: Eisenhower, Shivers, and the Crisis at Mansfield High* (Austin: University of Texas Press, 1997); and Ricky F. Dobbs, *Yellow Dogs and Republicans: Allan Shivers and Texas Two-Party Politics* (College Station: Texas A&M University Press, 2005). For a more detailed examination of the importance of the *Brown* case and desegregation in Texas, see Ben Keppel, *Brown v. Board and the Transformation of American Culture: Education and the South in the Age of Desegregation* (Baton Rouge: Louisiana State University Press, 2016); Richard Kluger, *Simple Justice: The History of Brown v. Board of Education and Black America's Struggle for Equality* (New York: Vintage Books, 2004); Charles J. Ogletree Jr., *All Deliberate Speed: Reflections on the First Half-Century of Brown v. Board of Education* (New York: W. W. Norton & Company, 2005); Merline Pitre, *In Struggle against Jim Crow: Lulu B. White and the NAACP, 1900–1957* (College Station: Texas A&M University Press, 1999); Anna Victoria Wilson and William E. Segall, *Oh, Do I Remember! Experiences of Teachers during the Desegregation of Austin's Schools, 1964–1971* (Albany: State University of New York Press, 2001); Green, *Establishment in Texas Politics*; and James T. Patterson, Brown v. Board of Education: *A Civil Rights Milestone and Its Troubled Legacy* (New York: Oxford University Press, 2002).

29. Shabazz, *Advancing Democracy*, 138–217; Goldstone, *Integrating the 40 Acres*, 36–111; Ronald E. Marcello, "Reluctance versus Reality: The Desegregation of North Texas State College, 1954–1956," *Southwestern Historical Quarterly* 100 (October 1996); Richard B. McCaslin, "'Steadfast in His Intent': John W. Hargis and the Integration of the University of Texas at Austin," *Southwestern Historical Quarterly* 95 (July 1991); Glenn Linden, *Desegregating Schools in Dallas: Four Decades in the Federal Courts* (Dallas: Three Forks Press, 1995); Calvert et al., *The History of Texas*, 371–72. For the make haste slowly comment, see William Henry Kellar, *Make Haste Slowly: Moderates, Conservatives, and School Desegregation in Houston* (College Station: Texas A&M University Press, 1999). For an analysis of the barriers that prevented unified civil rights efforts by African Americans and Tejanos, see Brian D. Behnken, *Fighting Their Own Battles: Mexican Americans, African Americans, and the Struggle for Civil Rights in Texas* (Chapel Hill: University of North Carolina Press, 2011). Although resistance and disruption marked the desegregation efforts of most Texas universities and colleges, one exception was Texas A&M University, which desegregated rather uneventfully. This can be found in Christopher B. Bean, "James Earl Rudder: A Lesson in Leadership" (master's thesis, University of North Texas, 2003); and Thomas M. Hatfield, *Rudder: From Leader to Legend* (College Station: Texas A&M University Press, 2011).

INDEX

Abilene, Taylor County, 214, 286, 289–290, 331
Acosta, Rudulfo "Rudy," 132
African Americans: 9, 15, 22, 25, 43–78, 172, 211–212, 216, 260, 333, 332–333; activism and civil rights, 9, 44–45, 50, 56–57, 66–67, 70–71, 74, 331; African-American women, 51, 54–55, 60, 67–69, 85n20, 116–117; African-American children, 51; Camp Logan Riots (1917), 63; domestics, 53–54, 85–86n23, 216; Double V Campaign, 10, 44–45, 51, 56, 69–72, 77–78, 83n10; government employment, 52; racial integration, 48, 333–334; military service, 48–50, 55, 59–61, 89–90n33; mobilization, 51–52, 72–73, 85n20; "New Negro," 43, 45, 50, 55, 77–78, 79–80n5; numbers in military service (Texas), 10, 44; patriotism, 56–57; post-war, 10, 76–78; racial violence, 22, 63, 96n53, 168; racism and Jim Crow, 9, 21–23, 43–44, 47, 49–50, 53–54, 57–59, 62–67, 71–72, 73–77, 89–90n33, 164, 168, 154, 325; Second Great Migration, 72–76; sharecropping, 55; slavery, 43; teachers and education, 70, 333; unions, 10, 52, 74–75, 154, 163–172; WACS, 53, 59; WAVES, 52, 59
Afrika Korps, 291
Aguillón, Julia, 134
Agricultural Extension Service. *See* Texas A&M University
agriculture and farming: 9, 18–19, 254–272; African-American women, 67, 260; Bracero Program, 140, 142, 260–261; children, 255; cotton, 256–257; diversification and mechanization, 5, 257–259, 262; farm population, 256, 320; grain sorghum, 255; irrigation, 258; livestock, 5, 207, 274n5, 262–65; peanuts (goober), 5, 267; drought, 317–319; poultry, 266–267; production, 256; sharecropping, 55, veterinarians, 270–271; victory gardens, 255; women, 206–207, 264–265
Air Defense Center, 321
Alaska, 18
Alger, Representative Bruce, 328
Alpine, Brewster County, 207, 265
Amarillo College, 334
Amarillo, Potter County, 27, 189, 208, 323
American Association of Retired Persons (AARP), 237
American Federal of Labor (AFL). *See* labor and unions
American GI Forum (AGIF), 141–142. *See* also Tejanos
American Red Cross, 51, 55, 100, 135, 205, 237, 331
American Veterans Committee (AVC), 329
Anderson, Mary Bingham August, 69
Apollo 11, 321
Arlington National Cemetery, 297, 331
Armendáriz, Jesús L., 132
Army Nurse Corps, 67, 134, 205
Arnold, General Henry H. "Hap," 112, 287
Atlanta, Georgia, 73
Atlas Intercontinental Ballistic Missiles, 331

Australia, 50
Avenger Field, 101, 110–111, 239, 250n21, 287
Aviation Enterprises, 104
Axis Powers, vii, 3–4, 8, 17–18, 23–24, 29–31, 45, 54, 56, 58, 60, 76, 115, 119, 128, 131–134, 137, 139, 153, 159, 185–186, 205, 233, 240, 254, 261, 265, 267, 281–282n19, 284–287, 290, 293–302, 329
Austin, Travis County, 20, 27, 51–52, 132–133, 214, 219, 296, 331

Baker, Annie Rucker, 52
Baker Family, 79–80n5
Baker, H. F., 167
Baker, Herbert, 43, 48
Baker, James Otis "Pap," 43, 46–48, 50–51, 78, 79n4, 99n60
Baker, Jesse and Fannie, 43–44, 46
Baker, Judge James Addison, 43
Baker, Wendell Harold, 43–44, 99n60
Basie, Count, 70
Bastrop, Bastrop County, 65, 206
Bay Town, Harris County, 160
Beahan, Kermit, 296
Bean, Alan, 322
Beaumont, Jefferson County, 20, 29–30, 73–74, 153, 219, 323
Beaumont Race Riot. *See* African Americans
Bell Aircraft Corporation, 321
Benavides, Duval County, 133
Bennett, Leon, 295
Bennion, Captain Mervyn, 60
Bethune, Mary McLeod, 68, 116
Big Spring, Howard County, 134
Biggs Army Air Field, 286
Bilbo, Senator Theodore, 19
Boggs, Eva, 67
Bond, Major General Charles, 296
Bonham, Fannin, 54
Botello, Eduardo, 133
Boy Scouts of America, 237
Bracero Program. *See* agriculture. *See* Tejanos
Brackettville, Kinney County, 65–66
Brady, McCulloch County, 290, 298
Bradley, Hervie, 160
British Flying Training Schools (BFTS), 287
Brooke General Hospital, 26
Brooks Field, 27, 286
Brooks-Lewallen, Nita Boyd, 214
Brown & Root Company, 322
Brown v. Board of Education of Topeka, Kansas (1954), 333
Brown Shipbuilding Corporation, 154
Brownsville, Cameron County, 18, 211, 286
Brownwood, Brown County, 26, 66, 285, 300
Bryan, Brazos County, 27
Bullard, Lieutenant General, Robert Lee, 55
Bush, President George H. W. Bush, 321, 329
Bush, President George W., 246
Bush, Wanda Harper, 207
Butler College, 71
Bynner, Harold Witter (Emanuel Morgan), 58–59

California, 45, 51, 53, 69, 135, 321
Cadena, Hermaninia Guerrero, 206
Camp Barkeley, 26–27, 286
Camp Bowie, 26, 66, 285, 291, 300
Camp Hood, 286, 291. *See also* Fort Hood
Camp Hulen, 25–26
Camp Huntsville, 59
Camp Kenedy, 239
Camp Lejeune, North Carolina, 120
Camp Logan Riots of 1917. *See* African Americans
Camp Maxey, 291
Camp Wallace, 25, 62
Camp Wolters, 62
Candelaria, Richard G., 131
Castañeda, Carlos, 137, 139, 170
Castro, Ladislao L. C., 132
Castro, Mary (Valfre), 117
Caucasian Race Resolution. *See* Tejanos
Cementville, Bexar County, 132
Central Flying Training Command CFTC), 107–108

Césarez, Teresa Herrera, 214
Chance Vought Aircraft, 321
Chennault, Claire Lee, 296–297
China, 17, 267, 296–297
Churchill, Prime Minister Winston, 184
Clements, Governor William "Bill," 328
Clark, General Mark, 300
Clinton, President William "Bill," 89–90n33
Cochran, Jacqueline, 8, 101–104, 1 08–112, 122–123n5, 287
Cold War. *See* Texas and Texans (post-war)
Cole, Nat King, 70
Comal Springs, 318
Congress of Industrial Organization (CIO). *See* labor and unions
Conde, Guadalupe, 132
Congressional Medal of Honor (CMOH), 60, 62, 89–90n33, 134, 246, 295–298, 312n19, 331
Cole, Hugh M., 230
Columbia University, 296
Commerce, Hunt County, 297
conscription. *See* Selective Training and Service Act of 1940
Consolidated Aircraft Corporation, 24
Consolidated Steel Corporation, 25, 210
Consolidated Vultee, 170, 321
Cooremans, Delfina, 211
Cooremans, Wilhelmina, 211
Corpus Christi, Nueces County, 4, 26–27, 61, 142, 219, 286, 323
Cortez, Hernan, 299
Countee, Staff Sergeant Samuel Albert, 94n48
Crawford, Roberta Dodd, 54
Crisis (NAACP official magazine), 64–65
Crossland, John, 158
Crystal City Alien Enemy Detention Facility, 294
Crystal City, Zavala County, 239, 294–295
Cuero, DeWitt County, 60

Dalhart, Dallam County, 18, 286
Dallas, Dallas County, 2, 3, 6, 12, 18, 20, 24–25, 27, 29–30, 52, 54, 71, 74, 135, 139, 153, 205, 216, 219, 257, 286, 298, 322–325
Dallas Morning News, 191
Daughters of the American Revolution, 237
Dealey, Samuel D., 298
Deaton, Leoti "Dedie," 104, 109
DeGolyer, Everette Lee, 5, 191, 193–194
Delgado v Bastrop (1948), 141, 342
Democratic Party, 31, 71, 328
De la Luz Sáenz, José, 137
Del Mar College, 334
DeLoach, William G., 267
Del Rio, Val Verde County, 134, 215
Denison Day–Lake Texoma, 292
Denison, Grayson County, 296
Denton, Denton County, 214
Des Moines, Iowa, 118
Dewey, Thomas, 328
Dickson, Anna Mae, 215
Dies, Congressman Martin, 18
Double V Campaign. *See* African Americans
DuBois, W. E. B., 55
Dyess, Air Force Base, 331

Eaker, General Ira Clarence, 296
Earhart, Amelia, 101
Ebey, George, 329
Eden, Concho County, 297
education. *See* Texas and Texans (pre-war). *See* African Americans. *See* Texas and Texans (post-war)
Eisenhower, General Dwight, 296, 328, 333
Elmo, Kaufman County, 71
El Paso, El Paso County, 18, 20, 26, 65, 131–132, 168, 205, 219, 238, 285–286, 321, 323
Ellinger, Don, 74
Ellington Army Airfield, 27, 104
Ellington, Duke, 70
Enola Gay, 114
espionage. *See* Texas and Texans (pre-war)
Espy, Pansy Evans, 264
Esquivel, Rafaela Muñiz, 135

Estrada, Herlinda Mendoza Buitron, 206
Executive Order 8802, 74, 139, 169
Euless, Tarrant County, 321

Fair Employment Practices Committee (FEPC). *See* labor and unions
Fálcon, Enrique Rodriguez, 299
Ferguson, Governor Miriam "Ma," 19
Fisk University, 46, 54
Fitzgerald, Ella, 70
Florsheim, Marion, 105
Flossenbürg Concentration Camp, 302
"Flying Tigers." *See* Claire Lee Chennault
Fort Bend County, 70
Fort Bliss, 26–27, 65, 285, 291, 293, 321
Fort Crockett, 25–26
Fort Davis, 131
For Hood, 330. *See also* Camp Hood
Fort Leonard Wood, 94n48
Fort Sam Houston, 26, 63, 285, 291, 293
Fort Worth, Tarrant County, 2, 6, 12, 20, 24–25, 29–30, 52, 103, 153, 208–209, 238, 321, 323–324, 330
"Four Freedoms," 91n40
Fourteenth Amendment, 333
Fowler, Thomas W., 295
4-H, 51, 214, 254–255, 260
France, 17, 23, 135, 296–297
Fredericksburg, Gillespie County, 296
Fuller, Maud A. B., 51

Gainesville, Cooke County, 219
Galveston Army Airfield, 286
Galveston, Galveston County, 6, 25–26, 62, 153, 207, 219
García, Héctor P., 141, 332
Garcia, Macario, 331
Garcia, Willie, 299
Garner, Speaker of the House John Nance "Cactus Jack," 18
Garza, Guadalupe, 132
General Dynamics, 321
Geneva Convention of 1929, 290, 293, 312n16
Georgia, 5
Gilchrist, Gibb, 270
Gillespie, Dizzy, 70
Gonzales, Manuel S., 131
Gonzales, M. C., 137
González, Henry B., 143
Good Neighbor Commission (GNC), 140–142, 261
Good Neighbor Policy, 139–141
Grand Prairie, Dallas County, 27, 154, 157, 321
Great Britain, 17, 23, 28, 267
Great Depression, 17, 30, 43, 104, 188, 234, 237, 239, 284, 299, 319, 322, 325
Greenville, Hunt County, 65, 219, 238, 286, 290
Grenn, Leola, 67
Grovey, Richard, 164, 166
Guerra, Elena Pimentel, 119
Guerrero, Victoria Partida, 207
Gulf Coast Training Command (GCTC), 106, 108
Gutiérrez, Ramón G., 131

Hamby, Pete Evans, 300
Hardin Simmons, 214
Harmon, Leonard Roy, 60
Hastie, Judge William, 56
Hawaiian Islands, 133
Hearne, Robertson County, 291
Henry, Isabella Martin, 116
Hereford, Deaf Smith County, 291
Hernández v. Texas (1954), 141, 332
Hernández, Candelario, 133
Hill, Celia Ann Smith, 207, 265
Hill, Fanny Christina, 69, 212
Hill, John Luke, 328
Hispanics and Mexican Americans. *See* Tejanos
Hobby, Oveta Culp, 30, 68, 100, 116
Hobby, Governor William P., 30, 68, 100, 116
Hondo Army Air Field, 62, 239
Hondo, Texas, 62
Horne, Lena, 70
Hoover, J. Edgar, 25–26
House Un-American Activities Committee (HUAC), 18
Houston County, 268, 295
Houston, Harris County, 2, 3, 6, 20, 24–25, 29–30, 47, 52, 66, 68, 70,

72–73, 75, 103–106, 109, 111, 114, 135, 153, 156, 209, 239, 262, 293, 321, 323–324, 329–331, 333
Houston Informer, 67, 164
Houston Post, 100
Houston, Sam, 297
Houston Ship Channel, 154
Hueneme Naval Base, 49
Hughes, Lloyd D., 295
Hughes Tool Company, 157, 161, 163, 166, 168, 171, 209
Humble Oil Company, 154, 166
Humphery, Gladys, 52
Hunt, Annie Mae, 54, 216
Hunter, Aller, 69
Hunter College, 120
Huntsville, Walker County, 43, 46–47, 99n60, 291
Hurst, Tarrant County, 321

Ickes, Secretary of Interior Harold L., 188, 190–192, 195
Immigration and Naturalization Service (INS), 293–294, 302
Independent Metalworkers Union (IWM), 157
Iowa, 259
Irwin, Dona, 212
Italy, 23, 297, 299
International Association of Machinists (IAM), 162–163
International Brotherhood of Boilermakers. *See* labor and unions

Jackson County, 332
Jackson, Andrew Webster, 70
Japan. *See* Axis Powers
jazz, 70
Jim Crow. *See* African Americans
Johnson, Clyde, 165, 181n22
Johnson, Lyndon B., 18–19, 27, 52, 143, 269, 279–280n12, 328, 332
Jones, Jesse H., 18

Kai-Shek, Chiang, 297
Kelly Field, 27, 134–135, 211, 286
Kenedy Alien Detention Camp, 293
Kerrville, Kerr County, 214
Kilby, Jack, 322
Killeen, Bell County, 286
Kingston, Hunt County, 297
Knight, O. A., 159
Knox, Secretary of Navy Frank, 28
Krueger, Lieutenant General Walter, 285
Ku Klux Klan, 73
Kyle, Edwin Jackson, 270

La Marque, Galveston County, 159
labor and unions: African Americans, 6, 52, 69, 74–76; American Federatio of Labor (AFL), 76, 155–156, 161–162, 165, 322; attitudes toward unions, 6; aviation, 69, 154; Congress of Industrial Organization (CIO), 75–76, 156–157, 159–161, 164–167, 170–172, 182n29, 183n32, 214, 322; difficulties in unionizing, 156–164, 166–172; Fair Employment Practices Committee (FEPC), 71, 74, 139, 142, 169–172, 210; International Brotherhood of Boilermakers, 75;
labor rights, 6, 138–139, 154–172; Oil Workers Industrial Union (OWIU), 76, 156–161, 165–172; number of Texans entering workforce, 7; prisoners of war (POWs/German), 292railroads, 155; shipbuilding, 5, 153; Tejanos, 168–170; unions and race, 6, 154, 154, 163–165, 167–172; United Auto Workers (UAW), 162, 170; United Steelworkers of America (USWA), 76, 156–157, 161; War Labor Board (WLB), 158–159, 165–166, 168; women, 7, 162–164
Lackland Field, 27, 286
Lacy, Mary, 213
Lamb County, 256, 260, 268
Lampasas County, 330
Laredo, Webb County, 27, 117, 133–134,
293
League of United Latin American Citizens (LULAC), 130, 137–142. 332
Lee, Robert E., 297
Liberty, Liberty County, 262
Library of Congress, 235–236

Lindbergh, Charles, 101
Long, Senator Huey P., 19
Longoria, Félix, 142, 331–332
Los Angeles, California, 18, 48, 69, 212
Louisiana, 19, 29, 48, 330
Love, Nancy, 102
Lubbock, Lubbock County, 27, 323
Lufkin Foundry, 209
Lyndon B. Johnson Space Center, 321

Majors Field, 65, 219, 286, 290
Mailer, Norman, 312n28
Manhattan Project, 116
Mansfield, Tarrant County, 333
manufacturing, 5
Marshall, Harrison County, 21
Marshall, General George C., 30, 296
Marshall, Lieutenant Colonel Samuel Lyman Atwood, 230
Martinez, Elsie Schaffer, 117
Martinez, Raúl Mata, 132
Marx, Lester M., 50
Mauldin, Bill, 27
McArthur, General Douglas, 116, 133, 296, 298, 301
McCreary, Walter L., 296
McLean, Gray County, 290
Memphis, Tennessee, 73
memory and oral history, 10–11, 229–238, 238–239, 239n13, 238n11, 238n12, 239n13, 240–247, 247n3, 251n57, 253n33
Menotti, Camella, 207
Mexia, Limestone County, 291
Mexican Expeditionary Air Force, 286
Michigan, 48
Midland Army Flying School, 289
Miller, Conery, 66
Miller, Doris "Dorie," 59, 66, 298
Mineral Wells, Palo Pinto County, 62
Minnesota, 259
Minute Women of the USA, 330
Mireles, Rodolfo, 133
Mississippi, 19
Missouri, 117
Mitchell, Ruby Wyatt, 52
Mount Holyoke College, 120
Muhammad, Elijah, 276–277n9
Murphy, Audie L., 297
Music Hall (Houston), 70

Nacogdoches, Nacogdoches County, 118
Nagasaki, 296
Nash, N. Richard, 335n4
National Aeronautics and Space Administration (NASA), 321
National Association for the Advancement of Colored People (NAACP). *See* African Americans
National Industrial Recovery Act (NIRA). *See* Texas and oil
National Labor Relations Act (NLRA). *See* New Deal
National Labor Relations Board (NLRB). *See* New Deal
Naval Air Station Corpus Christi, 286
Naval Air Station Grosse Ile, 48
Navasota, Grimes County, 261
Nazi Germany. *See* Axis Powers
Needville, Fort Bend County, 135
Ness Eliot, 219
Netherlands, 17
New Deal, 17, 21; Agricultural Adjustment Administration (AAA), 319; Civilian Conservation Corps (CCC), 22–23, 25–27, 293; Federal Art Project (Public Works Administration), 31; Federal Loan Agency, 18; National Labor Relations Act (NLRA), 155–156; National Labor Relations Board (NLRB), 156, 161; National Industrial Recovery Act (NIRA), 189, 191; National Recovery Administration, 189; National Youth Administration (NYA), 18, 46, Reconstruction Finance Corporation (RFC), 18, 288; Rural Electrification Administration, 320, 336–337n8; Works Progress Administration (WPA), 26
New Mexico, 264
"New Negro." *See* African Americans
New Orleans, Louisiana, 73

New York City, 18, 25
Newson, Mary, 69
Nimitz, Admiral Chester, 60, 296
Noguess, Aileen, 210
Norfolk, Virginia, 48
North American Aviation, 69, 154, 157, 212
North Atlantic Treaty Organization (NATO), 296
North Texas State University (University of North Texas), 214, 237, 333–334

Obama, President Barack, 115–116
O'Daniel, Governor W. Lee "Pappy," 3, 19, 76, 157
Odessa, Ector County, 289
Odlum, Floyd, 101
Office of Economic Stabilization, 264
Office of the Petroleum Coordinator (OPC), 190, 194
Office of Price Administration (OPA), 190, 214, 262, 268–269, 271, 278–279n12, 279–280n12
Oklahoma, 29
oil. *See* Texas and oil
Oil Workers Industrial Union (OWIU). *See* labor and unions
Oral History Association, 233
Orange, Orange County, 18, 25, 77, 210, 238
Osborne, Estelle Massey Lidele, 67
Oxnard, California, 49

Pampa, Gray County, 329
Palacios, Matagorda County, 25
Palestine, Anderson County, 67
patriotism. *See* Texas and Texans (World War II)
Patton, General George S., 60, 184
Pennsylvania, 51
Perales, Alonso, 137
Peréz, Ester, 135
Petroleum Administration for War (PAW), 190
Philadelphia, 25
Pittsburg Courier, 44
Plosser, Joe B., 107–108, 124n14
Pogue, Forrest C., 230, 237n6
polio, 325
Port Arthur, Jefferson County, 167
post-traumatic stress disorder (PTSD), 298–299, 314n23
Potsdam, 234
Prairie View (Normal and Industrial College/A&M), 21, 46, 51, 68, 71–72
Price, Representative Robert C., 329
Prince, Charles A., 107–108, 124n14
prisoners of war (POWs/German), 57–59, 261–262, 290–293. *See* also labor and unions
Provost Marshal General's Office (PMGO), 291
Pueblo, Colorado, 117
Pyle, Ernie, 240
Pyote Air Force Base, 239

Quintana, Carlos, 133

Randolph, A. Philip, 74
Randolph Air Force Field, 27, 134, 255, 286
Rayburn, Speaker of the House Sam T., 292
Raytheon Corporation, 286
Red River, 292
Richmond, California, 69, 211, 235
Richmond, Fort Bend County, 331
Reagan County, 264
Reconstruction, 44, 77, 79–80n5, 327–328
Republican Party, 31, 327–328
Roach, Nessye Mae Proffitt, 264
Roberts, George, 159
Rochester, New York, 50
Romania, 296
Rommel, General Erwin, 184
Roosevelt, First Lady Eleanor, 56, 101–102, 204, 287
Roosevelt, President Franklin D., 18, 22–23, 26–28, 56, 91n40, 119, 139, 153, 158, 169, 184, 190, 284
Rosie the Riveter/World War II Home Front National Historic Park, 235
Royal Air Force, 286, 295

Rubin, Teddy "Tibor," 246, 253n34
Rudder, Colonel James Earl, 297–298
Rutherford, Madge, 110

Salazar, Maria Sally, 117
Salk, Jonas, 325
Sam Houston High School, 46
San Angelo, Tom Green County, 27
San Antonio, Bexar County, 2, 3, 20, 26, 29, 116–117, 119, 134–135, 137, 211, 219, 260, 285–286, 290, 293, 296, 318, 323
San Benito, Cameron County, 132
San Francisco, California, 18
San Marcos Army Air Field, 62
San Marcos, Hays County, 27
Sánchez, George I., 137–138
Seagoville, Dallas County, 294, 312n16
Seagoville Enemy Alien Detention Station, 294
Second Great Migration. *See* African Americans
Selective Training and Service Act of 1940, 28–29, 40n24, 48, 135, 260
Servicemen's Readjustment Act of 1944 (GI Bill of Rights), 76, 115, 271
Sessions, Roy, 165
Shell Oil Company, 156
Sheppard Army Airfield, 27
Sheppard, Janie "Tex," 120
Sheppard, Senator Morris, 19
Shivers, Governor Allan, 333
Smith v. Allwright (1944), 332
Smith, A. Maceo, 71
Smith, Representative Chris, 236
South Texas College of Law, 29
Semper Paratus (SPARS), 100
So Proudly We Hail, 205
Solis (Thomas), María Isabella, 211
Southern Methodist University (SMU), 334
Stalin, Joseph, 184
Standard Oil of California, 187
Standard Oil of Indiana, 187
Standard Oil of New Jersey, 187
Standard Oil of New York, 187
Stephen F. Austin State College, 118
Sterling, Governor Ross, 189
Stevenson, Governor Coke, 19, 140
Stilwell, General Joseph, 297
Stimson, Secretary of War Henry L., 65
Sudetenland, Czechoslovakia, 302
Supply Priorities and Allocation Board, 195
Sweatt, Heman, 332
Sweatt v. Painter (1950), 332–333
Sweetwater, Nolan County, 101, 107–112, 239, 250n21, 252n29, 287

Taylor County, 286
Thai-Burma "Death Railway," 301
Texas Almanac, 26
Tejanos, 9, 25, 128–144; activism, 137–143; American GI Forum (AGIF), 141–142, 331; Bracero Program, 140, 142, 260–261; Caucasian Race Resolution, 140–141, 261; discrimination, 9, 215; labor rights, 168–170; military service, 9, 117, 120, 128–134, 299; patriotism, 128–129; post-war, 141–144. *See also* Texas and Texans (World War II)
Temple, Bell County, 299
Terrell, Kaufman County, 287
Texarkana College, 333
Texas and Southwestern Cattle Raisers Association, 264
Texas A&M University, 5, 28–30, 254–255, 269–270, 295, 298, 319, 321
Texas City, Galveston County, 158–159, 161, 165–166, 288–289
Texas Company (Texaco), 187
Texas Council of Negro Organization, 71
Texas Court Reporters Association, 237
Texas Grain & Feed Association, 262–263
Texas Historical Commission, 238
Texas Instruments (TI). *See* Texas and Texans (post-war)
Texas and oil: importance, 5; industry, 153–158, 160–165, 184–196, 321, 331; production, 5, 186–188, 190, 194–195; industry-government

cooperation, 187–189, 191–194; industry-government friction, 5; National Industrial Recovery Act (NIRA), 189, 191; overseas markets, 185; post-war, 331; Texas Railroad Commission (TRC), 189–191; transportation, 195
Texas and Texans (pre-war): education, 19–20, 22, 32; entertainment, 29–30; espionage, 26; history of state, 1; labor and mobilization, 155–157; modernization, 21; pre-war Texas, 3, 17–32; self-identity, 18, 34n4
Texas and Texans (World War II): African Americans, 10, 44, 47, 49, 51–52, 57, 59–61, 68–69, 72–73, 8, 85n20; 89–90n33, 116–117.333–334; economy and consumerism, 325–326; housing issues, 73; military and military service, 55, 68, 100–121, 128–134, 284–302; mobilization, 7–9, 23–25, 85n20, 100, 137, 153, 204, 207–209, 220; number of Texans who fought, vii, 4, 295–297, 301; number of Texans who died, vii, 4; number of military facilities, 4, 285; patriotism, 31, 56–57; population and demographics, 320–321, 326; post-war effects, 7, 326–327, 331; significance of war, 1–3, 285, 288–289; Tejanos, 9, 117, 120; war production, 4, 52
Texas and Texans (post-war): Texas, 317–334; African Americans, 76–78, 331, anti-communism, 329–330; Cold War, 12, 286, 321–322, 329–331; demographics and population, 11, 317, 323–325; farming difficulties, 318–319, 335 336n5; industry, 12, 319, 321–322, 331, 335–336n5; politics, 327–328; urbanization, 11, 317, 325; Tejanos, 141–144
Texas Railroad Commission (TRC). *See* Texas and oil
Texas Rangers, 73, 333
Texas State College for Women (Texas Women's University), 117
Texas Western College (University of Texas, El Paso), 334
Texas World War II Oral History Project, 241–245, 252n32
The Rainmaker (1956), 335n4
Thompson, Cadet Colonel Mayo J., 28–29, 40n26
Three Rivers, Live Oak County, 331
Tibbets, Paul, 114
Todd Shipbuilding Corporation, 25, 47, 75, 154
Tower, Senator John G., 328
Tuskegee Airmen, 62, 233, 296
Tuskegee University, 46,

unions. *See* labor and unions
United Auto Workers (UAW). *See* labor and unions
United Service Organizations (USO), 51, 62, 100, 118, 135, 214–215
United States (military branches): Army, 26, 120; Army Air Corps/Forces, 27, 102, 111–112, 132, 287, 295, 299, 109, 329; Coast Guards, 120; Marine Corps, 21, 59, 100, 119–120, 133; Navy, 26–27, 48, 59, 118, 120, 321–322; United States Air Force, 331
United States (military campaigns and battles): Anzio, 295, 300; Bulge, 297, 301; Guadalcanal, 60, 133; Iwo Jima, 133, 184; Gilbert Islands, 60, 133, 298; Italian, 300; Java, 301; Mashall Islands, 133; Makin Island, 230; Midway, 133; New Guinea, 117, 133, 301; Normandy (D-Day), 131, 133, 230, 301, 297, 301; North Africa, 132, 296–297, 299; Okinawa, 133–134; Omaha Beach, 297; Pearl Harbor, 70, 102, 128, 133, 139, 184, 192, 203, 205, 209, 234, 237, 254, 284–285, 295–296, 298; Philippines, 117, 133–134, 205, 331; Rapido River, 131, 300; Rhineland, 301; Saipan, 133; Salerno, 131–132; Sicily, 132, 296–297; Sunda Strait, 301
United States (units): 1st Infantry

Division, 132; Second Army, 55; 2nd Ranger Battalion, 297; Third Army, 285; 6th Infantry Division, 36; Fifth Army, 399; Sixth Army, 285; 7th Infantry Division, 29; Eighth Air Force, 296; Ninth Army, 285, 295–296; Ninth Air Force, 295–296;
Tenth Army, 285; Fifteenth Army, 285; 24th Infantry Regiment, 63, 65; 28th Infantry Division, 297; 32nd Infantry Division, 133; 334th Naval Construction Battalion, 48–50; 36th Infantry Division, 131–132, 240, 299–300; 45th Infantry Division, 26, 286; 79th Infantry Division, 133; 82nd Airborne Division, 330; 90th Infantry Division, 301–302, 312n28; 109th Infantry Regiment, 297; 112th Cavalry Regiment, 27, 301; 124th Regiment, 301; 131st Field Artillery Regiment, 300; 165th Infantry Regiment, 133; 318th Army Air Forces Flying Training Detachment, 109; 319th Army Air Forces Flying Training Detachment, 109; 761st Tank Battalion, 60–61

United States Army Command and General Staff College, Leavenworth, Kansas, 29
United States Department of Justice, 293
United States Department of State, 293
United States Latino and Latina World War II Oral History Project, 237
United States Marine Corps Women's Reserve (Women's Reserve), 100, 120
United States Supreme Court, 332
United Steelworkers of America (USWA). *See* labor and unions
University of California, Berkeley, 235
University of Texas at Austin, 71, 139, 189, 237, 332, 334
USS Harder, 298
USS Houston, 301
USS Liscome (Liscomb) Bay, 60
USS Neosho, 295
USS San Francisco, 60
USS West Virginia, 59–60

Veach, Dorothy Ann, 116
Veterans Administration, 152, 332
Veterans History Project (VHP), 235, 237, 250n19
Veterans of Foreign Wars (VFW), 238
Veterans' Oral History Project Act, 235–236
Victoria, Victoria County, 332
Vinson, Fred, 264

Waco, McLennan County, 20, 67, 117
Wade, Lance Cleo, 295
Walker, Major General Fred Walker, 300
Walker, Josephine Ledesma, 134
Walton, Keith, 53
Ward, Felix, 75
War Department, 23, 26, 27, 30, 52, 55–56, 60, 64–65, 68, 261
War Labor Board (WLB). *See* labor and unions
War Manpower Commission, 74, 163, 210
War Production Board, 159, 178n11, 190
War Supply Administration, 262
Warwick Hotel, 105
Washington County, Texas, 51
Washington, D.C., 18
Weaver, Robert, 74
Wesley, Carter, 164
West Point, 296
Wichita Falls, Wichita County, 104, 257
Wickard, Secretary of Agriculture Claude R., 255
Willow Run (Ford Motor Company), 24
Wingate, Julia, 210
White, Edward H., II, 322
White, Ella Ruth, 52
White, Lulu B., 10, 71
Wichita Falls, Wichita County, 295
William P. Hobby Airport, 105
Williams, Elizabeth "Tex," 68, 117
Wilson, Lucy, 205
Wise County, 189

women: anti-communism, 330; numbers in military, 8; sexism and difficulties experienced, 8, 120–121, 209–211; gender roles and marriage, 208–209, 216–217, 225n15, 339–340n17; home front/domesticity, 203–221, 212–213, 215–216; labor and unions, 162–164; mobilization, 100, 203–204, 207–209, 220, 212; morality and prostitution, 217–220, 228n21, 290; rationing, 268–269; service in military, 4, 8, 30, 41n28, 57, 68, 100–120, 121, 125n26, 34–135, 204–205, 220. *See also* African Americans
Women's Army Corps (WAC/WAAC), 8, 30, 41n28, 68, 100, 110, 116–119, 134, 204
Women Accepted for Volunteer Emergency Service (WAVES), 8, 57, 100, 118–120, 204
Women's Air Force Service Pilots (WASP), 4, 8, 100–116, 121, 125n26, 204, 220, 239–240, 287–288, 305–306n7
Women's Auxiliary Ferrying Squadron (WAFS), 102, 103
Women's Defense Corps, 214
Women's Flying Training Detachment (WFTD), 102, 103
Women's Land Army (WLA), 206, 259–260

Yarborough, Ralph, 143